Lecture Notes in Computer Science   9379

Commenced Publication in 1973
Founding and Former Series Editors:
Gerhard Goos, Juris Hartmanis, and Jan van Leeuwen

More information about this series at http://www.springer.com/series/7410

Bruce Christianson · Petr Švenda
Vashek Matyáš · James Malcolm
Frank Stajano · Jonathan Anderson (Eds.)

Security
Protocols XXIII

23rd International Workshop
Cambridge, UK, March 31 – April 2, 2015
Revised Selected Papers

Springer

Editors

Bruce Christianson
University of Hertfordshire
Hatfield
UK

Petr Švenda
Masaryk University
Brno
Czech Republic

Vashek Matyáš
Masaryk University
Brno
Czech Republic

James Malcolm
University of Hertfordshire
Hatfield
UK

Frank Stajano
University of Cambridge
Cambridge
UK

Jonathan Anderson
Memorial University of Newfoundland
St. John's, NF
Canada

ISSN 0302-9743   ISSN 1611-3349 (electronic)
Lecture Notes in Computer Science
ISBN 978-3-319-26095-2   ISBN 978-3-319-26096-9 (eBook)
DOI 10.1007/978-3-319-26096-9

Library of Congress Control Number: 2015953244

LNCS Sublibrary: SL4 – Security and Cryptology

Springer Cham Heidelberg New York Dordrecht London

Printed on acid-free paper

Springer International Publishing AG Switzerland is part of Springer Science+Business Media
(www.springer.com)

Preface

This volume collects the revised proceedings of the 23rd International Security Protocols Workshop, held at Sidney Sussex College, Cambridge, UK, from March 31 to April 2, 2015.

The theme of this workshop was "Information Security in Fiction and in Fact."

Fiction can become fact: mobile phones look and operate the way they do because the engineers who design them watched Star Trek when they were children. But yesterday's facts also become today's fictions: today most privacy protocols are theatrical performances, albeit not always playing to a live audience.

How is information security handled in fiction, and what aspects of this could we emulate in next-generation technology if we tried? And how much of what we do now should actually be relegated to writers of historical fiction?

As with previous workshops in this series, each paper was revised by the authors to incorporate ideas that emerged during the workshop. These revised papers are followed by an edited transcript of the presentation and ensuing discussion.

Our thanks to Lori Klimaszewska for the initial transcription of the recorded workshop discussions, and to all authors for their kind and timely collaboration with revising these transcripts and their position paper. Particular thanks to Simon Foley and Virgil Gligor for joining us on the Program Committee.

We hope that these proceedings will inspire you to turn a fictional security protocol into fact — or back again — in time for next year's workshop.

September 2015

Vashek Matyáš
Petr Švenda
Bruce Christianson
James Malcolm
Frank Stajano
Jonathan Anderson

Previous Proceedings in This Series

The proceedings of previous International Security Protocols Workshops are also published by Springer as *Lecture Notes in Computer Science,* and are occasionally referred to in the text:

22nd Workshop (2014)	LNCS 8809	ISBN 978-3-319-12399-8
21st Workshop (2013)	LNCS 8263	ISBN 978-3-642-41716-0
20th Workshop (2012)	LNCS 7622	ISBN 978-3-642-35693-3
19th Workshop (2011)	LNCS 7114	ISBN 978-3-642-25866-4
18th Workshop (2010)	LNCS 7061	ISBN 978-3-662-45920-1
17th Workshop (2009)	LNCS 7028	ISBN 978-3-642-36212-5
16th Workshop (2008)	LNCS 6615	ISBN 978-3-642-22136-1
15th Workshop (2007)	LNCS 5964	ISBN 978-3-642-17772-9
14th Workshop (2006)	LNCS 5087	ISBN 978-3-642-04903-3
13th Workshop (2005)	LNCS 4631	ISBN 3-540-77155-7
12th Workshop (2004)	LNCS 3957	ISBN 3-540-40925-4
11th Workshop (2003)	LNCS 3364	ISBN 3-540-28389-7
10th Workshop (2002)	LNCS 2845	ISBN 3-540-20830-5
9th Workshop (2001)	LNCS 2467	ISBN 3-540-44263-4
8th Workshop (2000)	LNCS 2133	ISBN 3-540-42566-7
7th Workshop (1999)	LNCS 1796	ISBN 3-540-67381-4
6th Workshop (1998)	LNCS 1550	ISBN 3-540-65663-4
5th Workshop (1997)	LNCS 1361	ISBN 3-540-64040-1
4th Workshop (1996)	LNCS 1189	ISBN 3-540-63494-5

No published proceedings exist for the first three workshops.

As a result of various delays, volumes in the Security Protocols series since the 16th edition have appeared in an order different to that in which the corresponding workshops were held. For reference, the actual order of publication is volumes 16, 19, 20, 17, 21, 22, 18, 23. In all cases, the volume number of the published proceedings corresponds to the sequence number of the workshop.

Throughout the catching-up process, the authors have cooperated with the editors in bringing their position papers up to date prior to publication, leading in some cases to closed time-like loops in the citation graph.

The publication of these proceedings (volume 23) brings the sequence back into serial order.

Introduction: Information Security in Fiction and in Fact (Transcript of Discussion)

Bruce Christianson

University of Hertfordshire

Hello everyone, and welcome to the 23rd Security Protocols Workshop. Our annual theme is not intended to constrain the contents of the discussions, but more as a suggestion for an unconventional point of view from which to look at them: this year our theme is Information Security in Fiction and in Fact.

Fiction can become fact. Sometimes this happens spontaneously, because the idea is already in the air, fiction picks up on it first, and fact just takes a few years to follow. Sometimes it takes more than a few years, I've still got a jet pack on back order since 1963. Sometimes, however, the link is causative. The reason that clamshell mobile phones look the way they do is because the engineers who designed them watched Star Trek when they were little.

But the movement can be in the opposite direction: fact can become fiction just as easily. The fact of the unbreakable Enigma machine became fiction without the Germans realising that it had. Secure public-key cryptography might, if you believe some people[1], have already gone the same way. Or, if you prefer to believe Ross Anderson and his collaborators[2], all of our algorithms for quantum computers may be about to be re-catalogued as works of speculative fiction, set in an alternate reality where magic is real. And what if it turns out[3] that P = NP, and there aren't actually any exponentially hard cryptographic puzzles at all? The whole of cryptography would join the long-bow as something that we can enjoy reading about in tightly plotted works of historical fiction.

I have alluded to the fact that fiction comes in a number of different genres, and sometimes we're perhaps a little careless at failing to distinguish these. The historical fiction genre is where we try to be as careful about the facts of history as we can, subject to the small number of changes we have to make to get the plot to work. Gothic novels, in contrast, are not subject to such constraint.

The same goes with the future. On the one hand we have what used to be called hard SF, where we try and respect the currently received laws of physics, apart from one or two innovations needed in order to make the plot work, and at an opposite extreme we have space opera, where it's OK to just push an entire alien civilisation in

---

[1] apps.washingtonpost.com/g/page/world/a-description-of-the-penetrating-hard-targets-project/691/

[2] Ross Anderson and Robert Brady, 2013, Why Quantum Computing is Hard - and Quantum Cryptography is Not Provably Secure, arxiv.org/abs/1301.7351

[3] www.claymath.org/millennium-problems/p-vs-np-problemwww.travellingsalesmanmovie.com/

through the wall whenever we feel like it. Maybe a lot of the developments that we dismiss (rather disparagingly) as security theatre are actually intended as security opera, and trying to look for a sensible plot in the background is to completely misunderstand the nature of the entertainment on offer.

So. What can we learn from the way information security is presented in fiction? In particular, can we learn something interesting about what people *believe* to be true? And what could we achieve, if we put our minds to it, in terms of making things that are currently fiction become fact in the future? In the other direction, what could those who write fiction learn from us? Particularly those who compose *convenient* fictions, people like politicians, and the civil servants who advise them. And what sort of genre do we want our own work to occupy? Do we really see everything we currently do as falling into the little niche market of fiction called Early 21st Century Noir, or should we be trying to break out of that genre and into the mainstream?

This is, as always, a workshop and not a conference. We've got a mixture of people that we have had before, and people that we haven't. We try to put a few people who've been at least once before up at the front of the programme, to help those here for the first time to get an idea of what to expect, but if you come and give the talk that you planned to give when you planned to come, then something has gone terribly wrong. Please expect to be interrupted, even if you're in the middle of interrupting somebody else.

This is intended to be a low friction arena, and if you break somebody's protocol during their talk, it is polite to try and help them fix it afterwards. You'll get a chance to revise your position paper, in the light of these interactions with the other participants, before you have to resubmit it.

We also publish transcripts of these discussions, but they too are works of fiction, because they are heavily edited, and we won't let you say anything stupid on the record. So this is a safe environment in which to take risks.

Frank Stajano: Yes. On the subject of the fact that this is a safe environment in which to try things out, the proceedings are then going to be heavily edited for taking out any stupidities and so on. What you say is going to be recorded multiple times.

Reply: Yes, we have a kind of Minority Report thing going.

Frank Stajano: The recordings are going to be made available to you and, for practical access control reasons, to everybody else who is also an author, but they are not going to leave that group. The primary person to revise your thing, to edit out the stupidity[4] is going to be *you*!

---

[4] Except when it is essential to the plot.

Contents

The Dark Side of the Code

Olgierd Pieczul[1,2] and Simon N. Foley[2]($\boxtimes$)

[1] Ireland Lab, IBM Software Group, Dublin, Ireland
olgierdp@ie.ibm.com
[2] Department of Computer Science, University College Cork, Cork, Ireland
s.foley@cs.ucc.ie

Abstract. The literature is rife with examples of attackers exploiting unexpected system behaviours that arise from program bugs. This problem is particularly widespread in contemporary application programs, owing to the complexity of their many interconnected parts. We consider this problem, and consider how runtime verification could be used to check an executing program against a model of expected behaviour generated during unit testing.

"Beware of bugs in the above code; I have only proved it correct, not tried it."
—Donald Knuth. Notes on the van Emde Boas construction of
priority deques: An instructive use of recursion, 1977

1 Introduction

Contemporary application systems are implemented using an assortment of high-level programming languages, software frameworks and third party components. While this may help lower development time and cost, the result is a complex system of interoperating parts whose behaviour is difficult to fully and properly comprehend. This difficulty of comprehension often manifests itself in the form of program coding errors that are not directly related to security requirements but can have a significant impact on the security of the system [16]. For example, while an application may enforce the correct access controls, its programmer may have mistakenly relied on the software development framework providing particular code injection defenses; alternatively, the framework developer may have mistakenly relied on its users implementing their own injection defenses, or, simply, that nobody had anticipated and/or understood the injection vulnerability. In a study of developers by Oliveira et al. [23], it was found that 53 % of its participants knew about a particular coding vulnerability, however they did not correlate it with their own programming activity unless it was explicitly highlighted. It is, therefore, not surprising that all of the OWASP Top 10 security risks [26] relate to implementation flaws, with the majority in the form of common coding mistakes. Two security vulnerabilities that received wide media coverage in 2014, Heartbleed [2] and Shellshock [1] are further examples of such mistakes.

© Springer International Publishing Switzerland 2015
B. Christianson et al. (Eds.): Security Protocols 2015, LNCS 9379, pp. 1–11, 2015.
DOI: 10.1007/978-3-319-26096-9_1

Given the complexity of contemporary applications, and the manner of their development, we argue that there will always be some aspect of their behaviour (ranging from application level to low-level system calls) that a programmer may not have fully considered or comprehended. We refer to this as the dark side of the code; a *security gap* that can exist between the expected behaviour and the actual behaviour of the code. Improper or incomplete comprehension means that security controls may not have been considered for the security gap and, as a consequence, the unexpected behaviour arising from the code may give rise to a security vulnerability. One might argue that encapsulation and programming by contract [21] could eliminate these security gaps; or, that one might attempt to model all unexpected behaviours in the security gap in terms of a Dolev-Yao style attacker [13,30] and verify that the application code is in turn robust to failure against this attacker. However, these approaches still require a full and proper comprehension of system components and their interoperation (in terms of formal specification) which, in itself, can have security gaps, regardless of the challenge of scaling these techniques to contemporary application systems.

In this paper we explore the dark side of the code and show how security gaps can emerge in applications. We argue that the security gap can be reduced by using anomaly detection style techniques to monitor the expected behaviour, against the actual behaviour, of individual applications and components. Our preliminary experimental results suggest that this approach can be used to identify a variety of security vulnerabilities that arise from programming error.

2 Contemporary Application Development

Current software frameworks enable developers to focus on the high-level functionality of the application by hiding low-level detail. System infrastructure detail such as DBMS, local file systems and memory is encapsulated as object storage; network connectivity is abstracted in terms of remote resource access, and user interaction and presentation is supported via a range of standard interfaces. In this paper we use a running example to explore the coding of a contemporary application. Despite being simple, the example is sufficient to illustrate some of the challenges in using these frameworks and to identify some of the unexpected vulnerabilities in the security gap.

Consider a web application that provides an online facility for users to manage and organize website bookmarks that is synchronised across different user devices. The application provides a web interface and REST API, supporting website snapshot images and metadata, browsing, searching and tracking bookmark use. The application can be built with little effort using contemporary tools, frameworks and libraries. For example, Listing 1 provides the code implementing bookmark creation request. The application is hosted on a web application server that handles network connection along with HTTP request. We assume that the application uses a web MVC framework to parse request parameters `address` and bookmark `title` and calls `addBookmark`. The framework is also responsible for exception interception, error rendering and providing

```
1  void addBookmark(String address, String title) throws
       Exception {
2      Image small = WebUtils.snapshot(address, 160, 120);
3      Image large = WebUtils.snapshot(address, 1200, 800);
4      Bookmark b = new Bookmark(address, title, small,
           large);
5      DataStore.save(b);
6  }
```

Fig. 1. Web application - bookmark creation

responses to the client. Inside the method **addBookmark**, a utility library [4] is used to render website snapshot images (lines 2–3) and a persistence framework (such as Hibernate [3]) to save the bookmark in a relational database (line 5) (Fig. 1).

While the high-level application code is clear and easy to follow, the program abstractions that are used mean that the typical programmer will not overly concern themselves with the specifics of the low-level behaviour of the underlying framework infrastructure. For example, at Line 5 the application uses the persistence framework to save a bookmark. The developer expects that the framework will make a connection to a database (or reuse an existing one), formulate an SQL statement from the bookmark object fields and execute it. Similarly, creation of website snapshot images (lines 2–3) is handled using a single call to an external library. The documentation, such as javadoc provided with the WebUtils.snapshot() source code in Listing 2, provides limited information about the method behaviour. From this, the developer can learn that it accesses the website specified by the URL, renders it and returns an image of specified dimensions. The programmer can expect that the library will verify the correctness of the provided address (as an exception is thrown for an "incorrect URL"), and that it will check for "communication problems" while the website is being accessed.

Studying the source code of WebUtils.snapshot() method in Listing 2 (Fig. 2), we can see that the library, used by the application, is also implemented at a similarly high level of abstraction. All of the logic related to accessing the remote website in order to create the snapshot is covered by lines 13–15 using the Java Platform API URL and URLConnection classes. Looking at the first lines of its documentation [24], the developer learns that a *"Class URL represents a Uniform Resource Locator, a pointer to a "resource" on the World Wide Web"*. The documentation informs its reader that in the case of a malformed URL, the constructor will throw an exception, which they decide to forward to the consumer to handle. Furthermore, the documentation [25] specifies that URL.openConnection() method returns *"a connection to the remote object referred to by the URL"*. And that URLConnection.getInputStream() *"returns an input stream that reads from this open connection"*. The documentation also states that a SocketTimeoutException is thrown *"if the read timeout expires before data is available for read"*.

```
1   /**
2    * Create an image snapshot for a website
3    * @see    #render(InputStream)
4    *
5    * @param  website URL address of the website
6    * @param  w        image width
7    * @param  h        image height
8    * @return          Image containing website snapshot
9    * @throws IOException communication problem
10   * @throws MalformedURLException incorrect URL
11   */
12   static public Image snapshot(String website, int w, int
         h) throws IOException, MalformedURLException {
13       URL url = new URL(website);
14       URLConnection connection = url.openConnection();
15       InputStream input = connection.getInputStream();
16       Image image = render(input, w, h);
17       return image;
18   }
```

Fig. 2. Library method

3   Securing What Is Understood

The convenience of using abstractions and their ability to handle security threats relieves the developer from having to consider much of the low-level details. For example, because object persistence frameworks do not require construction of SQL queries, the programmer need not consider sanitizing user input with respect to the SQL language. Similarly, letting the MVC framework provide the Web presentation layer can reduce programmer concerns about application output interfering with the output context, such as HTML, XML and JSON. This does not excuse the programmer from considering security issues entirely, rather the emphasis is on the security controls that are relevant to the application code.

Regardless of the effectiveness of the programming abstractions, it is reasonable to expect that the developer does understand some of the underlying system operation in order to identify possible threats and to counter them with adequate security controls. For example, although not directly referenced in the application code, it may be anticipated that the application will communicate over HTTP with the remote website in order to create a snapshot. Thus, the application should be permitted to make HTTP connections that are, to some degree, controlled by application users through the URLs they enter, and this may be a security threat. In this case, the application could be used to access systems—in the local network where it is hosted—that are not normally accessible from the Internet. A malicious user may, by adding a bookmark to the URL in the local network, such as http://10.0.0.1/router/admin, attempt to access systems that he should not have access to. In order to address this threat, the developer can code a security control in the application that verifies that the URL's host does not point to a local IP address, before calling the library to create a snapshot. For example, the `addBookmark()` method can begin with:

```
// [...]
InetAddress addr =
    InetAddress.getByName(url.getHost()));
if (addr.isSiteLocalAddress())
    throw new SecurityException();
// [...]
```

4   The Security Gap

To a casual reader, the bookmark application (or even the `WebUtils` library) code does not openly perform TCP/IP operations. The above threat was identified based on the programmer's expectation of low-level application behaviour. Correlating high level application behaviour (accessing URLs) with the threat (user-controlled network traffic) is a human task and, as such, is prone to human error. Failure to implement adequate security controls may not necessarily mean that the developers are unaware of the threat or neglect security. As observed previously, despite understanding a security vulnerability, a developer may unwittingly write code containing the vulnerability [23]. The cognitive effort that is required to anticipate security problems is much greater if the details are abstracted.

Consider again the bookmark application extended with the security control to prevent local URL access. Despite appearances, an attacker can bypass this check as follows. We first note that the HTTP protocol [12] allows a server to redirect the client to another URL in order to fulfill the request through a defined status code (such as 302) and a header.

- An attacker sets up a website that redirects to the local target machine and adds a bookmark to that website.
- The attacker's website (public) URL will be accepted as not local and action `WebUtils.snapshot()` is called.
- The Java library will access the website and in `url.openConnection()` in the implementation of `snapshot` effectively follow the URL, effectively connecting to a local address.

In order to prevent this attack it is necessary for the programmer to modify the utility library to explicitly handle redirects and verify the IP address each time, before accessing the URL. This approach, however, may suffer a TOCT-TOU vulnerability. In this case, there is a time gap between the verification of the IP address and the HTTP connection to the corresponding URL. Within that time gap, the mapping between host name and IP address may be modified. While past responses will typically be cached by the resolver, the attacker may prevent the caching by creating a record with lowest possible Time To Live value supported by Domain Name System [22], that is, 1 s. This is a variant of a DNS Rebinding attack [17].

Perhaps, and rather than trying to implement the network-related security controls in the application, a better strategy is to consider this a matter for system network configuration. In this case, it should be the systems and network administrators, not the developers, who need to handle the problem by implementing adequate firewall rules. While transferring administrative burdens to the consumer is a common practice [11], it also pushes the abstraction further and may make the threat equally difficult to identify.

Regardless of how this network protection is implemented, the web application still contains an even more serious and unexpected vulnerability. It allows application clients to access custom files from the web server's file system. The root cause is the fact that RFC3986 [9] specifies that a Uniform Resource Identifier can be `file:`, in addition to `http:` and `https:`. In this case,

- an application client, may create a bookmark for the address URL such as `file:///etc/passwd` and,
- the application generates an image representing file contents.

This behaviour may not have been anticipated by the application developer who, upon reading the documentation, understood that `WebUtils.snapshot()` should be called with a *"website address"* and which throws an exception if that address is *"incorrect"*. Similarly, the library developer might have been misled by the Java `URL/URLConnection` documentation and method names referring to *"connections"* and *"sockets"* and did not expect that their code could be used to access regular files. While, the `URL` class javadoc [24] includes a reference to `file:` URL scheme, it appears only once, in one of the constructors' documentation. Other platforms include similar, often misleading, features. For example the function `file_get_contents` in PHP, despite its name, allows accessing remote resources if the URL is provided as a file name [27].

To avoid this vulnerability, the developer must implement specific code that checks whether the URL specifies a website address. However, other URL-related problems may emerge. For example, in another part of the application, it may be required to verify whether a URL matches a list of accepted URLs. The Java `equals()` method can be used (explicitly or implicitly via the `List.contains()` method) as a standard way to test object equality. Using this method is convenient when comparing URL objects, as it respects that a host name and protocol are case insensitive and some port numbers are optional. For example, http://example.com/, http://example.com:80/ and http://example.com/ are equal URLs despite their different string representation. What may not be anticipated by the programmer, is that when comparing two URL objects, the method resolves their host names and considers them equal if they point to the same IP address. In this case http://example.com/ is considered *equal* to http://attacker.com/, provided that the attacker has targeted their host to http://example.com/'s IP address. This unexpected behaviour may lead to security vulnerabilities if URLs are for used for white/black listing, or to ensure the Same Origin Policy [8]. While the behaviour of `URL.equals()` is documented and the corresponding security issues are considered [10], a developer may not consider checking that part of documentation to be necessary, especially if the code may not explicitly invoke the method.

This example demonstrates how programming oversights, in what seemed to be trivial, high-level application code, can result in series of security issues whose identification and prevention requires an in-depth understanding of low-level libraries and a number of network protocols. In today's systems of interoperating components, the security gap between the expected behaviour and the actual behaviour is unavoidable. Pushing the responsibility to understand everything onto developers is expecting them to be omniscient, is not realistic, and is in effect, security theatre.

5   Verifying Expectation

An application system program has a security gap when a developer's misunderstanding means that an attacker can exploit the difference between its expected behaviour versus its actual behaviour and, for which security controls do not exist. In this section we outline our ongoing investigation on how the gap can be reduced by checking the runtime behaviour of the component against a predefined model of its expected behaviour. Runtime verification [7] is the process of observing system execution and validating that specified properties are upheld, or that the execution is consistent with a testing oracle. For example, a predicate stating that each **acquire** has a matching **release** in a (re-entrant) Lock class [19]. However, based on our earlier observations, we argue that a typical developer would still be unable to capture all properties about expected behaviour; a security gap remains. The challenge is to construct a model of expected behaviour that helps to reduce the security gap.

We use data mining techniques to infer patterns of expected behaviour from execution traces that are generated during the testing phase of the development lifecycle. Such system trace mining techniques have been used elsewhere to infer acceptable behaviour/policies for anomaly detection [14,28] process mining [5,6], security policy mining [15,20] and fault detection [18]. Expected behaviour is not exactly the same as the *normal* behaviour upon which anomaly detection is typically based. Normal behaviour is system-specific, and relates to system configuration, infrastructure, usage patterns and so forth. Typically, it is established for a particular instance of the system based on monitoring its operation under normal circumstances. The expected behaviour corresponds to the anticipated behaviour of the system under all expected circumstances. It represents all of the activity that the system is capable of performing. Some activity may be expected, recognized as possible in the system in general, but not considered normal in a particular system instance.

An approach for inferring behavioural models from system logs was proposed in the seminal work of Forrest et al. [14]. System behaviour is modeled in terms of a set of *n-grams* of system call operations present in the system log. As the system executes, its operations are compared against this model of 'normal' and, if the sequence does not match known n-grams, it may be considered anomalous. This approach is limited to identifying short-range correlations between operations in traces and can miss interesting behaviours by not considering transactional behaviour [29]. In our work we use the richer behavioural norms [28,29] which can identify repeating patterns of parameterized behaviour from the system trace.

Intuitively, behavioural norms are sequences of parametrized actions. For example, one of the norms that represent the actions that result from accessing an `http:` URL is the following sequence of method invocations:

```
net.url("get","http",$1,$2);
socket.connect($1,$3);
socket.resolve($1);
socket.connect($4,$3);
socket.read();
...;
socket.close()
```

The norm represents a repeating pattern of behaviour discovered in a system trace. It is not generated by static analysis of the code. Action parameter attributes are identified as static values (such as `"get"`) or free variables (such as `$1`) that can be bound to some value when matching an instance of the norm against runtime behaviour. In mining a system trace, our analysis algorithm [28] has proven quite effective in identifying the action attributes that remain static versus those that can change, and how they correlate, each time the norm is matched. For example, the norm above is the outcome of a `get` on an `http:` URL to some host `$1`, resulting in a socket `connect` and `resolve` on involving the same host and subsequent `connect` on a resolved IP address `$1`.

We carried out a preliminary evaluation of the use of behavioural norms as a means of identifying coding errors in the security gap. A set of conventional unit tests were run against the `WebUtils` library, testing both positive and negative cases. For example, the website image snapshot was tested with a number of URLs and expected error conditions, such as incorrect URL, unresolvable host, interrupted connection, and so forth. Note that none of the tests attempted to open `file:` URLs, as such behaviour was not expected as possible. The Java build process for the library was extended to capture a trace during test execution. This trace is a sequence of the low-level actions that result from testing `WebUtils`, and contain not just those actions from the snapshot library, but also all others, such URL methods, etc. This trace of all method invocations was analyzed for behavioural norms and the resulting model of expected behaviour was included in the library manifest. A Java aspect was used to provide runtime verification using the Java security manager. Note that neither generating the behavioural model nor its runtime verification requires any change to the original library code and is applicable to any Java component.

The web application was redeployed with its new library and tested. While the original positive and negative test cases were still effective (testing expected behaviour, such as creating images from websites) we found that the unexpected behaviour, such as creating images using local files, was no longer possible. In this case, the behavioural norm model permitted snapshot transactions that involved `http:` URLs, but identified a snapshot transaction using `file:` URLs as anomalous. Note that the generated model does not prevent the application from carrying out all `file:` URL operations, just those that occur within a snapshot transaction. In practice, other parts of the bookmark web application may be expected to access files, and general file accessing behaviour is part of the expected behaviour of the application as a whole.

We are currently investigating how this approach can identify other coding errors that lead to security vulnerabilities. In preliminary experiments, we have observed that a number of typical programming errors, including Insecure Direct Object Reference, TOCTTOU, access control flaws and broken authentication manifest themselves through distinguishably different low-level behaviour and, as such, could be detected using that technique.

6   Conclusion

Given the complexity of contemporary applications, we argue that there will always be a security gap between the code's actual behaviour and the behaviour expected by the programmer. The cognitive overload on the programmer increases with the level of the programming abstractions used and increases the likelihood of errors that lead to security vulnerabilities. We propose taking a runtime verification style approach to check an executing program against a model of expected behaviour that is generated during unit testing. While our initial experiments provide some evidence that this approach has potential, we note that its effectiveness depends greatly on the completeness of the unit testing at exercising expected behaviour.

Acknowledgements. This work was supported, in part, by Science Foundation Ireland under grant SFI/12/RC/2289 and the Irish Centre for Cloud Computing and Commerce, an Irish national Technology Centre funded by Enterprise Ireland and the Irish Industrial Development Authority.

References

1. Bash Code Injection Vulnerability via Specially Crafted Environment Variables. https://access.redhat.com/articles/1200223
2. The Heartbleed Bug. http://heartbleed.com/
3. Hibernate. http://hibernate.org
4. The Spring Framework. https://spring.io
5. Accorsi, R., Stocker, T.: Automated privacy audits based on pruning of log data. In: EDOCW, pp. 175–182 (2008)
6. Agrawal, R., Gunopulos, D., Leymann, F.: Mining process models from workflow logs. In: Schek, H.-J., Saltor, F., Ramos, I., Alonso, G. (eds.) EDBT 1998. LNCS, vol. 1377, pp. 469–483. Springer, Heidelberg (1998)

7. Barringer, H., Goldberg, A., Havelund, K., Sen, K.: Rule-based runtime verification. In: Steffen, B., Levi, G. (eds.) VMCAI 2004. LNCS, vol. 2937, pp. 44–57. Springer, Heidelberg (2004)
8. Barth, A.: The web origin concept. Request for Comments 6454, Internet Engineering Task Force, December 2011. http://www.ietf.org/rfc/rfc6454.txt
9. Berners-Lee, T., Fielding, R., Masinter, L.: Uniform resource identifier (URI): generic syntax. Request for Comments 3986, Internet Engineering Task Force, January 2005. http://www.ietf.org/rfc/rfc3986.txt
10. Carnegie Mellon University: CERT secure coding standards - VOID 2 MET21-J. Do not invoke equals() or hashCode() on URLs. https://www.securecoding.cert.org/confluence/x/5wHEAw
11. Davis, D.: Compliance defects in public-key cryptography. In: Proceedings of the 6th Conference on USENIX Security Symposium, Focusing on Applications of Cryptography, SSYM 1996, vol. 6, p. 17. USENIX Association, Berkeley (1996). http://dl.acm.org/citation.cfm?id=1267569.1267586
12. Fielding, R., Gettys, J., Mogul, J., Frystyk, H., Masinter, L., Leach, P., Berners-Lee, T.: Hypertext transfer protocol - HTTP/1.1. Request for Comments 2616, Internet Engineering Task Force, June 1999. http://www.ietf.org/rfc/rfc2616.txt
13. Foley, S.: A non-functional approach to system integrity. IEEE J. Sel. Areas Commun. **21**(1), 36–43 (2003)
14. Forrest, S., Hofmeyr, S., Somayaji, A., Longstaff, T.: A sense of self for unix processes. In: IEEE Symposium on Security and Privacy, pp. 120–128 (1996)
15. Frank, M., Buhmann, J., Basin, D.: On the definition of role mining. In: Proceedings of the 15th ACM Symposium on Access Control Models and Technologies, SACMAT 2010, pp. 35–44. ACM, New York (2010). http://doi.acm.org/10.1145/1809842.1809851
16. Gollmann, D.: Software security – the dangers of abstraction. In: Matyáš, V., Fischer-Hübner, S., Cvrček, D., Švenda, P. (eds.) The Future of Identity. IFIP AICT, vol. 298, pp. 1–12. Springer, Heidelberg (2009)
17. Jackson, C., Barth, A., Bortz, A., Shao, W., Boneh, D.: Protecting browsers from DNS rebinding attacks. In: Proceedings of ACM CCS 07 (2007). http://crypto.stanford.edu/dns/dns-rebinding.pdf
18. Jiang, G., Chen, H., Ungureanu, C., Yoshihira, K.: Multi-resolution abnormal trace detection using varied-length N-grams and automata. In: Second International Conference on Autonomic Computing, ICAC 2005, Proceedings, pp. 111–122 (2005)
19. Jin, D., Meredith, P.O., Lee, C., Roşu, G.: JavaMOP: efficient parametric runtime monitoring framework. In: Proceedings of the 34th International Conference on Software Engineering, ICSE 2012, pp. 1427–1430. IEEE Press, Piscataway (2012). http://dl.acm.org/citation.cfm?id=2337223.2337436
20. Kuhlmann, M., Shohat, D., Schimpf, G.: Role mining - revealing business roles for security administration using data mining technology. In: Proceedings of the Eighth ACM Symposium on Access Control Models and Technologies, SACMAT 2003, pp. 179–186. ACM, New York (2003). http://doi.acm.org/10.1145/775412.775435
21. Meyer, B.: Applying "Design by Contract". IEEE Comput. **25**(10), 40–51 (1992). http://doi.ieeecomputersociety.org/10.1109/2.161279
22. Mockapetris, P.: Domain names - concepts and facilities. Request for Comments 1034, Internet Engineering Task Force, November 1987. http://www.ietf.org/rfc/rfc1034.txt

23. Oliveira, D., Rosenthal, M., Morin, N., Yeh, K.C., Cappos, J., Zhuang, Y.: It's the psychology stupid: how heuristics explain software vulnerabilities and how priming can illuminate developer's blind spots. In: Proceedings of the 30th Annual Computer Security Applications Conference, ACSAC 2014, pp. 296–305. ACM, New York (2014). http://doi.acm.org/10.1145/2664243.2664254
24. Oracle: Java Platform API Specification - URL (2014). http://docs.oracle.com/javase/7/docs/api/java/net/URL.html
25. Oracle: Java Platform API Specification - URL Connection (2014). http://docs.oracle.com/javase/7/docs/api/java/net/URLConnection.html
26. OWASP Foundation: OWASP Top 10 2013. https://www.owasp.org/index.php/Top_10_2013
27. The PHP Group: PHP Manual – file_get_contents. http://php.net/manual/en/function.file-get-contents.php
28. Pieczul, O., Foley, S.: Discovering emergent norms in security logs. In: 2013 IEEE Conference on Communications and Network Security (CNS - SafeConfig), pp. 438–445 (2013)
29. Pieczul, O., Foley, S.: Collaborating as normal: detecting systemic anomalies in your partner. In: Christianson, B., Malcolm, J., Matyáš, V., Švenda, P., Stajano, F., Anderson, J. (eds.) Security Protocols 2014. LNCS, vol. 8809, pp. 18–27. Springer, Heidelberg (2014)
30. Ryan, P.: Mathematical models of computer security. In: Focardi, R., Gorrieri, R. (eds.) FOSAD 2000. LNCS, vol. 2171, pp. 1–62. Springer, Heidelberg (2001)

The Dark Side of the Code
(Transcript of Discussion)

Simon N. Foley[1]([✉]) and Olgierd Pieczul[1,2]

[1] Department of Computer Science, University College Cork, Cork, Ireland
s.foley@cs.ucc.ie
[2] Ireland Lab, IBM Software Group, Dublin, Ireland
olgierdp@ie.ibm.com

Bruce Christianson: Right, I think it was Dijkstra[1] who said that if you don't formally specify a system it can never be insecure, it can only be surprising. The obvious course of action is for the European Commission to make formal specification illegal and then announce victory. But here to put the other side of that particular argument are Olgierd and Simon.

Simon Foley: Thanks Bruce. This is a joint talk. I'm going to give a brief introduction and some context, and then Olgierd will take over with more detail.

Following up on Bruce's comment, I remember Bob Morris would sometimes describe security as absence of surprise and we've been looking at the security surprises that result from programmer error. For a programmer, an implementation fails if there's a surprise in its execution where its actual behaviour is not as required or expected. Thinking of this in terms of security, the implementation is not secure if there's an attack whereby the system's actual behaviour is not consistent with its required or expected behaviour. For example, a replay attack in the actual behaviour of a security protocol is not what the programmer expected.

No surprise means that the actual behaviour of the program matches its expected behaviour. Of course this assumes that the programmer fully understands the expected and actual behaviour. In practice, the programmer is likely to take a flat view of the system, thinking only in terms of the APIs he uses, and he may not think about what happens under the hood. For example, a protocol developer thinks in terms of messages and crypto operations, and might not think too much about what happens in the low-level code behind the API. At the extreme, this developer lives in a two-dimensional world that we can think of as flatland.

Edwin Abbot, who was a Shakespearian scholar, wrote *"Flatland: A Romance of Many Dimensions"* in 1884 as a saritical science-fiction exploration of life in a two-dimensional world, how its citizens managed with just two-dimensions and the difficulties that they had in comprehending other dimensions. For example, there's an account of the author, a flatlander, who gets visited by a Sphere and can't comprehend how the Sphere can cause things to disappear in the

---

[1] Or perhaps Bob Morris, see LNCS 6615, p 120. However, I searched the Internet and found attributions to "apocryphal" and to "Brian Kernighan" as well as use without any attribution at all.

© Springer International Publishing Switzerland 2015
B. Christianson et al. (Eds.): Security Protocols 2015, LNCS 9379, pp. 12–21, 2015.
DOI: 10.1007/978-3-319-26096-9_2

flatlander's 2-D world and then re-appear at a different location. Often, when we study security, take a flatland view.

Contemporary software development is not flat; what might seem like a simple API call in flatland, results in complex interactions within the underlying system and its infrastructure. A programmer writes code at the abstract API level (flatland), may understand some of the lower levels of the code, but does not understand everything that happens behind the API. This is what we call the dark side of the code: low-level program behaviour that is not known or understood by the programmer and this can cause security surprises.

For example, a flatlander programmer didn't understand that a database management system was behind an API call and as a result an injection attack occurs and percolates back up into some surprise in the programmer's flatland. This is like the two dimensional flatlander being surprised by the behaviour of the three dimensional Sphere. Of course, programmers can still make mistakes at their level. Surprises can also occur from programmer blindspots in things they understand but overlook. We think that the usual software development techniques can help us deal with the complexity of the system and ensure that the actual behaviour of the system is consistent with expectation. However, security vulnerabilities still persist. For example, even with abstraction we can still have attacks.

Bruce Christianson: [Just go for it Sandy]

Sandy Clark: Well, I would argue that it is only going to get worse, because currently it is difficult to finish an undergrad degree and not get through the your programme without specialising, and without specialising early, whereas previous generations didn't specialise, you learned the entire system.

Simon Foley: Yes, certainly. I'm not suggesting that abstraction, frameworks and everything else are the solution. I think that they are often put forward as some sort of solution, but they create as many problems as they solve. If we're to have secure systems where we don't have surprises, and the actual behaviour corresponds to the expected behaviour. It seems we need a developer who is expected to understand everything and with the result that there's no dark side of the code. Taking that argument to its conclusion, what we seem to be looking for are, omniscient coders, such as the beings from the Q continuum in Star Trek, who understand all dimensions, not just the few dimensions of the 'puny' human race, or indeed the programmer race. The Q understand everything. Of course its security theatre for us to think that programmers can be omniscient and understand everything. There will always be a dark side of the code.

I hand you over to Olgierd who will to walk you through a concrete example of this dark side in the code. He'll show how it is really easy for programmers not to appreciate what's happening in the low level details. He'll also talk a little bit about how we've been using run-time verification techniques to look at this problem.

Olgierd Pieczul: I will be talking about real developers that I am here to represent. I will use an example, a bookmark sharing application. It is a web application that can be used to create, browse and manage web bookmarks.

Among other things, it can be used to save snapshot image of a bookmark, which then can be viewed by a user. In the past implementing such an application required a lot of work. But today, with the many of tools and frameworks available it is very easy to implement. For example, all the code required to process bookmark creation can be contained just in a few lines. This code creates snapshot images of the website addresses provided as the parameters in the request, and saves them along with a bookmark information using persistence framework. In only four lines of code the application gets user provided data, contacts and retrieves the website, generates snapshot images and returns operation status.

But what exactly is the code doing? Is there anything that can potentially have impact on security? At the fourth line we see something that may be related to database operations. Perhaps there is potential security problem of SQL injection. Actually there is not, because the persistence framework protects against that. The first two lines, where application calls a library to create snapshot images of a bookmark, may cause security problems. The code makes network connections to a user-provided location. Why is should that be a security risk? It is expected that the application will connect to the public web server, to download the website, and create an image, and report back to the user. But there is also an expected threat, that instead of specifying a public website, a malicious user will provide an address to an internal site. This will cause the application to connect to that internal server (that may hold sensitive information), create a snapshot images and present them back to the user.

So what's in the code again? The listing presents very, very high level code, and there is nothing in it that relates to internal/external addresses. The code responsible for creating the image snapshot, provided by a third-party library, is also at a very high level. It takes the website URL as a parameter, and it seems to verify whether this URL is correct, as it throws an exception for a "malformed URL". According to Java documentation, the URL is a "resource to the World Wide Web". Further in the code, you can see that there is a "connection" that is "opened" and an input stream being created from that connection. Also, there is a possibility of "socket timeout" or some network related problem. Although this gives some hints about the code operation, the snapshot library code remains very high level. This is an example of security gap: the code does not openly perform any of the TCP/IP operations and the threat is based on *expectation* regarding low level application behaviour. That this is possible is not apparent by simply inspecting the application code in isolation. It is a human task to correlate the high-level application behaviour with this low level threat.

The most obvious solution is also low level. The application may try to verify that the address of the bookmark is not a local address. But, as you can see in the listing, this pushes the code to lower level of abstraction. Now, the developer needs to consider concepts such as local address, and public address in, otherwise high-level, code.

Alastair Beresford: Isn't there also an alternative solution at a different level?

Olgierd Pieczul: There is, I will present some of them. In fact, this particular solution is wrong. It is based on incorrect assumption that the address from the URL is the address that application will create the snapshot from. It may not be expected, that after the address is verified, and application connects to the HTTP server, that server may perform an HTTP redirect to arbitrary location, such as internal network server.

This problem can be fixed if the application, while verifying the address, followed all HTTP redirects and verified the final location. When implementing such protection, the developer may not expect that it can also be bypassed. A DNS rebinding attack may be used to redirect the connection to internal location after it is verified.

In order to identify all of those problems, the developer needs to go down the low level. For what was at first a very simple, high-level application, the developer now has to consider HTTP protocol, redirects, DNS protocol and so forth.

Often, the developer will just document the issue and expect the user or administrator to provide external security controls, and in this case, control the application's network access. But that does not really solve the problem, it only shifts responsibility from the developer to the administrator. As a result, the gap widens even more and the administrator needs to expect that the application that is installed with this default configuration can potentially endanger their local network. It is very unlikely they would expect that.

Assuming this is the most likely solution, an administrator deploys a firewall, or Java policy that prevents the access of specific local addresses. However, this same code has yet another vulnerability. A malicious user may create a bookmark to a URL with a file protocol, such as `file:///etc/passwd`. Although the URL handling code seems to be focused on network-related operations, it is actually capable of processing URLs with non-network schemes, such as files. In this case, rather than opening a website, the application will open a local file, and create an image, and render that image to the user. In order to avoid this vulnerability, the developer needs to understand the low-level details of the URL handling in Java, even though they never actually directly call it in their code.

This is what we call "the dark side of the code". An application may be able to perform operations that may not be expected by its developers. Expecting that developers can fully comprehend the application to the lowest level, including all its interoperating components, is unrealistic and, in our opinion, security theatre.

So what we propose is that, rather than preventing any possible unexpected behaviour by the application, we verify if the actual behaviour of the application is consistent with what is expected. The developer knows what is expected, because that's how the application should work, and our goal is to verify the actual behaviour against the expectation. Now, the question is, how we can capture and model this expected behaviour? We propose using a model of behavioural norms, an abstraction of application execution traces. The norms represent how the application behaves under normal circumstances. They can be discovered automatically from the logs, and capture unknown patterns of interaction between system components.

On this slide you can see some norms for HTTP and HTTPS connections, successful and failed. We performed an experiment, whereby by capturing all permissions checks, the Java Security Manager, can be used to generate a trace of application activity. We then used the WebUtils library unit tests to 'exercise' the library and capture a trace of expected behaviour. This trace was used to generate a norms model of expected behavior and this, in turn, is used by the runtime verification mechanism to check that current execution corresponds with this model of expected behavior. In the case of a violation, the mechanism can alert or stop the application code execution. In short, the result of running this experiment was that bookmarks with HTTP URLs, and many other expected scenarios execute correctly, while bookmarks with file URLs are prevented by runtime verification.

To wrap up. In modern applications there is a gap between expected behaviour and the actual behaviour. This gap is unavoidable, and expecting developers to fill the gap with their own knowledge and skill is an unrealistic expectation. Rather than preventing all the known unexpected behaviour we propose to capture the expected behavior and verify the application against that behaviour. The behaviour norms that we have developed can be used for that verification. Thank you.

James Malcolm: How are you going to tell the difference between unusual behaviour and bad behaviour? Lots of things are unusual but perfectly OK?

Olgierd Pieczul: There are two answers. One is test coverage: how much the application is being tested. Another one is the abstraction of the expected behaviour. The behavioural norms are not really exact traces of code, and provide a level of abstraction and flexibility within themselves. But yes, it's a good question, this is the intrinsic problem of our research.

Simon Foley: To add to that, one thing to consider about the models of expected behaviour that we are building is that they're not just the Flatland view of the program. That is, they are not just in terms of the API the programmer uses but also includes events in the underlying infrastructure. For example, if it was a web application then the model could include all of the HTTP traffic generated during the unit tests, not just the traffic that is explicitly coded by the application. Such a model may be sufficient to detect anomalies in HTTP traffic as the application executes. Alternatively, the model of expected behavior may be extended to include all local file system accesses. This more detailed model can be used to detect the anomaly in the application Olgierd described. At some point a judgement must be made about how much detail should be included in this model. If we limit ourselves to direct API events, its likely we won't find any surprises. We want to include enough detail to be able to detect the interesting surprises. As Olgierd mentioned previously, finding the right level of abstraction is a challenge in anomaly detection in general.

Dong Changyu: Have we considered the possibility that attacks might arise at the lookalike expected activity.

Olgierd Pieczul: Yes. Some attacks may not represent themselves through different behaviour. This is mostly a matter of how the behavioural model is built. It may consider only "action" attributes, but also other that provide more context. It may also include execution parameters and context that may result in much more precise model. This may, however, reduce the flexibility.

Dong Changyu: So, are the mimicry attacks possible?

Olgierd Pieczul: Yes, though they are more difficult here than in similar solutions, as the model is much more precise.

Keith Irwin: Is the application you use in the presentation the only example?

Olgierd Pieczul: Yes, it is only a proof-of-concept application we developed for this experiment.

Keith Irwin: I was going to say, because I would have trouble believing that the connection to the internal server would look different from a connection to the external server, from the app's perspective.

Olgierd Pieczul: That was an expected threat, that was something we did not try to protect against using norms.

Keith Irwin: Although you would expect you would sometimes run into HTTP redirecting.

Olgierd Pieczul: Correct.

Mohammad Dashti: Ideally you would like to be able to execute these norms and get rid of the problem, right? These norms are somehow restricting your program to what you want it to actually do, and if you could execute them then you could forget about the program.

Olgierd Pieczul: But they are not the actual programme, they are only an abstraction.

Bruce Christianson: But the question is, what's the difference between a program and implementation, and an executable specification.

Olgierd Pieczul: It is not a specification but only an abstracted trace, covering only some portion of application activity, such as permission checks. It is much more abstract than the actual code.

Mohammad Dashti: Sure, but if I see this norm as a regular expression, for instance, then it can be executed. I'm not suggesting that your norms could be executed, but if in principle we want to have an executable norm?

Simon Foley: Yes, I think in principle you could say: I'll take a log from the unit testing and from that I'll infer some state machine that's in some sense equivalent to the code that I have written to some degree of approximation. Then I could take that state machine, and execute it. Yes, in principle, but in practice that's not we're doing. We're working to some level of abstraction of the events under the hood: we're not going all the way down to the lowest-level of system operation. For our current experiments we're looking at the network as the level of abstraction, the TCP/IP operations. We make sure that when the program runs then we're validating against those particular sequences of network operations, everything else is abstracted away. The idea is that if there's a deviation from what's expected (in the network events), then you'll get a slight re-ordering of these sequences, and then that's what gets detected by runtime verification.

Bruce Christianson: But to what extent are you just trying to enforce the implementation to respect the abstraction at the specification then? And to what extent are you actually trying to verify that the abstraction is correct? Or is that a non-goal? Or are you finding them in parallel together?

Simon Foley: If we go back to the beginning of our talk when I argued that that programmers are like Flatlanders, and they think only in terms of their own APIs. If you consider the application that Olgierd talked about at the beginning, then that's their view of the system, their Flatland view of the world. They have no idea of, or pay little attention to, the underlying sequences of network interactions. When they think of expected behaviour, they think in terms of the high program APIs. Thinking formally, we'd might argue that functional requirements are specified at this high level, and we don't need to think too much about what's happening down at these lower levels of abstraction, which we're not even trying to model in our specification. We write our high level program as usual. During unit testing of expected behaviour, the application runs and we log not just on the high-level APIs, but also on the low-level calls under the hood, such as network events. The model of expected behaviour is built from these events.

Bruce Christianson: So it's actually your implementer who is working at the higher level of abstraction, and your specification is at a lower level.

Simon Foley: Yes, what's being generated is the stuff from the dark side.

Olgierd Pieczul: So just to clarify, all of those low-level norms correspond with a single line of the application code: create a snapshot of a website. Various norms capture different types of low level behaviour that developer may not expect.

Max Spencer: So I propose that the developer still has to know about the dark side of the code, because they need to be able to anticipate the places they input in their unit tests that would generate enough activity for the base line behaviour. The application can still do lots of useful stuff, they need to anticipate. So it might just be shifting your understanding, where instead of having to understand enough about checks in your actual program to prevent the bad behaviour, you would just know enough about it to make sure that your norm generating tests for good behaviour. So it just seems like a bit of a shift from one to the other, but you are still requiring developers to know about the dark side.

Olgierd Pieczul: Using unit tests is just one of a number of possible ways to generate the base line behaviour. Another could be to monitor application operating in a test or production environment.

Frank Stajano: He makes the valid point that you cannot come up with a unit test that tests the entire network for some scenario if you don't think about it, right? You're not going to come up with that at random.

Ross Anderson: It may be more general than that. The application will only work in those sorts of cases that were initially tested, you cannot use it to innovate, you can't use it to do new stuff. If you test an automated car to drive on the left-hand side of the road and you take it to France it will just freak out and it would stop, and all the gears will crunch, and smoke will come from the parts and it will expire. Now that may be OK for an application, but it's not OK for a platform, because the whole point of a platform is that other people can then build stuff on top of it to do entirely new stuff. This would be no good for testing Windows 11.

Alastair Beresford: So maybe one way to fix this is to record the application activity for the first 10 days in production, assuming that there are no attackers. I record how it is used and then flip the switch.

Olgierd Pieczul: Of course, the expected behaviour may be gathered in multiple ways.

Ross Anderson: So it gives new zest to the application development life-cycle, all the programs are a teenager that will try all sorts of new stuff, but by the time it's 25 it will be set it its ways, and it will never change.

Tom Sutcliffe: Do you feel this may risk breaking the abstractions that your library is trying achieve in the first place?

Sandy Clark: That is OK. If you break them, you find out where they are broken and then you understand the assumptions that were made in the first place that do not work.

Tom Sutcliffe: Yes, but it may be that it was an implementation detail, which really doesn't actually matter for your use base, but have to spend two days debugging it to establish that. I'm just thinking of the case where, for example, you upgrade a library and suddenly it starts caching the DNS requests somewhere such that you don't get your resolve step happening. And then it suddenly breaks your norms.

Olgierd Pieczul: We have thought about it as well. It is a question when behaviour is being captured. It may happen during development cycle of a new version of the library, but also, when the application is upgraded to the new library.

Tom Sutcliffe: If all those libraries are under your control and are bundled with your app then I guess you could do that. But if you're potentially deploying against different versions, and you don't necessarily know, you don't have a well specified environment to start with, it could get quite tricky.

Olgierd Pieczul: Yes, this is a problem, and a possible way to solve it was to limit captured behaviour on both high and low level and only build the norms for the things you control, or you know that are not changing.

Tom Sutcliffe: I suppose it does lead onto the fact that if you do control more of the stack then you're less likely to get unexpected behaviours if you are deploying against fixed versions that you've run and tested with, so yes.

Ross Anderson: So if you're got a big red button in your app that says, training now, and then the attacker is just going to socially engineer the user into pressing the big red button.

Mark Lomas: Can I suggest that part of the problem is that your internal network is too open. What we tend to do for testing applications, is to put them on an isolated VLAN where they have no external connectivity at all. Now clearly the application will not function, so the developer has to decide, as part of application design, that it will communicate with these other entities within the organisation. Then they have to set up a firewall, set up logging and verify if there's at least one test case that exercise that firewall rule. If there isn't one then the developer made a mistake, if there is one, and it's inconsistent, then if you change control to make that permanent rule, and then gradually, gradually open up control to allow the expected behaviour.

Olgierd Pieczul: That is true, but the problem is that the application may legitimately contact that server for other purposes. For example, application may be expected to contact a database server but not to contact it in context of creating snapshot images of its interface. Also, unexpected access to files, will still work regardless what network protection is used.

Bruce Christianson: So this gives you access to external behaviour, but not to information flows that are internal? Can you enforce information flow using a mechanism like this?

For example, most frauds are done by people doing things that the rules allow them to do, but then using the information for a purpose other than the purpose for which they're supposed to have access.

Olgierd Pieczul: So in some cases it's a question of granularity of all those protections.

Bruce Christianson: Yes.

Olgierd Pieczul: So for example, the firewall rules can be very specific to say that this application is only allowed access to this very limited set of targets. Or it may open files but only some classes may open class can open some files.

Bruce Christianson: Could you augment this by actual instrument, put an instrument in the application code, and follow in control paths through the application code, tracing that, and seeing whether that complied with what you expected.

Alastair Beresford: And maybe it's the broader question about what level or levels you actually try and track.

Bruce Christianson: Which is kind of where we came in, yes, that's fair, yes, OK. Right, thank you very much...

Redesigning Secure Protocols to Compel Security Checks

Keith Irwin[✉]

Winston Salem Sate University, Winston-Salem, USA
irwinke@wssu.edu

Abstract. In the study of secure protocols, we must both ensure that the design of the protocol is secure and that the implementation is correct. One implementation problem which has frequently occurred is that implementations fail to implement some of the checks which are needed for the protocol to be secure. For example, implementations may fail to validate certificates or fail to validate all aspects of the certificate. In this paper, we demonstrate that it is possible to change the design of a protocol to compel the implementation to carry out the checks. We assume that programmers will always do at least what is necessary to read and produce properly formatted messages. Then we use some simple cryptography to ensure that reading properly formatted messages essentially requires checking the parameters.

1 Overview

One of the ongoing problems of secure protocols is how to make the actual implementations secure. There have been two basic approaches to this problem. The first is to use formal logic to prove that an implementation correctly implements the protocol. This is a very effective idea which is hampered by the reality that very few implementers of software actually carry it out.

The second is to create well-vetted, secure, open libraries which implement secure protocols. This approach is similarly hampered by the fact that not all implementers use these libraries. And it can also be hampered by problems in correctly using the libraries. For example, some programs which used a popular TLS implementation accidentally turned off name checking due to confusion about the meaning of arguments passed to the library [1].

One common problem with security in protocol implementations is when checks mandated by a protocol are either not carried out or carried out incorrectly. This is a problem because it generally results in silent insecurity. From the perspective of the user, the lack of security checks does not cause any malfunction. For example, a web browser which forgets to check the signature on incoming TLS packets still renders the web page absolutely fine.

We propose tackling this problem by redesigning protocols to make this insecurity no longer be silent. Essentially, our basic technique is the take some important portion of a message and encrypt it using a key which is most easily derived as a side-effect of carrying out the security check. Currently, security checks

© Springer International Publishing Switzerland 2015
B. Christianson et al. (Eds.): Security Protocols 2015, LNCS 9379, pp. 22–29, 2015.
DOI: 10.1007/978-3-319-26096-9_3

which are necessary for protocol security are optional for interoperability. This allows the protocol designer to change those security checks from being optional for interoperability to being necessary for proper interoperability. This effectively requires that an implementer either do the checks properly or utilize a library which does so.

We assume, in this approach, that a protocol designer will provide for implementers a reference implementation which properly implements the protocol and that implementers will go at least as far as ensuring that their implementation properly interoperates with the reference implementation. This is normal practice in implementing common standards.

2 Example

To give a simple example of how our scheme might work, let us assume that we have a protocol which makes use of RSA signatures. Now, it is well known that RSA signatures on the value 0 should not be accepted because RSA signatures use modular exponentiation and 0 to any power is still 0. Thus the proper signature for the message 0 is always the value 0. A mandatory check for this protocol to be secure is that the value of the signature is not 0. (The Nintendo Wii failed to perform this check and it was used as part of an attack on their code signing scheme [2]). However, if the implementer fails to include this check, there will be no problems of interoperability or other difficulties visible to any user. By the nature of programming, it is always easier to omit this check than to include it since all he must do to omit it is to fail to write the code which does the check. We wish to change this.

In order to do so, we need to identify a value which is most easily computed by doing the check or whose computation implies that the check has been carried out. A simple example of this, for this check, is to specify a large constant, C, and make the encryption key be the result of the integer division of C by the value of the signature. In most implementations of integer division, a division by zero would return an exception rather than a result, thus, if the signature is 0, an error condition will be caused. If the original protocol called for sending the message $t, sig\{t\}$, we can now modify it to be $E_{C/sigt}\{t\}, sig\{t\}$.

If we modify the protocol in this way, the implementers have little choice but to ensure that their programs carry out the division, thus ensuring that the signature is not 0. We say little choice because the programmer has the option of carrying out a brute force attack to find the key or of finding a complex way to compute the quotient without actually doing the division. Both of these are possible, but should be unlikely. So long as the constant is somewhat larger than the maximum signature value, the range of quotient values should be large enough to avoid a brute-force attack.

As for the second possibility, finding the quotient without carrying out the division, this may be accomplished, but the implementer is unlikely to do it because it would entail a large amount of extra work and provide no benefit. We are trying to push the implementer into implementing the security checks, but the implementer has no particular reason to avoid the security checks. They are generally omitted because implementers are short on time or fail to realize what is required. They are not trying to avoid implementing them, just failing to do so. Allowing the implementer an option where they could go to great lengths to avoid the security checks is unlikely to be tempting to anyone.

3 Generalization

Above we used the example of calculating the quotient of a large number. To generalize this approach, we want to be able to describe keys which must be computed for a variety of different checks. For any particular check, we define a function G for that particular check which takes in the inputs needed to perform the check and outputs a key.

We wish our G functions to share certain properties. These are:

1. When the check fails, G should be undefined.
2. When the check succeeds, G should have a large range of possible values.
3. There should not be a small mistake that the programmer could make in implementing G which would result in the correct value of G when the check succeeds and a predictable value of G when the check fails.

In practice, we do not actually use the division from the example above because although it has the first two properties, it does not always have the third. In some division implementations, division by 0 can result in NaN or infinity or other similar values. These could either have their bit representations used directly as the encryption key or in some systems numeric type conversions can coerce these to integer values like 0 or MAX_INT.

Instead, we assume the availability of a simple cryptographic hash function H and use this to define a function Z which has the property that it does not return when its input is 0 and that this cannot be easily avoided except by explicitly checking for the input 0. Our Z function, as defined, only accepts integer input. In our Z function, we utilize two constants. b is a target value which should be chosen to be above the range of values for i. Our Z function is recursize and first doubles i and flips its sign in each step until it exceeds b and then approaches b by some amount between the distance between them and a quarter of the distance between them, rounded up in each successive step until b exactly is reached. The constant z_b is a constant which is then returned. Any choice of z_b is reasonable. Thus we define:

$$Z(i) = \begin{cases} z_b & \text{if } i = b \\ H(Z(-2i)) & \text{if } i < b \wedge i \neq 0 \\ H(Z(i - \lceil (i - b)\frac{i}{4b} \rceil) & \text{if } i > b \end{cases}$$

Note that with proper implementation, the third case will only be reached when i is greater than b and less than $4b$, so the fraction which is multiplied by the difference between i and b is between 1 and $\frac{1}{4}$. This means that in each step of the third case, the input will move at least a quarter of the way closer to b. We round up to ensure that progress is always being made. Also note that if either the second or third cases is given an input of 0, they will loop forever.

This function has all three of the desired properties. In the event that i is 0, this function will never terminate since no amount of doubling i will ever cause it to exceed b, thus its output when given 0 is undefined. When the i is not 0, then every possible integer value of i should produce a different path of values on its way to reaching the terminal case ($i = b$), and thus the output should have as wide a range of values as the input.

It is difficult to prove that the third property holds without more robust models of possible programmer mistakes than exist in the literature, but we assert that it does. If we check through simple mistakes such as not properly checking which case we are in or returning the wrong value, we can note that any such change will clearly result in significant and obvious differences when the check is successful (when $i \neq 0$).

We should also note that Z will make a limited number of hash function calls which is bounded by the length of b. Specifically, it will make no more than $\log_2 b + \log_{4/3} b \approx 3.4 \cdot \log_2 b$ recursive calls, and thus the same number of hash function calls. Assuming that a b value is chosen to not be much larger than the maximum anticipated value for i, this should not be very expensive. It should be noted that the hash functions for this scheme may be chosen with a goal of optimizing for speed rather than for security since we do not expect the programmer to attempt to attack the hash functions.

3.1 Inequality Checks

Once we have defined Z we can use Z to easily define a G function for generalized inequality checking. $G_{\neq}(x,y) = Z(x - y)$. This can be used whether y is part of a message or a constant, so it can be used to check known bad values such as the 0 signature in RSA.

We can also use Z to construct a check for the less than or equal to operator over integers. $G_{\leq}(x,y) = Z(y - (y \bmod x))$ where mod is the modular remainder operator. If $x \leq y$ then $y \bmod x \neq y$ and thus $y - (y \bmod x) \neq 0$. Note that this only works for positive x. However, we can easily modify this test when x is negative if we know its range is bounded below by some constant $-C$ by testing $x + C \leq y + C$ instead.

Because are working with integers we can also simply define $G_{<}(x,y) = G_{\leq}(x, y - 1)$.

3.2 Combining Checks

We can also easily combine different checks using boolean AND and OR operations. We do not support NOT because, quite obviously, no scheme could prove that a check was not carried out.

If we have two checks c_1 and c_2 which must be completed on argument pairs (x_1, y_1) and (x_2, y_2), we define our encryption key $k = G_{c_1}(x_1, y_1) \oplus G_{c_2}(x_2, y_2)$ where $\oplus$ represents bitwise XOR. Thus, both G functions must be computed to know k.

If we have two checks c_1 and c_2 for which it is only required that one of them be completed, we instead let k equal a random number r_k and then include $E_{G_{c_1}(x_1, y_1)}\{r_k\}$ and $E_{G_{c_2}(x_2, y_2)}\{r_k\}$ in the message. This way, if either check is carried out, r_k may be computed.

3.3   Equivalent Encoding Check

Although it would appear that we could use our scheme as outlined so far to define an equality check $G_=(x, y)$ as $G_\le(x, y) \wedge G_\le(y, x)$, this unfortunately is not so (even if we use two different constants in our Z functions to avoid a result of 0). This is because doing an equality check which is immune to programmer mistake is impossible regardless of how it is designed. This is because any $G_=$ function must have the property that $G_=(x, y) = G_=(x, x)$ when $x = y$, so there is always an easy way for the programmer to accidentally skip the check. They can simply accidentally call the function $G(x, x)$ rather than $G(x, y)$.

Because the equality check is impossible, we instead describe an alternate check where one or both values are instead re-encoded into a different encoding scheme with randomness added and then the function checks that the two encodings have the same value. An equivalent encoding check will not have the property that $G_{enc}(x, y) = G_{enc}(x, x)$. This can be substituted for equality checking in most but not all situations where equality checking would be needed.

In some cases, values need to be human readable or are fixed by digital signature. For some of those, equivalent encoding cannot be substituted for equality checking, but for many it can.

There are many possible ways to do the equivalent encoding check. We have chosen this one for this paper because it is easy to understand and implement and has all the required properties. It, however, unlike some other possible choices, only allows checking a normally encoded message against a specially encoded one, not two specially encoded messages against each other. We plan to present additional options for encoding which can be used in equivalent encoding checks in future papers.

To encode a number x, we first chose a random number r. Then we break x into digits in some number base and then hash each digits together with its position and r. We then scramble the order of the hashes. The encoding of x, which we will call x_{enc} is the set of hashes (in scrambled order) and r.

This will usually result in x_{enc} being quite a bit larger than the original representaion of x. x_{enc} should be transmitted in the message in place of x. As such, this will increase the message size. In the long run, more complex equivalent encoding schemes which do not increase the message size as much are likely to be preferable.

To check if x_{enc} is an encoding of y (which it will be if $x = y$) we simply break y into digits the same way we did for x and the hash the digits of y

with their position and r the same way. Each hash of a digit from y is matched against the list of hashes from x_{enc}. If all are present and no extra hashes are present, then x_{enc} is an encoding of y and thus $x = y$. To define $G_{enc}(x_{enc}, y)$ we take the hashes from x_{enc} in order and compile a list of which position in y they correspond with. We also take each digit in y and find which hash from x_{enc} it corresponds with and make a list of those positions. Then we define $G_{enc}(x_{enc}, y)$ as the hash of those two lists, concatenated.

This G function has our three properties. There is no sensible answer to which positions the hashes of x correspond to and the digits of y correspond to when x does not encode y. There will be a range of values when the check succeeds. And, lastly, there does not appear to be any simple mistake that a programmer could make when implementing this algorithm which would result in correct values for G when the check succeeds but incorrect ones when it fails.

4   Related Works

On the whole, there is very little work related to this work. The closest work we have been able to find is that there do exist some key-management protocols which use cryptography to derive shared keys which are specific to uses or parties and thus implicitly check that the uses or parties are correct when the other party attempts to derive the same key. In the incorrect circumstances, an incorrect key is generated, thus preventing an opponent from substituting valid keys not meant for those circumstances. When done with parties, it is called key notarization [4]. When done with uses, this is called control vectors [3].

Our approach is similar in that it makes checking more implicit, but is much more general because unlike either control vectors or key notarization, it can be applied to any check in virtually any protocol. Both key notarization and control vectors only provide exact equality checks in these limited cases whereas we support a larger variety of checks.

5   Conclusion

In conclusion, our approach is novel and promising, but we have not yet been able to test it in the real world. To our knowledge, it is the first paper to propose using cryptography purely as a means to modify the behavior of implementers to be more secure.

However, we should note that there are some drawbacks to this approach. It does include an increase to the processing power required to process incoming messages. This scheme does not include any public key operations, and in general, we would argue that the security benefits outweigh the costs.

Another drawback is that the G functions described in this paper have data-dependent timing and power consumption. This is not necessarily an inherent requirement of the scheme, but it is a property of these particular functions. It is possible that this may lead to side channel attacks in some cases. By the nature of the scheme, no information which is known to just one party is used.

All keys and data must be known to both parties in order for the message to be able to be created and read. Thus a side-channel attack would only arise when a third party had access to the side-channel information and either additional information about the messages or a means to influence them. We expect this to be uncommon, but this is definitely an issue which should be kept in mind during protocol design.

Another drawback is that the complexity is increased. This may increase the difficulty of static analysis of implementations of the protocol. However, the increase in both complexity and apparent complexity may lead to an increase in usage of libraries which implement secure protocols, thus helping solve the problem that not everyone uses the well-vetted libraries.

The increased complexity of the protocol and commonality of backwards compatibility in real-world implementations may also make it difficult, in practice, to add this scheme to an existing protocol and have it be adopted. That is, if version 1.0 of a scheme does not have the compulsory security checks and version 2.0 does, an implementer who is pressed for time may simply continue to use the 1.0 version of the protocol. We recommend this scheme primarily for new protocols unless there is other pressure which would lead to upgrades being likely.

It may also be the case that updating a protocol which is already using this scheme to add additional checks could have the same problem. Our suspicion is that small additions would not produce large resistance, but empirical evidence would be needed to know for certain.

A benefit of this scheme not yet mentioned is that it should make it easier for code auditing to detect situations where security checks are avoided or ignored. Avoiding the security check will require complex code and doing it and then ignoring the results should be fairly obvious. This is designed to prevent accidental security bugs but could also sometimes help in recognizing intentional backdoors if those backdoors involve avoiding or ignoring the security checks.

5.1   Future Work

Currently, we are working on more empirical testing to validate that this approach does result in fewer missed security checks in practice. We also have G functions designed for additional checks which will be presented in the future. These include list membership, list non-membership, and regular-expression compliance. Beyond that, we are still working on G functions for other checks such as substring matching or substring equivalent encoding.

We also are working to make the protocol transformation more automated. Ideally, we would like to have a process where a protocol designer could write a protocol specification, identify which checks needed to be carried out, identify which portions of the message should be encrypted, and have a tool which creates a machine-readable description of the enhanced protocol. This description of the enhanced protocol could then be fed to a library which could be recieved incoming messages, do all the security checks and transform the message into the simpler form of the original specification.

References

1. Georgiev, M., Iyengar, S., Jana, S., Anubhai, R., Boneh, D., Shmatikov, V.: The most dangerous code in the world: validating SSL certificates in non-browser software. In: Proceedings of the 2012 ACM Conference on Computer and Communications Security, CCS 2012, pp. 38–49. ACM, New York (2012)
2. marcan and bushing. Console hacking 2008: Wii fail. In: 25th Chaos Communication Congress, 25C3. Chaos Computer Club (2008)
3. Matyas, S., Abraham, D., Johnson, D., Karne, R., Le, A., Prymak, R., Thomas, J., Wilkins, J., Yeh, P.: Data cryptography operations using control vectors in a data processing system, 17 April 1990. US Patent 4,918,728
4. Smid, M.E.: A key notarization system for computer networks. Number 54. US Dept. of Commerce, National Bureau of Standards: for sale by the Supt. of Docs., US Govt. Print. Off., (1979)

Redesigning Secure Protocols to Compel Security Checks (Transcript of Discussion)

Keith Irwin[✉]

Winston-Salem State University, Winston-Salem, USA
irwinke@wssu.edu

So my talk today is "Redesigning Secure Protocols to Compel Security Checks". To set up the problem: a lot of secure protocols require certain checks to be performed. You write up the protocol, that's perhaps your fiction And then later we have an implementation, that's fact, one way or the other. And there are certain checks that are supposed to be in these protocols. You might, say, check that the signature matches the message, check that a timestamp was within a certain range, check that certain values or keys, which are known bad values or known bad keys, are not being used. You might check that names in different parts of a message match each other or in different certificates match each other. You might check that you get back the same nonce you sent out. And of course, if you don't do these checks, what happens, you wind up with an insecure implementation.

And implementations sometimes leave out these checks. So, a couple of examples: in SSL and TLS delegated certificates which say you can sign for *.foo.com, for quite a while Safari on iOS, for basically about the first three to four years that IOS existed, the version of Safari there failed to check that the name of the actual website you were going to matched the restrictions of the delegated certificate. So you could send it one for *.foo.com, and then also use that same key to sign for Citibank.com, and it was perfectly happy with that, because it said, "oh you've got a delegated certificate, so that means you can sign for certain other domain names, oh here's another domain name," and it wasn't checking that the postfix matched the way it should have.

The Nintendo Wii had a bug where it accepted RSA signatures on the value 0, and if you remember RSA from whenever you covered that, RSA is done via exponentiation [3]. So to prove that I can actually sign something, I take a number, I raise it to the power of my secret key. So if the initial number is 0, what's that signature going to be? It's going to be 0. So you shouldn't accept a 0 as a signature. Now this is not necessarily unto itself a horrible problem.

Bruce Christianson: 1 is good as well.

Reply: Yes, 1 is not very good. The equivalent of negative 1, not real good either, right? You do have to know whether the private key is even or odd, but that's sort of the extent of it and really it's n-1, but yes. Those are the only three bad values, but they are kind of doozies and necessary. Taking a 0 may not actually be a big problem in a lot of things because you are often signing a hash, and it was in this case too, but they used strncmp to check the hash. Yes,

© Springer International Publishing Switzerland 2015
B. Christianson et al. (Eds.): Security Protocols 2015, LNCS 9379, pp. 30–40, 2015.
DOI: 10.1007/978-3-319-26096-9_4

I see someone gets it right away. Strncmp, that's using C style strings. They stop when you get a null. So if you've signed 0 and it stops when it gets a null, any hash that starts with a 0 will automatically match. It will go, "oh these are both empty strings, we're done." And so this allowed them to build a fake-sign which would, if you give it the code you want it to sign, it would change one character on average about 256 times until it came up with something for a hash whose first byte was 0, and then the Wii would happily accept it. I bring this one up in particular because I have a good check for 0, but it's certainly not the only thing we can do.

So why did they get left out? Well programmer mistake is a part of it. Sometimes the programmers, as best as they might try, they're just not going to understand everything. That's what we were talking about last talk: programmers don't always understand everything at all levels. Some of this can be poor protocol documentation. I was watching a talk the other day where someone was talking about the, it turns out that several of the ECC implementations have trouble because they don't necessarily verify that the point you gave them is on the curve, and it turns out that was in a footnote for the specification, and not everyone happened to read that footnote. There was also another talk [2], they were talking about problems in TLS Libraries that were available, and there was one, I believe it was for either Python or PHP, I forget which, but it took us an argument for whether or not it was going to do the name-checking, either a 0, a 1 or a 2, and 0 means you don't do it, meaning the application would do it instead, which can make sense because sometimes what's the same name is specific to your application. 1 meant do it this way. 2 meant do it the other way. And what was happening is people were passing true, and the problem is in this language true maps to 0, which means don't do any checking. So it wasn't that the library — I mean it was sort of doing what you told it, but it's not an obvious way to write it: so that true means, don't do any checking. I'm going to set name verification to true. Yes?

Alastair Beresford: But the situation is worse, they don't just leave them out, programmers put them in the sense that there's a great paper called Eve And Mallory about Android SSL, where programmers actually put these vulnerabilities into their apps [1]. The default implementation is secure.

Reply: Right, I was going to reference that one down when I got to this kind of section here, but yes, I read that paper too. Actually I was there for that one, I was happy about that, that was in my home town, very convenient. I wish they'd put more in my home town.

Anyway, and we also have time crunches going on. And so sometimes you do the insecure way now, and you make a note to yourself that later you're going to come back and do this the real secure way. And later never happens, because the application has to ship now. We can't ship later. And in general, of course, the reason they leave them out is because they can leave them out.

Well the time crunch one also I think went with the paper. They showed that in a lot of Android apps you can override some of the parts of the verification process, and they found that a startling number of the free apps they had pulled down, like 30 %, 35 %, something like that, overrode at least one part of it to not do it. They had code in them that would skip the verification. But in some cases that might have been from debug time, and this is, of course, a problem you run into. It's like, "Oh, well, in our debug environment we don't have the real certs yet. We can't really validate them. The certs we do have don't really validate, so for the time being we're going to skip the validation. And before we ship it we'll put that back in." And when they actually went and did a survey of 100 particular ones (this was over thousands of apps) to really do the complex code analysis, they actually found that most of them, although they contained the code to skip it, they weren't using that code. So a lot of them put it in temporarily and then remembered to take it back out before they shipped it. I mean, it's still compiled in there, but it was separated off by a if debug kind of statement, or something like that.

But the problem, of course, is we do forget this. Programmes without the checks, they still run fine in every way. As far as the user can tell they go open up an app, they go pull up your website — the people using Safari on IOS where it wasn't doing the name matching, they had no idea, and every web page they would load, it loads fine, and it shows it to them fine. If you're using email, and it's supposed to be verifying your PGP/GPG signature, and it doesn't, how do you know? As long as it looks like it does, you can still read the email message. If it doesn't do the decrypt when you have a decrypt that's kind of obvious. But if it doesn't do the checks that it needs to do, unless some security researcher comes along and tries to figure out whether or not it does the checks, you probably don't know. And the checks also, the checks sometimes reveal other problems, so the people who wrote that, Eve and Mallory Android paper, also found some message boards where people were asking, "Hey, when I try and run this my certificate is not validating," and the answers they were getting back from the developers were, "here's how you turn off certificate validation." Which, depending on your situation, might actually be easier than getting your IT guy to go fix the problems with your certificate.

So the real root problem is that testing isn't generally going to show these problems. If you're testing your app using only well-formed messages, not malicious messages, or files, or so forth, you're not going to find this. And if you're testing a malicious one you have to find like the exact ones that cause the problem. Users aren't going to notice if there's no difference in the behaviour unless they actually get hacked in some form. And code without the checks is always simpler to write than the code with the checks, right? It's very simple: it's the same code but with slightly fewer lines because you don't do the checks.

There are some existing solutions to try and handle this sort of problem, and I wanted to talk about those briefly before I talk about my solution. Because my solution in some ways is a little weird, which is part of how I got invited here, hooray. But the existing solutions: formal verification of code is a big one. You can do a formal verification, make sure your code actually matches a protocol, has all the checks it should. And that's terrific, and it works really well if people use it. The problem is almost no-one uses it. And I don't know how to change that. What mostly happens, I've submitted this paper at another conference, and they're like, "oh everybody should just do formal verification," and I'm like, "yes, they should, but they're not." So let's talk about what we can do in the real world.

The other one is a good standard library that does checks for you. The standard library has been written very carefully. It does all the checks. You can be the high-level abstraction guy and not worry about what the library is doing because it's doing the right thing. And again, this is a very good solution if people use it and don't try and roll their own library. Which, let's face it, people sometimes roll their own code. And if it's easy to use correctly, like that example where you set the name checking to true and it turns it off. So you still potentially have issues with documentation and interface, and stuff like that here, but there are some good libraries, and there are some where they've put a lot of thought into making it very hard to use it incorrectly for particular situations. And we don't necessarily want to say, "oh we don't want people using standard libraries." We'd like people to use standard libraries, and one of the roles of my solutions is to actually leverage people to make them more likely to use standard libraries.

So, how are we going to solve this problem? What we want to do is we actually want to make changes to our protocols. We're going to take the observation that the code is not unrelated to the protocol. Changes we make in the protocol are going to result in changes to the code in some form. And so we have to try and get this to result in the kind of changes in the code we want. And we want tests to be likely to show that there's a lack of checks. We want checks to be something that are visible to the users. It's not that we're ever going to make programmers write perfect code, but when they skip a security check we want this to show up as a bug in a way that's obvious. Now, this doesn't fix every possible thing you could do wrong. This is focused on the security checks in particular. And so what we want is we want it to make it essentially more complex to write functional software without the security checks (that actually interoperates with the things it needs to interoperate with) than code with the security checks. We want this version with the security checks to actually be the simpler, easier version.

Our assumptions we're making here in the solution is that we can design a protocol. So this is really something aimed at people developing protocols, preferably from scratch. And the reason I say preferably from scratch is we are going to make the protocol more complicated, and so if you have a 2.0 version, which is much more complicated than a 1.0 version, sometimes people just go, "ah, we're just going to stick with 1.0, everybody is going to have backwards compatibility." So we're probably assuming this is our 1.0 version, this is our first version out there, and so people are going to do whatever the thing is we're putting the protocol out for, they're going to kind of have to live with our protocol to a certain extent.

And in particular we're going to say that the implementer is going to attempt to implement the protocol faithfully. This is not the implementer really trying to subvert things. We're going to assume we've got some kind of reference implementation out there. They're going to write their code. Their client or their server is going to interact with the reference client or server, and if it basically looks right they'll probably say, "yes, this is good." But they're not going to be like, "oh I've built my new web browser, and I point it to google.com, and it doesn't work but that's probably Google's fault, so I'm going to go for it." So they're going to make that, and they're not going to just go say, "we're just going to go and redesign our protocol, and ignore everything you've done and design a new thing."

The fundamental idea here is: we're going to find this special function G. I call it G because it's kind of a little game that we're forcing the programmer to play in order to be able to read the messages. G should be pretty easy to compute when you're carrying out the check. It should be pretty complex to compute when you're not carrying out the check. In the process of doing the checks, you're going to be able to compute G, sort of as a side effect. You'll have to add a few extra operations, but if you're trying to do this without carrying out the check at all, you're going to really have to, you know, as they say, trying to get from your thumb to your index finger by going around your elbow. So it's not that it's impossible to do without, you might be able to calculate G without carrying out the check, but in general it's going to be a really complicated thing. And ideally G is in fact undefined in the situation that the check fails.

What we're going to do on the next slide, we'll do kind of a quick example, and then I'll talk about why I don't actually use the quick example, and we'll go on to a slightly more complicated version. And it shouldn't be vulnerable to small implementation mistakes. If there's a very small implementation mistake you can make that makes it work right when the check succeeds, but not work right when the check fails, that's a bad thing. So we want it to basically be likely to work right either way, or not work right either way, because, you know, bugs happen.

In the protocol we take the result of this G function, and we're going to use it to encrypt some other part of the message. So this is not encryption for security against hackers. It's just encryption so that the guy implementing it is going to have to compute G, because if he doesn't compute G part of the message will still be garbled. So we can choose our encryption function here for speed rather than for security, we just want something that no reasonable implementer is going to be like, "oh let me try and brute-force this."

So here's an example, this is our simple example. So we have a message, m and we're going to assume it's got two parts, m_0 and m_1, and the check in this is we want to make sure that $m_1 \neq 0$. We've just said m_1 not allowed to be 0, so maybe it's the Wii signature kind of case, or maybe it's something else. So m_1 is not allowed to be 0, so this is the G function that's going to go along with checking values to make sure they're not 0. This one is a fairly simple one. We're going to have some large constant C, quite a bit larger than the possible range of values for m_1, and we're going to take C and we're going to divide it by m_1, and this will give us our G function. And then our new message, so this will be sort of the simple version of the protocol, the amended version of the protocol where we're using my approach is we're actually going to take m_0, and we're going to encrypt it using that.

So what happens if m_1 is 0? Well we should get a divide by 0 error here. So what we need to do is, before we do that division, we're going to have to actually do the check. The programmer will have to do the check that we're trying to force them to do. They'll say, "ah, is it equal to 0, okay." Now maybe after they've done that check they might just completely ignore it, that is always a possibility. I can make them do the check, I can't make them do the right thing after they've done the check. It's, "ah, this message is probably fakesigned, I'll take it anyway." That at least is likely to be found if there is a code review, if somebody else is looking over it. "I found this problem here, why didn't you do anything?"

So it's not a perfect approach. I can kind of force them to do the check. So if the code doesn't check for the 0 value, it's either, we've got an uncaught exception of some sort, or we didn't bother computing G, and if we didn't bother computing G, we can't decrypt m_0, and so we can't display the message. So this means the code is effectively forced to check the 0 value if it wants to display the message to the user. If it displays an encrypted version of m_0, the user is going to notice.

So does that simple example make sense to everybody? So there are some problems with this. There are some languages or implementations of languages that handle division by 0, there are a few that will set it to none or null. The standard floating point sets it to infinity. So I don't actually really want to use division by 0. I do want something where it's undefined. So in those languages the check could still be omitted. And so we actually want a slightly more complicated function that also still has this property.

And I realised as I was looking at the paper I submitted, and my slides last night, that I did the version of Z that I was using for a very long time, and I forgot that I'd come up with even a slightly different version of Z. So this one is pretty good, but the one in the paper is actually better. This one is sort of vulnerable to the possibility of loop unrolling. Now I sort of assume most people aren't going to manually write an unrolled loop, but the other one is slightly better because it's harder to predict how long it's going to take.

So the other one actually, it starts with a number and it doubles it until it's over some constant, and then it moves it back down to the constant through repeated calls, with an extra hash at each step until it gets there, and that's even slightly better than this one. And I realise actually my explanation in the version of the paper, I have a couple of constants in there that I forgot to say anything about, I somehow didn't notice that. So in the revised version I promise I'll explain what those constants are. They're not really that important. But if you're looking at my paper and you see the Z formula, and you're like, "what's that constant?", it's just a big constant of some sort.

So we're defining $Z(i)$, so Z is going to be a function that gives you a completely different value for almost every i, but is undefined if it's 0. So if $i \mod 2$ is 1, so if i is an odd number we calculate the hash of i and we're done. We have some hash function, again it should be fast, it doesn't have to be super secure. And if $i \mod 2$ is 0, so we've got a 0 in the last bit, the least significant bit, we divide it by 2, and then we call it recursively. So as long as i is not 0 this will terminate after however many 0 s we have in the least significant bits. But, of course, if i is 0 this will loop forever. So really before you call this we should check if $i = 0$. So this is what we'd actually use as a Z function, or the modified version in the paper, because this one, if you know exactly how many bits i had, you can kind of write an unrolled loop. I don't know anyone would, but, you know, or do a loop for this where you just put the number of bits as a stopping point. And so the other one makes it a little more complicated to figure out how long it's going to run. Although it's still bounded we don't want it to be running infinitely. We're going to have some extra CPU overhead, you don't want it to be very much.

So if the check is not done of course we're going to get an infinite loop. And if we're trying to calculate this value without doing any loop at all, it's not impossible, but it's really weird and complicated. So we're going to assume that programmers are not intentionally trying to defeat this system. They're trying to implement the protocol faithfully, and they might make some mistakes. So if we make it weird and complicated enough for them to do it without doing the check, they're going to do the check.

So I have some other checks that can be done. The simple one for if you want to check that two values are not equal to each other, you simply calculate the Z of their difference. If you want to say x is less than y, assuming x and y are both positive integers (this does not work for negative numbers), we'd use $Z((y \mod x) - y)$. If x is bigger than y, $y \mod x$ will just be y, and that will be 0. If x is not bigger than y it will give you some other number. I have some other ones, list membership and list non-membership, I actually worked out a conformity to regular expression one. You can't really do equality, because the problem is the G function of x, y for equals, is always going to be the same as the G function x, x when the message is well formed, when they are equal. So instead you can do this thing where you instead take one or both of those values and encode them in some other form rather than just a regular integer, and then you do a check to make sure that this value is an encoding of the other value. I didn't include that in this talk because I didn't want to be up here forever.

Last couple of slides. So I want to talk about what I see as the downsides and the upsides of my approach, And then, I mean, obviously it's kind of open anyway, but we'll throw open for questions. So the downside is more computational overhead. When I've sent this out for review in a couple of other places a lot of people said, "this is more computational overhead." I said, "Yes, but we're not usually CPU bound in kind of ordinary things." You have to calculate G, and of course, some things are encrypted, so you want to decrypt them. We don't want to use any public key cryptography. We want this all to be secret keys so it can be nice and fast, and we can even choose the fastest secret key we can find, since we're just working against making the programmer not try and brute-force it. It's more work of course to implement. And formal verification of these sort of, it may actually be harder for protocols that include this kind of stuff. I'm not sure.

But, of course, the upsides, when you leave out the security checks this should break your implementation in a pretty obvious way. You'll get something like an infinite loop, or you'll get a value that comes up as nonsense because it wasn't decrypted before it was displayed. And by making the whole thing a little more complicated I think you actually make it more likely that people are going to look at that and go, "This is complicated, let me see if I can find a standard library," and then actually use the standard libraries. When it looks easy people are more likely to go, "Oh, I can do this." If it looks complicated it's more likely to push them to standard libraries. And it's not hard build this sort of thing into a standard library. So okay, that's what I've got.

Changyu Dong: I think one problem might be that it creates a compatibility problem, for example, older version don't use the check, and then in the new versions you find something you need to check, and in the new version you can verify that but in older software you have to complete ...

Reply: Yes, that's true, if you don't have a perfectly solid idea of what checks are necessary at the time you're designing your protocol, it's a difficulty. It's hard to add new checks to the protocol and guarantee that people will actually do them.

Ross Anderson: This is a nice idea. We've seen something vaguely similar already, for example, in some payment protocols, and in TLS, where at the end of the initial protocol run you use hashes of everything to date basically as MAC keys. But this in tension with the robustness principle, which is that when you do a security protocol you should toss in everything you can think of, including even the kitchen sink, in case you have to check them later. An example of this is the NorPEN attack on EMV, where if you use a middle person to dupe a chip and PIN terminal to believe that a transaction was verified by a PIN, while the card thought it was verified by a signature, you can against most banks use a stolen card without knowing the PIN. However, the information from the card and from the terminal goes to the card-issuing bank, and it can, if it is bothered, write the code to check these, and thereby block the attack. Which one of the UK banks, HSBC, now does. Now if you had to try and make every single aspect of a protocol that could possibly be checked bulletproof, it would be very difficult to provide that.

Reply: That's true, and I mean, I think right now though we're basically not forcing any of the checks. And so I think a situation where we identify as many of the checks as we can think of, and make them mandatory essentially, or nearly mandatory, certainly very strongly, you know, a big hassle to not have, in the protocol, I think is better than one in which right now it's just kind of, it's open season. You can do whatever checks you want or not do whatever checks you want, and it's not really noticeable to anyone.

Bruce Christianson: The think I like about your approach is that it provides the lazy programmer with the incentive to produce a perfect implementation.

Reply: Yes, and actually my working title for this when I was doing it was, Lazy Programmer Protection.

Dylan Clark: You made the assumption that the programmer wouldn't deliberately want to get round the check, and I think in some cases that may not be. I've seen instances like the contractors who deliberately weaken the system to exploit it later. However, what your system does do is it makes it easy to audit that.

Reply: Yes, I think that's true. And I think in the end, I think there's not really going to be a general solution to somebody trying tp back-door something. It's just, that's a lot harder. Whereas, of course, a lot of the problems we're actually seeing in the real world right now are not intentional back-doors. They're accidental back-doors, and when you close that I think that's good.

Dylan Clark: I think with your system, when somebody comes to test it and they're all going to say, "Why've you written this in this really convoluted way? It seems really not obvious." That gives you big advantages.

Reply: Or "why did you perform this check to calculate G but then ignore the results?"

Dylan Clark: Yes.

Mark Lomas: I like your idea, but what I'm about to say isn't a criticism, it's some extra motivation for it. When they were developing the Minix operating system, there was a very good design idea which was to encrypt each port with a supposedly different key, in order to make sure that you were authorised. But the first implementation used the identity function as the encryption function, and therefore a lot of the implementations skipped calling the encryption function, which meant that you couldn't actually turn on the security feature that they designed into it. So had they used your principle they would have been forced to actually do it.

Michael Roe: An example of something similar I think I've seen before is, well, you know, if you had an encrypted MAC message the thing you worry about is the programmer will not check the message authentication code, and will just unbundle the message verification part. And the defence against that is to use encryption mode where the message authentication bits cascade through the decrypted site, through the encryption process.

Reply: Right, like Galois Counter Mode or one of those, yes. And there are some other ways to do things where you can — so actually like the elliptic curve example I used, there actually winds up being an easier solution than checking to make sure that your points are on the curve. In that one you can actually, if you send the x coordinate that will narrow it down to two points, and then you can use one bit to specify the y coordinate, to say, well it's the top point, or it's the bottom point. And, of course, that's even better than having to go through this check. So in situations where you can redesign it to just say, "It's just implicitly part of what's going on so we don't even have to check this," that's even better. But I don't think in the end we can ever get rid of all of that, because sometimes you're going to have certificate chains, and things like that.

Bruce Christianson: The point Ross made also extends to checks on shared context, that very often an attack on a protocol works because either the protocol itself doesn't check that the context that needs to be shared, is shared, and each implementer says, "Well it's simpler if I just assume the other end has got it right." And if you say, "Well I'm going to take all the context that should be shared, hash it together, and XOR that hash with the message I send you," that forces you to check whether you've got the same shared context right now.

Reply: And in TLS recently they've had a couple of different ones where they've figured out that you have, the sort of expected state machine that is described by the protocol, is not actually being implemented by their implementations. It turns out you can kind of jump from message to message without having necessarily done the in-between messages. And having a formal FSA and then saying, "Okay, I know where you ought to be in this FSA, and you know where I ought to be, and so we're going to put this into the message in some form," I think makes sense, too. But I haven't figured out how, if that's something that goes with my approach, or something that should be done slightly separately, or so on.

Bruce Christianson: I think it would go nicely with, actually.

Reply: OK, so the one last plug is, I teach at a teaching university where our students are very lovely and friendly, but most of them are terrible coders. So I would love to do a large trial or a decent size trial, where you get people to implement the same protocol with these checks, with this technique, and without this technique, to actually say, "Okay, how many of our, say, masters students in computer science miss the checks when they have to do this way? How many miss the checks when they have to do it this way? Did any of them miss a non-obvious check?" etc. And the problem is my students. I love them, but they are terrible at coding. If I gave 20 of them this, I broke them into two groups, I gave 10 do it this way, 10 do it this way, I would be lucky if I got one working implementation from either side. So if anybody has better students and would like to work with me on testing this, trying to actually get some empirical data that shows us this works, because obviously I've given you — this is how I think it ought to work. And I think most people agree with me. But it would be nice to actually have some empirical data so that when I send this out to some people — because I get some people who say, "This is weird and complex," and I've had some difficulty getting it published as a result. So if anybody wants to work with me please come let me know, or send me an email, or whatever. I would love, you know, even if you're like, I've got five students, and we put together some students from different places and just try it out, that would be great.

Thank you.

References

1. Fahl, S., Harbach, M., Muders, T., Baumgärtner, L., Freisleben, B., Smith,M.: Why eve and mallory love android: an analysis of android ssl (in)security. In: Proceedings of the 2012 ACM Conference on Computer and Communications Security, CCS 2012, pp. 50–61. ACM, New York (2012)

2. Georgiev, M., Iyengar, S., Jana, S., Anubhai, R., Boneh, D., Shmatikov, V.: The most dangerous code in the world: validating ssl certificates in non-browser software. In: Proceedings of the 2012 ACM Conference on Computer and Communications Security, CCS 2012, pp. 38–49. ACM, New York (2012)
3. Marcan, Bushing: Console hacking 2008: Wii fail. In: 25th Chaos Communication Congress, 25C3. Chaos Computer Club (2008)

Derailing Attacks

Saša Radomirović[(✉)] and Mohammad Torabi Dashti

Institute of Information Security, Department of Computer Science,
ETH Zürich, Zürich, Switzerland
{rsasa,torabidm}@inf.ethz.ch

Abstract. We introduce derailing attacks, a class of blocking attacks on security protocols. As opposed to blunt, low-level attacks such as persistent jamming, derailing only requires a minimal, application-level intervention from the attacker. We give a simple definition of derailing attacks in an abstract formal model, and demonstrate that derailing attacks are viable in practice through examples from two application domains, namely radio-frequency identification and fair exchange protocols.

Keywords: Formal models · Availability · RFID · Fair exchange

1 Introduction

Alice and Bob play correspondence chess by postal mail. They are both absorbed in and obsessed with their game, which has been ongoing for several months. Charlie, Alice's boyfriend, is not happy with the situation: he feels he has lost Alice to chess. If only he could stop their game! Charlie thinks of intercepting the posts coming from Bob, and destroying them. This is however an expensive and risky solution. Charlie knows that Alice would get suspicious if no mail from Bob arrived for a while, and she might even get worried about Bob, which Charlie would not like. She would perhaps start calling up Bob or even consider to travel to meet Bob. Charlie's interception would therefore work only if he can cut off Alice and Bob's communication through *all* means (e.g. telephone, emails, and homing pigeons) and for an indefinite length of time. This, of course, is infeasible.

Charlie realizes that there is a much simpler and cheaper solution: he just needs to make Alice believe that Bob is playing wrong moves. Then Alice would stop playing with Bob, because she would think that he is either trying to cheat or he has lost his total devotion to the game and is making mistakes. To reach his goal, Charlie only needs to make their chess boards inconsistent. For example, Charlie could modify a post from Alice to Bob so that Bob would think Alice makes a certain move, while Alice makes another. This would change Bob's chess board in one direction, while Alice's would change in another. Once they lose the consistency of their chess boards, Charlie can sit back and observe Alice's growing frustration. She will eventually give up on playing with Bob, and Charlie will win back Alice.

B. Christianson et al. (Eds.): Security Protocols 2015, LNCS 9379, pp. 41–46, 2015.
DOI: 10.1007/978-3-319-26096-9_5

This correspondence chess scenario illustrates blocking attacks, where the adversary's goal is to prevent, or prematurely terminate, communication between two parties. A trivial means of blocking is simply to disable the communication media altogether. This is a blunt approach because it does not allow the attacker to selectively block communication. It could moreover be unsustainable if the attacker incurs the prohibitive costs of, say, jamming a signal indefinitely. A more refined approach is to exploit the features of the communication protocol for terminating the exchange of information. Examples include the Chinese firewall's use of TCP packets for resetting TCP sessions, and using IEEE 802.11 standard "deauthentication" packets for ending a wireless session. In this paper, we introduce *derailing attacks*, a class of more elaborate blocking attacks on communication protocols. A derailing attack on a protocol disrupts the communication between the protocol's participants by corrupting their internal states. Charlie's clever trick is a simple instance of these: Charlie injects a message that adversely affects Alice and Bob's states, namely it makes their chess boards inconsistent.

In Sect. 2, we describe two instances of derailing attacks on published protocols, and in Sect. 3, we discuss how derailing attacks can be thwarted. There we also formally define derailing attacks. We conclude the paper in Sect. 4.

2   Derailing Attacks in Practice

Below, we give two examples of derailing attacks. These attacks have been studied in the literature, but they have not been recognized as belonging to the same class of attacks.

Our first example comes from the domain of radio frequency identification (RFID) protocols. RFID tags are inexpensive devices that communicate wirelessly with RFID readers. A large class of RFID protocols store correlated "state information" on the tag and on the reader's side. RFID reader and tag are said to be *synchronized* if the tag's state information allows the reader to uniquely identify the tag. For privacy concerns, this information is updated after each transaction between a tag and a reader. The update cannot be carried out atomically due to concurrency. An adversary can exploit a flawed update protocol to force the tag and the reader into a desynchronized state. Once they are there, they can no longer communicate. Desynchronization resistance has been formally defined in [3] and a number of protocols vulnerable to desynchronization attacks have been investigated in [4]. Desynchronization is an instance of derailing attacks.

Note that, similarly to Charlie's hesitation to destroy the posts, the desynchronizing adversary would prefer a derailing attack over perpetually blocking the communication between the tag and the reader. The latter is not only unsustainable and practically infeasible, it is also intrusive and overt, thus more likely to raise an alarm. For example, the owner of the RFID tag might become concerned about the stalker who shows up around all RFID readers. We remark that Charlie's trick and the RFID desynchronization attacks do not take effects immediately. This is in contrast to the Chinese firewall scenario where the attacker can tear down a session immediately by sending a TCP FIN or RST packet.

Our second example pertains to fair non-repudiation protocols. Zhou, Deng and Bao [6] proposed a protocol where P sends a message to Q containing a certain key k encrypted with the public key of a trusted third party T. The encrypted key is meant to enable Q to achieve fairness with the help of T. That is, Q and T should be able to generate a non-repudiation token whenever P and T are able to generate such a token; we do not need to further specify the token for our purpose. Now, since Q cannot check if the cipher text he receives is in fact k encrypted with the public key of T, a malicious P can derail the protocol by sending a fake key to Q after having received a non-repudiation token from Q. Consequently Q cannot achieve fairness; indeed, Q and T cannot successfully communicate. Boyd and Kearney [1] discovered the flaw, and proposed a fix for it. However, their fixed protocol suffers from a similar derailing attack. Then, Zhou [5] proposed another way to mitigate the flaw; his mitigation is not effective either. The story of the protocol is summarized by Gürgens, Rudolph and Vogt [2].

Note that in the example of fair non-repudiation protocols a derailing attack undermines a security requirement of the protocol, namely its fairness. In the RFID example an availability requirement is violated. However, the RFID authentication requirement is not necessarily affected by the attack. Suppose that an RFID protocol is deployed in a building to keep out unauthorized people. The reader would open a protected door only if it can authenticate a person by identifying the tag the person carries. Now, derailing attacks do not undermine the "security" of the building: an unauthorized person is kept out. So are authorized ones if the attack succeeds.

In the next section, we discuss how derailing attacks can be mitigated.

3   Thwarting Derailing Attacks

Authentication and integrity protection are seemingly sufficient for thwarting derailing attacks. For example, if Alice and Bob were able to recognize the tampered messages, then Charlie's trick would be fruitless. Similarly, the aforementioned RFID desynchronization attacks are mitigated by ensuring that the protocol satisfies Lowe's agreement property. This would however run contrary to the resource constraints of low-cost RFID tags. A detailed description of this point falls outside the scope of this note.

Note that, in the aforementioned fair non-repudiation example, even if all the messages exchanged between P and Q were authenticated, the attack would still be possible. This is because T cannot determine whether P or Q was the origin of the fake encryption of k. By modifying the protocol such that P must send to Q not only the encrypted key k but also its signed hash, the derailing attack is mitigated. This is intuitively because then T is able to identify the origin of a malformed token: if P were the origin, then T would issue an affidavit to Q, as a replacement for the non-repudiation token; cf. [2].

In short, an evidence of tampering in the correspondence chess problem and the RFID example allows the participants to detect, and thus thwart, derailing attacks. Similarly, in the fair non-repudiation example, requiring P's signature would provide Q with an evidence of tampering, and would enable T to identify the culprit. This discussion illustrates that protection against derailing cannot be readily reduced to well-understood security requirements such as message authentication. Below, we give a simple definition of derailing attacks in an abstract formal model.

A Formal Model

A formal definition of derailing attacks can be given through a notion of safe and unsafe configurations. We start by defining a simple protocol model.

A participant executing a protocol is a state machine that exchanges messages over an asynchronous communication medium and changes state upon reception of a message. We assume the presence of an additional state machine, the *outsider*. We distinguish between two types of messages. The green messages, which are sent by a protocol participant, and the red messages, which are sent by the outsider. State transitions that occur due to reception of a green message are called green transitions and similarly for red transitions.

The set of configurations C (global states) of a protocol is the Cartesian product of the sets of states of the protocol's participants. The state transition of participants induces a natural transition relation on the set of configurations. A protocol's security requirements define a *safe* set of configurations $S \subset C$. Intuitively, these are the configurations in which all security requirements are met. The safe configurations are not closed under the transition relation due to asynchrony of communication. During the execution, the protocol may therefore leave the set of safe configurations. We define the set of *transitional configurations* $T \subset C$ as configurations from which the protocol can reach a safe configuration without taking any red transitions. The transitional configurations trivially contain the set of safe configurations. The set of *unsafe configurations* U is the complement of the set of transitional configurations. Figure 1 illustrates these three sets.

A protocol is susceptible to *derailing attacks* if there exists a sequence of transitions (green or red) that takes the protocol from a safe configuration to an unsafe one. We assume that by making use of secure communication channels, we can eliminate the red transitions from the set of transitions induced by a protocol execution. We illustrate these notions on our two protocol examples.

Example 1. Consider the RFID protocol. The security requirement is that the RFID tag can authenticate itself to the reader. The set of safe configurations consists of pairs of states, where the tag and reader are synchronized. For simplicity we assume that they are synchronized when they store the same key. The outsider is an attacker with the standard Dolev-Yao capabilities except for the ability to indefinitely block communication. To update their keys the protocol participants must leave the set of safe configurations due to asynchrony. The outsider can interfere with the protocol, by injecting a red message, so that the tag

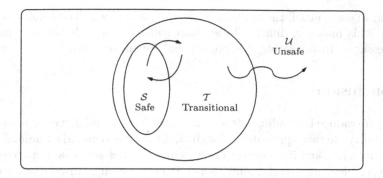

Fig. 1. Safe, transitional and unsafe configurations.

and reader update their keys differently. This prevents further communication and leaves the protocol in an unsafe configuration.

If the communication channels were secure, the red message would not be accepted by the protocol participants. That is, the set of unsafe states would not be reachable for a well-engineered protocol. An unrestricted Dolev-Yao attacker could, of course, block the communication between reader and tag and keep them in a transitional configuration. As discussed before, this is unsustainable.

Example 2. Consider the aforementioned fair exchange protocol. The security requirement to be satisfied is that Q can obtain a non-repudiation token whenever P can and vice-versa. Therefore the set of safe configurations consists of pairs of states in which either both P and Q have a non-repudiation token or neither of them has.

Note that if only P, but not Q, receives a non-repudiation token, restarting the protocol by instructing Q to "forget" about the current exchange does not result in a safe configuration. Moreover, the attack described in Sect. 2 still succeeds even if all communication channels are secure, i.e., only green transitions are possible. The attacker in this example is not an outsider.

Derailing attacks can be characterized as the reachability of a configuration from which all paths to safe configurations include a red transition. That is, in its abstract form derailing poses a *nested reachability* problem: Can the system reach a configuration from which no safe configuration is reachable (only using green transitions). Let us write $\rightarrow_g \subseteq \mathcal{C} \times \mathcal{C}$ for the set of green transitions, and $\rightarrow_r$ for the set of red ones. Let $\rightarrow = \rightarrow_g \cup \rightarrow_r$, and write $\mathcal{C}_0$ for the set of initial configurations. Then, the system is susceptible to derailing if and only if

$$\exists C_0 \in \mathcal{C}_0, C \in \mathcal{C}. \ \left(C_0 \rightarrow^* C \ \wedge \ \neg \exists C_S \in \mathcal{S}. \ C \rightarrow_g^* C_S\right).$$

Here, $\rightarrow^*$ is the transitive closure of the relation $\rightarrow$ and $\mathcal{S} \subset \mathcal{C}$ is the set of safe configurations.

The formalization of this property in a security protocol verification tool is not straightforward, due to the aforementioned nested reachability problem.

Moreover, in such a tool, the outsider is often identified with the communication network. This makes it difficult to automatically distinguish between red and green messages. Investigating this point is left for future work.

4   Conclusion

We have introduced derailing attacks on availability, and have demonstrated their viability in two application domains. Derailing demands minimal effort from the attacker, and it is covert. These characteristics set derailing apart from blunt, overt blocking attacks, such as persistent jamming. In contrast to common denial of service attacks on availability, derailing cannot be fully addressed through replication. Formal verification techniques can mitigate the problem by assisting protocol designers to find the flaws that enable derailing. While the primary purpose of this note is to bring attention to this class of attacks, we have also given a lightweight formalization of derailing. Further investigations in this direction are left for future work.

Acknowledgments. We thank Jan Cederquist and Sjouke Mauw for insightful discussions.

References

1. Boyd, C., Kearney, P.: Exploring fair exchange protocols using specification animation. In: Okamoto, E., Pieprzyk, J.P., Seberry, J. (eds.) ISW 2000. LNCS, vol. 1975, pp. 209–223. Springer, Heidelberg (2000)
2. Gürgens, S., Rudolph, C., Vogt, H.: On the security of fair non-repudiation protocols. Int. J. Inf. Secur. 4(4), 253–262 (2005)
3. van Deursen, T., Mauw, S., Radomirović, S., Vullers, P.: Secure ownership and ownership transfer in RFID systems. In: Backes, M., Ning, P. (eds.) ESORICS 2009. LNCS, vol. 5789, pp. 637–654. Springer, Heidelberg (2009)
4. van Deursen, T., Radomirović, S.: Attacks on RFID protocols (version 1.1). Cryptology ePrint Archive, Report 2008/310, August 2009. http://eprint.iacr.org/2008/310
5. Zhou, J.: Achieving fair non-repudiation in electronic transactions. J. Organ. Comput. Electron. Commer. 11(4), 253–267 (2001)
6. Zhou, J., Deng, R.H., Bao, F.: Evolution of fair non-repudiation with TTP. In: Pieprzyk, J.P., Safavi-Naini, R., Seberry, J. (eds.) ACISP 1999. LNCS, vol. 1587, pp. 258–269. Springer, Heidelberg (1999)

Derailing Attacks (Transcript of Discussion)

Mohammad Torabi Dashti[✉]

Department of Computer Science, Institute of Information Security,
ETH Zurich, Zürich, Switzerland
mohammad.torabi@inf.ethz.ch

I'm going to talk about Derailing Attacks. This is joint work with Saša, who's in the audience, my name is Mohammad. Our story starts with correspondence chess. This is how geographically distant people used to play chess. Imagine Alice is playing chess with Bob, in this case let's say Bobby Fischer. This is how they play. They have a deck of postcards. When Alice makes a move, she indicates it on a card and sends it to Bob. After a few days Bob receives the post, sees what move Alice has made, he replicates the move on his board, and then makes his own move, and sends it back to Alice. In this scenario we are considering the case that Charlie, say Alice's boyfriend, is jealous of Alice playing chess with Bob, you can think of many reasons why that could be, and we leave this up to you to decide. So, Charlie wants to disrupt their game.

Peter Ryan: But Charlie doesn't realise that Bobby Fisher's dead.

Reply: Well it's a bit like Elvis, right? Some people just don't get it.

So what can Charlie do to disrupt their game? The easiest way probably is to block the posts. Charlie makes sure that he wakes up everyday early, checks the mailbox, and if there is a letter from Bob he just destroys it. This has disadvantages. First, it is blunt because if Alice does not receive any letters from Bob, she will notice it. It is overt, and it is expensive because Charlie needs to be all the time around the mailbox, he needs to know when a letter arrives. And if Alice gets suspicious she might consider calling Bob, or sending him homing pigeons, or somehow try to contact him, and that would not be in Charlie's favour.

This sort of blocking is expensive. Charlie figures he can do it differently by trying to corrupt their states. The idea here is simply that these guys are playing chess, so their chess boards should have some sort of relation to each other. They can be at most one move away from each other. If you think of these chess boards as their states, if their state is corrupted they cannot continue playing with each other, it doesn't make sense anymore. So what Charlie can do is to observe Alice making one move. He can then indicate another move, send a post to Bob, assuming that he can forge Alice's signature, and Bob will make Charlie's instead of Alice's move. Alice and Bob continue playing for a few steps. If Charlie injects the wrong move in a clever way, then after a few steps Alice and Bob will reach a dead end. For instance, Alice would notice that Bob is doing something that is not legal according to their protocol, in this case chess, and she might think that Bob is trying to cheat, or he is not paying enough attention. Either way she is going to be upset and will not continue playing with him.

© Springer International Publishing Switzerland 2015
B. Christianson et al. (Eds.): Security Protocols 2015, LNCS 9379, pp. 47–49, 2015.
DOI: 10.1007/978-3-319-26096-9_6

Virgil Gligor: Can Charlie intercept the post in both directions?

Reply: For doing this attack he just needs to inject the message on behalf of Alice, and make sure that the letter that Alice sends will not arrive at Bob's.

Virgil Gligor: But if Bob's post quotes Alice's last move, Alice would have a record of the previous message Bob received.

Reply: Right, in that case, Charlie actually has to intercept the post in both directions and modify two messages instead of just one.

The nice thing about this attack is that it is cheap. Charlie needs to just once inject a message, maybe two, and then he can sit back and wait to see what happens. And it is covert in the sense that Alice is not going to be suspicious of the communication media, because she is going to receive letters from Bob, but they are not going to make sense at some point. We call this sort of attacks *derailing attacks*, and the idea is that through derailing an attacker can disrupt communication between two participants.

You might wonder if these attacks actually appear in practice, if there is anything real that resembles this correspondence chess story. One of the cases that we have seen is in RFID protocols. In a typical RFID system, you have an RFID reader and RFID tags and they keep some sort of state, for instance by means of a cryptographic key that they use to communicate. After each transaction these keys are updated. Because the transaction is not synchronous, the keys are updated one by one. So let's say first the key on the card is updated, and then the key on the reader is updated. If the attacker manages to inject a message that causes these two updates to go in two different directions, the transaction will still appear to complete successfully. But the next time the tag is presented to a reader, the reader cannot communicate with the tag. Not because the messages are jammed, or the communication is blocked, but because the keys stored on these two components are not the same, so the tag and reader cannot comprehend each other's messages. And essentially what this means is that the availability of the system is broken. There are indeed RFID protocols with a key update phase that suffer from this problem. An attacker could inject messages to update their states in two different directions.

In the correspondence chess and the RFID key update scenarios, it is clear that if the integrity of these messages is protected, this sort of injection cannot happen. If the recipients know that the message that they're receiving was actually sent by the other participant, and it hasn't been tampered with, then the attack is not possible. But integrity protection is not sufficient in general.

Another class of protocols that are also vulnerable to these sort of problems are fair exchange protocols. Here you have two participants and they want to exchange some valuable items, for instance, one of them has a token, another one has another token, and they want to exchange these in a fair way. This means that if Alice gets the token that Bob has, then Bob gets the token that Alice has, or none of them get the token of the other participant. In this class of protocols you usually have a trusted party also, and this trusted party is supposed to resolve problems if the fairness property is broken. In these protocols we also have seen examples where you can derail the protocol by corrupting the states of the participants. This happens as follows. Alice sends a message to Bob promising her token. Bob then sends to Alice his token, and then it is Alice's turn to send her token. But Alice, contrary to her promise, doesn't send back her token to Bob. At this point Bob goes to the trusted party to resolve the case. But when he presents the promise that Alice sent, it turns out to be incomprehensible to the trusted party. Alice has performed a derailing attack.

In these sorts of protocols you cannot prevent derailing by just protecting the integrity of the messages, because the participants who are involved in the protocol can be dishonest in this case, and just making sure that their messages are not tampered with does not help you with derailing. We have seen also these sorts of examples in the literature.

To summarise what derailing attacks are, they are a class of attacks on availability, they demand minimal effort on the attacker's side. They are covert in the sense that the participants are not going to be suspicious of the communication means. A lot of attacks on availability can be addressed through replication. This is not true for derailing attacks. Even if you have many Bobs that are playing chess, if all of them are derailed it doesn't matter how many there are. We have seen derailing attacks in different domains. We like to think of them as a class of attacks, such as man-in-the-middle attacks, and we would be interested to know if other instances appear in other domains. An open question that we have is how to detect these attacks automatically. What would be a good formal definition of derailing, and how can we verify a protocol for the absence of these sort of problems?

Establishing Software-Only Root of Trust on Embedded Systems: Facts and Fiction

Yanlin Li[1], Yueqiang Cheng[1], Virgil Gligor[1]([⊠]), and Adrian Perrig[2]

[1] CyLab, Carnegie Mellon University, Pittsburgh, PA, USA
gligor@cmu.edu
[2] Computer Science Department, ETH Zurich, Zürich, Switzerland

Abstract. Establishing SoftWare-Only Root of Trust (SWORT) on a system comprises the attestation of the system's malware-free state and loading of an authentic trusted-code image in that state, without allowing exploitable time gaps between the attestation, authenticity measurement, and load operations. In this paper, we present facts and fiction of SWORT protocol design on new embedded-systems architectures, discuss some previously unknown pitfalls of software-based attestation, and propose three new attacks. We describe the implementation of the first attack on a popular embedded-system platform (i.e., on the Gumstix FireStorm COM), establish the feasibility of the second, and argue the practicality of the third. We outline several challenges of attack countermeasures and argue that countermeasures must compose to achieve SWORT protocol security.

1 Introduction

An adversary who can insert malware into a system poses a persistent threat. Malware can survive across repeated boot operations and can be remotely activated at the adversary's discretion. Attempts to detect persistent malware in a system usually require off-line forensic analysis and hence do not offer timely recourse after a successful attack. In contrast, on-line detection of adversary presence in a system can be fast (i.e., a matter of minutes), but typically requires some form of hardware- or software-based attestation by an external device that the system state (e.g., RAM, CPU and I/O registers, device-controller memory) is malware-free. Attestation of malware freedom is particularly important in establishing *SoftWare-Only Root of Trust* (SWORT) since the loading of a trusted-code image in the presence of malware would compromise trust assurances.

When strong guarantees are sought in attestation despite malware presence, designers usually rely on secrets protected in tamper-resistant hardware and standard cryptography; e.g., the private keys of a Trusted Platform Module (TPM) [29]. In contrast, SoftWare-based ATTestation (SWATT) aims to avoid management of secret keys and their protection in hardware. Nevertheless, some SWATT approaches that attempt to provide security assurance still use *some* secrets. For example, early research suggests that, to obtain guarantees of untampered code execution on an adversary-controlled machine, one should use

B. Christianson et al. (Eds.): Security Protocols 2015, LNCS 9379, pp. 50–68, 2015.
DOI: 10.1007/978-3-319-26096-9_7

software agents that encapsulate *hidden* random addresses at which the check-sum execution is initiated [7,14]. Other work requires the use of *obfuscated* check-sum code [17,24]. More recent research shows that if a remote system can be initialized to a *large enough secret*, malware cannot leak much of the secret before it is changed by a remote verifier, and malware-free code can be loaded on that system [32].

Facts and Fiction. Although tempting, attestation based on secrets is fraught with risk when performed in the presence of a skillful and persistent adversary. Hardware-protected private keys can still be successfully attacked by exploiting compelled/stolen/forged certificates corresponding to these keys [11,19], side channels [30], and padding oracles [3]. Equally important, managing hardware-based attestation (e.g., TPM-based) poses significant usability challenges; e.g., the Cukoo attack [18]. Using a software-protected secret (e.g., checksum obfuscation technique) is particularly dangerous since the secret may be implicitly used for verifying millions of user machines and its discovery may affect many sensitive applications. Annoyingly, secrets can be subpoenaed by oppressive authorities leading to loss of privacy precisely where one needs it most; i.e., in censored computing environments. Hence, attestation based on secrets combines facts, such as the strong cryptographic guarantees available for trusted-image authenticity, with fiction; e.g., long-term protection of secrets can be assured despite advanced persistent threats.

In contrast, traditional SWATT protocols [2,14,20–23] do *not* need secrets for SWORT establishment. These protocols use external system verifiers, which are assumed to be free of malware, to challenge adversary-controlled systems with the execution of checksum functions whose output is verified and execution time is measured. Hence, these protocols must assure that their checksum functions have *accurately measurable* execution-time bounds. Inaccurate verifier measurements would allow an adversary to exploit the time gap between the verifier's expected measurements and the adversary's lower actual execution time.

In practice, however, accurate measurements of checksum execution times are more fiction than fact. For example, to avoid numerous false alarms on realistic system configurations, a verifier's attack-detection threshold must be extended past the average execution-time measurement to account for a checksum's execution-time jitter. This includes clock variation due to static skew and dynamic (e.g., peak-to-peak) jitter, each of which can easily extend a processor's clock period by 3–8 % [27], and execution-time jitter due to hard-to-predict Translation Lookaside Buffer (TLB) and cache behavior. Since threshold extensions can lead to successful attacks, previous SWATT approaches set low values for them; e.g., less than 1.7 % over the average execution time in the no-attack mode of operation in [14,22]. However, low values will cause false-positive malware detection on new embedded-system platforms, which SWATT aims to avoid[1]. Extending the threshold

---

[1] Repeating the SWATT protocol only a half a dozen times to identify and disregard false positives would be unrealistic for embedded-system platforms such as the Gum-stix FireStorm Com where a single checksum execution takes about thirteen minutes; viz., Sect. 4.1.

to only 3 % over the average execution time to avoid false positives would certainly introduce added vulnerabilities (viz., Sect. 3.2), and thus SWATT would have to counter new attacks on these platforms.

Furthermore, modern embedded platforms have became increasingly complex and diverse. Thus the belief that a traditional checksum designs (reviewed in Sect. 6), perhaps with provable properties [2], will suffice for different architectures and scale is based on more fiction than fact.

An additional fact, which is sometimes ignored by past research, is that SWATT must be uninterruptably linked to other functions to be useful in SWORT. Otherwise, SWORT becomes pure fiction: an adversary could pre-plan unpleasant surprises for a verifier *after* successful SWATT and *before* system boot. For example, the adversary could violate the authenticity of the trusted image by returning a correct image-integrity measurement and yet load an adversary-modified image in a malware-free state; viz., Sect. 3.1. This type of attack is enabled by hardware features on modern embedded platforms that enable attackers to create a time gap between SWATT and authenticity measurement of the loaded image.

Contributions. In this paper, we show that the new embedded system architectures pose significant challenges to software-only root of trust (SWORT) protocols by enabling new attacks launched primarily against software-based attestation (SWATT). In particular, we make the following three contributions.

1. We present new architecture features of embedded system platforms that pose heretofore unexpected challenges to traditional SWATT protocols and their use in SWORT.
2. We define three new attacks against SWORT protocols that are enabled by both new architecture features (e.g., future-posted events, L1 caches relying on software-only coherence mechanisms) and scalability considerations (e.g., jitter caused by caches during randomized memory walks, clock jitter) on embedded platforms.
3. We present the implementation of the first attack on a popular embedded-system platform (i.e., on the Gumstix FireStorm COM), establish the feasibility of the second, and argue the practicality of the third. We outline several challenges of attack countermeasures, find dependencies among them, and argue that these must compose to achieve SWORT protocol security.

Organization. The remainder of this paper is organized as follows: Sect. 2 provides a brief overview of typical SWORT protocols and known attacks against SWATT designs. Three new attacks against SWORT protocols on modern embedded platforms are described in Sect. 3. Section 4 establishes the feasibility of these attacks, and Sect. 5 illustrates the challenges of effective countermeasures for these attacks. We describe related work in Sect. 6, and present our conclusions in Sect. 7.

2   Software-Only Root of Trust

A SoftWare-Only Root of Trust (SWORT) protocol comprises three distinct steps: (1) the establishment of an untampered execution environment (aka. a malware-free system state) via SoftWare-Based ATTestation (SWATT), (2) the verification of trusted-image authenticity, and (3) the loading of the authentic image onto the malware-free state, without allowing exploitable *time gaps* between the three steps.

2.1   Architecture and Protocol

In SWORT, a verifier program runs on a *trusted* machine and performs SWATT on a prover device using a nonce-response protocol; viz., Steps 1 – 2 of Fig. 1. The verifier program comprises a checksum simulator, a timer, and a cryptographic hash function. The checksum simulator generates pseudo-random *nonces* for attestation, constructs a copy of the device memory contents, and computes the expected response (i.e., checksum result) by simulating the checksum computation on the prover device. The timer measures the elapsed time of the nonce-response reception. An authentic, trusted code image (i.e., a correct, malware-free device image) is available on the verifier machine, and the hash function is used to compute its digest for the integrity measurement of the *device image*.

On the prover device, a prover program is installed and includes a checksum function, a communication function, a hash function, and other functions, such as those of the boot code. The checksum function disables interrupts on the device, resets system configurations to a known state, computes a checksum over the prover program and other critical memory contents (e.g., page table, stack, exception handler table, and communication buffer), and establishes an untampered execution

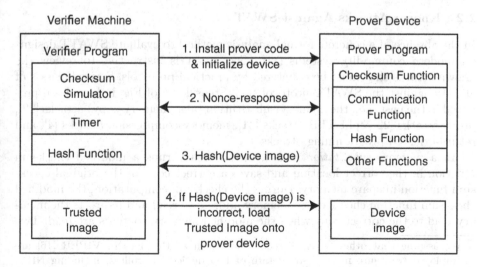

Fig. 1. SWORT system architecture and verification protocol.

environment for the device image. The checksum function must be designed such that modifications of its code or additions of malware instruction would invalidate the checksum result or cause a detectable computation overhead.

The verifier program checks the validity of the prover's response (i.e., the checksum result) and the elapsed time of the nonce-response pair. If the checksum result is correct and the measured time is within a detection threshold, the verifier program obtains the guarantee that an untampered execution environment has been established on the prover device, and subsequent results sent by the prover device are obtained in a malware-free state and are trusted. Please note that SWORT assumes that attackers cannot physically change the hardware configuration of the prover device, such as adding additional memory, replacing the device's CPU with a faster CPU or over-clocking the device's CPU frequency. In addition, the SWATT component (i.e., Steps 1 – 2 of Fig. 1) of the SWORT protocol *assumes* that attackers cannot optimize the checksum function to run it faster or find an alternative algorithm to compute the result faster.

After sending the checksum result to the verifier program, the checksum function calls a hash function to compute an integrity measurement (i.e., cryptographic hash) of the entire device image and sends the measurement to the verifier program. The verifier program checks the integrity of the device image, and if the device image has been changed, the verifier program loads the authentic, trusted image onto the prover device. Subsequent loading of this image in the malware-free memory state establishes the root of trust on the prover device[2].

In SWATT, the checksum function can also fill the spare memory space with pseudo-random values and then compute a checksum over the entire memory contents (instead of only over the prover program and other critical memory contents). In this way, the verifier program can prevent attackers from using the spare memory space on the prover device to perform malicious operations.

2.2   Known Attacks Against SWATT

In the absence of a concrete formal analysis method to evaluate SWATT designs on modern commodity systems (viz., Sect. 6), it is instructive to review the known attacks that must be countered by practical protocols. Several classes of attacks against the SWATT protocol (i.e., Steps 1 – 2 of Fig. 1) have been proposed in the past; i.e., the memory-substitution (aka. memory-copy) attacks [22], proxy attacks [22], split-TLB attacks [31], memory-compression attacks [4], and return-oriented programming attacks [4].

In a *memory-substitution attack*, an adversary runs a modified checksum function in the correct location and saves a correct copy of the original checksum function in spare memory. During the checksum computation, the modified checksum function checks every memory address to read and redirects the memory read to the correct copy when the modified memory contents are read. Two

---

[2] We assume that other SWATT techniques, such as the ones in VIPER [16] are employed to assure malware-free state of I/O device controllers, including NICs, GPUs, and disk, keyboard, and printer controllers.

types of such attacks have been identified in the past. In the first type, attackers run a modified checksum function at the correct memory location, and save a correct copy of the original checksum function in spare memory space. During the checksum computation, the malicious checksum function computes the checksum over the correct copy. In the second type, attackers load the original checksum function to the correct memory location, but run a malicious checksum function in another memory location that computes the checksum over the original copy. To defend against these attacks, the Program Counter (PC) and Data Pointer (DP) values (the memory address to read) are incorporated into the checksum computation. Thus, the malicious checksum function has to forge both the correct PC and DP values to compute the expected checksum, thereby causing a computation overhead.

In a *proxy attack*, the prover device asks a remote faster computer (a proxy) to compute the expected checksum. The proxy attack can be detected if the user monitors all the communication channels of the prover device. For example, the user can use a Radio Frequency analyzer (e.g., RF-Analyzer HF35C) to detect any wireless communications of the prover device, thus detecting wireless proxy attacks.

In a *split-TLB attack*, an adversary configures the Instruction Translation Lookaside Buffer (I-TLB) and the Data Translation Lookaside Buffer (D-TLB) such that the entries for the checksum function memory pages point to different physical addresses in the I-TLB and the D-TLB. Thus, the adversary can execute a malicious checksum function, but compute the checksum over the correct copy of the checksum code. However, the adversary must guarantee that the carefully configured entries in the D-TLB and the I-TLB are preserved during the checksum computation.

When the checksum function fills the spare memory space with pseudo-random values and computes a checksum over the entire memory contents, attackers cannot find the free memory space for a memory-copy or memory-substitution attack or a split-TLB attack. In this case, attackers might be able to perform a *memory-compression attack* whereby a malicious checksum compresses the memory contents of the prover program (to get spare memory space), and then decompress the compressed content to get the expected value when the compressed memory content is checksumed.

In a *return-oriented programming attack*, an adversary modifies the stack contents to break the control flow integrity of the prover program. Because the stack contents are incorporated into the checksum, the adversary has to perform additional operations (e.g., a memory-copy attack) to compute the expected checksum result.

3   New Attacks Against the SWORT Protocol

New attacks against the SWORT protocol include those that create and exploit timing gaps between correct execution of SWATT and subsequent integrity measurements; i.e., between the correct completion of Step 2 and the execution of

Step 3 in Fig. 1. New attacks also include those that exploit vulnerabilities of traditional SWATT introduced by new architecture features of embedded-system platforms. The balance of this section illustrates both types of new attacks.

3.1 Future-Posted Event Attacks

Some modern embedded-system platforms allow the configuration of *future-posted* events. These events can be set during system configuration (e.g., during Step 1 of Fig. 1) and trigger at a future time when the system runs (e.g., after Step 2 of Fig. 1). Leveraging the *future-posted* events, attackers can create a timing gap between the SWATT steps and subsequent integrity measurements. An example of such an event is the *future-posted Watch-Dog Timer (WDT) reset*. Other examples include the future-posted DMA transfers.

On some embedded platforms, attackers can configure the WDT to reset the device after a specific timer period. For example, on TI DM3730-based platforms, the CPU [28] supports the future-posted WDT reset, and the specific time period to reset the device can be configured as between about 62.5 μs and 74 h and 56 min. As a result, attackers can perform *future-posted WDT reset attacks*.

Figure 2 shows the timeline of this attack. Suppose that malware controls the platform during the installation of the prover code (i.e., Step 1 of Fig. 1) and configures the WDT to reset the device after the *correct checksum result* is sent to the verifier program; i.e., after Step 2 of Fig. 1. Then the malware erases itself from memory and invokes the prover program. During the SWATT steps, the prover program calls the checksum function to compute a checksum over the memory contents based on the nonce from the verifier program, and then sends the correct checksum result to the verifier program. After the checksum result is sent, the WDT reset event is triggered and the platform boots from an adversary-modified device image. After reboot, the malware of the device image controls the platform and sends a forged hash result (i.e., integrity measurement of the device image) to the verifier program.

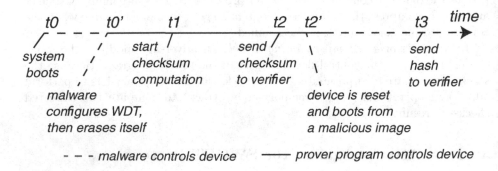

Fig. 2. Timeline of a WDT reset attack.

3.2   Attacks Exploiting High Execution-Time Variance

In SWATT protocols, the measured time of one nonce-response round is utilized to detect malicious operations on the prover device; e.g., malicious operations to forge correct checksum results. Typically the attack-detection threshold is set based on the overhead caused by possible attacks. If a measured time exceeds the threshold, it is highly likely that malicious operations are performed on the prover device. However, the measured time may exhibit significant variance caused by CPU clock variance, Translation Look-aside Buffer (TLB) misses, and possibly cache misses. Hence, to avoid false-positive malware detection, the attack-detection threshold must be extended over the maximal value of the measured time in normal (no-attack) conditions.

Recent research [27] shows that the modern CPU clock variance can be up to 3–8% and it increases with program execution times. Furthermore, because the traditional checksum functions read the memory contents in a pseudo-random pattern, the resulting TLB misses could increase the measured execution time significantly. To account for these types of execution-time jitter, the maximal value of the measured time in normal (no-attack) conditions must be extended significantly; e.g., by nearly 3 % of the average execution time.

Previous software-based attestation schemes did not have to account for *high* execution-time variance in setting the maximal execution time threshold. Their

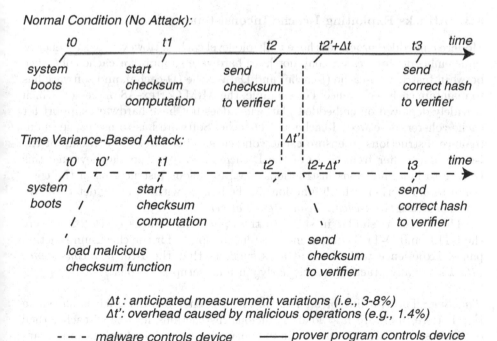

Fig. 3. Timeline of normal condition and time-variance based attack.

designs made cache behavior fairly predictable; e.g., the checksums fit into the cache and random access patterns resulted in predictably high overheard. TLBs need not be used since measurements were taken in physical RAM, and clock jitter was small because checksum execution times were short for relatively small memory configurations. In contrast, some of the new embedded-system processors force virtual memory (and hence the TLB) use whenever caches are used, and large memory configurations (i.e., GB size) cause checksum functions to execute for minutes instead of tens of milliseconds. Consequently, attackers can now exploit the high execution-time jitter on embedded systems to launch successful time-variance based attacks with *non-negligible probability*.

Timeline. Figure 3 shows the timeline of a *time-variance based attack*. Here, malware that controls the platform loads a modified checksum function that computes the expected checksum result. To protect the modified contents (i.e., malicious code) from being detected, the modified checksum function performs additional operations to forge the expected checksum, and these operations cause an overhead $\Delta t'$. However, as shown in the figure, under normal (no-attack) conditions, the anticipated measured time variation is Δt (i.e., the timing detection threshold), is larger than $\Delta t'$. Consequently, the verifier receives the correct checksum result within the timing detection threshold, and hence the verifier cannot detect this attack; i.e., a false-negative detection result.

3.3   Attacks Exploiting I-cache Inconsistency

Modern embedded processors have multiple-level caches. However, to save energy, some embedded processors may not have hardware support for cache coherence between Instruction-cache (I-cache) and Data-cache (D-cache), and software has to maintain cache coherence. For example, the ARM Cortex-A8 processor, which is widely deployed on embedded platforms, does not have hardware support for cache coherence between I-cache and D-cache. Software has to use cache maintenance instructions to ensure cache coherence. Therefore, the contents of the I-cache may differ from those of the D-cache, and attackers can leverage this feature to hide malicious instructions (e.g., malicious instructions in the communication function or hash function) in the I-cache without being detected. We call this attack the *I-cache inconsistency attack*.

This attack is similar in spirit to the Split-TLB attacks (Sect. 2.2), where the I-TLB and D-TLB contain inconsistent mappings for the checksum function pages. Experience with those attacks suggests that the *I-cache inconsistency attack* is equally practical, particularly since its setup is simpler.

Timeline. The timeline of an I-cache inconsistency-based attack is shown in Fig. 4. Here, malware first loads malicious instructions into the I-cache, then overwrites the malicious content in memory with the original values to guarantee that only legitimate contents are in the memory during checksum computation. The malicious code needs to comprise only a few instructions of the hash

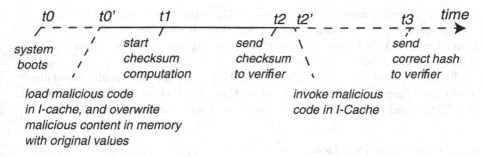

Fig. 4. Timeline of an *I-cache inconsistency attack.*

or communication function. The checksum function is computed over the legitimate memory contents and the correct checksum result is sent to the verifier program. After the checksum result is sent to the verifier program, the malicious instructions in the I-cache are invoked, and then the adversary controls the system.

4   Checksum and Attack Implementation

We implemented our SWATT protocol checksum and attacks based on future-posted events and execution-time variance using a Gumstix FireStorm COM[3] as the prover device and a HP laptop as the verifier machine. We leave the implementation of the *I-cache inconsistency* attack to future work.

The Gumstix FireStorm COM is a TI DM3730-based platform [28] with 512 MB SDRAM, 64 KB SRAM, and 512 MB NAND Flash. The TI DM3730 Central Processing Unit (CPU) is equipped with an ARM Cortex-A8 core (MPU) [1] running at 1-GHz. The ARM Cortex-A8 core has two levels of caches without hardware-support for cache coherence in the first-level caches. The first level (L1) has a 32 KB I-cache and a 32 KB D-cache while the second level (L2) has a 256 KB unified cache. The Gumstix COM runs a Linux operating system (based on Yocto Poky Dylan 9.0.0[4]) with the Linux kernel version 3.5.7. The HP laptop is connected to the Gumstix COM directly via an Ethernet cable. The laptop has an Intel Quad-Core i5 CPU running at 2534 MHz, 4 GB of RAM, and runs 32-bit Ubuntu 12.04 LTS as the guest OS.

We implemented the prover program as a loadable kernel module, which includes the Ethernet communication function, checksum function, and SHA256 hash function. The checksum implementation for the ARM Cortex-A8 core is based on the checksum function of PRISM [6]. The prover program uses an AES-based Pseudo-Random Number Generator. Using part of the pseudo-random nonce sent by the verifier machine as the seed, the prover program generates

---

and fills all spare memory space on the Gumstix COM with pseudo-random values before the checksum computation. On the verifier machine, we run a verifier program that measures the time of one nonce-response round using the *RDTSC* instruction.

In this section, we first describe our checksum function implementation in detail, and then present the implementation of attacks exploiting the Watch-Dog Timer and the execution-time variance of our checksum.

4.1   Checksum Function

Checksum Implementation. We implement the checksum function as 32 code blocks where each code block updates a 32-bit checksum-state variable (out of a total 32 checksum-state variables) comprising 33 ARM instructions that strongly order *AND, XOR*, and *SHIFT* operations. Each code block takes as input: the other checksum-state variables, the memory address being read (Data Pointer), memory contents, current processor status (i.e., the Current Processor Status Register (CPSR) value), Program Counter (PC), the pseudo-random numbers generated by a T-function [12], and a counter. The strong ordering of the checksum instructions guarantees that they cannot be executed in parallel.

In the checksum function, the 32-bit T-function is used to build a Pseudo-Random Number Generator (PRNG) to construct the (random) memory addresses used by the *read* instructions. Each code block performs two memory *reads*: one from the 512 MB SDRAM and the other from the 64 KB SRAM. Multiple iterations of checksum code-block executions cover the entire memory content of our system. The checksum function uses all 30 available ARM General Purpose Registers (GPRs) (nb., 2 GPRs in monitor mode are not available to access on ARM Cortex A8) as follows: 25 GPRs are used to save checksum states; r0 stores the pseudo-random value from T-function; r1 and r2 are used as temporary variables; r3 stores the counter value; $r12$ stores the current checksum state. (We also use available Save Processor Status Registers [1] to save checksum states.) Fig. 5 shows the assembly code of a single checksum block.

Checksum Execution Time. To include every randomly picked memory location in the checksum computation at least once with high probability, we set the checksum code-block iteration number (i.e., the number of checksum code blocks that execute on the Gumstix COM) to $0xb0000000$ based on the Coupon Collector's Problem [5]. Our verifier measurements show that a single nonce-response round (i.e., Step 2 of Fig. 1) takes 765.4 s on average with 2.9 s standard deviation over 371 measurements under normal (no-attack) condition. The maximal execution time of the nonce-response round is 768.1 s while the minimum value is 745.0 s. Seven measurements out of the 371 measurements take less than 750 s while the other 364 measurements take between 765 to 769 s. Thus, the measured time variance of the seven measurements is about 2.6 %.

To get consistent timing results using the *RDTSC* instruction, we configure the HP laptop (the verifier machine) running at a constant CPU frequency (2534

$r0$	Pseudo-Random Number (PRN) in T-function
$r1$	tmp and memory address to read
$r2$	tmp
$r3$	counter
$r4$ to $r14$	checksum states
C	Carry flag
Assembly Instruction	Explanation
umull r2, r1, r0, r0	$tmp = PRN \times PRN$, T-function computation
orr r1, r2, #0x5	$tmp = tmp \mid 5$
add r0, r0, r1	$PRN = PRN + tmp$
and r2, r0, 0x1FFFFFFC	$offset = PRN \ \& \ mask$
adds r1, r2, 0x80000000	$addr\_sdram = base\_addr + offset$, update C
ldr r2, [r1]	$tmp = mem[addr\_sdram]$
adcs r12, r12, r2	$r12 = r12 + tmp + C$, update C
eor r12, r12, r13	$r12 = r12 \oplus r13$
adcs r12, r12, r15	$r12 = r12 + PC + C$, update C
eor r12, r12, r14	$r12 = r12 \oplus r14$
adcs r12, r12, r4	$r12 = r12 + r4 + C$, update C
eor r12, r12, r0	$r12 = r12 \oplus PRN$
adcs r12, r12, r5	$r12 = r12 + r5 + C$, update C
eor r12, r12, r6	$r12 = r12 \oplus r6$
adcs r12, r12, r1	$r12 = r12 + addr\_sdram + C$, update C
mrs r2, spsr	$tmp = SPSR$
eor r12, r12, r2	$r12 = r12 \oplus tmp$
adcs r2, r12, r0	$tmp = r12 + PRN + C$, update C
movt r2, #0x4020	$tmp = (tmp \ \& \ 0xFFFF) \mid 0x40200000$
and r1, r2, #0xFFFFFFFC	$addr\_sram = tmp \ \& \ mask$
ldr r2, [r1]	$tmp = mem[addr\_sram]$
adcs r12, r12, r2	$r12 = r12 + tmp + C$, update C
eor r12, r12, r7	$r12 = r12 \oplus r7$
adcs r12, r12, r8	$r12 = r12 + r8 + C$, update C
eor r12, r12, r1	$r12 = r12 \oplus addr\_sram$
adcs r12, r12, r9	$r12 = r12 + r9 + C$, update C
eor r12, r12, r10	$r12 = r12 \oplus r10$
adcs r12, r12, r11	$r12 = r12 + r11 + C$, update C
mrs r2, cpsr	$tmp = CPSR$
eor r12, r12, r2	$r12 = r12 \oplus tmp$
adcs r12, r3, r12, ROR #1	$tmp = rotation\_shift\_right\_1\_bit(r12)$
	$r12 = tmp + counter + C$, update C
adcs r0, r0, r12	$PRN = PRN + r12 + C$, update C
sub r3, r3, #1	$counter = counter - 1$

Fig. 5. Assembly instructions for a single checksum block.

MHz); we also configure the ARM Cortex-A8 processor on the Gumstix COM running at its maximal CPU frequency (1 GHz).

4.2   WDT Reset Attack Implementation

The implementation of the WDT reset attack against our prover code comprises two critical steps: the first is the setting WDT timer to reset the device, and the second is the generation of the correct hash result and its sending to the verifier program when the system boots up.

Before setting the WDT timer, we must wake it up. Specifically, we have a dedicated kernel module *malmod*, which is installed exactly before the attestation kernel module. The *malmod* sets *EN_WDT2* bit (i.e., Bit 5) in the *CM_FCLKEN_WKUP* register and *EN_WDT2* bit (i.e., Bit 5) in the *CM_ICLKEN_WKUP* register to wake up the WDT timer. A WDT timer has a large reset period, from 62.5 μs to 74 h 56 min, and the time of one nonce-response round under normal (no-attack) condition (i.e., 765.4 s) is within the reset period. In addition, the SHA256 hash computation (i.e., the interval $t3 - t2$ in Fig. 2) takes about 76 s. The *malmod* configures the WDT to reset the device between times $t2$ and $t3$ on the time line of Fig. 2, and then starts the WDT by writing its start/stop register (WSPR) twice using the sequence *0xAAAA* followed by *0x5555* [28]. Before checksum computation starts, the prover kernel module replaces the memory contents of the *malmod* with the required pseudo-random values.

After the correct checksum result is sent to the verifier machine, the Gumstix COM reboots from an attacker-modified device image. In the modified device image, we place a script file in the */etc/init.d/* directory, which automatically executes a malicious program after reboot. In our implementation, the prover kernel module and the verifier program communicate via ICMP packets. The malicious program generates the expected ICMP response message including the correct hash value, and sends the ICMP message to the verifier program.

4.3   Feasibility of the Time-Variance Based Attack

We evaluated the feasibility of time-variance based attacks by measuring the overhead of a *memory-substitution* attack (viz., Sect. 2.2) in which an adversary saves a correct copy of the prover code on the NAND Flash. Then the attacker-modified checksum verifies every randomly generated memory address to be used by the *read* instructions and redirects the *reads* to the original copy on the NAND Flash whenever they attempt to use the attacker-modified checksum contents.

In this attack, the attacker-modified checksum function reads the entire SDRAM (512 MB) in a pseudo-random pattern. Note that the attacker-modified SDRAM content (i.e., the modified checksum code blocks) represents only a small fraction; i.e., about 4 KB or 0.00076 %[5]. Consequently, the main over-head of this attack is caused by the instructions that verify the pseudo-random

---

[5] $\frac{4}{512 \times 1024} = 0.0000076.$

SDRAM memory address and redirect the *reads* when necessary. In the evaluation, we ignore the small and relatively rare overhead caused by the actual reading the NAND Flash, and evaluate the frequent overhead caused by the additional instructions that check the randomly generated SDRAM address.

We added six instructions in each modified checksum block to verify every pseudo-random SDRAM memory address used by the *read* instructions; i.e., one instruction to jump out of the modified checksum code block to avoid changing the PC value incorporated into the checksum; four instructions to check if the memory address is within the modified memory space and to restore the previous Current Processor Status Register (CPSR) value; and one instruction to jump back to the checksum block. We measured the time of one nonce-response round of the SWATT protocol (i.e., Step 2 of Fig. 1) using the modified checksum function on the Gumstix COM. The measurement results show that the overhead caused by the six additional instructions is only 1.4 %[6], which is much smaller than the time variance under the normal (no-attack) condition; i.e., 2.6 %, as shown in Sect. 4.1. Consequently, this instance of a memory substitution attack will succeed with non-negligible probability.

5   Challenges for Effective Countermeasures

Challenges. To counter attacks exploiting *future-posted events*, the checksum function needs to capture the values of *all* critical configuration registers in the checksum result. Thus the setting of future-posted events would cause an incorrect checksum result. This countermeasure is less straight-forward than it might first appear, for two reasons. First, modern embedded platforms have a large numbers of configuration registers with complex configuration options; e.g., there are thousands of I/O device control registers in the Gumstix ARM Cortex-A8 platform that must be analyzed. Thus, finding *all* critical configuration options that may enable such attacks becomes a non-trivial exercise. Second, the assurance of a correct setting that disables future-posted WDT events depends on effective countermeasures to attacks that exploit high execution-time variance and I-cache inconsistency (discussed below).

To counter attacks that exploit *I-cache inconsistency*, a possible approach is to design a checksum function whose size is larger than the I-cache. Thus during checksum execution, the code blocks in the I-cache will be evicted and replaced. However, attackers may be able to compress the checksum code blocks (e.g., by removing duplicate instructions), add malicious instructions and run the compressed checksum code blocks in the I-cache instead of the original, larger blocks. It is extremely challenging to guarantee that a checksum function cannot be compressed to fit into the I-cache. For example, one might include the cache-miss counter, which is used by the system performance monitor, to the checksum computation [10], in an attempt to prevent attackers from running

---

[6] The primary reason the overhead added by the six instructions is so small is that the instruction which *reads* from a pseudo-random memory address in every code block consumes many more CPU cycles than six instructions.

a smaller checksum function that will change the cache-miss counter. However, this countermeasure would require that the cache replacement policy be deterministic. Otherwise, the verifier program could not predict and verify the checksum results. Unfortunately, on the TI DM3730 platform, the ARM Cortex-A8 processor utilizes a random-replacement policy for the I-cache.

Yet another possible approach to counter attacks that exploit *I-cache inconsistency* is to utilize dynamically modified instructions in the checksum code blocks. Then, one could insert instructions into these code blocks that invalidate all I-cache blocks. For example, the ARM Cortex-A8 instruction set includes an instruction that invalidates all I-cache blocks. However, attackers may perform *read-decode-execute* operations to handle dynamically modified checksum instructions and avoid the invalidation of the I-cache blocks. That is, in a *read-decode-execute* operation, adversary-modified (i.e., malicious) checksum code in the I-cache can read the dynamically modified instructions, decode them, and execute code based on the decoded information. Thus, the modified (i.e., malicious) checksum function can avoid the instruction that invalidates I-cache blocks. Obtaining demonstrable countermeasures for attacks that exploit *I-cache inconsistency* is extra challenging because they depend on other countermeasures; i.e., on those for the time-variance based attacks (discussed below).

To counter attacks that exploit high *execution-time variance*, one could modify the checksum design to force attackers to perform complex operations and cause an unavoidable increase of execution overhead. A possible approach would be to add performance-monitor values (e.g., the executed instruction counter, the TLB-miss counter) in the checksum computation. Unfortunately, this might not increase the attack overhead sufficiently for detection. For example, attackers may need only several additional instructions to calculate the correct instruction counter. In addition, attackers may run the malicious code in the same page with the checksum function, thereby avoiding changes to the TLB-miss counter. The I-cache-miss counter may force attackers to perform a large number of operations to obtain the expected value; e.g., by simulating the I-cache replacement. However, this also requires that the I-cache replacement policy be deterministic, which is not the case for the ARM Cortex-A8.

Effectiveness. To be effective, a countermeasure for a given attack must not only deny the attacker' goal but must also compose with countermeasure for other possible attacks; e.g., a countermeasure can be effective for an attack only if other countermeasures are effective against other attacks [8]. Composition requires that all dependencies between countermeasures be found and cyclic dependencies removed [9].

Countermeasure dependencies exist for our attacks. For example, the countermeasures for the future-posted WDT reset attack depend on the countermeasures for attacks that exploit high execution-time variance and I-cache inconsistency. Unless these two attacks are countered effectively, the adversary can modify the checksum code to erase the instructions that disable future-posted WDT events. Furthermore, a dependency exists between the countermeasures for the I-cache inconsistency attack and that for time-variance attack. The former depends on the latter, since the time-variance attack can be used to modify the checksum code so that the I-cache resetting instructions are erased.

6 Related Work

Reflection [26] is a software-only approach to verify program code running on an untrusted system. *Reflection* fills the spare memory with pseudo-random content, resets the system state, and computes a hash over the entire memory. A verifier machine checks the hash results and the execution time. Genuinity [10] validates the system configuration of a remote machine using software-based mechanisms. Genuinity reads memory in a random pattern to cause a large number of TLB misses, and incorporates the number of TLB misses in the checksum result, preventing attacks based on the observation that simulating the hardware operations (e.g., TLB block replacement) is slower than the actual execution. However, Genuinity is vulnerable to memory-copy attacks [25]; viz., Sect. 2.2.

SWATT [23] performs software-based attestation for embedded systems. In SWATT, a checksum function computes a checksum over the entire memory contents using strongly-ordered *AND*, *ADD*, and *XOR* operations. An external verifier checks the checksum results and the execution time. The main idea was that malicious operations would either invalidate the checksum results or cause detectable timing delays, or both. However, this protocol does not aim to counter attacks caused by future-posted events, cache (in)coherence, or high execution-time variance; e.g., CPU clock variance, cache- and TLB-caused jitter.

Pioneer [22] establishes an untampered execution environment over a small piece of memory on an AMD Opteron K8 architecture platform. The Pioneer checksum disables all interrupts, and computes its result over a small piece of memory. Naturally, the Pioneer design could not anticipate the future hardware features of embedded platforms that we address in this paper. PRISM [6] used software based attestation to establish untampered code execution on embedded ARM platforms. However, PRISM does not address the possible challenges of cache (in)coherence and high execution-time variance presented in this paper.

SBAP [15] verifies the firmware integrity of an Apple aluminum keyboard that has limited resources using software-only approaches. VIPER [16] verifies the integrity of peripherals' firmware on commodity systems using software-based attestation mechanisms. VIPER describes the possible mechanisms to prevent proxy attacks in software-based attestation protocols. Like Pioneer, the VIPER design could not anticipate the impact of future hardware features on software-based attestation. Kovath *et al.* [14] propose a comprehensive timing-based attestation system that verifies the system integrity of machines in enterprise environments. It successfully detects attacks that have only 1.7 % overhead. However, the low detection threshold may cause a significant number false-positive detection of malware because of the CPU clock variance, which can reach 3 % of execution time on some embedded-system platforms.

Armknecht *et al.* [2] propose an abstract security model for design and analysis of software-based attestation protocols. However, this model does not aim to address SWORT protocols nor to offer *concrete* checksum designs that could counter the the attacks of new hardware features described in this paper.

7   Conclusions

Embedded system platforms are used pervasively in security-sensitive applications, and consequently are becoming attractive targets of attack [13]. Yet, existing software-based attestation protocols designed for such applications cannot address the newly introduced complex hardware features that enable new attacks. As a result, attackers can leverage these features to break the security of SWORT protocols. This paper presents new attacks whose countermeasures appear to require a significant redesign of traditional software-based attestation protocols. In particular, we find dependencies among countermeasures, which show that countermeasures must compose to achieve SWORT protocol security.

Acknowledgements. We are grateful to David Brumely, Tom Forest, Di Jin, and Maverick Woo for their comments and suggestions on the research reported herein. This work was supported in part by the Defense Advanced Research Projects Agency (DARPA) under contract N66001-13-2-404 and by a grant from the General Motors (GM) Corporation at CyLab, Carnegie Mellon University. The views and conclusions contained here are those of the authors and should not be interpreted as necessarily representing the official policies or endorsements, either express or implied, of CMU, GM, DARPA, or the U.S. Government or any of its agencies.

References

1. ARM. Cortex-A8 technical reference manual. Revision:r3p2, May 2010
2. Armknecht, F., Sadeghi, A.-R., Schulz, S., Wachsmann, C.: A security framework for the analysis and design of software attestation. In: Proceedings of ACM Conference on Computer and Communications Security, pp. 1–12 (2013)
3. Bardou, R., Focardi, R., Kawamoto, Y., Simionato, L., Steel, G., Tsay, J.-K.: Efficient padding oracle attacks on cryptographic hardware. In: Safavi-Naini, R., Canetti, R. (eds.) CRYPTO 2012. LNCS, vol. 7417, pp. 608–625. Springer, Heidelberg (2012)
4. Castelluccia, C., Francillon, A., Perito, D., Soriente, C.: On the difficulty of software-based attestation of embedded devices. In: Proceedings of the ACM Conference on Computer and Communications Security, November 2009
5. Erdos, P., Renyi, A.: On a classical problem of probability theory. In: Proceedings of Magyar Tudomanyos Akademia Matematikai Kutato Intezetenek Kozlemenyei, pp. 215–220 (1961)
6. Franklin, J., Luk, M., Seshadri, A., Perrig, A.: Prism: enabling personal verification of code integrity, untampered execution, and trusted I/O or human-verifiable code execution. CyLab Lab Technical report CMU-CyLab-07-010, Carnegie Mellon University (2007)
7. Garay, J.A., Huelsbergen, L.: Software integrity protection using timed executable agents. In: Proceedings of ACM Symposium on Information, Computer and Communications Security, pp. 189–200 (2006)

8. Gligor, V.: Dancing with the adversary: a tale of wimps and giants. In: Christianson, B., Malcolm, J., Matyáš, V., Švenda, P., Stajano, F., Anderson, J. (eds.) Security Protocols 2014. LNCS, vol. 8809, pp. 100–115. Springer, Heidelberg (2014)

9. Kailar, R., Gligor, V., Gong, L.: Effectiveness analysis of cryptographic protocols. In: Proceedings of IFIP Conference on Distributed Computing for Critical Applications. Springer, January 1994

10. Kennell, R., Jamieson, L.H.: Establishing the genuinity of remote computer systems. In: Proceedings of the USENIX Security Symposium, pp. 295–308 (2003)

11. Kim, T.H.-J., Huang, L.-S., Perrig, A., Jackson, C., Gligor, V.: Accountable Key Infrastructure (AKI): a proposal for a public-key validation infrastructure. In: Proceedings of International World Wide Web Conference (WWW) (2013)

12. Klimov, A., Shamir, A.: A new class of invertible mappings. In: Kaliski, B.S., Koç, K., Paar, C. (eds.) CHES 2002. LNCS, vol. 2523. Springer, Heidelberg (2002)

13. Koscher, K., Czeskis, A., Roesner, F., Patel, S., Kohno, T., Checkoway, S., McCoy, D., Kantor, B., Anderson, D., Shacham, H., Savage, S.: Experimental security analysis of a modern automobile. In: Proceedings of IEEE Symposium on Security and Privacy, pp. 447–462 (2010)

14. Kovah, X., Kallenberg, C., Weathers, C., Herzog, A., Albin, M., Butterworth, J.: New results for timing-based attestation. In: Proceedings of IEEE Symposium on Security and Privacy, pp. 239–253 (2012)

15. Li, Y., McCune, J.M., Perrig, A.: SBAP: software-based attestation for peripherals. In: Acquisti, A., Smith, S.W., Sadeghi, A.-R. (eds.) TRUST 2010. LNCS, vol. 6101, pp. 16–29. Springer, Heidelberg (2010)

16. Li, Y., McCune, J.M., Perrig, A.: VIPER: verifying the integrity of peripherals' firmware. In: Proceedings of ACM Conference on Computer and Communications Security, pp. 3–16 (2011)

17. Martignoni, L., Paleari, R., Bruschi, D.: Conqueror: tamper-proof code execution on legacy systems. In: Kreibich, C., Jahnke, M. (eds.) DIMVA 2010. LNCS, vol. 6201, pp. 21–40. Springer, Heidelberg (2010)

18. Parno, B., McCune, J.M., Perrig, A.: Bootstrapping Trust in Modern Computers. SpringerBriefs in Computer Science, vol. 10. Springer, New York (2011)

19. Sagoian, C., Stamm, S.: Certified lies: detecting and defeating government interception attacks against SSL. In: Proceedings of ACM Symposium on Operating Systems Principles, pp. 1–18 (2010)

20. Seshadri, A., Luk, M., Perrig, A., van Doorn, L., Khosla, P.: SCUBA: secure code update by attestation in sensor networks. In: Proceedings of ACM Workshop on Wireless Security, pp. 85–94 (2006)

21. Seshadri, A., Luk, M., Qu, N., Perrig, A.: SecVisor: a tiny hypervisor to provide lifetime kernel code integrity for commodity OSes. In: Proceedings of ACM Symposium on Operating Systems Principles, pp. 335–350 (2007)

22. Seshadri, A., Luk, M., Shi, E., Perrig, A., van Doorn, L., Khosla, P.: Pioneer: verifying integrity and guaranteeing execution of code on legacy platforms. In: Proceedings of ACM Symposium on Operating Systems Principles, pp. 1–16, October 2005

23. Seshadri, A., Perrig, A., van Doorn, L., Khosla, P.: SWATT: software-based attestation for embedded devices. In: Proceedings of IEEE Symposium on Security and Privacy, pp. 272–282 (2004)

24. Shaneck, M., Mahadevan, K., Kher, V., Kim, Y.-D.: Remote software-based attestation for wireless sensors. In: Molva, R., Tsudik, G., Westhoff, D. (eds.) ESAS 2005. LNCS, vol. 3813, pp. 27–41. Springer, Heidelberg (2005)

25. Shankar, U., Chew, M., Tygar, J.: Side effects are not sufficient to authenticate software. In: Proceedings of the USENIX Security Symposium (2004)
26. Spinellis, D.: Reflection as a mechanism for software integrity verification. ACM Trans. Inf. Syst. Secur. **3**(1), 51–62 (2000)
27. Tam, S.: Modern clock distribution systems. In: Xanthopoulos, T. (ed.) Clocking in Modern VLSI Systems, Chap. 2. Integrated Circuits and Systems, pp. 6–95. Springer, USA (2009)
28. Texas Instruments. AM/DM37X multimedia device technical reference manual. Version R, September 2012
29. The Trusted Computing Group. TPM Main specification version 1.2 (revision 116) (2011)
30. Wollinger, T., Guajardo, J., Paar, C.: Security on FPGAs: state-of-the-art implementations and attacks. ACM Trans. Embed. Comput. Syst. (TECS) **3**, 534–574 (2004)
31. Wurster, G., van Oorschot, P., Anil, S.: A generic attack on checksumming-based software tamper resistance. In: Proceedings of IEEE Symposium on Security and Privacy, pp. 127–138 (2005)
32. Zhao, J., Gligor, V., Perrig, A., Newsome, J.: ReDABLS: revisiting device attestation with bounded leakage of secrets. In: Christianson, B., Malcolm, J., Stajano, F., Anderson, J., Bonneau, J. (eds.) Security Protocols 2013. LNCS, vol. 8263, pp. 94–114. Springer, Heidelberg (2013)

Establishing Software-Only Root of Trust on Embedded Systems: Facts and Fiction (Transcript of Discussion)

Virgil Gligor[✉]

Carnegie Mellon University, Pittsburgh, USA
gligor@cmu.edu

This presentation is based on joint work with Yanlin Li, Yueqiang Cheng, and Adrian Perrig.

Let me start by defining what I mean by root of trust, and then its software-only variant. Suppose that one has, on the one hand, an authentic system image that's trustworthy, and on the other, a system that is supposed to load that image in a verifiable manner. Also suppose the system may have *persistent* malware, which survives repeated secure- and trusted-boot operations. Our task is to ensure that either the trustworthy image is loaded in the malware-free system state or we detect the existence of malware. This task provides the root of trust on that system.

Frank Stajano: If you are in a definitions mode, what does *secure* and *trusted* boot mean if it allows the system not to be secure?

Reply: Let's start with *trusted boot*. Trusted boot, as understood by most people since the Trusted Platform Module (TPM) was invented – or even earlier as defined by Gasser, Goldstein, Kaufman, and Lampson [1] in 1989 and more formally by Lampson, Abadi, Burrows, and Wobber [2] in 1992 – means that a software module $S_i, i \geq 1$, measures the next software module to be loaded onto the system, S_{i+1}, by computing its hash before transferring control to it. The first software module, S_1, is measured by a trusted hardware component; e.g., by the TPM. Each hash value accumulates the results of the previous hash operations in the TPM, and the final hash is signed by TPM and returned to an external verifier whenever an *attestation protocol* is performed.

The attestation protocol for trusted boot starts with the verifier sending a nonce to the TPM, which computes a signature over the nonce and the final hash and returns it to the verifier. The verifier checks whether that the received signature is correct, and if it is, that means that the system state contains the *expected* software. However, the expected software is *not* necessarily bug-free and the system state is *not* necessarily malware-free. For example, malware may still exist in peripheral device firmware or device controllers, so even if the CPU and primary memory are malware-free, the overall system may not be.

Secure boot, simply put, means that the system boots off a "white list" of approved software modules such that the signature of each module is verified by a trusted system component before the module is booted. In contrast with trusted boot, the booting process stops as soon as a signature is found to be

© Springer International Publishing Switzerland 2015
B. Christianson et al. (Eds.): Security Protocols 2015, LNCS 9379, pp. 69–79, 2015.
DOI: 10.1007/978-3-319-26096-9_8

invalid. Again, while all booted software is approved, the overall system state in which the boot takes place may be infested with malware.

In *root of trust establishment* one has a system image that must be measured before boot, perhaps as in trusted boot, for instance. In addition, the boot process requires an attestation protocol that obtains a "proof" (e.g., some verifiable evidence) that the state in which one boots is malware free. If the proof fails, then there is malware in the system. In some sense, if one establishes a root of trust, one gives system malware a choice that it cannot refuse: either it disappears, because the system boots in a malware-free state, or one detects the presence of malware in the system, and eventually one can take remedial action; e.g., taking the system off-line and cleaning it up of malware using appropriate tools. So that's basically what I mean by establishing root of trust.

SoftWare-Only Root of Trust (SWORT) says that one establishes root of trust using only software. For example, there is *no* special hardware to support the verification of the booted image authenticity. Furthermore, there are *no* secrets in the system. In fact, saying that one does not have to rely secrets is making virtue out of necessity, since secrets don't help here. Although using a secret one can establish the authenticity of the image that is booted, the secret cannot tell a verifier anything about whether the system state is malware-free. One can't establish malware-free state exclusively with secrets, so root of trust needs additional properties that hardware-protected secrets, like those of the TPM, cannot offer. Software secrets, such as obfuscated code or hidden initial checksum addresses offer insufficient protection. Discovery of software secrets may also jeopardize large numbers of machines. Nevertheless, if the attestation protocol uses a remote verifier, the security of the system's communication with the verifier (e.g., remote system's authenticity) will require software-maintained secrets described in our SPW 2013 paper [3].

The basic building block for SWORT is the notion of the *software-based attestation*, which was studied extensively by Adrian Perrig and his students at Carnegie Mellon University starting with 2004. In essence, software-based attestation attempts to establish malware-free system states, by producing evidence a checksum code ran untampered by malware in the system. Briefly, the checksum design aims to produce incompressible checksum code and execution sequences. The code is loaded into the system's cache where it occupies all the cache space. The checksum execution is started by receipt of a *nonce* from a local verifier and is timed by the verifier. The verifier can tell whether system malware affected the checksum execution, since execution of any malware instructions would modify either the checksum's timing or result, or both.

In our recent project on SWORT using software attestation we encountered three challenges that arise when one uses new embedded-system architectures, which has not been addressed in prior work. The first challenge is that SWORT must link the establishment of malware free states with the measurement and loading of the system image in an atomic (i.e., uninterrupted) way. Yet, new architectures enable postdating events that may break that link and establish an exploitable time gap whereby malware can substitute the loading of the authentic image with a corrupt one after software attestation establishes a malware-free state.

The second challenge is that the checksums designed for the past ten years do not scale to gigabyte memory sizes (e.g., they execute for about 13 min for a 0.5 GB RAM and 64K SRAM) and their execution time includes jitter; e.g., caused by clock, cache, and TLB variations. This enables an adversary to exploit the lenient verifier time measurements that account for execution-time jitter and execute extra malware instructions. Non-lenient measurements would cause false positive malware detection and require repeating the measurements several times, which is impractical in many embedded applications given the long latencies; e.g., 13 min.

The third challenge is that, to save energy, some new embedded-system architectures do not maintain cache coherence in hardware. Instead they require software-based mechanisms that use knowledge of the application and systems code to maintain the coherence of instruction and data caches. This enables malware to lunch new memory substitution/copy attacks, which require new defense countermeasures. In this talk, I will describe three types of attacks that are enabled by the features of these new embedded-system architectures.

Perhaps the most challenging aspect of SWORT is that prior work has not developed concrete assurances for the software-based attestation protocols to date; i.e., we don't have high assurances of the determination of malware-free state. There is some theory, which was developed in a recent model by Armknecht et al. [4], but like most abstract models, this model does not deal with the realities of new systems. For example, the model assumes the existence of ideal oracles that model checksum properties without concrete evidence that these properties can be implemented on modern architectures. Furthermore, the model relies on taking snapshots of systems states and comparing them by computing Hamming distances, which could easily take upwards of 20 min on modern embedded-system architectures. We clearly need new theory for establishing formal assurances of software-based attestation. However this is the topic of ongoing research.

For the purpose of this presentation, I rely of the simple protocol description presented in Sect. 2 and illustrated in Fig. 1 of the accompanying paper. In this protocol, the verifier machine is an HP laptop and the system (i.e., the prover device in Fig. 1) is a Gumstix FireStorm COM, which a TI DM3730 CPU is equipped with an ARM Cortex-A8 core running at 1-GHz. The Gumstix FireStorm COM platform has two other processors in the integrated video-audio (IVA) sub-system with their local memory as well as access to the main RAM. The HP laptop is connected to the Gumstix COM directly via an Ethernet cable.

The SWORT protocol comprises two phases, namely a typical software attestation phase (Steps 1–2 of Fig. 1) followed by a device-image measurement and booting phase (Steps 3–4 of Fig. 1). In Step 1, the verifier sends a request for system initialization to the prover device comprising checksum, communication, hash function, and booting code and along with PRNG code and a random seed. The prover device is supposed to initialize its all random access memory (RAM) with the code received and a string of random numbers generated by the PRNG and seed. In Step 2, the verifier sends a random *nonce* to the prover device and expects the correct result of the checksum computation on the input nonce to return within a given time. The nonce randomizes the checksum result and, presumably, malware could not anticipate/guess the result without the nonce with more than negligible probability. During its execution, the checksum disables all interrupts, sets all I/O registers to known values, and computes its result by reading all memory content (i.e., all code and random numbers) from randomly generated addresses. To ensure that all n RAM (i.e., SDRAM and SRAM) words are read at lease once, the checksum computation generates $n \times log\, n$ random addresses, as suggested by the Coupon Collector's Problem. If the checksum result is correct and returned within the expected time to the verifier, a malware-free memory state – aka., an untampered execution environment – is achieved, and the verifier begins executing Step 3. In this step, the prover device measures the device image in the untampered execution environment, (i.e., by computing the hash of the device image stored on the NAND flash memory) and returns the result to the verifier. If the measurement fails, the verifier executes Step 3 whereby it transfers the authentic trustworthy image onto the NAND flash and restarts the protocol. Otherwise, the verifier initiates the loading of the device image in malware-free memory. This establishes the root of trust.

Alastair Beresford: If the prover device is connected by an Ethernet what stops it offloading the computation to a faster device somewhere else?

Reply: Indeed, what happens if one faces a "proxy attack"? In a proxy attack, the prover device offloads a computation to a faster machine (i.e., the "proxy"), gets a result in less time than expected by the verifier, executes malware during the free time made available, and it replies in time to the verified device. In principle, one can handle such an attack in two ways. The first, which does not work very well, is to physically disconnect the device from the network. However, malware could surreptitiously turn on WiFi communication and still contact the faster external machine(s). To handle this problem, one could use a RF frequency analyzer (e.g., HF35C), which would enable one to figure out is there is any WiFi communication during the attestation protocol. The reason why that doesn't work well is that if there is a lot of ambient WiFi communication at the location of the verifier and device prover, one could not easily avoid false positive communication detection.

The second way to handle a proxy attack is ensure that external I/O communication can be sensed by the verifier's time measurement. This requires that we use a fast version of the Ethernet with a small transmission-time variation. Also, the checksum's executing time jitter together with the communication variation on the Ethernet cable must be smaller than a single round-trip transmission on the external I/O communication channel to the proxy. Otherwise, the external I/O communication could not be sensed by the verifier's time measurement.

Keith Irwin: Before you said, we're going to use a very fast version, I was going to say, it doesn't necessarily have to be WiFi, it could be audio.

Reply: Yes, the device malware could use audio communication, not just WiFi.

Keith Irwin: But my other question was, when you talk about the initial RAM, the flash memory, were you also verifying any of the sub-systems, because, as you said, we have more than one processor, and sometimes these have separate flash?

Reply: Absolutely. Let me point out the challenge there. Although we've known how to verify some sub-systems (i.e., peripherals) in addition to the main CPU and RAM since Yanlin Li *et al.*'s 2011 paper [5], the Gumstix FireStorm COM has two other processors within the IVA sub-system that can access the shared RAM. The way we handle them during the checksum execution is to have the checksum verify that the configuration registers indicate that the IVA processors cannot access the RAM. In other words, the CPU exercises its priority to disable the access of those two other processors while its checksum computation is going on. This has to be done, because otherwise malware that hides in these processors could help speed up the checksum computation.

Keith Irwin: But I guess I don't see how that stops malware. I see how that stops malware hiding in the other processors from impacting this process. I don't see how this rules out there being malware.

Reply: Yes, it doesn't. It is not intended to eliminate that malware yet. Once we establish a malware-free execution environment on this CPU, RAM, and I/O registers, we can go and handle the other two processors. First, however, we have to exclude those processors' access while we compute the checksum, so that we can sequentially handle the other processors next. And in fact there is a way to eliminate malware from the other processor, which I can explain to you off-line, but it's obviously somewhat more complex.

Keith Irwin: Does this work with something like a baseband processor which basically get to veto the other processor?

Reply: No. Very briefly, it's based on the fact that once the checksum excludes the other processors and the verifier checks that there is an untampered execution environment, the verifier can run another program that establishes the malware freedom of the next fastest processor and its memory; i.e., this program becomes the verifier that processor, and while this is done the third processor is excluded. And then one goes to the third processor and repeats the process.

Tom Sutcliffe: What's to stop your malware from sitting in the bit of your main memory, which was otherwise not very empty, so that it can easily calculate what the contents of that memory should have been, and when it's running the checksum on what's actually there, it could, over some simple calculation, compensate for the difference and produce the correct result in expected time.

Reply: You have to wait few minutes, because this is essentially the second attack I will present.

The first attack. So let's now see how the first attack against software attestation on our embedded systems works. One of the things we noticed is that on modern devices there is a watchdog timer that can be programmed to reboot the device image from the NAND flash at some point in the future. The reboot event can be programmed to occur at any time between $62\,\mu s$ and $76\,h$ and $56\,min$ from the time of its setting.

Now assume that the prover device has persistent malware on it. At Step 1 of the SWORT protocol (see Fig. 1 of the accompanying paper when the prover device receives the system initialization message), malware configures the watchdog timer to reset the device and reboot it immediately after attestation succeeds; i.e., after the checksum returns the correct result at Step 2 of Fig. 1. A malware-infested device image is booted from the NAND flash, gains control of the device, and responds to the verifier's image-measurement request with a correct hash result (at Step 3 of Fig. 1). The verifier has no way to detect that, although the software-based attestation was correct, the SWORT protocol failed to establish root of trust. Another version of this attack may use future-posted DMA transfers.

The second attack. Let us recall Tom's earlier question and present an example of a similar attack, which we call the "memory substitution" attack. Recall that each RAM word is randomly read by the checksum computation at least once. This means that the instructions of all prover code, namely the checksum, communication, hash function, and boot code, are captured in the checksum result.

Now suppose that the adversary wants to modify some of the code in a region of the device prover's RAM (e.g., insert a few malware instructions) and yet cause the checksum to compute the correct result. To do so, the checksum code is changed to include a couple of instructions that checks whether the random address generated for the next *read* operation comes from the modified region, and if so, it redirects the *read* to the original correct memory content on the NAND flash. Thus the correct checksum result is computed and yet malware is left undetected in the device's RAM.

The reason why this is possible is because the verifier's measurement of the checksum's execution time must be lenient. That is, it must account for execution time jitter; e.g., the clock jitter may extend the clock period by about 3%–8% on some processors but not in other processors of the same type. Similarly, non-determinism in the cache and TLB behavior may also add some jitter that may occur once in, say, one hundred protocol runs. To avoid false positive time measurements because of jitter, the verifier ends up adding an extra δ units of time (i.e., the leniency) to the average checksum execution time t, and the expected execution time become $t + \delta$.

Now it turns out that if malware adds only six instructions to the checksum to verify whether the random addresses for the *read* operations come from the modified region (and if so, redirect them to the NAND flash), the overall added overhead is only about 1.4% to a checksum computation of $13\,min$ over the prover device's RAM. Yet, the jitter that we measured is about 2.6% of the execution time. So if we set the δ to 2.6% of the total checksum execution time of, say, $13\,min$, turns out that within $t + \delta$ period malware can execute the six instructions undetected and compute the correct result by reading from the NAND flash, when necessary. Is that what you had in mind, Tom?

Tom Sutcliffe: Pretty much, I was just thinking that you may be able to find the bit of memory where you didn't even need to do the NAND *read* in that the memory was predictable enough that you could reconstruct it without consulting the NAND.

Reply: Well, that would be difficult to do, since there are no memory bits left that are uninitialized to a random number. However, we tried other attacks where we wanted to exploit the fact that, if the random address is generated by a random *permutation* instead of a *function* and *read* once, that address would not be read again so its content could be modified undetectably. These attempts did not work because our checksum touches every memory location close to two times. So while such attacks are theoretically possible, they are very difficult in practice.

Frank Stajano: Why did the attacker have access to the NAND Flash? Or was it discovered by the checksum as well?

Reply: The attacker substituted the original code that the verifier wanted to have loaded with modified code, at initialization. So while the device RAM stores malware-modified code (i.e., the red region denotes modification), the NAND flash has the original code; i.e., the green region denotes the original code.

Frank Stajano: Yes, but it means that he has spare space he can use in the green region. Why would you not be checking that as well with all your checks?

Reply: The green region is on secondary storage (i.e., the NAND flash), and one doesn't check secondary storage.

Bruce Christianson: The question is, why not?

Reply: Because it can be huge. It turns our secondary storage is fairly small, namely half a gigabyte. Typical secondary storage is about 100 GB, and to read every word of it would take forever. Recall that reading every location of half a gigabyte of SDRAM to compute the checksum, which is very simple, takes about 13 min.

Tom Sutcliffe: And you've got to validate the primary memory before you can verify secondary storage.

Reply: Yes.

Bruce Christianson: No you don't, because if you filled everywhere with random values the attacker is stuffed.

Tom Sutcliffe: Yes, but that's not [nb., practical...]

Bruce Christianson: Well the checksum will do that, it's just it will take forever.

Alastair Beresford: OR

Tom Sutcliffe: Yes, and you're going to lose power while this happens ...

Bruce Christianson: Well yes, ...

Keith Irwin: A related question, did you say the prover code is assumed to not be compressible?

Reply: Yes, the prover's checksum code is assumed to be incompressible, and that assumption is questionable. We did not launch any attacks in that area, but I'm almost positive we could.

Nevertheless, the reason why this checksum is assumed to be incompressible, is because the original version (designed by Adrian Perrig and his students) used the T-function code of Klimov and Shamir [6] which is incompressible. However, our checksum design invokes it repeatedly in a much longer computation, so we no longer have a proof that the resulting checksum is incompressible. Nevertheless, I think Adrian and his students did a very good job with the original design, so this is not the first place where one would try to attack. Furthermore, the T-function appears hard to parallelize. The only reason I said that this assumption is questionable is because I could not prove to myself that the resulting checksum is incompressible.

The third attack. This attack exploits the fact that the coherence of the instruction cache (I-cache) and data cache (D-cache) is not maintained by the ARM processor hardware, apparently because this feature was considered to be too energy intensive. To establish cache coherence, one could execute a special instruction that invalidates the cache contents. Now imagine that during device initialization (Step 1 in Figure1 of the accompanying paper) malware loads this piece of malicious code in RAM, and perhaps in the unified (level 2) cache. The problem arises because after the malicious code gets loaded somewhere into the I-cache, it erases its copy from the RAM and de-synchronizes the I-cache from the D-cache. At this point, the original unmodified code is restored in the RAM and unified cache. But in fact the actual instructions that are executed out of the I-cache contain the malware, and yet the checksum result is computed on the RAM contents and hence is correct.

Although we have solutions to these attacks that appear feasible, we are still in the same vulnerable position we've been in for the past 10 years. Researchers come up with some clever attacks, we handle them one by one, but so far we don't have a theory that tell us that software attestation with concrete assurance is possible for innovative architecture features that are introduced so frequently today. And this is a significant challenge because now we have to face malware persistence, which is exploited by government funded/encouraged/tolerated individuals worldwide. As Ross once pointed out, if one gets persistent malware on one's system, just about all one could do is to throw away the hardware and start over.

Basically, we want to do somewhat better than that. We want to come up with a system which would enable us to carry out real proofs of correctness for SWORT.

Mark Lomas: One of your assumptions is that you know how much memory there is in there.

Reply: As a matter of fact that is the first the assumption that we made and the first challenge that we have.

Mark Lomas: There is an annoying habit of saying, we have new expanded versions that got an extra bit of memory ...

Reply: We struggled with finding out what's the real content of the systems that we bought. And I'm not talking about malicious hardware. I would just want to know the true configuration of the system that I bought, and have assurance it corresponds to the specs. Discovering one's system configuration is a non-trivial exercise.

Even simpler questions one faces require a great deal of work. For example, we had to find how many I/O registers a system has, we had to figure out which are writable and readable. And after we finally found all the registers, we also had to find all the dependencies and side effects among these the write and read operations. This took a graduate student nearly six months of work. It is certainly a challenge posed by new embedded-system architectures.

Ross Anderson: Hardware in devices nowadays vary so severely, and so unexpectedly, and unpredictably, as stuff is made up of hundreds of components including dozens [nb., of different versions].

Reply: From different suppliers.

Ross Anderson: From different suppliers who change their specs all the time. But while this is interesting work, it avoids the question of whether it's actually economic to do it this way, or do we just presume a TPM, and some kind of word chaining trust from one CPU to another. Or alternatively to use one of the existing CPUs as a TPM, or to use multiple CPUs one after another as progressive TPMs. Try using your phone from this processor, then from that processor and then from the next processor.

Reply: Right. We tried that and the problem is that, and while the functionality of the TPM gives you a very good thing, namely the authenticity of boot images, it cannot give one assurance of the malware freedom of the (complete) system state in which the TPM helps you boot. So that's really the problem with the TPM, as I mentioned at the beginning of this presentation. In fact, the TPM itself could be exploited by malware to falsely indicate that a corrupt BIOS is pristine, as shown by Butterworth et al. in 2013 [7].

Ross Anderson: It's actually worse that than because if the chip in your phone that does word spelling on your non volatile memory has got NSA malware, then you're completely dead, even if you're doing this and of TPM and everything else.

Reply: The scope of SWORT is limited to software and firmware, and doesn't include malicious hardware devices.

Before I end, the problem that you raised earlier, namely same processor spec implemented by three different manufacturers may exhibit significant time variability in instruction execution, is pretty common in practice. Why? The three may handle static clock skew differently in the implementation/manufacturing process. And some of them don't address the dynamic (peek-to-peek) clock jitter. So one can certainly expect some variation among different versions of the same processor.

Ross Anderson: There's also the issue of potentially malicious peripherals. We recently bought another car from a main dealer, and it had supposedly been sanitised from the previous owner. The first thing that happened, you know, once I mated my phone to Bluetooth, is that the previous owners' contacts, and previous owners' directions within the GPS, appeared. Sanitising modern complex electronic devices is a hopeless task.

Reply: It's too expensive to do, since it requires user's attention.

Ross Anderson: And if the main dealers can't do it, you're dead. So you make your phone virtually trustworthy, but as soon as you connect it to your car, goodness knows...

Reply: Yes. Talking about cars, I forgot to acknowledge that this work was funded in part by General Motors and DARPA.

Tom Sutcliffe: Something else occurred to me that a lot of modern processors do allow quite dynamic flop frequency scaling such that you could put your processor into a boosted mode whereby you have more cycles than you were expecting.

Reply: We can take care of this attack. First, to put the processor in a boosted more (i.e., over-clock it) requires a particular register setting, and our checksum continuously reads and captures the settings of all configuration registers in its result. However, it may still be possible to modify the checksum code and bypass the reading of the clock setting register. Hence, this would require prevention of all memory substitution attacks; viz., the second attack above and in the accompanying paper. Second, the verifier can measure the execution time at the highest possible clock rate and force the device to use this rate, so no further boosting is possible. So, at least in principle, we can handle such attacks.

References

1. Gasser, M., Goldstein, A., Kaufman, C., Lampson, B.: The Digital distributed system security architecture. In: Proceedings of the National Computer Security Conference, Baltimore, MD (1989)
2. Lampson, B., Abadi, M., Burrows, M., Wobber, E.: Authentication inn distributed systems: theory and practice. ACM Trans. Comput. Syst. **10**(4), 265–310 (1992)
3. Zhao, J., Gligor, V., Perrig, A., Newsome, J.: ReDABLS: revisiting device attestation with bounded leakage of secrets. In: Christianson, B., Malcolm, J., Stajano, F., Anderson, J., Bonneau, J. (eds.) Security Protocols 2013. LNCS, vol. 8263, pp. 94–114. Springer, Heidelberg (2013)

4. Armknecht, F., Sadeghi, A.-R., Schultz, S., Wachsman, C.: A security framework for the analysis and design of software attestation. In: Proceedings of the 2013 ACM Conference on Computer and Communications Security. ACM (2013)
5. Li, Y., Mccune, J.M., Perrig, A.: VIPER: verifying the integrity of PERipherals firmware. In: Proceedings of the 18th ACM Conference on Computer and Communications Security. ACM Press (2011)
6. Klimov, A., Shamir, A.: A new class of invertible mappings. In: Kaliski Jr., B.S., Koç, Ç.K., Paar, C. (eds.) CHES 2002. LNCS, vol. 2523. Springer, Heidelberg (2003)
7. Butterworth, J., Kallenberg, C., Kovah, X., Hertzog, A.: BIOS Chronomancy: fixing the core root of trust for measurement. In: Proceedings of the 2013 ACM Conference on Computer and Communications Security. ACM (2013)

Mind Your (R, Φ)s: Location-Based Privacy Controls for Consumer Drones

Tavish Vaidya and Micah Sherr[✉]

Georgetown University, Washington, DC, USA
{tavish,msherr}@cs.georgetown.edu

Abstract. This position paper explores the threat to individual privacy due to the widespread use of consumer drones. Present day consumer drones are equipped with sensors such as cameras and microphones, and their types and numbers can be well expected to increase in future. Drone operators have absolute control on where the drones fly and what the on-board sensors record with no options for bystanders to protect their privacy. This position paper proposes a policy language that allows homeowners, businesses, governments, and privacy-conscious individuals to specify location access-control for drones, and discusses how these policy-based controls might be realized in practice. This position paper also explores the potential future problem of managing consumer drone traffic that is likely to emerge with increasing use of consumer drones for various tasks. It proposes a privacy preserving traffic management protocol for directing drones towards their respective destinations without requiring drones to reveal their destinations.

1 Introduction

The proliferation of consumer drones raises a number of important security and privacy questions. Citizens may rightfully ask "What/Who will govern the movement of drones and prevent them from crashing into each other? Will there be a constant hoard of drones hovering over people's backyards? Will there be a drone police to monitor the drones?" Drone operators may pose a different set of questions: "Is my drone allowed to fly over my not-so-friendly neighbor's yard? Am I allowed to operate a drone in a particular vicinity? How do I become informed about flight restrictions? Are there restrictions on flight parameters such as speed and altitude? When am I allowed to record audio or video? To what legal risks am I being exposed by operating a drone?"

Despite the increasingly widespread use of drones, there is surprisingly little existing work that examines technical means by which ordinary citizens may protect their privacy from intrusive drone use, nor is there adequate existing literature that presents technical approaches that drone operators may apply to prevent accidental privacy (or legal) violations due to drone use. Also, with the increasing popularity and usage of consumer drones, the problem of managing drone traffic in areas of allowed drone operations will emerge.

© Springer International Publishing Switzerland 2015
B. Christianson et al. (Eds.): Security Protocols 2015, LNCS 9379, pp. 80–90, 2015.
DOI: 10.1007/978-3-319-26096-9_9

In this position paper, we propose a policy-based access control language for specifying rules governing the operation of drones in a geographical area. We then describe how the access control mechanism might be realized in practice with current consumer drones and provide a discussion on enforcement challenges with respect to adherence to the specified policies. Further, we describe a protocol for managing drone traffic that can be realized by modifying the proposed access control mechanisms.

Background. Currently available consumer drones offer various capabilities with respect to onboard sensors and navigational control. Most consumer drones are now equipped with multiple cameras, GPS, accelerometer and other sensors to ensure smooth operation and various flight capabilities. The majority of drones provide a real-time video feed using an onboard camera; this feed allows navigation when the drone is far or not in view of the operator. Some more recent drones with onboard GPS can fly autonomously once their flight path is marked with GPS coordinates [2,7]. Other drones can autonomously follow a paired device having a GPS antenna [4,5]. We believe that the set of onboard sensors will increase in future consumer drones, much as has been the case with smartphones and other mobile devices. These new highly equipped drones will enable more functionalities, which in turn pose addition privacy and security risks.

2 Privacy and Security Challenges of Widespread use of Drones

Present day consumer drones pose several privacy and security challenges:

Threat to Privacy. Consumer drones are equipped with high resolution cameras that can continuously record and relay live video streams to their operators. Microphones can easily be placed on these drones to record audio. Although such sensors provide diverse functionalities, misuse of drones can have serious consequences to privacy. Widespread use of drones will also raise issues concerning illegal surveillance and stalking. A prime motivation of this position paper is that such privacy concerns should be carefully addressed *before* drones become ubiquitous.

Security and Safety Issues. Operating in the physical world, the drones themselves pose safety hazards. Many incidents have been reported by commercial airline pilots with drones coming in close proximity of aircraft during landing and takeoff [3]. Some consumer drone manufacturers have made efforts to prevent such incidents by hardcoding the locations of major airports onto the drones and adding controls that prevent their use in the vicinity of these locations [6]. However, such a solution clearly addresses only a specific issue and does not scale. Additionally, such protections are brittle: we tested one of the consumer drones available in the market and were able to take control from the operator by spoofing the control packet stream. More generally, the lack of device authentication and other security mechanisms allow an attacker to hijack drones and potentially cause physical damage to infrastructure and injury to persons.

We argue that there is a strong need for a standard policy language and secure enforcement mechanism for limiting the flight paths of drones.

Threat Model and Goals: Our threat model considers the adversary to be the users of consumer drones who, with unrestricted use of drones and their capabilities, can pose a threat to security, privacy and the safety of other individuals and cause damage to property. Even in the absence of any malicious intent, consumer drones can inadvertently invade personal privacy or operate in restricted areas due to lack of any active guiding/restricting signals that can inform the drones (and their operators) of any such restrictions.

Ideally, all drones will have tamper-resistant components that enforce authenticated policies and cannot be overridden. Unfortunately, such a scheme is likely impossible to achieve in reality. However, the current status quo—i.e., a total lack of security and privacy protections—is also clearly undesirable. In this position paper, we consider drones produced by law-abiding manufacturers (as opposed to home-built drones that can clearly be constructed to ignore advertised policies). Our claim is that by developing *and widely adopting* flexible standards for expressing drone restrictions, meaningful privacy protections can be achieved that benefit both the general public and drone operators.

3   Policy-Based Location Access Control

This position paper proposes a policy-based location access control mechanism for consumer drones. Our approach requires sub-mechanisms for (i) specifying policy-based restrictions, (ii) communicating these restrictions to the drone and (iii) enforcing these restrictions on the drones. For specifying policy-based restrictions, we propose a policy language which can be used by a privacy conscious individual to specify restrictions on the usage of drones and/or their allowed capabilities near a particular location (e.g., his house).

Figure 1 motivates our proposed system model. Here, a homeowner specifies a policy as to whether a drone can operate over his property, and if so, what restrictions are in place. To be useful, the policy language clearly needs to define both geographic boundaries and be sufficiently flexible to support authorizations over a large set of actions (see below). Once the user has written a policy, he configures his wireless access point (WAP) to periodically broadcast it over WiFi. WiFi-equipped drones listen for such policy "beacons" and verify that their current state and their planned actions do not violate the advertised policy. As we discuss in more detail below, drones that lack GPS-capabilities (or more generally, the ability to accurately and precisely determine their current locations) can use the signal strength of the beacons to estimate its distance to WAP.

Policy Language. We describe a simple policy language for specifying location access rules as a context-free grammar $L = (V, \Sigma, R, S)$. The rules for L are provided in Fig. 2.

Grammar L generates strings that define location based access policies for various capabilities. Once the user specifies the values to be assigned to the

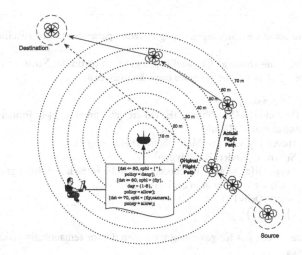

Fig. 1. System Model: A homeowner specifies a location access policy for various capabilities, distances and day of the week. His WAP broadcasts the policies for that particular day and time as beacons. The dashed line indicates the original intended flight path; the solid line denotes the adjusted path that conforms to the homeowner policy.

variables, the generated policy strings will be translated into rules before being broadcasted.

Examples. Let us consider the following example with policies specified in decreasing order of priority from top-to-bottom:

(a) $0900 - 1400 : Mon; Tue; Wed; Thur : \epsilon :$ Sphere $: (10, 10, 10) : \epsilon :$ Allow
(b) $\epsilon : Sat; Sun : Fly :$ Cylinder $: (10, 12, 13) : 60 :$ Allow
(c) $\epsilon : \epsilon : \epsilon :$ Sphere $: (20, 10, 15) : 0 :$ Deny

Policy a allows all capabilities between 9 AM to 2 PM, Monday to Thursday at any distance greater than 10 m from the beacon without any limit on noise levels. Policy b only allows drones to fly at a distance of 10 m and 12 m high from the beacon while implicitly restricting other capabilities on Saturdays and Sundays and also places a limit of 60 decibels on the drone's noise level. Policy c denies any use of drones and their capabilities within 15 m of the beacon throughout the day for every day of the week and has a zero noise tolerance policy. Use of drones nearby airports can be restricted by using policy c. Policy c also acts as the default policy in this case, restricting the use of drone outside of the time interval specified by policy a and on Fridays.

4   Towards a Practical Realization

To communicate with drones, beacons broadcast the specified policy for that particular day and time. Any interface that can successfully communicate with the drones can be used as a beacon, with 802.11 WiFi being an obvious choice.

- V is the finite set of variables representing different parameters to be specified in location access rules.
  $V = \{S, \text{Day}, \text{Time\_Interval}, \text{Capability}, \text{Region}, \text{Coordinate}, \text{Noise\_Limit}, \text{Policy}\}$
- Σ is the finite set of values the variables can take, such that:

  $\Sigma = \{d|d \text{ is a day}\} \cup$
  $\{\text{hhmm-HHMM—hhmm,HHMM are valid times in 24-hr format and hhmm} < \text{HHMM}\} \cup$
  $\{\text{Hover, Fly, Camera, Microphone, IR-Imaging}\} \cup$
  $\{\text{Sphere, Cylinder, 3D-Polygon}\} \cup$
  $\{(x,y,z)|(x,y) \text{ are GPS coordinates and } z \text{ is the height from ground}\} \cup$
  $\{k|k \text{ is the noise limit in decibels}\} \cup$
  $\{\text{Allow, Deny}\} \cup$
  $\{\epsilon\} \cup \{:,;\}$

- R is the finite set of rules for governing the generation of semantically valid access rules. The set of rules R is:
  - $S \rightarrow$ Time_Interval : Day : Capability : Region : Coordinate : Noise_Limit : Policy
  - Time_Interval $\rightarrow hhmm - HHMM$; Time_Interval$|hhmm - HHMM|\epsilon$
  - Day $\rightarrow d|d$; Day $|\epsilon$ (where d is a day of week)
  - Capability $\rightarrow$ Hover | Fly | Camera | Microphone | IR-Imaging | ϵ
  - Region $\rightarrow$ Sphere | Cylinder | 3D-Polygon
  - Coordinate $\rightarrow (x,y,z)$; Coordinate $|\epsilon$
  - Noise_Limit $\rightarrow k | \epsilon$
  - Policy $\rightarrow$ Allow | Deny
- $S \in V$ is the start variable.

Fig. 2. A CFG for a location access control policy language for drones. We remark that our proposed policy language is designed to be extensible. New capabilities of future drones can be easily incorporated by adding a new value to set Σ.

We tested the feasibility of communicating with a drone from its operating environment by using a bottom of the line Parrot AR 2.0 consumer drone and performing a toy experiment. The drone is equipped with an 802.11 wireless interface which acts a WiFi hotspot to which any 802.11 supporting client device can connect. In our toy experiment, we connected two devices: the first was the operator that controlled the drone and the second acted as the beacon. The beacon sent ping broadcasts which were received by the operator via the drone. This toy experiment shows that any device supporting 802.11 can be used as a beacon to relay information to the drone or the drone's controller. Relaxing the security constraint, the drone can estimate the distance from the beacon using the observed signal strength and compare it with the distance specified in the access rule broadcast [8,9,14]. In a practical setting, a beacon can keep trying to connect to a drone. When a drone is in range, it can then broadcast the specified rules thereby relaying access control information to the drone.

Higher-end drones are GPS enabled and can therefore better estimate their positions. The beacons can also broadcast GPS coordinates specifying a space perimeter in the access control rules and drone can learn the restrictions on its operation in that space perimeter. Future drones equipped with other sensors (e.g., proximity sensors) can gather data from multiple sources to get more accurate estimates of their position in space with respect to the beacon and the policy specified region in space.

5 Enforcement?

An obvious challenge — and one that we do not claim to completely solve — is to *enforce* the access control policies.

One potential approach is to rely on tamper-resistant hardware [22]. Our proposed approach requires the drones to act on the access control information relayed by the beacon. To enforce the restrictions on the drone, we propose a tamper-resistant "enforcer" module that manufactures could incorporate into the design of their drones. The enforcer would intercept data from drones' sensors and would act as a security layer, similar to SELinux's Linux Security Module architecture for regulating the use of system calls. The enforcer decides which sensor is allowed to operate in the current environment based on the received access control rules (Fig. 3). With respect to movement, the enforcer can directly send navigation commands to the actuators to ensure compliance to broadcasted restrictions or slowly land the drone as a failsafe mechanism.

We do not yet know how to build a policy enforcement mechanism when the adversary can build their own drones with custom hardware and software. We likely will never be able to stop such an adversary from posing a threat to others' privacy and safety.

Despite this important shortcoming, we argue that there are clear benefits for standardizing an access control language and enforcement mechanism: First, including enforcement mechanisms on commodity drones raises the bar for violating access control policies by requiring drone operators to either build their own hardware or defeat the tamper-evident features of commodity drones. Second, and most importantly, including an automated enforcement system *aids* well-intentioned drone operators by ensuring that they do not mistakenly violate federal, state, or local laws or ordinances concerning the use of drones. For example, the U.S. Federal Aviation Administration (FAA) bans all use of

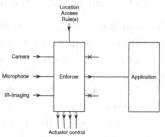

Fig. 3. Enforcer layer between sensors and application layer. Based on the location access rule(s), only allowed sensor data is passed to the application.

drones in Washington, DC [1]; it is unlikely that these rules were intended for hobbyist drone operators located miles away from federal buildings, and indeed such restrictions are not widely publicized. Including integrated policy enforcement mechanisms protects drone operators from unintentionally violating others' privacy and helps ensure compliance with legal restrictions.

6 Privacy Preserving Traffic Management for Consumer Drones

Autonomous drones are not a distant reality and will be seen flying in neighborhoods doing various tasks. As the number of drones operating in an area increases, the lack of coordination on flight parameters among the drones may lead to collisions causing physical harm and other undesirable consequences. (Consider, for example, the perils of ten drones simultaneously approaching an intersection without any coordination.) A potential solution for coordinating movements is to have each drone communicate with every other drone in its vicinity. Such solution will clearly scale poorly as the number of drones increase.

A better approach for managing drone traffic at regions of contention is to have a central coordinator, i.e., a drone *traffic controller*, that regulates the movement of all drones passing through that region and directs them to towards their respective destinations. Such drone traffic controllers are feasible by extending the use of beacons for broadcasting navigational directions instead of (or in addition to) access policies.

Additional Assumptions. We assume that drones can securely communicate with the beacon, e.g., via TLS. We note that this may require beacons to obtain a verifiable certificate, e.g., from LetsEncrypt[1]. We further assume that the beacon is connected to the Internet and can provide a communication link between drones and the Internet. This latter assumption allows us to offload computations to the cloud on behalf of the drone.

A Non-privacy-preserving Protocol. Beacons act as drone traffic controllers for contentious regions and route incoming drones towards their respective destinations. The controllers require destination information for each incoming drone to make scheduling and routing decisions. Each drone approaching the contentious region broadcasts its destination information encrypted using the beacon's public key. Beacons maintain state information about traffic—for example, the number of drones previously directed in each direction.

For regulating traffic, beacons compute a routing function that takes into account the state information and the destination of the drone. The routing function is computed for each incoming drone request and outputs the flight parameters to be passed on to the requesting drone. The scheduling of drones can be controlled by injecting time delays in broadcasting the response to each drones' request for directions.

A Privacy-Preserving Traffic Management Protocol. The above protocol allows for managing drone traffic using beacons. However, it requires the drones to

---

[1] https://letsencrypt.org/.

reveal their final destinations to beacons. This may be problematic for future uses of drones. (Consider, for example, package delivery systems in which purchasers may not want their locations broadcast during the delivery process.)

We propose the use of secure-multiparty computation (SMC) for computing the routing function, such that drones never reveal their final destinations to the beacons. SMC is of course resource intensive and drones have limited computational resources. We remark, however, that Carter et al.'s recent work on off-loading resource intensive steps of SMC to the cloud [11] can be directly applied in our drone setting.

A drone is able to communicate with the cloud infrastructure via communication relayed through the beacon. We note that this link can be secured using end-to-end encryption between the drone and cloud, e.g., using TLS. A drone, with the help of cloud, and the beacon perform a two-party SMC for calculating the routing function without revealing their inputs. The Whitewash protocol [11] allows for off-loading the garbled circuit generation for the routing function on behalf of the drone to the cloud, while the beacon evaluates the output of the circuit. The inputs to the routing function, the state information and drone's destination, are garbled and supplied by the beacon and the drone respectively to the cloud. Thus, no party learns the original inputs of any other party. After evaluating the garbled circuit for the routing function, the beacon releases the outputs of the function to the drone. The outputs of the routing function will be the flight parameters to be sent to the drone. The beacon will distribute the results of protocol runs to each drone, encrypted with the ephemeral key provided by the respective drone, at pre-scheduled intervals to prevent collisions.

The proposed protocol leverages the cloud infrastructure to benefit resource-constrained consumer drones, allowing the dissemination of flight parameters without revealing drones' final destinations.

7   Related Work

Mechanisms for detecting malicious applications and limiting their access to various functionalities and sensitive data have been thoroughly researched [10,12, 15,18,25], with the primary aim of protecting the privacy of device owners from malicious applications. Other works on permissions and privileges in operating systems have focused on providing minimum privileges to applications by default and granting access to sensitive data only when required to protect the user [21, 23,24]. On the contrary, our work focuses of protecting the privacy of *other individuals* from the drone operators.

Jana et al. [16] proposed fine-grained access permissions for augmented reality application to protect user privacy by allowing the user to specify permissions at the object level. However, the user who wants to protect his privacy himself specifies the permissions, unlike the case with the operation of drones.

Our work is closely related to the work done by Roesner et al. [22] that proposed the use of external indicators to convey permission information of allowed capabilities to wearable devices, freeing the device user from the burden of managing permissions in changing environments. Our work builds off of a similar idea to allow individuals to specify location access control rules that restrict the use of drones in a specified geographical region.

Policy languages have been proposed for specifying security policies with complex constraints in different applications such as firewalls, file permissions, etc. [13,19,20,26]. Of particular note, GeoXACML is an extension to eXtensible Access Control Markup Language (XACML) that allows the declaration of location-specific access rights [17]. These policy languages are too general and verbose to be well-suited for specifying simple policies for the drones. Our proposed language is purposefully compact and is specifically tailored for users of consumer drones with ease-of-use in mind.

8   Conclusion

This position paper discusses the potential issues and questions that will be raised as consumer drones become more commonplace. We argue that the community's emphasis should be on finding solutions to privacy problems *before* drones become ubiquitous. Towards this end, we propose a policy-based location access control mechanism to counter the privacy and safety threats posed by consumer drones. We believe that further discussion and research is required to realize the balanced use of drones and their capabilities.

We also address the issue of managing consumer drone traffic, set to arise with ubiquitous use of drones in the future. We propose the use of drone traffic controllers, and sketch a privacy preserving protocol for directing drone traffic without requiring drones to reveal their destinations.

Acknowledgements. This work is partially supported by the National Science Foundation through grants CNS-1064986, CNS-1149832, CNS-1223825 and CNS-1445967. The views expressed are those of the authors and do not reflect the official policy or position of the National Science Foundation.

References

1. NOTAM number: FDC 0/8326. http://tfr.faa.gov/save_pages/detail_0_8326.html. Accessed 4 January 2015
2. DJI Phantom 2 (2014). http://www.dji.com/product/phantom-2/feature. Accessed 3 January 2015
3. Near-collisions between drones, airliners surge, new FAA reports show (2014). http://www.washingtonpost.com/world/national-security/near-collisions-betwe en-drones-airliners-surge-new-faa-reports-show/2014/11/26/9a8c1716-758c-11e4-bd1b-03009bd3e984_story.html. Accessed 3 January 2015
4. HEXO+ (2014). http://hexoplus.com. Accessed 3 January 2015
5. IRIS+ (2014). https://store.3drobotics.com/products/iris. Accessed 3 January 2015
6. No FLY zones (2014). http://www.dji.com/fly-safe/category-mc. Accessed 3 January 2015

7. Parrot bebop drone (2014). http://www.parrot.com/usa/products/bebop-drone. Accessed 3 January 2015

8. Blumenthal, J., Reichenbach, F., Timmermann, D.: Minimal transmission power vs. signal strength as distance estimation for localization in wireless sensor networks. In: 2006 3rd Annual IEEE Communications Society on Sensor and Ad Hoc Communications and Networks, SECON 2006, vol. 3, pp. 761–766, September 2006

9. Bulusu, N., Heidemann, J., Estrin, D.: GPS-less low-cost outdoor localization for very small devices. IEEE Pers. Commun. **7**(5), 28–34 (2000). ISSN 1070–9916

10. Burguera, I., Zurutuza, U., Nadjm-Tehrani, S.: Crowdroid: behavior-based malware detection system for android. In: Proceedings of the 1st ACM Workshop on Security and Privacy in Smartphones and Mobile Devices, SPSM 2011, pp. 15–26, New York (2011)

11. Carter, H., Lever, C., Traynor, P.: Whitewash: outsourcing garbled circuit generation for mobile devices (2014)

12. Enck, W., Gilbert, P., Chun, B.-G., Cox, L.P., Jung, J., McDaniel, P., Sheth, A.N.: Taintdroid: an information-flow tracking system for realtime privacy monitoring on smartphones. In: Proceedings of the 9th USENIX Conference on Operating Systems Design and Implementation, OSDI 2010, pp. 1–6, Berkeley (2010)

13. Fundulaki, I., Marx, M.: Specifying access control policies for XML documents with XPath. In: Proceedings of the Ninth ACM Symposium on Access Control Models and Technologies, SACMAT 2004, pp. 61–69, New York (2004)

14. Han, D., Andersen, D.G., Kaminsky, M., Papagiannaki, K., Seshan, S.: Access point localization using local signal strength gradient. In: Moon, S.B., Teixeira, R., Uhlig, S. (eds.) PAM 2009. LNCS, vol. 5448, pp. 99–108. Springer, Heidelberg (2009)

15. Hornyack, P., Han, S., Jung, J., Schechter, S., Wetherall, D.: These aren't the droids you're looking for: retrofitting android to protect data from imperious applications. In: Proceedings of the 18th ACM Conference on Computer and Communications Security, CCS 2011, pp. 639–652. ACM, New York (2011)

16. Jana, S., Molnar, D., Moshchuk, A., Dunn, A., Livshits, B., Wang, H.J., Ofek, E.: Enabling fine-grained permissions for augmented reality applications with recognizers. In: Presented as part of the 22nd USENIX Security Symposium (USENIX Security 13), pp. 415–430, Washington, DC (2013)

17. Matheus, A., Herrmann, J.: Geospatial extensible access control markup language (GeoXACML). Open Geospatial Consortium Inc., OGC (2008)

18. Nauman, M., Khan, S., Zhang, X.: Apex: extending android permission model and enforcement with user-defined runtime constraints. In: Proceedings of the 5th ACM Symposium on Information. Computer and Communications Security, ASIACCS 2010, pp. 328–332, New York (2010)

19. Ni, Q., Xu, S., Bertino, E., Sandhu, R., Han, W.: An access control language for a general provenance model. In: Jonker, W., Petković, M. (eds.) SDM 2009. LNCS, vol. 5776, pp. 68–88. Springer, Heidelberg (2009)

20. Ribeiro, C., Ribeiro, C., Zúquete, A., Ferreira, P., Guedes, P.: SPL: an access control language for security policies with complex constraints. In: Proceedings of the Network and Distributed System Security Symposium, pp. 89–107 (1999)

21. Roesner, F., Kohno, T., Moshchuk, A., Parno, B., Wang, H., Cowan, C.: User-driven access control: rethinking permission granting in modern operating systems. In: 2012 IEEE Symposium on Security and Privacy (SP), pp. 224–238, May 2012

22. Roesner, F., Molnar, D., Moshchuk, A., Kohno, T., Wang, H.J.: World-driven access control for continuous sensing. In: Proceedings of the 2014 ACM SIGSAC Conference on Computer and Communications Security, CCS 2014, pp. 1169–1181. ACM, New York (2014)

23. Shirley, J., Evans, D.: The user is not the enemy: fighting malware by tracking user intentions. In: Proceedings of the 2008 Workshop on New Security Paradigms, NSPW 2008, pp. 33–45, New York (2008)

24. Stiegler, M., Karp, A.H., Yee, K.-P., Close, T., Miller, M.S.: Polaris: virus-safe computing for windows XP. Commun. ACM **49**(9), 83–88 (2006)

25. Xu, R., Saïdi, H., Anderson, R.: Aurasium: practical policy enforcement for android applications. In: Proceedings of the 21st USENIX Conference on Security Symposium, Security 2012, pp. 27–27, Berkeley (2012)

26. Zhang, B., Al-Shaer, E., Jagadeesan, R., Riely, J., Pitcher, C.: Specifications of a high-level conflict-free firewall policy language for multi-domain networks. In: Proceedings of the 12th ACM Symposium on Access Control Models and Technologies, SACMAT 2007, pp. 185–194, New York (2007)

Mind Your (R, Φ)s: Location-Based Privacy Controls for Consumer Drones (Transcript of Discussion)

Tavish Vaidya and Micah Sherr[✉]

Georgetown University, Washington, D.C., USA
ms955@cam.ac.uk

Micah Sherr: Thanks for the introduction. Today I'm going to talk about privacy controls for consumer drones. This is going to be another split talk: I'm going to let my PhD student take over at some point.

This talk is about consumer drones and their privacy implications. And just to sync up about what we're talking about, we're talking about consumer drones. We're not talking about the other types of drones (for example, military drones) where privacy is a second order issue that you might have.

So consumer drones, what are they? They basically have a bunch of rotors and fly around. I'm sure everybody has seen these. They can range from about $300 at the low end. The high end ones cost several thousand of dollars. They have different capabilities. Almost all of them that I've seen include the ability to record video. They're used a lot by hobbyists. Some of them offer the ability to record audio. Some of them support live streaming. They typically communicate with a controller over 802.11. Some of the more fancy ones (the more expensive ones) allow for autonomous flight. There is a rich developer community for many of these, where people have leveraged the fact that the controller protocols are open or reverse engineered. Importantly, these protocols offer no security whatsoever. They are unencrypted.

Sandy Clark: You can telnet in drones.

Reply: They run BusyBox. You can telnet into them, and break them in about two seconds.

They're gaining in popularity because these things are relatively cheap. There is a clear drone interest from industry, and by that what I mean is they're used for things like delivery services. As I strongly suspect most of you have heard, Amazon, at least in the United States, would like to have some sort of same day delivery service where lightweight packages are delivered by drones, which is somewhat laughable, and definitely fits with today's theme.

Consumer drones are becoming increasingly problematic as they are more widely obtained. There are many, many stories about drones misbehaving. They're great for drug smugglers—they are a good way to get drugs across the border.

A few months back, there was a big issue where an owner of a drone, who was a hobbyist, who may or may not have been drunk at the time, and lived nearby the White House, was flying his drone. To misquote him, "I lost control

© Springer International Publishing Switzerland 2015
B. Christianson et al. (Eds.): Security Protocols 2015, LNCS 9379, pp. 91–104, 2015.
DOI: 10.1007/978-3-319-26096-9_10

of the drone, I don't know where it went, I went to sleep, when I woke up in the morning it was all over the news that the drone had crashed into the White House lawn." And this came right in the middle of other issues that the Secret Service is having.

A serious problem is that a number of near collisions have happened between drones and aeroplanes, at both major airports and also smaller airports. I don't know if any collision has actually occurred yet, but that would not be a good thing. There are also incidents of drones being flown in areas that they're clearly not supposed to. One was spotted buzzing beneath the London Eye, others at French nuclear sites, also a big no-no. And from today's Washington Post there's a story about whether in Maryland the police have a right to restrict reporters' use of drones over crime scenes.

So these point to a number of problems, both in terms of clearly illegal use of drones where the intent is malicious (i.e., to break the law) as well as careless use of drones. By "careless use of drones", I'm assuming that the drones aren't used for terrorism-related purposes. Rather, they are used by someone who's not so bright flying a drone near an airport, or someone who just loses control of their drone, or someone who may not be aware of the legal restrictions that are in place.

We depict the different uses of drones in this (fairly subjective) graph[1]. It shows the different types of security problems that we want to consider for drones. At one axis we have the intent of the drone operator—this is with respect to the operator of the drone—so their intent to do harm. I'm going to define harm fairly loosely, and by loosely, I mean I'm not going to define it.

We have at one end of the spectrum, operational safety issues. For example, you probably don't want to get hit on the head by the Amazon drone that's delivering a package. You probably don't want drones to collide over your house and cause damage to your roof.

Then there are obvious privacy issues. There are legitimate privacy issues both in terms of accidental and malicious uses.

There is misuse of the drones, flying drones in areas where you're not supposed to, maybe because you're just ignorant about local regulations concerning drone use, or you're just not a particularly skilled drone pilot.

And then at the other extreme is physical security. These entail the kind of terrorism-related scenarios in which someone straps something to a drone. Drones are hard to shoot down–you probably don't want to have Secret Service agents shooting into the sky right next to the White House where hundreds of tourists are located.

So there's a whole spectrum of security issues, and I'm sure this is an incomplete list.

In this talk, we're going to concentrate on two particular security issues:

We're going to focus on the privacy issues of drones in terms of how can we protect the general population from having their privacy violated by drones. And also misuse: how can we actually protect ignorant drone operators from getting into trouble?

---

[1] The slides for this talk are available on request from the authors.

Admittedly, this is somewhat of a weird problem, but I think it's a legitimate and under-explored one, particularly as drones become more commonplace. Put succinctly, *how do I know as the user of a drone whether or not I'm actually allowed to use it?*

And so our "adversary" is the drone operator. I call this the honest but ignorant model, where the operator is non-malicious. They're not terrorists. They're not building their own drones—we can't do much about that; they're using out-of-the-box, common off-the-shelf, commodity, consumer drones. They are generally fairly law-abiding, but they're oblivious as to what those laws might be.

Let me give a concrete example of this. I teach in Washington DC. It's perfectly legal for me to purchase drones on-line, to have them delivered to work, but flying them in Washington DC is illegal because of poorly written FAA restrictions. Washington DC is a no-fly zone in the United States, except for the military. So technically speaking, flying a drone anywhere in the District of Columbia is considered an FAA violation.

So does ignorant, illegal use of drones regularly occur? I asked Tavish to see if he could find evidence of this on YouTube. After about 5–10 min, he found a number of interesting videos. This is someone flying their drone next to the US Capitol, right on the Washington Mall. Here's a different video where someone is buzzing the Washington Monument, also clearly right in the epicenter of a no-fly zone. Here's a picture of the guy who did it, after he landed his drone. He captured his image, which is clear on the monitor here, and he posted this on-line for the world to see. And there are numerous other examples. These are all examples of people who buy drones, fly them, are probably ignorant to the fact that they aren't allowed to fly them in a particular area, and could probably benefit from having some enforcement mechanism that at least alerted them to the fact that they're operating drones in areas that don't allow it.

Let's look at how we expect this problem to scale as drones proliferate. We see a trippling of sales for low-end drones. We estimate about 130,000 drones sold last year for GJI; 3D Robotics, which are high-end drones sold 30,000. And Amazon is selling about 10,000 a month within the United States.

To reiterate, there are certain things that are not part of our attack model for this presentation. Again, we're not considering terrorism-related attacks where the adversary is carrying bombs, or constructing homemade drones. We aren't going to talk about Star Wars-like defenses such as surface-to-consumer-drone missiles, although that's kind of a fun project. And while our solutions could benefit from tamper resistant hardware, it's probably not an effective technique, particularly since hobbyists can go out and just build their own drones that don't have this hardware.

So what's actually in scope for today's talk? We're going to talk about a voluntary protocol that drone manufacturers can embed into their drones that help drone operators become aware of the privacy wishes of the general population. We are developing a language, if you will, for expressing as a citizen whether or not I want my particular area to be photographed, have it audio recorded, etc. It's an initial step towards protecting the public's privacy from drones.

There are solutions that exist today that aren't very good. You can go to a centralised website and enter your home address, and then in theory a drone manufacturer in the next update could bake into the firmware a hardcoded list of where not to fly. Drone manufacturers are doing this today for airports and other government facilities, but this obviously isn't a scalable solution. So we're trying to come up with a way to do this that makes sense and that scales.

Our solution nicely blended itself towards doing something that was more future looking, and I think appropriate for today's theme. Our privacy-preserving language also provides mechanisms to perform traffic control for autonomous drones. If you're Amazon, for example, and you want to deliver packages using drones, you probably can't afford to hire a pilot for every one of your tens of thousands of drones that you're going to deploy. Instead, what you're going to do is you're going to install some autonomous software so that these drones could fly themselves to their destinations. And this obviously has significant hurdles in terms of how you manage traffic management. We do this in two ways, which Tavish will talk about. So with that I'm going to hand this off to my Ph.D. student, Tavish.

Tavish Vaidya: Thanks Micah. For privacy protection against consumer drones and drone operators, we think these are the three requirements that need to be fulfilled, each requiring its own solution to get to a complete solution. The first step is how to specify access controls; second, how to communicate the specified access rules to the drones; and lastly, how to make sure that the access rules are respected by the drones. Before going into the details of what we propose, I will briefly describe the current state of technology with respect to each requirement.

In general, we know access control refers to limiting access to some servers, a process or devices. For this problem, access can be for geographical locations, let's say the London Eye, Buckingham Palace or a city, etc.—locations where drones are not allowed to go. Additionally, access control can also mean placing limits on actions or capabilities of sensors on board these drones. Can a drone fly, can it take pictures, record audio near a landmark? We believe that the number of sensors on board the consumer drones will grow in the future. They might have infrared imaging, heart rate sensors, etc. We might see real-time face recognition as well, which will be a scary situation from a privacy perspective. Therefore, we would like to place limits on such capabilities. To do that, there must be ways to specify the constraints.

Currently, manufacturers of consumer drones are hard-coding GPS coordinates of sensitive locations like airports, military bases, etc. GPS coordinates of such locations are baked into all the drones before they are supplied to the consumer. However, this way of specifying constraints makes the approach inflexible. Second, only the drone manufacturers can specify the rules. (By rules I mean the GPS coordinates, where they don't want the drones to fly.) And access control is only for geographical locations with no consideration or way to address privacy issues. Therefore, there needs to be way(s) for specifying rules for limiting the various capabilities of consumer drones.

Once the rules are in place, they need to be communicated to the drones. With current hardcoding techniques, the drones already have all the information, because the GPS coordinates are baked in, so they don't need any external information, and thus no communication is required. And this again has scalability issues. Once you've shipped a drone, that's all the information it can have. To wait for the new information to get added they have to get a mandatory update. For example, in the case of the White House incident, the drone manufacturer DJI rolled out a mandatory update the very next day to add the White House's coordinates to the list of coordinates baked into the drones. However, such a strategy won't work in every case and is not a scalable solution. We need something better to communicate the rules.

The third step is to ensure that drones obey the access rules. What it means is that drones must respect and adhere to access policies governed by the rules. This requires on-board mechanisms. Currently, the baked-in GPS coordinates are compared with the current location of the drone to check if it's near any prohibited location. DJI claims that if the drone is within a region of the geofence, the drones will just not fly, once it gets a GPS lock. So someone might argue that you can break the GPS, but that's particularly hard. And this is the part that we think is the hardest to achieve in practice.

Now I'm going to talk about our proposed approach for each of these three steps. Instead of specifying the access rules by the manufacturers, or hardcoding them, we believe that access rules must be specified by the stakeholders. Stakeholders in this case can be homeowners, airport authorities, universities, management operating the London Eye, or any entity that wants to restrict access to drones, or to their capabilities, at a particular location. We propose a policy language to specify these rules.

Let's say that a guy wants to protect his privacy from the drones. So he comes up with a rule saying around my house within a 15 m radius, I don't want any drones to fly. He can also specify that from Monday to Friday I don't want anything, but I will allow the drones to fly from 9 to 5 because I'm not home so I don't care, I'm a good Samaritan, I would allow the use, but when I'm home I don't want them to fly. We propose a language in a way a user can specify these rules.

Simon Foley: So how would I know, or how would the manufacturer know whether I had control or owned this address. So access to your house or to my house?

Tavish Vaidya: The manufacturer has nothing to do with it and the question directly refers to the issue of authorization. Who is allowed to set up such rules and is he allowed to do it at a particular location? I will be talking about this challenge and possible ways to address the issue.

Frank Stajano: What is the incentive for the guy with the red hair not to say just "don't fly over my house at all", instead of going to the trouble of learning the syntax for doing all these things and saying "I will allow flying at this time"? Why do I care? Why don't I just say "Fuck off and just don't fly"?

Tavish Vaidya: Yes, the guy can say don't ever fly. But the incentive is just like any community driven project. Or maybe, the guy can make money by allowing drones to fly over yard!

Sandy Clark: Well you can fly your own drone at home.

Tavish Vaidya: Yes.

Max Spencer: What about if my neighbour says he wants them to fly all the time.

Tavish Vaidya: The neighbor can do it on his property.

Audience: Do you have any provision for saying like, I don't know, some specific drone can fly off my lawn to deliver stuff, but like my neighbour's spy drone can't? Can the language help with help?

Audience: Like ones without cameras?

Tavish Vaidya: Yes, so you extend the policy language to incorporate complex rules like this that take into account the identity of the drones. This, however, will require additional steps with respect to identification and verification of drone identity. You will need to know which drone is which.

Ross Anderson: But if I can cause a drone to fly 200 feet above ground level on my own property, I can watch my neighbour's wife sunbathing nude on the lawn, so this appears to be a kind of futile exercise anyway doesn't it?

Tavish Vaidya: Yes, you can do that, but consumer drones aren't even close to be able to see your neighbour's wife from 200 feet. That will require a high-res camera to be put on the drone, and the shear weight of the camera would prevent the drone from getting airborne.

More to the point, we are proposing a voluntary standard that will help drone operators understand and respect other people's privacy wishes. What we aren't trying to accomplish is a fool-proof access control enforcement mechanism that can stop a highly motivated person from spying.

Audience: Then there's a higher level issue, which is that other areas where technology has restricted things previously like region code DVDs, and the most popular DVD players to buy are those where you can disable the region code. So similarly I would imagine that in the drone market where there will be drones that are popular, where you can press the red button three times and suddenly it's just stuck, it's disabled.

Tavish Vaidya: Possibly true, however, it might be bad for drone manufacturers not to enable the features due to legal consequences.

Audience: Yes, it seems like maybe that's slightly too broad to include anybody who wants to impose any kind of policy. Then we should get them involved, whereas maybe if it were more focused on airports, and FAA restrictions, and such, then you're less likely to have people wanting to bypass it.

Sandy Clark: But in that way it's similar to constellations in money in that Adobe Photoshop and copying machines and printer companies have gone with– they are coded into their systems that if you see this particular constellation you can't make a copy of that. It would be very similar to that sort of philosophy.

JF: But I don't think there is some general right to restrict others from seeing you, I mean, for example, if I'm out in public and somebody takes, and I'm not a public figure, and someone takes a photo of me, that person is allowed to use this photo, that photo is part of his life. My point is that some specific thing is allowed and some other specific thing is not allowed, then what is the underlying legal theory here for who's allowed to restrict what? I'm not sure why offhand, everyone who is a stakeholder should have the right to restrict other stakeholders.

Tavish: Right, there is the issue of authorization as to who is allowed to specify the rules.

Audience: Who's allowed to restrict other people's behaviour.

Tavish: Yes, and under what conditions you're allowed to do that.

Frank Stajano: Besides the technology, my question very similar to Joan's: if I own a house, do I own the airspace up to infinity above it? I don't think so, right?

Joan Feigenbaum: No!

Frank Stajano: If I see a drone and I don't like it, and it's not obeying my policy, can I take my shotgun and take it down? How does it *work*, before you develop the technology?

Ross Anderson: Well the Department of Transport does consider the regulation of drones to be the highest issue on its agenda, and they say that this is the place of the greatest regulatory stress, and therefore the greatest regulatory opportunity. They would actually like to make a law in the next Parliament that would enable ministers to issue regulations on just this issue.

Frank Stajano: So this basically translates to there is no rule as of right now.

Ross Anderson: No, that's not what I said. The government would like to make another law specifically for this.

Audience: Presumably existing flights, you know, at the level of aircraft flights heights, is regulated, but...

Reply: But it's not regulated by the homeowner.

Tavish Vaidya: I would say no, but without any specific knowledge of the law.

Tavish Vaidya: The second step is to communicate the rules to the drones. Beacons can be used for this purpose, where a beacon is any interface that's capable of communicating with the drone. Beacons broadcast the access rules for drones in their reach, and this is definitely better than hardcoding. With this approach, drones will learn all the access rules from the environment. Therefore in this case, once the homeowner specifies the rules, the beacon on top his home will start broadcasting the rules. A good example of this will be the London Eye. You can put a beacon on top of it which will start emitting the access policies. Clearly, the environment is providing the policy information, and nothing needs to be hardcoded on the drones. When a drone comes nearby, within a certain range, the drone will learn the access policy from the environment, and can fly around it and respect the policy. Now the question that remains is, how do you make sure the drone respects the policy?

Frank Stajano: How do you make sure that the policies of the London Eye, and the Houses of Parliament, and Big Ben are compatible? Because they overlap the same reception area.

I think I may have mentioned this earlier but you didn't say anything about it. What if it's a building that is not just a detached house but a building like this one? It might have 30 people, and each one of them could set their own policy. Who guarantees that there is a compatible intersection between those policies? If everybody does theirs, what happens?

Tavish Vaidya: The system can be designed to follow the most restrictive policy. So, if there are multiple policies, the drone can adhere to the most restrictive one.

Tavish Vaidya: The third requirement for the solution to work is to ensure that drones respect the access policies. Our threat model assumes that drone manufacturers are law abiding, they want to stay in business, and they would follow any rules or regulations proposed by the government for protecting consumer privacy. Any non-compliance can be bad for business, and we think that like the CE standards for electronic consumer goods, which all the electronic manufacturers around the world follow, there can be some standards which the drone manufacturers would like to follow if they are in place.

Keith Irwin: Is that really sort of the earlier point though that you made about, you know, you're talking about restriction on this. I buy the fan with the CE label on it because I know it's not going to burn my house down, it's not that it doesn't have this extra fourth speed of fan that I'd really like to use. Whereas in this case you're basically making the drones less capable than current drones, drones that go anywhere.

Tavish Vaidya: No, we're not talking about limiting the capabilities of the drones, but we are trying to make the use of drones friendlier and less invasive to other's privacy.

Keith Irwin: But that is a restriction of the capabilities of the drone, right now the drone can anywhere, you'll probably want it to go anywhere.

Sandy Clark: It's a restriction on its behaviour, not on what it can do.

Tavish Vaidya: Yes, it's on the behaviour of the drone. It can still have all the capabilities.

Keith Irwin: Well if you're the drone owner you might, if I want to go buy a drone I might want the drone that can do that.

Tavish Vaidya: Yes but you certainly want to respect the privacy of others. If someone does that to you how would you feel?

Keith Irwin: You're assuming people are much more altruistic than people actually are. So I might want to, but you know, why am I, I'm being asked to give up something, which is that now I'm going to have to, my drone is going to be, if it's adhering to these rules then it's not just that I know that I won't violate some privacy, and also it might be that, you know, maybe the privacy I want to violate is a business that's saying, you know, a farmer saying, we don't want you flying a drone over here and documenting our use of, you know, slave labour. And my drone is saying, oh yes, I can't go fly over there so I can't show that it's slave labour, right, so this drone is less capable of doing certain things if it's going to respect those rules.

Tavish Vaidya: I think the vast majority of drone operators would want to be informed when they are breaking the law. But it's certainly true that there may be instances in which violating someone else's advertised policy is warranted—for example, an investigative journalist who is investigating this farm. We're describing a mechanism for propagating access control policies. It may very well be a good idea to allow drone operators to override these policies, but doing so may often be at their own peril.

Audience: Well the solution there presumably is to make this, say a discretionary thing such that if your drone is infringing these rules then it feeds a message back to the user controlling it saying, you are in violation of a rule, and then it is up to the law abidingness of the user as to whether they then land or divert, or whether they ignore it because they have damn good reason in their own mind for flying the drone where they are. So, you know, you don't necessarily want the drones themselves to be enforcing this behaviour–you want to be pushing it onto the user because it's the user's responsibility to be in control of the drone.

Ross Anderson: Yes, Sudo make me a sandwich.

Audience: Yes, basically.

Audience: Maybe it comes back to what you were saying about, at the beginning, about like users accidentally flying like into some restricted area.

Audience: Well quite, so if you need to be telling the users that they aren't allowed here.

Audience: It seems like then they've actually got some good reason to not do what they were trying to do, i.e. like the police may come round if they're flying over an airport.

Audience: I don't understand why it's such a problem to understand why it makes sense to restrict it? I mean, you buy a car, you own it, you're allowed to run people over with it, but the law restricts it right? So the mere fact of buying a drone should not restrict the things it can do or places it can go?

Tavish Vaidya: Yes, you can run people over. But the crime, in the majority of cases, will leave evidence, like a dead body. However, in the case of drones, the recording of videos from distance, may not leave any evidence that it recorded a video. So, I think the argument of running people over with a car just because you can do it, doesn't apply too well for the drones.

There's another important difference. If you plow someone down in a car, it's obvious that you are breaking the law. If you are flying a drone in a public park, it's not at all obvious what local ordinances might restrict your flights.

Keith Irwin: Well it's a question of how that regulation is enforced and in what way, right? And if we're saying we'd have an access control policy that usually, when I have an access control policy on my computer that means if I get on a computer it means if I ask the computer to do certain things, it's just not going to do those. It's going to say, "I'm sorry I'm not going do that," right? Whereas my car, for instance, if I say I want to drive on the sidewalk, my car still drives on the sidewalk.

Sandy Clark: Until we get stopped, like people?

Audience: Right, and we may run into the same issue down the line. That's not to say there might be legitimate reasons even at that point where I might want to drive on the sidewalk at times. It's like I've got this giant delivery, it's the middle of the night, the sidewalk is clear. I have driven a car on the sidewalk, right, it was on a college campus in the middle of the night, because we needed to deliver something

Keith Irwin: Right, and we may run into the same issue down the line, right, and that's not to say, you know, and there might be legitimate reasons even at that point where I might want to drive on the sidewalk at times, right, it's like I've got this giant delivery, it's the middle of the night, the sidewalk is clear, I'm just trying to get it to, it's the only way I'm going to be able to get it, I mean, you know, I have driven a car on the sidewalk, right, it was on a college campus in the middle of the night, because we, they said, oh you need to deliver this, drive on the sidewalk, you know.

Bruce Christianson: I think we've leapt straight from describing a mechanism to arguing about how best to use it.

Audience: Well that's what's going to happen. It's quite a big topic isn't it?

Bruce Christianson: Let's hear about, form a view about what the mechanism can and can't do.

Audience: So if I have a drone and it does fly over Westminster, what actually happens, so have I violated the policy?

Tavish Vaidya: It depends on what the policy is. If they are broadcasting a no fly zone, yes you would have violated a policy. What happens next is off topic. But yes you would have violated a policy.

Tavish Vaidya: Moving forward, we did a toy experiment to check the feasibility of using beacons, and to see what actually happens if the drone comes within a certain range and you send it some messages. The majority of drones today have 802.11 interfaces and are controlled by Smartphone applications. You connect to the drone from the smartphone, establishing a communication channel between the controller and the drone. So we set up a beacon and a controller, both being two different laptops. We reverse engineered the protocol and connected to the drone from the controller laptop. Once we connected the second laptop (the beacon) to the drone, we sent a ping broadcast to the broadcast IP which was received by the controller. Therefore, the capability that exists today can be used to pass policy information to the controller. As someone previously said, "what happens like if you get into restricted airspace?" Yes, you can send an alert to the controller, something that says that you are entering a restricted airspace, just go away, or something bad will happen to you. So yes, there is a mechanism to do it with the current drones on the market.

In the future, when drones are autonomous or if they have that much capability to process this information on their own, certain actions can be taken depending on what capabilities they have in future.

The next question is–how do we respect access rules on board? We believe that the drone manufacturers will be law-abiding, and not just give away their business if the government just bans all their imports. And I think in this case tamper-resistances might be helpful. We are not claiming it's a perfect solution, but it might be a solution. This is the toughest part as to how we can make sure that the rules are respected by the drones. Our threat model doesn't assume an adversary which can construct its own drone. Definitely, yes, you can make your own drone and and fly it anywhere. Our model considers the drones that can be bought from the market or Amazon, like the drone that crashed in to the White House. Such incidents can be prevented with this particular model.

Summarizing, a guy programs the beacon, which then broadcasts the policy, and the drone comes into the the vicinity of the beacon. So this is the original flight path, which it should have taken, but because of the policy in place the drone can't. The controller can take some actions to respect that policy on board, and go around that region towards its destination. Questions with respect to the legality of specifying access policies and the extent and ownership of airspace above one's property are outside the scope of this work and since we are not legal experts, we don't have a definite answer.

Lack of authentication is another challenge. Anyone can set up a beacon and just broadcast the deny policy, and prevent any use of the drones. Preventing such denial of drone use requires authenticating the policy broadcast. To do this, a PKI can be leveraged. It is the least worst option, as we all know that, PKI has its own problems. A good thing that PKI provides is offering verifications. The root certificates can be baked into the drones and the policy that's being specified by the beacon coming with a certificate signed by a trusted party. The policy can then be authenticated by drone. However, authentication doesn't solve all of the problems. We also need authorisation. I can get a certificate for my house that places a no-fly zone around my house. But what if I take that beacon and start broadcasting the policy from my neighbour's house, or from a different neighbourhood? This requires the beacon to be associated with a GPS coordinate from where it is authorized. Currently a website called noflyzone.org is making an effort to do this. It asks for your address along with some proof, to check for authorization and then collaborates with drone manufacturers for baking in your home's GPS coordinates into the next update.

Another challenge is enforcement, something we can't claim to solve, but the drone manufacturers have an incentive to minimise the incidents and stay away from liability claims.

Audience: You're assuming that people that want to prevent drones are willing to give the address. If I've got a number of very sensitive sites scattered around the country I might want to have a beacon that says, do not fly over my terribly sensitive site, but I'd rather want that nobody has a list of where the sensitive sites are.

Tavish Vaidya: In that case you are better off shooting down the drone.

Frank Stajano: Could you not certify them individually, as each one being independent of the others?

Audience: I may, but the fact that they even exist would be a secret.

Frank Stajano: Right: you want to communicate with WiFi but not put it in the database?

Tavish Vaidya: It's better to stay silent with total radio silence if you want to keep the locations secret!

Tavish Vaidya: Back to the point on adherence to policies by the drones. We think that tamper resistant hardware can be used, that respects the access control operation, and it raises the effort required for violation in case of tinkering. But it does not completely solve the problem. Also, it is a tough challenge to tackle custom built drones.

Tom Sutcliffe: Well the thing with that is that you could just go down the route of getting involved in the Open Source software that's running on those. You're never going to get an Open Source project through force to accept mandatory access control, but you might well be able to get them to put in the framework for the discretionary stuff that will display on the screen that you're in a no-fly zone. I mean, that would be probably an easier approach than trying to get lots of drone manufacturers to all cooperate. I mean, it's just a possible approach.

Tavish Vaidya: Yes, that can be an approach to start with.

Frank Stajano: In the Open Source environment, the best thing that would work is to actually write the code and say: "Here is the piece that does that already! Why don't you just link it in?"

Bruce Christianson: It also gives you a partial solution to the problem with multiple occupancy. You can send the user a message that says, welcome to Sydney Sussex College, by 42 votes to 18 with 3 abstentions.

Ross Anderson: Well you're also imposing on house-holders, the expense of buying a beacon, assuming that their domestic WiFi can't be repurposed for this because BT is already repurposing it for ten other purposes of its own. And presumably one of the things that people would want would be a means of declaring their house to be a no-fly zone, and just expecting the manufacturers to bake it into the drones at the next upgrade. In other words, why should I have to go to the expense of running a beacon in my house just to say, no. If my decision to say no is a considered, permanent and public decision.

Sandy Clark: We can't get that as a default state for anything. Look at web tracking privacy, everything has to be an individual selection. That's what we want for a default, but we don't get it.

Ross Anderson: Well yes, but even in the sense of wanting an opt-out as the minimum necessary thing you can get away with, perhaps under the data protection regulation, so I want an effective means to opt out.

Bruce Christianson: It's no worse than having to put a cat scarer in your garden.

Sandy Clark: But I wondered: could you create a drone trap by setting up a whole bunch of no-fly beacons and forcing them to fly into my house because there's no protection, you can simply take over somebody else's beacon if they're close enough.

Audience: Yes.

Sandy Clark: Can I collect drones?

Ross Anderson: Perhaps you have the manufacturers subsidise the sale of drone reparts? That says, give away all drones beacons that people can buy for a nominal amount, and then a subsidy for the electricity as well.

Tavish Vaidya: So you are saying that homeowners should give their addresses to drone manufacturers and then ask them to bake it in? But that solution will raise a bigger privacy concern as you will be giving all the information to one drone manufacturer, or lets say ten drone manufacturers.

Ross Anderson: Some people might not care about that, some people might like to say, I am anti-social, I don't believe in this new drone-based world economy, I am a no-fly-zone. People might walk around labeled with ribbons on their jackets saying, "I am a no-fly type person". So what about people who publicly come out as being against drones, is there not a shortcut for them?

Tavish Vaidya: Sure, it is an option for the anti-socials.

Sandy Clark: How is that different from any sort of surveillance? You're walking down the street, then you've got a camera watching you. Isn't that the same? You'd be able to make the same argument for not being watched by any sort of surveillance camera.

Ross Anderson: I have somewhere a T-shirt that Privacy International produced about 20 years ago. It's got a big copyright mark on it, and it says that if you take a photograph of me you're violating the DMCA.

Frank Stajano: When I was on sabbatical with Google in Germany they had to hire legions of people who were taking up most of one floor to click on places that they would then have to blur out because people had posted a request that their house should not be on Street View, and because Germany was more sensitive to privacy than other places.

Ross Anderson: So how will this work out in Germany then? Will Google have to share that blur me out map with all the drone makers?

Frank Stajano: Well the point is that in the days of Google it was done the proper way, which as you correctly advocated, is that the onus should be on the people running around with cameras to try not to take photos of people, not the people who have a house to go to the trouble to buy the beacon. I agree with that viewpoint.

Ross Anderson: So given that in Germany this blur me out map already exists, the first thing to do is simply for the Germany Bundestag to pass a law obliging all drone manufacturers to use it.

Frank Stajano: Look it up on Google. If it's blurred, don't fly there.

Mark Lomas: But Germany has already set a legal precedent. There's a court that has ruled that you're not permitted to put a camera, a videocamera in your car. The courts will not use video evidence generally by people who put cameras in their car.

Sandy Clark: But one of the very first drones was built by a German, the 'octopod'; it could fly 500 m straight up in seconds, and then just hover there for a while, and then head to wherever the GPS coordinates you programmed in it, and then stop there and stay there until you wanted it to come back, and it could carry a two kilogram payload.

Michael Roe: or **Mark Ryan:** or **Max Spencer:** Just quickly, I wonder if we should consider the kind of opposite: a kind of framework is somehow in place, as with this experiment, like a drone trap. So the drone flies along and says, ah, a lot of people around here, and actually ends up in a little circle, and another beacon turns on, and the drone is stuck inside?

Tavish Vaidya: Since we are out of time, I will summarise. We proposed an idea for addressing the privacy concerns that will emerge with increasing use of consumer drones. There are various non-technical issues of legality, ownership of airspace that are unresolved. In the second part of the paper, we talk about privacy preserving automatic traffic management of drones, which is based on the whitewash protocol. The idea is to use beacons as traffic controllers that route drones to their destinations without requiring the drones to reveal the destination coordinates.

Thank you.

Location-Private Interstellar Communication

Hugo Jonker[1], Sjouke Mauw[2(✉)], and Saša Radomirović[3]

[1] Open University of the Netherlands, Heerlen, The Netherlands
hugo.jonker@ou.nl
[2] University of Luxembourg, Luxembourg, Luxembourg
sjouke.mauw@uni.lu
[3] ETH Zürich, Zürich, Switzerland
sasa.radomirovic@inf.ethz.ch

Abstract. Mankind is actively trying to communicate with extraterrestrial life. However, historically the discovery of new civilizations has led to war, subjugation, and even elimination. With that in mind, we believe that for any attempted contact with extraterrestrials *our location must not be revealed*. Therefore, we focus on the problem of location-private interstellar communication. We approach this as a security problem and propose to work towards solutions with tools from the domain of secure communications. As a first step, we give proposals for adversary models, security requirements, and security controls.

1 Introduction

Scientists have been working to find evidence of extraterrestrial life both passively and actively. Passively, by listening for radio signals in the SETI project and detecting the "Wow! signal", for instance, and actively by sending out signals such as Cosmic Call and a reply to the Wow! signal, as well as objects such as the Voyager and Pioneer space probes. The two Pioneer probes carry a golden plaque[1] and the two Voyager probes contain a golden record with information pointing out the location of Earth.

Our view is that in any attempts at communications with extraterrestrials, our location must not be revealed lest the receiving party be hostile. We therefore propose to develop methods and technology to support communication with extraterrestrials while keeping the Earth's location secret. The ability to keep our location secret depends on the capabilities of the involved parties and the physical laws involved. Even with an imperfect knowledge and understanding of these, we can explore the relationship between assumptions on adversary capabilities and the possibility of location private communication. This work takes a first step in the problem of *location-private interstellar communication* by viewing it as a security problem and working towards a solution from the domain of secure communication. We provide first proposals for security requirements, security controls and for classifying adversary capabilities.

---

[1] Note that revealing possession of rare minerals to foreigners has historically not worked well on Earth.

B. Christianson et al. (Eds.): Security Protocols 2015, LNCS 9379, pp. 105–115, 2015.
DOI: 10.1007/978-3-319-26096-9_11

2   To Communicate or Not to Communicate?

The problem of communicating with extraterrestrials is of an interdisciplinary nature and, consequently, it has been studied in disciplines that range from signal processing to futurology [12]. Interestingly, information security specialists have hardly touched upon the topic, even though our community may have valuable input on various aspects of this problem.

The potential benefits from contact with extraterrestrials are significant. Any contact would lead to an increase in knowledge on Earth. It could give an answer to the fundamental question "are we alone or is there life out there?", provide evidence that our physical theories are incomplete, and lead to an actual exchange of knowledge with extraterrestrials.

However, contact with extraterrestrials carries risks and ethical issues. Discovery of new countries and new indigenous people on Earth has often led to subjugation or even elimination. There is no reason to assume that extraterrestrials are selfless. Extraterrestrials might accidentally ruin mankind. For example, mankind may not be ready to handle technology that is normal to extraterrestrials. Is it ethical for a group of people to try to actively contact extraterrestrials when the result could impact Earth's entire population? Any contact with extraterrestrials will only occur tens, if not hundreds of centuries after the initial attempt. Can our generation make such a profound decision for (distantly) future generations?

Another side to the discussion is that it is useless to worry about contact with extraterrestrials. One argument on this side is that mankind has been sending radio and TV signals for a while now. However, such signals have not been sent with high power and were not directed, meaning the information in them is too dissipated to decipher. In fact, Billingham and Bedford [1] make a case that even the highly powered, focused interstellar messages mankind has already sent are undecipherable (but still detectable as artificial) by the most current Earth technology after a few dozen light years. Moreover, even the artificial nature of the signal is too dissipated after a few hundred light years.

To date, the transmission of nearly a dozen interstellar messages has been made public [9]. These messages may not only reveal our location, they also contain information about mankind that may make us vulnerable as has been argued by Lestel [6]. This information includes, for instance, an indication of our level of scientific achievements: we are able to send out such a signal, but not able to travel so fast to obviate the need for these signals. It also contains an upper bound on our energy budget, i.e., the total of the Sun's output.

3   Adversary Model

One might argue that any communication with extraterrestrials must inevitably give away our location. For instance, successful communication requires that a message sent must reach its destination. The extraterrestrials could follow the messages until they find us.

However, impossibility of Location Privacy is not necessarily a tautology. Any proof that location privacy is impossible in a communication with extraterrestrials must make assumptions regarding physical laws as well as the computational and technological capabilities of both communication partners. Such assumptions therefore constitute a model for the impossibility of location privacy. By modifying the assumptions so as to weaken the extraterrestrials' capabilities sufficiently, and strengthening our own capabilities, we can find a model that does support location-private interstellar communication. Therefore, while we do not know what exact capabilities extraterrestrials may have and our understanding of physics in space may be limited, we can still explore the relationship between these assumptions and the possibility of location private communication.

We now present an initial adversary model for intergalactic communication. The model is defined by the capabilities an adversary is assumed to have.

3.1   Adversary Types

We distinguish the following types of adversaries.

(a) extraterrestrial communication partner;
(b) third party extraterrestrial;
(c) local (Earth-bound) party.

In the remainder of this paper, we will focus on extraterrestrial adversaries, although all three types of adversaries can attack our location privacy. For instance, any Earth-bound party can broadcast our location, breaking Earth's location privacy.

3.2   Technological Capabilities

For extraterrestrial adversaries, we can furthermore classify a civilization according to its capabilities with respect to detection (of electromagnetic waves and objects), communication and travel. We propose a categorization of these capabilities on an increasing scale in Table 1, similar to the Kardashev scale [5].

The table denotes the extent (within home planet, own stellar system, home galaxy, and intergalactically) to which a civilization is able to perform a task reliably. For instance, we do not consider unintentionally leaked signals to constitute a capability to communicate. However, the exact threshold for reliable

Table 1. Scales for estimating a civilization's capabilities for different categories.

	Detection	Communication	Travel
1. Planet	Type D_1	Type C_1	Type T_1
2. Stellar system	Type D_2	Type C_2	Type T_2
3. Galaxy	Type D_3	Type C_3	Type T_3
4. Intergalactic	Type D_4	Type C_4	Type T_4

performance in a given category is out-of-scope of this paper. Moreover, these broad categories need to be refined in any specific instance, as any communication attempt will rely on both sender and receiver capabilities. For example, a civilization capable of sending devices into the galaxy (Type T_3 concerning devices) may send devices that emit radio waves within a stellar system. These waves will only be detected by a civilization that can detect radio waves within their stellar system (Type D_2 with respect to radio waves), while the device itself will be detected by a civilization that can reliably detect devices entering their stellar system (Type D_2 for devices). In the rest of the paper, we consider detection capabilities for satellite-sized devices unless clearly indicated.

The classifications of Table 1 help us determine the effect an adversary may have. For example, if mankind attempts to communicate by sending a probe that transmits radio messages, a Type T_3 civilization is able to travel to the probe to examine it in detail, while a Type D_1 civilization will not detect the probe, and might even not be able to detect the attempted communication. Note that there are relations between the capabilities. For instance, communication is at least as fast as travelling, since messages may be delivered by a travelling device or being.

We classify mankind as reliably able to detect satellite-sized devices near Earth (notwithstanding the occasional unexplained disappearances of large scale structures such as airplanes). While mankind has sent messages and devices beyond the Solar system, such communication and travels are neither easy nor timely. Thus our present abilities are between a Type D_1-C_1-T_1 and a Type D_1-C_2-T_2 civilization.

From an anthropomorphic point of view, it makes sense to consider extraterrestrial adversaries with capabilities more advanced but close to ours, that is, a Type D_2-C_2-T_2 civilization. Type D_3 adversaries would be able to detect device launches on galactic scales. Maintaining location privacy against such an adversary without a pre-existing galaxy-wide infrastructure (a Type C_3 capability) to support location privacy might be impossible. On the other hand, a Type D_2-C_2-T_2 adversary (or more primitive) is restricted in travel and detection capabilities, and is therefore unlikely to physically interact with any device sent from Earth. For such adversaries outside our Solar system, we can focus on how much location privacy is attainable without considering what a physical communication device may reveal about Earth's location.

4   Envisioned Controls for Location Privacy

To illustrate the possibility of interstellar location-private communication, we discuss two potential privacy controls, cf. Table 2. The proposed controls are able to provide location privacy against certain adversary capabilities. The effectiveness of any specific control depends not only on the capability of the adversary, but also on the distance between the adversary and the sender. A D_2 adversary can only reliably detect transmissions within a stellar system. This is enough to pinpoint communications originating from other planets in the same system, but

Table 2. The discussed approaches for location-private interstellar communication.

Approach to location-privacy	Protects against adversaries up to
1. Private Communication Probes	D_2-C_2-T_2
2. Random Relay Network	D_3-C_3-T_3

insufficient for any communications originating from beyond the stellar system. In the remainder of this section, we consider a setting where the sender is in a different stellar system than the adversary.

Communication Strategies. The search for extraterrestrial intelligence can be performed *passively* or *actively*. Passive search is currently conducted with low impact devices, such as telescopes and radio receivers. Such devices are relatively small in relation to the current footprint of intelligent life on Earth and the devices themselves will not contribute to the already existing risk of revealing our location. However, there are even risks involved in passive search. We list three examples of such risks:

- *Size.* Larger devices, of stellar size possibly, might be needed to detect a particular type of extraterrestrial signals. Such devices may be detectable at interstellar distances.
- *Malicious payload.* Received signals may have a payload that can trigger actions on Earth that lead to revealing our location.
- *Targeted message.* Any reply to a received message will probably relate to the received message, for instance by quoting some parts. Revealing this link carries a risk, as the initial message may have been keyed to our solar system. Thus, any reply may allow the senders to determine which message the reply was to, and hence what stellar system must have sent this reply.

In the case of active search, we will distinguish *direct* from *indirect* transmissions. Direct transmissions require sending and receiving devices for the communication partners, but do not require an interstellar communication infrastructure. Examples of direct communication are the emission of electromagnetic or gravitational waves. Indirect transmissions require an interstellar communication infrastructure to relay the messages. Such an infrastructure can consist of already existing natural artefacts in space, such as stars and planets, or may be constructed by humans. An extreme example of the use of natural artefacts for indirect communication is to cause a stellar explosion[2]. Possibilities of setting up a dedicated interstellar infrastructure have been proposed, such as von Neumann probes, Bracewell probes, and Sandberg probes [4]. Below, we discuss some points related to setting up and using such an infrastructure, and we provide two examples of security controls that establish location privacy against certain adversaries using indirect transmissions.

---

[2] Admittedly, with the drawback of a relatively low bitrate and quite significant APBDC (Average Per-Bit Delivery Cost).

4.1   Private Communication Probes

To communicate a message to extraterrestrials we assume the existence of self-replicating probes, which we call *private communication probes (PCPs)*. The PCPs replicate with the aid of resources found in their vicinity. After a successful replication, the original probe self-destructs to avoid being traced back to its origin, see Sect. 4.3. The probes replicate into $n > 1$ descendant probes. Descendants "fly off" into different directions. If a probe has contact with extraterrestrials, it takes an answer from the extraterrestrials and communicates it back with the same algorithm: The probe replicates such that each of its descendants (reply probe) has a copy of the reply and each descendant flies off in a different[3] direction. We must ensure that there is a significant probability that a reply probe finds us.

However, it would be unwise to reply due to the *Targeted message* risk mentioned before: the received message might have only been sent to one location, so acknowledging that message would reveal one's location. As extraterrestrials might reason similarly, we should not expect a reply via the same probe system. Thus, in order to not reveal their location, both sender and receiver would have to disperse "mailbox" probes throughout the galaxy. The contact of a "sender" mailbox probe with a "receiver" probe would allow both parties to communicate without revealing the location of their home planets.

For PCPs to provide location privacy, the adversary must not be able to trace the original message to its source, nor the reply to its intended receiver. Thus, barring implementation errors, the PCPs should provide location privacy against an adversary located in our galaxy, as long as the adversary is of at most Type D_2-C_2-T_2. PCPs would not be effective against a D_3 adversary, because such an adversary could detect the initial launch of the PCPs.

4.2   Random Relay Network

Our second proposal borrows ideas from the area of *wireless sensor networks*. We assume the existence of a number of probes as in the previous solution sketch. Rather than letting the probes carry a message through the universe, we assume that the probes transmit messages that can be picked up either by other probes or by extraterrestrials. To achieve this, the probes must be capable of determining the artificiality of received signals, and capable of transmitting a directed signal to the N nearest stellar systems. Each probe has a buffer for M messages. Periodically, the probe sends one of the buffered messages (according to a predefined probability distribution) in the direction of a randomly chosen neighboring stellar system. Upon detection of an artificial signal that is not yet buffered, the signal is stored in the buffer. In case the buffer is full, the oldest stored message is deleted.

Initially, the buffer contains one predefined artificial message. This is to notify any potential recipients that there is intelligent life in the universe, capable of

---

[3] This increases the burden of extraterrestrials trying to trace their reply back to us.

communicating via such signals. Implicitly, this invites any recipient to reply via a similarly artificial signal. Figure 1a depicts the transmission of a message from Earth. Any response from extraterrestrials could be routed as depicted in Fig. 1b.

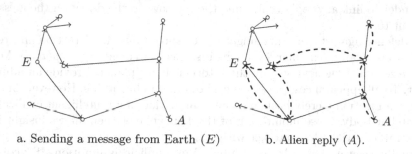

a. Sending a message from Earth (E)   b. Alien reply (A).

Fig. 1. Example of a Random Relay Network.

For a Random Relay Network to provide location privacy, the adversary must not be able to trace the original message to its source, nor the reply to its intended receiver. Since each node in the network acts as a source for any received signal, this in turn implies that an adversary who does not have a global view of the network (i.e., which messages exist in the network, and which node sends what message when and where to) cannot determine the origin of a signal. An adversary could establish such a global view in various ways: either by having sufficient detection capabilities, or by travelling to each node of the network and eavesdropping. Therefore, for long-distance communication where both sender and receiver reside in the same galaxy, a Random Relay Network provides location privacy against adversaries with less detection capabilities than D_3, and less travel capabilities than T_3.

4.3   Some General Observations on Privacy Controls

Any interstellar communication must inherently leave some traces of its origin: for indirect communication, the physical infrastructure leaves such traces, e.g., a tell-tale matter signature; for direct communication, the propagation properties of the signal itself provide some guidance to its origin. A mitigating counter-measure is a "generational" probe approach, where a device flies to an ore-rich stellar body and constructs new probes from the raw material. This approach provides security from any civilization with travel capabilities below T_3. From T_3 on, the extraterrestrials could trace each generation back to its point of origin. For direct communication, a mitigation is to emit a signal such that there are multiple possible origins (i.e., multiple stellar systems on the line from the receiver in the direction of the sender). This will work for civilizations below D_3. A D_3 civilization has sufficient detection capabilities to distinguish the genuine origin amongst the candidates. Thus, probes and signals inherently carry some traces leading back to their point of origin.

Message *contents* may carry such a trace as well. It is already common practice for some companies to tailor their web presence to the visitor [8]. Similarly, each message sent out could carry a distinct element (e.g., a nonce). This allows the sender to link any reply containing the message to the direction the message was sent to.

A defence against such shenanigans is to spread out the detection and reply capabilities on an interstellar level. One instance is to create *honeyplanets*. Much like the so-called "honeypots" on the Internet, honeyplanets provide an alluring target. To all appearances, these planets contain intelligent life. However, in reality such a location merely hosts a careful simulation of an intelligent civilization on a stellar body. Close monitoring of the honeyplanet then allows insight into the extraterrestrials that interact with it.

Finally, security controls may be based on implicit assumptions. By considering typical controls in an extreme setting such as interstellar communication, their limitations are clarified, allowing researchers to work on further improving such controls.

5   Additional Security Requirements

Setting up a communication with extraterrestrials requires a coordinated effort. There should be agreement on a wide range of issues including who speaks for the Earth and what should be said [7,10]. Protocols and policies to that effect have been discussed and proposed [3,11]. However, even if a so-called post-detection policy is agreed upon by all nations, there still may be dissenting cabals.

Communication with extraterrestrials requires therefore protection against both Earth-bound and extraterrestrial adversaries. We have described first ideas for location-private communication in the preceding section. However, the security requirements that first come to mind in a communication protocol are authentication of the communication partners and integrity and confidentiality of communicated messages. Here we briefly discuss these requirements.

We start by considering these requirements against an extraterrestrial adversary and note that all three of these properties are probably too much to hope for. To authenticate an entity *ET* we must be able to distinguish between *ET* and a potential impostor. When we make first contact, we cannot know with whom the contact was established. We therefore have to settle for a weaker property, namely *sender invariance* [2]. That is, we can try to verify that subsequent messages originate with the same communication partner, and we conversely provide evidence that the sequence of messages sent from us has a single origin. Earth-bound protocols that achieve sender-invariance employ public key cryptography and assume that the communicating parties execute the same protocol. For integrity protection of a message, the communicating party must know how to verify the integrity. If an attacker relays all messages between us and the extraterrestrials and strips off the protections, the receiving party will not be aware of the existence of an integrity protection and will not be able to detect any tampering. Similarly, no standard notion of confidentiality appears to be achievable. Any key received by a party could be received and modified by an extraterrestrial attacker. Protocols that establish a shared key by taking advantage of the sender-invariance property are conceivable, but appear to lead to a very weak notion of confidentiality.

If we consider terrestrial attackers, we have to assume that they are able to eavesdrop on all communication and that they can send arbitrary messages to the extraterrestrials. It seems plausible to assume that a terrestrial attacker will not be able to imperceptibly modify transmissions and to act as a man-in-the middle. We may moreover assume that the terrestrial adversary has comparable computational resources. Under these conditions it appears easier to achieve sender-invariance, integrity protection, and confidentiality (against terrestrial adversaries), but it is still an open problem. It is unclear whether any scheme offering computational security (with insanely large keys) could possibly be used, as it depends on our present computational ability, the extraterrestrials' computational ability in a distant future, and our descendants' adversaries' abilities in a further distant future. To be on the safe side, any security and privacy controls would need to be based exclusively on the laws of nature. Unfortunately, mankind's understanding of these laws is imperfect, and any security control we devise may thus be circumvented.

Given the time scales involved, any long-distance interstellar communication faces additional problems. For one, how to ensure that the receiver is not accidentally replying to an old message sent by himself? This requires that the existence, importance, and operational details of the system are kept alive over a very long period of time. This in turn requires reliable communication to humanity's future generations. How to reliably, authentically, or securely communicate information over very long periods of time is an interesting question in its own right and one that needs to be answered before an attempt at communication with extraterrestrials is started.

6   Conclusions

Establishing contact with extraterrestrial intelligence is attractive. It will answer the age-old question of whether there is life "out there", it will bring a new understanding, and it can potentially bring new technology and new ideas.

However, trying to contact extraterrestrials entails the risk of revealing our location. This paper approached this location-privacy issue as a secure communications problem, and provided some initial steps towards a classification of attacker capabilities in line with the Kardashev scale, and put forth initial concepts for security controls at intergalactic scales.

Notwithstanding the benefits of establishing contact, we reiterate that for now, **mankind must not attempt to contact extraterrestrials**. Without proper security provisions, we are not able to oversee the risks of exposing our location. Consequently, we should stop sending messages and even consider the destruction of space probes like the Pioneer 11, which are already on their way with a mission to reveal our location. During this moratorium the security and privacy aspects of communication with extraterrestrials must be researched. We suggest the following initial research questions:

– *What can be proven about the (im)possibility of location-private communication with extraterrestrials?*
Answers to this question must be in relation to specific adversary models and defender capabilities, for which we provided an initial proposal. For instance, it might be conceivable that location-private communication is impossible as long as mankind's travel capabilities do not exceed level T_2.

– *How can we scale up existing security solutions to a galactic scale?*
We proposed abstract security controls, that rely on self-replicating machines – technology that does not yet exist on macro-scale – to create the interstellar equivalent of sensor networks. Other security controls might be similarly scaled up, such as onion routing, or even honeyplanets. This will help mankind to understand the minimum requirements needed to achieve location privacy.

– *Which security requirements, in addition to location privacy, should be considered?*
We can consider the standard Confidentiality/Integrity/Availability properties, but also properties like fairness and detection of malicious content.

– *Can we develop a future-proof infrastructure?*
We observe that our technology develops fast in relation to the time scales expected for communication with extraterrestrials. As a consequence, all current communication attempts and corresponding infrastructure will be outdated long before we can even expect a reply to our messages. However, we may discover new vulnerabilities in our own infrastructure, requiring a protocol update, or even revocation of the whole infrastructure.

– *How to estimate the impact of extraterrestrial adversary capabilities?*
We took a first step towards a classification of adversary capabilities, to estimate the impact of adversary capabilities. This initial classification should be further extended. For example, there is a significant difference between the ability to detect significant changes in a wide area, and to focus detection capabilities on a particular spot.

References

1. Billingham, J., Benford, J.: Costs and difficulties of large-scale 'messaging', and the need for international debate on potential risks. arXiv:1102.1938 [astro-ph.IM] (2011)
2. Hankes Drielsma, P., Mödersheim, S., Viganò, L., Basin, D.: Formalizing and analyzing sender invariance. In: Dimitrakos, T., Martinelli, F., Ryan, P.Y.A., Schneider, S. (eds.) FAST 2006. LNCS, vol. 4691, pp. 80–95. Springer, Heidelberg (2007)
3. Harrison, A.A.: Speaking for Earth. In: Vakoch, D.A. (ed.) Archaeology, Anthropology, and Interstellar Communication. NASA, USA (2012)
4. Freitas Jr., R.A.: A self-reproducing interstellar probe. J. Br. Interplanetary Soc. **33**, 251–264 (1980)

5. Kardashev, N.S.: Transmission of information by extraterrestrial civilizations. Sov. Astron. **8**(2), 217–221 (1964)
6. Lestel, D.: Ethology, ethnology, and communication with extraterrestrial intelligence. In: Vakoch, D.A. (ed.) Archaeology, Anthropology, and Interstellar Communication, pp. 229–236. NASA, USA (2012)
7. Michaud, M.A.G.: Ten decisions that could shake the world. Space Policy **19**(2), 131–136 (2003)
8. Pariser, E.: The Filter Bubble: What the Internet is Hiding from You. Penguin, UK (2011)
9. Paul Shuch, H. (ed.): Searching for Extraterrestrial Intelligence: SETI Past, Presence, and Future. The Frontiers Collection. Springer, Heidelberg (2011)
10. Tarter, D.E.: Reply policy and signal type: assumptions drawn from minimal source information. Acta Astronaut. **42**(10–12), 685–689 (1998)
11. Tarter, J., Michaud, M. (eds.): Acta Astronautica, vol. 21(2). Elsevier, UK (1990)
12. Vakoch, D.A. (ed.): Archaeology, Anthropology, and Interstellar Communication. NASA (2012). http://www.nasa.gov/sites/default/files/files/Archaeology_Anthropology_and_Interstellar_Communication_TAGGED.pdf

Location-Private Interstellar Communication
(Transcript of Discussion)

Sjouke Mauw$^{(\boxtimes)}$

CSC/SnT, University of Luxembourg, Luxembourg, Luxembourg
sjouke.mauw@uni.lu

While the landing of a drone on the White House lawn is an issue, it is definitely not relevant if you relate it to the landing of a spaceship on that lawn. It reminds me of the movie *Mars Attacks*. These guys have an automatic translator which, to prevent problems, always translates into "we come in peace". So these aliens are running through the White House, "we come in peace", and blasting everybody with their phasers. OK, that's the scenario that I'm talking about, and clearly aliens are not going to worry about any of your access control mechanisms, and any of your legal enforcement tools that you may have. The only prevention from aliens taking over Earth is hiding. Hiding the entire planet *Earth* somewhere in the interstellar space. That's the topic of my presentation. On the one hand, this is more fictional than the other presentations, but on the other hand, the risks are so high that you may want to consider it anyhow.

The first question that you should ask yourself when thinking about this issue is: do we want to communicate or not? If you don't want to have any problems, don't communicate. We are happy with each other, we don't need extraterrestrials here. But we have the urge to know if we are alone in this universe, and we could always do with more knowledge than we have currently, and develop knowledge in a higher speed. So I assume that people will want to communicate with extraterrestrials if possible. And of course there are the risks. The risks are that the aliens come in peace, and leave us in pieces. Even if they don't come in peace, they will give us their technology, and of course we are too young as a species to deal in the right way with all this technology. Even if it's only cultural technology we will probably not be able to deal with it without setting the whole Earth on fire, or maybe getting other problems. We can also think of viruses, even active communication is very harmful. Maybe they can send viruses through their communications, either viruses that affect our communication system, or viruses that instruct us to build certain objects that turn out to be harmful.

Micah Sherr: I don't know if you are aware of this, but Slate Magazine had an article about viruses from outer space published today.[1]

There is a lot of work on this topic, but mainly by mathematicians, linguists, and archaeologists. I have not seen any papers, serious papers, by computer

---

[1] Dan Falk, *Is this thing on?*, Slate, March 29, 2015.
http://www.slate.com/articles/technology/future_tense/2015/03/active_seti_should_we_reach_out_to_extraterrestrial_life_or_are_aliens_dangerous.html.

© Springer International Publishing Switzerland 2015
B. Christianson et al. (Eds.): Security Protocols 2015, LNCS 9379, pp. 116–125, 2015.
DOI: 10.1007/978-3-319-26096-9_12

security experts. So this is why I want to invite you to take up my first push and to start thinking about what we can do for the world. This is in fact the statement that I would like to make: we should not engage in communication, not even in attempts to communicate, unless we have solved, whatever that may be, this location privacy problem for communication.

Sandy Clark: Isn't it too late, because one of the standard tropes is that we've been sending out radio waves since the invention of the radio?

Reply: Yes, well that brings me to the next slide of course, we have already started sending out messages. We started in 1962 with the Morris message, and we continue doing this. For example, this is the Arecibo message, where we clearly identify ourselves, there's a picture of us.

Sandy Clark: They were a lot fatter too?

Reply: What they did, this is a double helix if I remember correctly, and this is the location of the Earth relative to our sun, so they would be able to find us.

Max Spencer: Why does it have a gmail logo?

Reply: Which one is the gmail logo? This one?

Max Spencer: The one at the end.

Reply: Oh that's the radio dish.

Audience: Sorry, just correct me if I'm wrong, but with the kind of trope about the radio waves, they're actually not detectable beyond a certain distance because of the background radiation, whereas the more targeted messages are.

Reply: Yes, the current state of affairs is that if we send a message into space, then within maybe 10, 20 light years it will lose its information, and within 100 to 200 light years, it would even lose the information that it is artificial, assuming current technology.

Frank Stajano: So when you say you want location privacy, what is the size of the anonymity set? If I am on the next planet am I still anonymous, or do I have to be in the next galaxy?

Reply: Yes, that's the type of questions that you should answer. Yes, I'm reflecting most of the questions to you. I will come back to that later. I will try to make some kind of classification of the adversary capabilities which relate to the defendability capabilities. But that's typically a question we should pose ourselves.

It's not only about signals, but we have also started sending out objects. These objects carry golden plates. These are more realistic "Hey that's where we are, please attack us, you can find us between 9 and 5 at this place". It more or less looks like that. And you know what happens on Earth when people show their golden plates to invaders... Don't ever show your precious metals to other people.

That brings us to the adversary. So what we in effect want to understand is: what are the security requirements, what is the adversary model, and can we come up with some security controls. That's the first investigation of a very high level that I will propose to you.

So who is the enemy? In fact we can have three classes of enemies.

The first is the communication partner who tries to detect where we are and to find out if we have precious metals, and if we have other resources they want to have. But maybe they are trustworthy, and they want to exchange some information in a fair way. Then we have third party extraterrestrials, who want to snoop our communication with the good guys at the other side of the universe, and want to learn about whatever we discuss, and to wipe us out later. And then we have local parties, on Earth. Not everything is fully controlled by the USA I guess, so there will be bad guys on Earth, and they will either try to disrupt communications, or take over communications for their own profit. If you think of the current technology needed to communicate with aliens, you don't need to be a very rich country to set up a telescope, and some laser beams, or whatever you want to use. I will come back to that later as well.

The first observation is that there is a quite straightforward impossibility result on location privacy. If our enemy is really, really powerful, having control of space and time, having unlimited energy resources, then probably there is no point in trying to be location private. So let's decide what kind of people we are, and against what kind of enemies we could potentially get a bit of location privacy. In order to achieve that, inspired by the Kardashev scale of energy usage, we have made this table of potential capabilities of adversary classes. We consider the size of your activities: planetary scale, stellar system scale, galaxy wide, or even intergalactic. And then the typical types of activities, where your detection on a planetary scale would be any device of 5 meters wide can be detected on the planet. We've seen aeroplanes disappearing suddenly without us finding a trace, so we are almost there probably for large objects, not for small objects. Detection could also be related to electromagnetic waves. We can sort of detect all communication attempts on the Earth.

In a stellar system we are not capable of detecting anything, except for very, very large objects like meteors. Communication, we are typically a $C1$ society at the moment, we can easily and effectively communicate on the planet. We have started communication to other planets and moons. Travelling, we are also quite effective in travelling on the Earth, and we are transitioning into the $T2$ phase travelling into our Solar System. What you can expect is that we are somewhere between these two phases, and we may be able to get location privacy against an adversary who is, for example, $D2$-$C2$-$T2$, or maybe one more advanced even. Anything further I think is beyond what we can ever achieve in the next hundreds of years.

That brings us to potential controls of privacy. First of all, if we want to establish communication we are going to listen to potential signals. We can do that actively or passively. If you actively do it there are more risks than if you passively engage in listening only. Actively communicating to aliens means that you send out messages, maybe you send out directly, but here we sketched two ways to achieving communication with aliens which are indirect. Indirect in the sense that you are not aiming at a particular direction, and you don't give away the return paths of the communications. It's a bit like sensor networks or onion routing.

The first one is what we call Private Communication Probes. A probe is an object that you send out into space, and one of the risks of using probes is that the materials that you use come from the Earth. Probably it will be easy to detect from which part of the universe such a probe comes just by looking at the typical materials, objects, atoms, whatever you use for making the probes. If you want to build a kind of probe network, an interstellar probe network, you must use probes that simply copy themselves, they go to another sun and they copy themselves, and then they burn themselves into the sun, just to leave no traces of their origin. After a number of copies, probably the probes will lose any relation to their origin. The idea is that you put a message into a probe, and the probes that replicate themselves somehow reach out and enter the alien's visibility. Aliens then can reply, either they reply by a reply mechanism built into the probes, and then the probes will multiply further until somehow they come back to Earth, or they can set up their own probe infrastructure. Then the challenge is, of course, how to make the system in such a way that you don't give away your home base, whilst still having a reasonable chance that the answers reach you. So totally probabilistically sending out your probes in random directions is probably not going to work.

Micah Sherr: Sorry, this is a model where human kind has interplanetary communication, travel? And if so, can we build our probes not from, you know, Earth material, but maybe from some other planet?

Reply: This is with the current model where we can travel within our solar system but not outside. If you trace this back within one solar system you will find us easily I think, given the sun you will find any living species on any of the planets near the sun.

Micah Sherr: So the adversaries travel. . .

Reply: Yes.

Tom Sutcliffe: So as someone famous once said, space is really big, and we can't get probes far enough away from our solar system to effectively hide where we are, and we can't send them out fast enough for that to be a realistic way of hiding us, because it would narrow down to a trivial number of planets to scout because of just the distances involved.

Frank Stajano: Especially if you can see the density of the probes that you find in space increases towards the sun.

Sandy Clark: You could track lots, yes, if you counted lots of them.

Changyu Dong: I think one thing is that the communication probably had started long, long ago since the planet (Earth) was born. I read some reports saying that we have found some planetary systems where life could exist, so aliens can do the same I guess.

Reply: I'm not sure I understand.

Changyu Dong: Scientists have discovered certain conditions for life to develop on planets, and then they use those conditions to screen planets. For example, they can say that certain stars are too big or too small, there won't be any life on planets orbiting them. Similarly, if a planet is too close to or too far from its star, there won't be life. If some planets are in a habitable zone, then there is a high probability there would be life. Then scientists can analyse other observations, such as light from the planets, to narrow down the range of potentially habitable planets. even smaller. So basically that's...

Reply: They may have different criteria for life to exist.

Changyu Dong: Yes, that communication has already started. Since Earth came into being, the information mentioned above has already been observable from the outside (of our solar system).

Reply: Yes, clearly, if you look for life in the universe you will restrict your search to the obvious places, but let's not start from an anthropomorphic point of view. There may be different types of life that we cannot imagine even.

Changyu Dong: Yes, actually one question I have is why we haven't been invaded by aliens.

Reply: There's a huge pile of literature with many thousands of answers to that question.

Changyu Dong: But the universe is much older than Earth, and for some alien civilisations, the technology probably can progress to a stage where they can invade us.

Reply: Yes, so the argument is, they haven't invaded us yet, so we shouldn't worry about the future.

Peter Y.A. Ryan: This question might be slightly out of scope, but I'm quite curious about what the goal here is. So what, you're talking about sending out a message, so what sort of message, is it some, I'm leaving aside the issue how do we decode something they're likely to understand, or is it, please send us the theory of everything?

Reply: I think we should send out a simple ping to start with: "hello is there anybody out there?" I think that's the first message.

Frank Stajano: That sounds a slight contradiction with trying to maintain location privacy, right?

Reply: Well the fact that you exist is...

Frank Stajano: I think in one of the first slides you said "if you don't want to be found, then just shut up". So why do you want to send this ping now?

Reply: Well that's because the first slide also showed these two pluses, namely, are we alone, and we really want to have knowledge.

Tom Sutcliffe: Yes, I mean, you can want to talk to them without them knowing your home address potentially.

Bruce Christianson: It sounded like one of these blind dating networks, you know them a bit before you decide whether you want to go out with them or whether you're going to leave in a hurry.

Audience: What if we switch the two sides, what if we are the intelligent beings, and then we try to answer the second part of the slide, how should ET reply. Let's say we are ET and there are some planets where the single cell mechanisms have just started off. Then can we look at it from that perspective, like how can we find their location, and that's what we are trying to do.

Reply: Yes, certainly, so that's also part of the problems with this answer: should ET use the same probes that we sent to them to answer to us? Of course not. If we are clever and want to locate them, we will build in their location into the probe itself and they will never know that they sent back that information. And by replying to a certain message you already give away that you reply to that message, and maybe if the message were directed to a certain location, then you give away your location without knowing. So this in fact could even hint at an impossibility result: if the other guys are as anxious as you are, there will never be any communication. And that's one of the many arguments why we have never seen any attempt to communicate to us.

I especially focused on these probes since they are helpful in understanding, if you are very imaginative, the limits that we can achieve. A second way of using probes is what we call a Random Relay Network. You build this interstellar infrastructure. And then these probes are signalling messages to each other, and what they signal is either their initial message, which is the big ping from our side, or they forward any message that they consider artificial. So if they receive an artificial message they will simply send it out to a lot of other probes who will forward it, and forward it, and somehow it will reach us again.

These are just two directions of thinking from the same school of probes. We have played with other ways, blowing up suns in far solar systems, but that's a bit expensive. You can do it at a large distance maybe if you have enough technology, but to send one bit of information to the rest of the galaxy by losing one planet or one sun is a bit expensive. I think, we shouldn't do that. We've played with other thoughts to scale up things. If you have honeypots, we can make honey-planets. Try to attract as much as possible the bad guys, the Mars Attacks guys, and observe them, and to understand how they behave, and defend ourselves, or being attacked in the same thing. One of the problems is the timescale. If we talk about long distances, if we talk about light years, many light years means many years. Maybe we send out now a message and it arrives at its destination in 100 or 1000 years, and maybe a message comes back in 2000 years, and how are we going to tell our kid's children that there is still a message floating around and what to expect.

Sandy Clark: We can't read filesystems 15 years old.

Reply: Exactly. So in fact what you're doing, you're sending a message to the future, which is in itself a very interesting problem. And even worse in a 1000 years people living on Earth may get an answer, they think, but in fact it's just your own message bouncing back through one of the probes. You're going to talk to yourself, "hey there's intelligent life", but I don't know where it is, maybe on the planet. There are lots of ethical issues related to this issue, which I will not go into.

Frank Stajano: Given this timescale the message may be more like "there *was* intelligence".

Max Spencer: Should we consider the possibility that planet Earth is itself a honey-planet, seeded with life millennia ago, in order to test out some... We're the third party between two previous alien civilisations, one is just trying to test whether the other will be malicious towards us.

Reply: I didn't think about the possibility, and I don't want to consider it, because it doesn't make me happy. Of course you should not only look at location privacy. There are many more security issues that you want to achieve. For example, you want to authenticate your communication partner, but that's impossible if you have no previous interaction with that partner. And maybe you can defer to simpler, weaker requirements like sender invariance instead of authentication. Sender invariance means that the messages that you receive are all coming from the same sender, and that you prove to the other party that all messages that you send are indeed from you, without proving your identity. There are more requirements that you could consider.

Keith Irwin: The sender as an organisation, or a sender as a planet? Because that's clearly not necessarily sender as an individual, and we're talking about a timescale of hundreds of thousands of years.

Reply: Yes, this is related to the adversary model: who is the adversary. Of course now we have a lot of adversaries, we have political axes of evil. In the future there will be an evolution of all these adversaries, and I don't know if the descendants of us here are still the good guys. We happen to think of ourselves as the good guys, but will we stay the good guys? Will the bad guys of now have offspring that become the good guys? I don't know. So there's this notion of sender invariance, which is just a random notion of somebody who has control of the communication at that point in time. And we hope that that's an entity that has some power.

Sandy Clark: We're going to get some alien teenagers just doing a phone prank.

Reply: I would say let's stop sending messages for the next 10,000 years. Let's start doing research on how to set up communications in such a way that at least we know what our limits are, so that we know what we can do in our current state of technology, and assuming some just higher level adversary.

Jeunese Payne: So if you want to stop sending messages, do you also want to recall all the previous messages?

Reply: Yes. Quite seriously, I think we should.

Jeunese Payne: And to be honest the one you showed didn't make much sense to me as a human being, I'm not sure that it would make much sense to an alien either.

Reply: But I think we should send new probes to Pioneers and Voyagers, and simply take them down as soon as possible.

Max Spencer: Or maybe just take off the existing message and put a new one on that points somewhere else.

Jeunese Payne: Except that we haven't managed to send them very far, so they have to just look... Even if those messages didn't say much, the fact that they were intentionally sent – you can just look in their surrounding area, and, oh there, there is a planet, OK, we'll put one there.

Tom Sutcliffe: It's a pretty straight line as well on the trajectory...

Reply: So what would I like to research, or would I like you to research: let's try to find out what kind of possibility or impossibility results we can achieve for location privacy, given certain classes of adversaries or certain classes of defenders of their privacy. For example, if you have a $T1$ society can you get location privacy if you have these capabilities for $T2$ attackers, something like that.

Let's look at the idea of honeypots to honey-planets, what kind of solutions do we have already on this local scale. Access control for drones that we can use to get location privacy at a larger scale. Let's look at location privacy plus other requirements, maybe we can achieve some kind of fairness in exchanging information, scientific knowledge with aliens.

Jeunese Payne: Isn't that like a similar problem with some countries went into other countries and gave them some buttons in return for gold. How do you know that it's fair, based on the fact that aliens are probably going to have a completely different idea of what's valuable.

Reply: Yes, very true, that's one of the many arguments I've seen in this discussion by archaeologists and psychologists on the topic.

Luca Viganò: This is also the problem of the message that you're really sending. There's a new movie coming out[2] where aliens are attacking Earth as video-games because they interpret the capsules that we sent with arcade games as

---

[2] *Pixels*, Columbia Pictures, 2015.

a declaration of war. They attack the Earth with Packman and such. So it's a perfect example for misinterpretation, right.

Reply: Thanks.

Next step. How can we set up a future proof infrastructure? Maybe next week somebody will find out that P is equal to NP. Let's recall all cryptographic algorithms, please do it in such a way that we can recall them from other solar systems as well. Or you want to recall your messages by sending probes to the Voyagers to take them down. And we have made a start with thinking about capabilities of the extraterrestrials, but maybe you can refine it further, or have some other categorisation that's more effective in understanding what we can and cannot do. So that was sort of my voyage, I hope you enjoyed it. Any questions?

Peter Y.A. Ryan: So you said, quite rightly I think, that you can't have authentication with someone you've had no prior contact with. Then you went on to talk about this sender invariance, I think you called it, which sounds like a sort of notion of pseudo-authentication. That's not possible either is it?

Frank Stajano: That's the same as a Google playstore isn't it? You don't know who's providing the app, but you know that they keep signing with the same key and so they're the same guy who provided the app in the first place.

Bruce Christianson: Yes, and the second message is from the same civilisation that the first one was from.

Reply: So if they sent a public key and...

Peter Y.A. Ryan: So okay, they know about RSA.

Reply: Of course, there is this phase of getting the same frame of reference, and that takes a lot of communication before you have a common frame of reference, and from that point in time you may have some kind of sender invariance.

Max Spencer: And they're computationally bound with aliens.

Audience: And there should be a universally trusted third party.

Frank Stajano: Even God is not a universally trusted party, since everyone may have his own God.

Luca Viganò: So coming back to your point about the adversary models, I think you could look at a paper by Enrico Fermi where he discussed reasons why aliens have not contacted us yet, or why we have not found them yet.

Bruce Christianson: The usual one is because of their superior intelligence.

Luca Viganò: Well the first one is because they don't exist, which is a good possibility. The second one is because if they were almighty as you mentioned, then they would have contacted us already, or maybe they're using us as a honey-planet or whatever. But there are a list of reasons there, and I think you could reproduce at least some of them to discuss your models.

Reply: Yes.

Luca Viganò: Or they are so intelligent that they do not want to talk to us, because we are the ants and they are looking at us like we look at...

Audience: People who still think that P is not equal to NP.

Bruce Christianson: Not ready to eat yet.

Ross Anderson: Why go for a conspiracy? If the physics of such an interstellar travel were easy, then the first species to evolve intelligence would have colonised the lot. I mean, why go for a conspiracy theory when there's an obvious one. Observably, physics makes interstellar travel difficult.

Audience: So we've not colonised everything on Earth because we have good reasons for that. We're not really in the oceans because we can't, so the notion of colonisation is also something that we could discuss.

Ross Anderson: We've not colonised Afghanistan because it's too hard, they fight back.

Luca Viganò: Exactly.

Bruce Christianson: Any alien intelligence would assume that the dominant life-form on Earth were bacteria, so perhaps they're communicating with them.

Reply: I think we should continue discussing with a beer now. Thanks a lot.

The Lifetime of Android API Vulnerabilities: Case Study on the JavaScript-to-Java Interface

Daniel R. Thomas[1][(✉)], Alastair R. Beresford[1], Thomas Coudray[2],
Tom Sutcliffe[2], and Adrian Taylor[2]

[1] Computer Laboratory, University of Cambridge, Cambridge, UK
{daniel.thomas,alastair.beresford}@cl.cam.ac.uk
[2] Bromium, Cambridge, UK
thomas.coudray.fr@gmail.com, tom.sutcliffe@bromium.com,
adrian@bromium.com

Abstract. We examine the lifetime of API vulnerabilities on Android and propose an exponential decay model of the uptake of updates after the release of a fix. We apply our model to a case study of the JavaScript-to-Java interface vulnerability. This vulnerability allows untrusted JavaScript in a WebView to break out of the JavaScript sandbox allowing remote code execution on Android phones; this can often then be further exploited to gain root access. While this vulnerability was first publicly disclosed in December 2012, we predict that the fix will not have been deployed to 95% of devices until December 2017, 5.17 years after the release of the fix. We show how this vulnerability is exploitable in many apps and the role that ad-libraries have in making this flaw so widespread.

Keywords: API security · Android · WebView · Security updates · Ad-libraries · JavaScript · Java · Vulnerabilities · Network attacker · RCE

1 Introduction

The Android ecosystem today is a complex network of competing and collaborating companies. In addition to the main OS developer (Google) there are at least 176 additional open source projects whose code is used in the platform. There are also many manufacturers and network operators who customise Android for their devices and networks. For example, 20 300 study participants in the Device Analyzer project [17] use devices built by 298 distinct manufacturers and networks run by 1 440 different operators.

In this landscape, fixing security flaws is hard since it often involves the collaboration of open source developers, Google, the device manufacturers, the network operators and the user (who needs to approve the installation of updates). In this paper we explore Application Programming Interface (API) vulnerabilities in Android and quantify the rate at which these flaws are fixed on real

© Springer International Publishing Switzerland 2015
B. Christianson et al. (Eds.): Security Protocols 2015, LNCS 9379, pp. 126–138, 2015.
DOI: 10.1007/978-3-319-26096-9_13

devices. Such vulnerabilities often represent a security protocol failure, in the sense that the API designer had a particular protocol or API call sequence in mind, and the attacker repurposes those API elements to break the intended security model.

Fixing API vulnerabilities, like fixing deployed protocols, is often hard: fixes may require changes to the API, which breaks backwards compatibility. In our analysis we find that an exponential decay function provides a good model for predicting the rate of fixes for API vulnerabilities in Android. Unfortunately, the rate of decay is low: it takes nearly a year for half of the Android devices using the Google Play Store to update to a new version of Android. In other words, it takes a long time to move from the domain of security fiction (a new release is available which has fixed the vulnerability) to fact (devices are now secure). This is explored further in Sect. 2.

In order to ground our approach we have included a case study in Sect. 3 to investigate the timeline for fixing one API vulnerability in Android. We have selected the JavaScript-to-Java interface vulnerability for this purpose as it is particularly serious and affects all versions of Android prior to the release of version 4.2. The fixing release was first available in October 2012 and as such we now have sufficient data to quantify the speed at which updates have propagated.

2   API Vulnerabilities in Android

At the beginning of 2015 Android had revised its API twenty one times since version one was released with the first Android handset in 2008. We have manually collected the monthly statistics published by Google which record the proportion of devices using particular API versions when they connect to the Google Play Store since December 2009. These statistics[1] are plotted in Fig. 1. The API version distribution shows a clear trend in which older API versions are slowly replaced by newer ones.

In order to quantify the lifecycle of a particular API version we recalculate the API version data in two ways. Firstly, in order to understand the speed of adoption of a particular version of the API, we are interested in the number of days since release rather than specific calendar dates. Secondly, we are interested in the proportion of devices which have *not* upgraded to a particular API version or any successor. For example, when a new API version is first released, no devices could have already been updated to it and therefore the proportion which have not upgraded is one. As devices begin to upgrade to the new API version (or any subsequent release), the proportion not upgraded tends to zero.

We have replotted data from Figs. 1 in 2 to show the proportion of devices not upgraded to a particular version of Android against days since the API version was first released. These data show that all API version upgrades follow a similar trend: a slow initial number of upgrades in the first 250 days, then widespread adoption between 250 and 1000 days, followed by a slow adoption of the new API version by the remaining devices.

---

[1] We have made these available [13].

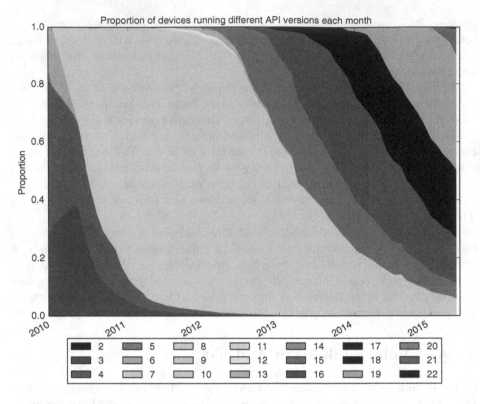

Fig. 1. Proportion of devices running different API versions.

Visually, these data appear to have an exponential decay as it tends to zero. We therefore decided to model this as $f(t)$, a combination of an exponential function together with a delay t_0 which offsets the start time:

$$f(t) = \begin{cases} 1.0 & \text{if } t < t_0 \\ e^{-\text{decay}(t-t_0)} & \text{otherwise} \end{cases} \tag{1}$$

Fitting $f(t)$ to these, we get a Root-Mean-Squared-Error (RMSE) of 0.182 with the parameters $t_0 = 80.7$ days, decay $= 0.0023$ days^{-1} across all API versions. This 2 degree fit gives a RMSE of 0.182, which compares favourably with a standard polynomial fit (3 degree polynomial fit gave an RMSE of 0.182) or a spline fit (3 degree fit gives a RMSE of 0.182) and gives a meaningful model of behaviour rather than a generic curve.

From this fit, the number of days from the release of a new version of Android until 50 % of devices are running that version or higher is 347 (0.95 years) and full deployment to 95% of devices takes 1 230 days (3.37 years). The same analysis using the Device Analyzer data on OS versions in use gives 324 days (0.886 years) and 1 120 days (3.06 years) respectively which is faster but not by much.

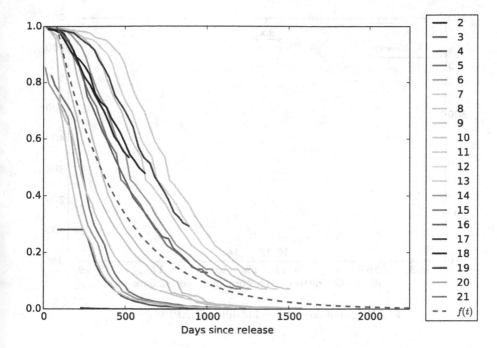

Fig. 2. Proportion of devices not updated to particular versions of Android or any later version. The best fit $f(t)$ is an exponential decay function.

Hence if a security vulnerability is fixed through the release of a particular API version it will be 1 230 days (3.37 years) after that until the fix is fully deployed.

Unfortunately, while this is a good predictor of average behaviour, individual API versions are systematically different from each other. Hence, we took the fit parameters from the global analysis and used them to seed a fit for each API version. This gave us the parameters in Fig. 3 with t_0 and 1/decay plotted as this means that larger values for both indicate a worse provision of updates. API versions 11, 12 and 13 were for Android 3.x which never saw widespread deployment because they targeted tablets and were not available for use on phones. Discounting those values, Fig. 3 shows a trend of updates taking longer over time as t_0 increases and 1/decay increases. This implies that the Android ecosystem is getting worse at distributing updates.

The differences between the predictions and recorded reality is shown in Fig. 4. It shows how the difference between our prediction and recorded behaviour oscillates around 0 with some systematic errors early on due to the simple model of $f(t)$. The errors are mostly less than 10 % and fall over time.

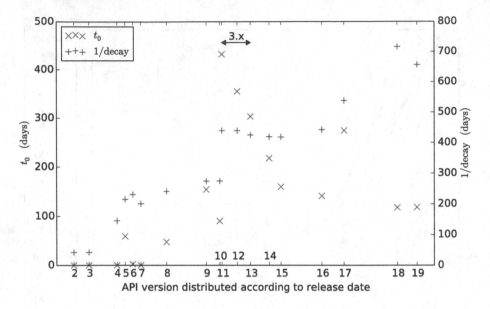

Fig. 3. Fitted parameters for different API versions.

3 Case Study: The JavaScript-to-Java Interface Vulnerability

The Android *WebView* provides a developer with a web browser UI component that can be controlled programmatically by a hosting app, including rendering dynamic HTML content driven by JavaScript. To allow convenient interaction between the WebView and the hosting app, a Java object instance can be bound to a JavaScript variable name, allowing the JavaScript code to call any public methods on the Java object. Prior to Android 4.2, the exposed public methods included those inherited from parent classes, including the `getClass()` method of `java.lang.Object`. This permitted the execution of arbitrary Java code from the JavaScript running inside the WebView. For example, Java reflection controlled from JavaScript can be used to execute Linux programs such as id, as shown in Fig. 5. This is a security vulnerability (CVE-2012-6636) which can be used to remotely run malicious code in the context of an app using the JavaScript-to-Java interface vulnerability and from there exploit other vulnerabilities to gain root privileges on devices and spread as an Android worm.

The attack is comprised of the following steps.

1. Content for WebViews in apps is commonly from untrusted sources or over an unauthenticated HTTP connection, so therefore an active attacker controlling the network (strategies for doing this are discussed in Sect. 3.1) can inject a malicious JavaScript payload into the HTTP stream, which is then executed inside the JavaScript sandbox.

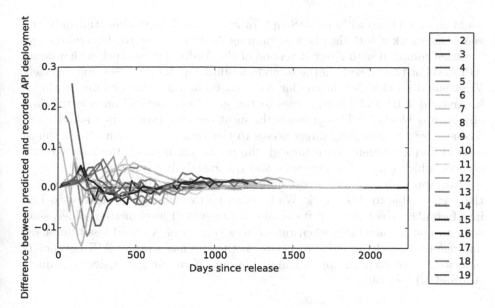

Fig. 4. Difference between predicted behaviour and recorded behaviour.

```
<script>
    Android.getClass()
        .forName('java.lang.Runtime')
        .getMethod('getRuntime',null)
        .invoke(null,null).exec(['id']);
</script>
```

Fig. 5. JavaScript attack, assuming *Android* is the JavaScript alias for the exposed Java object.

2. The malicious JavaScript can then use the JavaScript-to-Java interface vulnerability to break out of the JavaScript sandbox into the app context.
3. Then the malicious code can often use other known vulnerabilities to break out of the app sandbox and gain root privileges on the device. We know that, on average, approximately 88% of Android devices are vulnerable to at least one known root vulnerability [14].
4. Once an attacker has root on a device, he can use ARP spoofing or ICMP redirect attacks to reroute local traffic through the device and inject malicious JavaScript into any HTTP traffic, thereby starting step (1) above on a new device. Thus the attack has the potential to act as an Android worm.

Google has modified the Android API or its implementation twice in an attempt to fix the JavaScript-to-Java interface vulnerability. In the first modification, the function of the JavaScript-to-Java interface was modified in Android 4.2 to ensure that only public methods with the annotation @JavaScriptInterface could be called from within JavaScript for new apps. This modification only prevents the attack if *both* the phone is running Android 4.2 or greater *and* the app has been compiled with a recent version of the Android framework with a target API Level of 17 or newer. In the second modification, for devices using the Web-View based on Google Chrome for Android version 33.0.0.0 or later (included in Android 4.4.3 and later), access to the `getClass` method on injected Java objects was blocked.[2] This prevents the most obvious JavaScript-to-Java interface attacks by preventing direct access to the Java runtime. An attacker must instead find a different route through the public methods on the injected Java objects, which may not always exist and is certainly much harder.

Any app with a WebView containing a JavaScript-to-Java interface is potentially vulnerable to this attack. We label an app which uses JavaScript-to-Java interface *always vulnerable* if it contains a target API level of 16 or older, since such an app is vulnerable when run on any version of Android less than 4.4.3; and *vulnerable only on outdated devices* if the app has a target API Level of 17 or newer, since such an app is vulnerable only if running on a device running Android 4.1.x or older.

3.1   Threat Model

There are several different scenarios in which an attacker could inject malicious JavaScript to exploit the JavaScript-to-Java interface vulnerability.

1. An attacker could control the original server that supplied 'legitimate' HTML either through compromising it or by using some other means (such as buying ads) to supply the malicious JavaScript.
2. An attacker could control a node on the path from the original server allowing them to inject malicious JavaScript into the HTTP traffic.
3. An attacker could control traffic passing through the device's local network and inject malicious JavaScript. This could be achieved by either running a public Wi-Fi network, or compromising an existing network using ARP spoofing or ICMP redirect attacks to redirect all traffic via a machine under the attacker's control.

Level 1 attacks can be mitigated by better system security and input validation at the original server. Level 2 and Level 3 attacks can be mitigated by apps using HTTPS with proper validation of certificates [3] (for example using pinning [2]) to prevent an attacker from being able to inject malicious JavaScript. Level 3 attacks can also be mitigated through the use of a secure VPN to a trustworthy network and by better security on the local network (protection against ARP spoofing, ICMP redirect attacks and independently encrypted connections to the router).

---

[2] https://codereview.chromium.org/213693005/patch/20001/30001 committed as 261801 or afae5d83d66c1d041a1fa433fbb087c5cc604b67 or e55966f4c3773a24fe46f 9bab60ab3a3fc19abaf.

3.2   Sources of Vulnerability

To investigate the severity of this vulnerability we need data on which apps use the JavaScript-to-Java interface and where they use it. We analysed 102 174 APK files from the Google Play Store collected on 2014-03-10 and between 2014-05-10 and 2014-05-15. We found that 21.8% (22 295) of apps were always vulnerable, 15.3% (15 666) were vulnerable only on outdated devices, 62.2% (63 533) were not vulnerable and 0.67% (680) could not be analysed due to failures of our static analyser. These results are presented in Table 1 and show that most apps are not vulnerable, but that more apps are always vulnerable than are vulnerable only on outdated devices.

The static analysis was performed by decompiling the APKs using `apktool` and extracting the target API version from the Android Manifest. Apps using the JavaScript-to-Java interface were detected by string matching for 'add-JavascriptInterface' in the decompiled .smali files.

Of the 38 000 vulnerable apps, 12 600 were in the Device Analyzer data [17], those which are not in the Device Analyzer data are unlikely to be widely used, since they were not installed on any of the 20 300 devices in Device Analyzer data.

In the following analysis, values are given ± their standard deviation. We found that always vulnerable apps were started 0.6 ± 0.0 times a day between the disclosure of the vulnerability and the start of our APK file collection, with 8.34 ± 0.67 such apps installed.

We found that apps vulnerable only on outdated devices were started 0.78 ± 0.10 times a day between the disclosure of the vulnerability and the start of our APK file collection, with 7.27 ± 0.71 such apps installed.

Hence on an outdated device vulnerable apps were started 1.38 ± 0.11 times a day with 15.6 ± 0.9 vulnerable apps installed. Due to static analysis failures and the fact that not all the apps are observed by Device Analyzer, these rates are likely to be underestimates. It is also possible that the Device Analyzer data could be biased towards users with more apps than is typical, which might cause this figure to be an overestimate.

Table 1. Percentage of the 102 174 apps analysed which fell in each category.

Classification	Percentage	Count
Always vulnerable	21.8	22 295
Vulnerable only on outdated devices	15.3	15 666
Not vulnerable	62.2	63 533
Unscannable	0.67	680

Ad-Libraries. We tested a couple of dozen of the apps we had identified as always vulnerable by MITMing them and injecting JavaScript which exploited the JavaScript-to-Java interface vulnerability. We found that 50 % of these were actually exploitable. There are several reasons why we might not have been able to exploit the vulnerability: we did not activate the vulnerable activity, HTTPS was used for the request or the vulnerable code in the app was not exercised during our testing.

Inspecting the vulnerable HTTP requests revealed that ad-libraries were the the usual reason for vulnerable requests. We performed further static analysis on the APK files by reverse engineering the ten most downloaded apps that detect ads and constructing a list of pattern matches for different ad-libraries. The distribution of different ad-libraries is shown in Fig. 6.

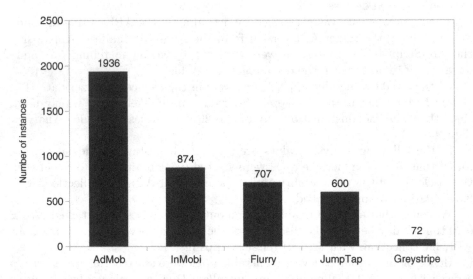

Fig. 6. Number of instances of each ad-library within the always vulnerable apps. Not all of these frameworks necessarily introduce the vulnerability and some versions of them may have been fixed: this plot just shows the distribution of the ad-libraries within the always vulnerable apps.

3.3   Lifetime of the Vulnerability

The vulnerability was first publicly recorded in December 2012 [1]. The proportion of devices that contacted the Google Play Store and are secure for apps vulnerable only on outdated devices are shown in blue in Fig. 7. In summary, in April 2015 70.6% of devices were running a version of Android that protects users from apps vulnerable only on outdated devices.

This vulnerability will cease to be problematic when all Android devices run API version 17 or later *and* all apps which use JavaScript-to-Java interface target API version 17 or later. Using our model for $f(t)$ from Eq. 1 and knowledge that API version 17 was released in October 2012 we expect 95% of all Android devices to be secure for apps vulnerable only on outdated devices by December

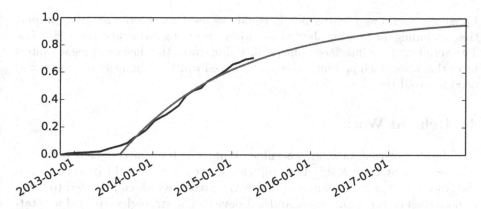

Fig. 7. Proportion of fixed devices with these data from Google Play given in blue and above it our prediction in green.

2017. This prediction is shown in green in Fig. 7. We do not have visibility into the way apps' target API versions on Android change over time and therefore it is harder to understand whether always vulnerable apps will continue to represent a significant risk after almost all Android devices support API version 17 or later.

3.4 Solutions

There are various strategies which could have been adopted to more rapidly mitigate this vulnerability. Android could have broken API compatibility and backported the fix to all versions of Android, however other work has shown that security updates are deployed slowly on Android [14]. Android could refuse to load JavaScript over HTTP and require HTTPS (with properly verified certificates) or use local storage which would make MITM attacks injecting malicious JavaScript much harder. Part of the problem is that the libraries (particularly ad-libraries) which developers bundle inside their apps target old API versions and developers need to update their dependencies to versions that target higher API versions.

If Android had a more comprehensive package management system, which handled dependencies, then apps could be loosely coupled with their ad-libraries and the libraries could be updated to fixed versions without the app developers having to re-release every app that used the library. Alternatively, to maintain backwards compatibility while fixing the vulnerability, apps could be automatically rewritten to fix the vulnerability.

Users could use a VPN to tunnel all their traffic back to a trusted network so that MITMs on local networks (such as open Wi-Fi access points) would not be able to mount this attack, but this would not protect against attackers on the network path to the ad-server, or malicious ad-servers.

The fix included in Android 4.4.3 discussed earlier in Sect. 3, where access to the `getClass` method is blocked, substantially mitigates this vulnerability.

Language solutions such as Joe-E could be used to enforce security properties, including preventing JavaScript from executing arbitrary code [8]. The JavaScript-to-Java interface vulnerability illustrates the danger of legacy interfaces that allow such protections to be bypassed which a language solution would need to avoid [18].

4   Related Work

The JavaScript-to-Java interface vulnerability has been investigated before. It was demonstrated by MWR Labs [6] who showed how it could be used to run the Android security assessment framework drozer, which can be used to run a remote shell on a compromised Android device. The strategies we used for statically analysing Dalvik bytecode to discover use of JavaScript-to-Java interface have also been used previously [19].

Attacks have been published against WebView [7] including those relating to the JavaScript-to-Java interface and vulnerabilities caused by the violation of the origin-based access control policy in hybrid apps [4].

There have been investigations of the behaviour of ad-libraries on Android. Stevens et al. demonstrated how attacks could be mounted on JavaScript-to-Java interface used by ad-libraries, but without realising the significance of get-Class [12]. However, unlike the vulnerability we have discussed, these attacks continue to work on fixed devices even for apps vulnerable only on outdated devices. Grace et al. have shown that ad-libraries require excessive permissions and expose users to additional risks [5], which are further compounded by the JavaScript-to-Java interface vulnerability.

To counteract the problems caused by ad-libraries being packaged within an app, and thereby inheriting all their permissions, there have been proposals to separate out the ad-libraries into separate processes by altering Android to provide an API [10] and then automatically rewriting apps to use such an API [11]. This improves security, particularly if it means that the ad-libraries can be updated independently of the apps, but it does not otherwise help if an attack on JavaScript-to-Java interface can be followed up with a root exploit.

We scanned 102 174 apps but the PlayDrone crawler was able to analyse over 1 100 000 apps, and found a similar but more comprehensive distribution of usage of different ad-libraries [16].

Nappa et al. have analysed the decay of vulnerabilities affecting client applications on Windows [9]. They used similar data to our analysis but collected it from information provided by hosts directly rather than using published summary data.

5   Conclusion

In this paper we proposed the exponential decay model for Android API vulnerabilities and we explored one case study: the JavaScript-to-Java interface vulnerability. By applying our model to our case study we find that for apps which are vulnerable only on outdated devices, 95% of all Android devices will be protected from the JavaScript-to-Java interface vulnerability by December 2017, 5.17 ± 1.23 years after the release of the fix. It is not known whether always vulnerable apps will continue to present a security risk and therefore it is unclear whether Android users will be safe from this vulnerability after this date.

Acknowledgements. This work was supported by a Google focussed research award; and the EPSRC [grant number EP/P505445/1]. Some of the raw data and source code is available [15]; the analysed APKs are not included as we do not have distribution rights for them. Thanks to Robert N.M. Watson for his insight and useful feedback.

References

1. Bergman, N.:. Abusing WebView JavaScript bridges (2012). http://d3adend.org/blog/?p=314. Accessed 09 January 2015
2. Clark, J., van Oorschot, P.C.: SoK: SSL and HTTPS: revisiting past challenges and evaluating certificate trust model enhancements. In: IEEE Symposium on Security and Privacy, pp. 511–525 (2013). doi:10.1109/SP.2013.41
3. Fahl, S., Harbach, M., Muders, T., Smith, M., Baumgärtner, L., Freisleben, B.: Why Eve and Mallory love Android: an analysis of android SSL (in)security. In: CCS, pp. 50–61. ACM (2012). doi:10.1145/2382196.2382205, ISBN: 9781450316514
4. Georgiev, M., Jana, S., Shmatikov, V.: Breaking and fixing origin-based access control in hybrid web/mobile application frameworks. In: Network and Distributed System Security Symposium (NDSS) (2014). doi:10.14722/ndss.2014.23323
5. Grace, M.C., Zhou, W., Jiang, X., Sadeghi, A.-R.: Unsafe exposure analysis of mobile in-app advertisements. In: Proceedings of the Fifth ACM Conference on Security and Privacy in Wireless and Mobile Networks (WiSec), pp. 101–112 (2012). doi:10.1145/2185448.2185464
6. MWR labs. WebView addJavascriptInterface Remote Code Execution (2013). https://labs.mwrinfosecurity.com/blog/2013/09/24/webview-addjavascript interface-remote-code-execution/. Accessed 19 December 2014
7. Luo, T., Hao, H., Du, W., Wang, Y., Yin, H.: Attacks on WebView in the Android system. In: Proceedings of the 27th Annual Computer Security Applications Conference (ACSAC), Orlando, pp. 343–352. ACM (2011). doi:10.1145/2076732.2076781, ISBN: 9781450306720
8. Mettler, A., Wagner, D., Close, T.: Joe-E: a security-oriented subset of Java. In: Network and Distributed System Security Symposium (NDSS) (2010)
9. Nappa, A., Johnson, R., Bilge, L., Caballero, J., Dumitras, T.: The attack of the clones: a study of the impact of shared code on vulnerability patching. In: IEEE Symposium on Security and Privacy, pp. 692–708 (2015). doi:10.1109/SP.2015.48.138
10. Pearce, P., Felt, A.P., Wagner, D.: AdDroid: privilege separation for applications and advertisers in Android. In: ACM Symposium on Information, Computer and Communication Security (ASIACCS) (2012). doi:10.1145/2414456.2414498
11. Shekhar, S., Dietz, M., Wallach, D.S.: AdSplit: separating smartphone advertising from applications. In: Proceedings of the 21st USENIX Conference on Security Symposium, p. 28 (2012). arXiv: 1202.4030

12. Stevens, R., Gibler, C., Crussell, J., Erickson, J., Chen, H.: Investigating user privacy in Android ad libraries. In: IEEE Mobile Security Technologies (MoST) (2012)
13. Thomas, D.R.: Historic Google Play dashboard (2015). http://android vulnerabilities.org/play/historicplaydashboard
14. Thomas, D.R., Beresford, A.R., Rice, A.: Security metrics for the android ecosystem. In: ACM CCS Workshop on Security and Privacy in Smartphones and Mobile Devices (SPSM), Denver. ACM (2015). doi:10.1145/2808117.2808118, ISBN: 978-1-4503-3819-6
15. Thomas, D.R., Coudray, T., Sutcliffe, T.: Supporting data for: "The lifetime of Android API vulnerabilities: case study on the JavaScript-to-Java interface" (2015). https://www.repository.cam.ac.uk/handle/1810/247976. Accessed 26 May 2015
16. Viennot, N., Garcia, E., Nieh, J.: A measurement study of Google Play. In: SIGMETRICS (2014). doi:10.1145/2591971.2592003
17. Wagner, D.T., Rice, A., Beresford, A.R.: Device Analyzer: large-scale mobile data collection. In: Sigmetrics, Big Data Workshop, Pittsburgh. ACM (2013). doi:10.1145/2627534.2627553
18. Wagner, D., Tribble, D.: A security analysis of the Combex DarpaBrowser architecture (2002). http://combexin.temp.veriohosting.com/papers/darpa-review/security-review.pdf. Accessed 08 March 2012
19. Wognsen, E.R., Karlsen, H.S.: Static analysis of Dalvik bytecode and reflection in Android. In: Master's thesis, Department of Computer Science, Aalborg University, Aalborg, Denmark (2012)

The Lifetime of Android API Vulnerabilities: Case Study on the JavaScript-to-Java Interface (Transcript of Discussion)

Daniel R. Thomas(✉)

Computer Laboratory, University of Cambridge, Cambridge, UK
daniel.thomas@cl.cam.ac.uk

Security protocols like TLS often have a two-sided upgrade problem, it takes a long time to upgrade, as both the client and the server must be upgraded. An API is a protocol, and there are a two-sided upgrade problems with APIs. We have evaluated a particularly nasty API vulnerability in Android for which we have data on the different approaches used to fix it and their deployment timeline. First I will describe the vulnerability, and why it is important.

Android apps display HTML, CSS and JavaScript based content, particularly for advertising. They often use a WebView, a UI element that displays a web page. This web page can contain JavaScript. The JavaScript code needs to communicate with the app's native Java code, for example, to collect information for ads. It might require access to location or contact details. It might provide interactivity such as taking a photo or recording audio. To support this, inside a Java app a developer can map a Java object into the JavaScript scope of the WebView, so that it can be accessed from JavaScript. Calls on this object are automatically mapped into equivalent calls on the Java object. This is the main mechanism for JavaScript code to communicate with Java code.

One use case is displaying a pop-up to the user. The developer could write a showToast method and inject the object into the WebView for the JavaScript to use. There is a problem with this interface: a security vulnerability. This vulnerability means that if you sit down in a coffee shop and use an app that displays an advert, your device is compromised, and the attacker can use your device to spread across the network infecting other devices. How does that happen?

All public methods on embedded Java objects are accessible from JavaScript, including inherited ones. Hence public methods on java.lang.Object are accessible. Object has some very powerful methods like .getClass which returns the class object, which has methods such as .forName, which allows reflection, which can be used to get the Runtime, which then gives you .exec, and that will run arbitrary shell commands. This could be used to run rm, or to write out binaries containing root exploits and then run them. In other work we found that on average 87 % of Android phones are exposed to known critical vulnerabilities since 2011 [1]. This means that arbitrary code execution is dangerous, because an attacker can then gain root and attack other phones using the same method. They could use ARP spoofing, or ICMP redirect attacks to intercept traffic and inject JavaScript, or exploit other remote code execution vulnerabilities such as one in DHCP.

© Springer International Publishing Switzerland 2015
B. Christianson et al. (Eds.): Security Protocols 2015, LNCS 9379, pp. 139–144, 2015.
DOI: 10.1007/978-3-319-26096-9_14

Google has made two modifications to Android to try and solve this problem. Firstly in 2012, they changed the API: from API 17 and onwards methods on the injected Java object are only accessible if annotated. This works if the phone is running API version 17 or higher, and the app has rebuilt against API version 17 or higher. However if the app has not been built to target that API version then for backwards compatibility, the old API is used. Therefore this fix only works if both sides are upgraded.

This fix splits into four categories, neither phone nor app upgraded, app but not phone upgraded, phone but not app upgraded, and phone and app upgraded. Only in the last case is the vulnerability prevented. We have looked at which categories apps fall into, and about 60 % of apps are not upgraded, and about 70 % of phones are running version of Android greater than API version 17. Those numbers are not completely comparable as they were not recorded at the same point in time but that is the ballpark.

This fix was not comprehensive, so Google made a second attempt at a fix in 2014. At this point Android had switched to a new version of the WebView based on Google Chrome rather than the old native browser. From Android 4.4.3 it blocks all calls to .getClass from JavaScript. Consequently it is no longer possible to automatically exploit any WebView using the JavaScript interface, without finding a new chain of methods leading to remote code execution. If the developer has only provided safe methods on the injected object, then no such chain will exist. This is a better solution, and from that point onwards security is improved, but this was more recent and so fewer phones have that fix.

To evaluate how this fix has been deployed, we investigated the distribution of API versions in use on Android. Google have published the proportion of devices running different API versions most months since December 2009, and I have gone through and looked at old blog posts from every month, and then more recently visited the site every month in order to record this information [2]. They provide this for developers so that they know what features are available on phones, and what proportion of devices will be compatible if they used a new feature. We can see that new API versions get deployed over time, but we cannot tell whether that is because people are buying new phones, or because old phones are updated, but new versions eventually come to dominate. We want to know what proportion of the devices are running a fixed version of the API, (that version or any later version) and how that varies for different API versions. If we normalize this for the release date of that API version we can compare different API versions in terms of their distribution process.

This gives us Fig. 2 from the paper. The curves look fairly similar, but while the general behaviour does not change much, there is variation between API versions. It looks like older API versions are deployed faster than new ones, implying that the deployment process is getting worse. To determine whether that is the case we fitted a curve. We chose the curve to have two meaningful parameters, the time when nothing is being deployed, and then the rate at which deployment happens at. We can then plot the fit for those parameters for all the different API versions. This gives us Fig. 3 from the paper. The values of both parameters have increased over time. It is takes hundreds of days for any deployment to happen, and then it is a slower process than before.

Another way of measuring deployment is to measure the vulnerability of apps rather than devices. We scanned 100 000 APK files from the Google Play Store, and performed a static analysis to see whether they were vulnerable. We check whether the apps use a WebView, if so, do they use the JavaScript interface, if so, are they targeting an API version higher than 17. We found that of the apps which use the JavaScript interface, about 60 % of them are targeting an API version of Android less than 17 and so are not fixed.

We also have some data from Device Analyzer, a project that we have been running since 2011 [3]. It is an Android app installed on user devices that collects data, including the apps installed and which apps they run. Hence we can take the list of apps we found to be vulnerable in our static analysis and see when they were run on user devices. We found that on an outdated device, which is running Android API version 16 or less, then a vulnerable apps are run 1.4 times a day, each of which provides an opportunity for an attack to occur. On a more recent versions of Android, a vulnerable app was run 0.6 times a day.

James Malcolm: Why are those numbers different?

Reply: 60 % of apps in our static analysis had not upgraded to the new API version, but 40 % had, so the 1.4 times a day number is higher because it includes the 40 % of apps which have had the fix, but are running on an old version of Android and so do not get the benefit of that fix.

Bruce Christianson: So the optimistic message is that the fix has made things better.

Reply: Yes. It is getting deployed, and the situation is much better now.

We are not surprised that two-sided fixes are hard. However one might expect that Google would be able to do better, as they both make the OS and control the Play Store, and so have influence over both the developers who make the clients, and they are the people who ship the server. They should be able to quickly make and deploy the fix, but we do not expect this to be happen until 2018, five years to fix a serious vulnerability.

Mark Ryan: Why has the deployment of new Android versions got worse over time?

Reply: We are not sure why it takes longer. Perhaps at the beginning Android was not that good, and so the new features in later versions made a big difference, providing a commercial incentive to deploy these new versions. Recently, most of the features have already been implemented, the new versions might be better, but they are not revolutionary, reducing commercial pressure.

Alastair R. Beresford: Maybe as the price has being driven down, cheaper manufacturers have entered the marketplace and do not provide updates.

Reply: There is a big difference between different manufacturers in how good they are at shipping updates how recent the version of Android they use is.

Mark Ryan: Should the world move towards automatic updates, out of the control of users, or should this be left to the discretion of users?

Reply: In other work [1], we have looked at the update process more closely. We found that for a particular device model, once an update reaches some devices, then within 26 days it has reached 50 % of the devices, and in a year it has reached almost all of those devices of that device model, which is relatively prompt delivery of updates; in comparison with the general distribution of all Android devices where it takes hundreds of days before 50 % of devices get a new version. It seems that when an update is available for a particular device model most people install it pretty promptly. Hence we think it is the update not being available rather than the update not being automatically installed is the primary problem, but it is hard to tell precisely.

Frank Stajano: There is the issue of regressions. The issuers of updates are not always thorough in checking that they do not break older things. I remember one time that an upgrade of Ubuntu broke the application that I used for my calendar and time management: I was so pissed off!

Reply: Theoretically manufacturers test things carefully, and then the operators then test it again. They certainly have a long period of time in which they could test it, and Android provides a well-defined API, and is careful about compatibility. We have not noticed the same level of apps breaking on new versions that you might see on Ubuntu, which does not make the same guarantees.

Frank Stajano: The fact is that the update may repudiate some older version of a library. It could be that an application (that has never been updated) only relied on that version because the new one did not even exist when it was written, and the author stopped developing it. And if I depend on that particular application, then I am screwed when the Ubuntu update repudiates the old but functioning version of the library on which the application depends.

Reply: We have apps that we wrote for Android 1.6, which is API version 4, and they still work fine on an Android 5. They do not look quite as shiny because they are not using the new features, but they do still work. Perhaps there are cases where this is not true, but there is good backwards compatibility. There are other reasons people might choose not to upgrade, such as, cheap phones not having enough disc space to install the update.

Paul Wernick: The phone I have got is not going to be updated, it is now fixed at two versions of Android old. Does that mean that the security updates are not going to be provided?

Reply: Yes.

Paul Wernick: Does that mean that Google needs to differentiate between must-have security updates, and would-be-nice business updates?

Reply: One thing that we could criticise Google for is, for some security updates, they have not shipped them at all, even to their Google Nexus devices, until they have a new version of Android to bundle them in. They tend to do this with things they think are not that important. For example, there was a vulnerability in APK signing, where an app could pretend to be signed by anyone, and that meant it could gain system permissions. This meant that an attacker could install a VPN, and do all sorts of nasty things like that, if you installed an APK from an untrustworthy source, but because the Google Play Store checked, and Google's model is, everyone uses the Google Play Store, but if you not one of those people then you are not safe.

Paul Wernick: Over time there will be an increasing number of machines that are not running the latest versions, and work fine but are increasingly vulnerable?

Reply: Yes. Or at least we cannot distinguish between devices getting updates and devices being replaced, and so we do not know what proportion of new versions becoming popular is new devices versus updates to the old ones. If people buy new devices every 18 months, which is certainly not what I do, then it is fine because maybe your device only has 6 months of updates, you are only vulnerable for a year after that, and then you have a new one.

Alastair R. Beresford: As a comparison point, if you bought Windows XP in 2001 you got free updates for 13 years. Many Android devices we see do not get any updates ever.

Reply: Including not during the 24 months of the contract which pays for the phone, you still have a contractual relationship with the company who sold you the phone, but you are not getting updates.

Petr Svenda: Is Device Analyzer data representative? Can you distinguish between geographic areas? Does that give different distributions?

Reply: We claim that it is representative. We have compared it with the Google Play API version data, and it is similar, with a similar update pattern. Device Analyzer is perhaps biased towards early adopters, so on average we see more recent API versions more in Device Analyzer than in Google Play, but the data we used in this work was from Google Play, and so is the ground truth.

In the Device Analyzer data we had a lot of users from Bangladesh due to a particular focused study that was run there, and one thing we noticed was that they were more likely to be running Android API version 17, which was a slightly old version at that time. They were also using manufacturers and operators which we have rated to be particularly poor. This possibly partly due these being cheap devices, if you own a cheap device maybe you do not get a good quality of service in terms of updates. We would expect that there to be a correlation between how much people pay for their phones, and whether they get security updates, and so if you are in Bangladesh, then maybe you get a worse service than if you are in the UK, but it is not clear how to solve that.

References

1. Thomas, D.R., Beresford, A.R., Rice, A.: Security metrics for the Android ecosystem. In: ACM CCS Workshop on Security and Privacy in Smartphones and Mobile Devices (SPSM), Denver, Colorado, USA (2015). doi:10.1145/2808117.2808118
2. http://androidvulnerabilities.org/play/historicplaydashboard
3. Wagner, D.T., Rice, A., Beresford, A.R.: Device analyzer: understanding smartphone usage. In: 10th International Conference on Mobile and Ubiquitous Systems: Computing, Networking and Services, Tokyo, Japan, December 2013. https://deviceanalyzer.cl.cam.ac.uk/

Challenges of Fiction in Network Security – Perspective of Virtualized Environments

Vit Bukac[(✉)], Radim Ostadal, Petr Svenda, Tatevik Baghdasaryan,
and Vashek Matyas

Faculty of Informatics, Masaryk University, Brno, Czech Republic
{bukac,ostadal,xsvenda,matyas}@mail.muni.cz, tatbagg@gmail.com

Abstract. The paper aims to start a discussion about challenges and possible caveats of performing network security experiments with high traffic volumes in virtual environment. A new framework for rapid evolution of denial-of-service attacks by genetic algorithms is presented. Issues with virtual environment that were encountered during initial work with the framework are listed.

Keywords: Virtualization · Framework · Genetic algorithm · Denial of service attack

1 Background

Virtualization has a significant impact on how network security experiments are performed. It allows for a high flexibility in both experiment design and scope setting, and it also supports experiment repeatability with quick restoration of predefined state. Virtualization enables a great utilization of available resources with a high scalability. Yet are the environments that were built over standard hypervisors (e.g., Xen, VMware, Hyper-V) truly representative? Are experiment results obtained in virtual environment applicable also in physical environment?

We have designed a new generic framework for quick automated evolution of denial-of-service (DoS) attacks in virtual environment. The framework is sufficiently universal to be used for evaluation of an arbitrary denial-of-service attack. However, we have encountered issues that could have a huge impact on the results collected in similar environments. We would like to initiate a discussion about issues that could change our perception of virtual environment as a helpful servant.

It has been known for a long time that network simulations do not reflect behavior in real networks correctly, especially when considering high-volume traffic. Research on denial-of-service attacks has been badly affected, because simulations assume ideal environment without limitations of the physical world (e.g., sizes of buffers on routers) [1]. As a response, emulation testbeds [2] and hybrid physical-virtual testbeds [3] have been built to support experimentation with large-scale attacks.

© Springer International Publishing Switzerland 2015
B. Christianson et al. (Eds.): Security Protocols 2015, LNCS 9379, pp. 145–151, 2015.
DOI: 10.1007/978-3-319-26096-9_15

2   Our Framework

The framework has been initially created to examine possible enhancements to the HTTP GET flooding attack by modifying HTTP request headers. The project aim was to search for such HTTP GET headers where their processing by the victim server would be significantly more resource demanding than the processing of HTTP GET headers from common web browsers.

The framework applies genetic algorithms to existing DoS attacks in order to discover advanced, more potent attack variants and also to identify DoS vulnerabilities in applications that are serving as targets. The architecture is outlined in Fig. 1.

The framework consists of a central management host and multiple physical computation hosts for conducting experiments themselves. Each computation host has a hypervisor installed and hosts two virtual machines attacker and victim. Each management unit can assign tasks to multiple computation hosts, therefore each generation can be evaluated on dozens of physical hosts simultaneously. Virtual machines (VMs) on different physical hosts are clones of attacker and victim initial source VM images. Thanks to snapshot restoration, each evaluation is performed in exactly the same virtual machine state.

The modular architecture enables seamless changes. Employed genetic algorithm, virtual machine operating system and target application can all be changed with minimal impact on the other parts of the framework. Once the task and its properties are fixed, the framework can be left to produce relevant results automatically.

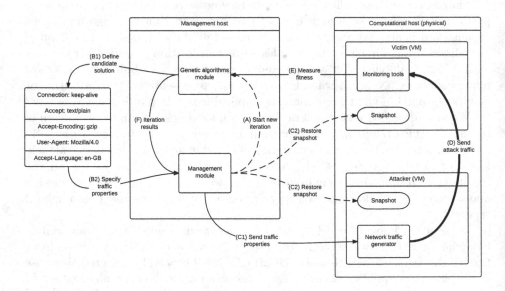

Fig. 1. Framework architecture

2.1   Workflow

A – Management module initiates evaluation of a new population.

B1, B2 – Genetic algorithms module creates a list of candidate solutions to be evaluated in the current round and provides the list to the management module. Each candidate solution provides a representation of network traffic that needs to be evaluated.

C1 – Management module maintains a list of active computational hosts. Candidate solutions are distributed equally to all available computation hosts in order to minimize the time required to evaluate the entire population.

C2 – Management module restores snapshots of all virtual machines on computation hosts. Restoring snapshots is quick and establishes a common initial state for evaluation of every candidate solution.

D – Attacker virtual machine contains a network traffic generator that can translate the received specification (i.e., candidate solution) into an arbitrary network traffic. The actual generated stream of packets is sent towards the victim virtual machine.

E – Monitoring tools on the victim VM measure the impact of received traffic on the host (e.g., consumption of RAM, CPU load or values of application-specific performance counters). Measured values are converted into a common format and sent as fitness function values (how well candidate solution satisfies the goal high load in our case) to the genetic algorithms module.

F – Genetic algorithms module evaluates all received fitness function values, chooses the best solution(s) and provides results to the management module for a manual review. Once enough results are received, management module starts a new round.

3   Scenarios

3.1   HTTP Requests

As mentioned before, our original goal was just to search for such HTTP GET headers that could create a burden on the victim server with significantly more resource demanding load than would be that of a processing of HTTP GET headers from common web browsers.

A candidate solution is an ordered list of pairs (HTTP header field, value). Candidate solutions differ in the chosen header fields, appropriate values and the order of pairs in the header. Each candidate solution is incorporated into HTTP GET request with a constant URL before being sent. The URL targets a copy of a well-known news webpage which is running on the victim VM. Each request is sent 10 000 times. Monitoring tools on the victim VM collect CPU time of all Apache processes.

Measured values were afterwards compared to CPU time of HTTP requests that were constructed to mimic requests from common web browsers (i.e., Google Chrome 35, Internet Explorer 11 and Mozilla Firefox 31).

3.2   HTTP Requests – Lessons Learned

We have encountered a number of problems to cope with:

- **Measurement Precision.** While the deviation of multiple measurements of the same phenomena was less than 3 % with physical hosts, the deviation increased up to 20 % when similar measurements were conducted in virtual environment.
- **No Relation of Results in Virtual Environment and Physical Machines.** We were unable to replicate some results from virtual environment on real hardware. The example could be the Fig. 2 with results from virtual environment. In virtual environment, Best 1, 2 and 3 requests require higher CPU load than the common IE request. When we sent the same HTTP headers on two separate physical machines, the difference between them and IE was negligible.
- **Different Interpretations on Physical Machine and in Virtualization.** We observed that the same version of Wireshark on the same version of operating system interprets the same network traffic differently, when running on real HW and when running in a virtualized environment. This behavior could influence any automated analysis of PCAP files that is based on the libpcap library.
- **Incomparable Performance from Hosts with Different Hardware Configuration.** Virtual machine performance is heavily influenced by underlying physical hardware. Two virtual machines running on different hardware will provide different measurement, even though the environment seems to be exactly the same when observed from inside. All candidate solutions must be evaluated on computational hosts with similar HW configurations. This presents a significant challenge for comparability of any cloud-based computations.
- **Cable vs. Wi-Fi Connection.** We also applied a variant where attacker VM and victim VM resided on separate physical hosts. Operating system performance counters values were distinctively different when attack traffic was sent through Wi-Fi and through cable connection.
- **Lower Precision Bound.** When using virtualized environment, there is always background noise (e.g., fluctuations of CPU load, OS native network traffic, RAM consumption varying in time). This noise sets a lower bound for useable precision of measurements. With less than 1000 HTTP requests during each run, the noise was too dominant for measurements to have any real informational value. We therefore used at least 10 000 HTTP requests. Noise in physical environment is arguably lower.
- **Results Interpretation.** Sometimes it was difficult to identify what parameters were key influencers of final results (e.g., VM configuration, physical host properties, network configuration, and internal application configuration). We had to employ try-error approach to interpret some of the observed anomalies. Also, it was helpful to collect fitness values for minimal size HTTP requests formed by the smallest possible HTTP request that still get non-error results,

together with one additional header field. Later we use these fitness values as guidance for mutual comparison of more complex headers with up to nine different header fields.

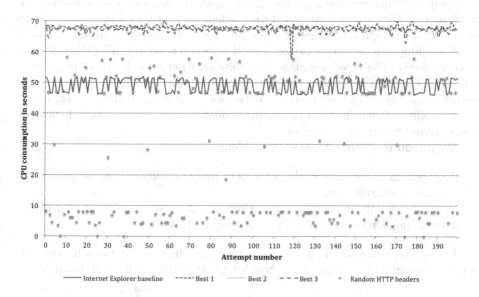

Fig. 2. CPU occupation by HTTP requests.

Figure 2 illustrates some of our findings. Random HTTP headers represent distribution of CPU consumption of 200 randomly constructed HTTP request headers. Cluster between 0 and 10 represents malformed requests that are responded with 400 error code. Cluster between 45 and 60 represents standard common requests. Best1, Best2 and Best3 show consistency of measurements of 200 iterations of 3 most demanding requests that we were able to construct. Measurement precision is sufficient for the purpose of selecting better performers by genetic algorithms. IE baseline represents consistency of measurements of 200 iterations from common Internet Explorer 11 request.

Our HTTP request project was eventually cancelled. Contrary to our hypothesis, we were unable to find a sequence of HTTP header fields and respective values whose CPU requirements would be significantly higher than computational requirements of standard browser requests. Apparently, the impact of HTTP header fields processing on a standard Apache webserver is negligible, with the exception of Accept-Encoding field. Accept-Encoding field value can significantly increase CPU consumption when zip compression is required. However, such behavior is default for common HTTP requests.

3.3 Slow Attacks

Although HTTP requests research project provided negative results, the framework proved to be both simple and effective. Currently we are adapting it for searching for slow DoS attack opportunities in common protocols. An inherent property of most network protocols is to proceed with next phase of protocol only when previous phase was completed. Meanwhile, each side has to allocate its computational resources for any (half-)open connection. Under normal circumstances, connections are closed only when they are no longer used, either explicitly with a close message or when an inactivity timeout expires.

For example, a webserver can only send response when full HTTP request has been received. The Slowloris attack exploits this behavior by sending a never-ending HTTP header. Therefore, the request is never finished and connection socket is effectively and indefinitely blocked for other users. If the attacker is able to maintain sufficient number of simultaneously opened connections, legitimate users cannot reach the webserver.

We intend to use our framework to identify:

- Time points of message exchange where artificial delays can be introduced into the communication.
- Separation points in each message where the message can be divided in two or more smaller messages (i.e., packet fragmentation).

Evaluation criterion will be the maximum time how long it takes to complete a given sequence of messages (e.g., how long it takes to finish a SSL handshake).

4 Open Questions

We are looking for inputs and both good and bad experiences in the following areas:

- What are other limitations of virtual environment and what are the differences between virtual environment and physical hosts? How to get consistent results from virtual environment running on different hardware?
- What protocols and applications may be interesting from the viewpoint of slow DoS attack verification?
- Where to get an extensive list of available HTTP request header key-value pairs?
- Are there any similar network security evolution frameworks? Is it possible to modify existing generic fuzzers such as Peach [4] to support genetic algorithms and (D)DoS principles?

5 Summary

We have designed a framework that can be used both for automated enhancement of existing denial of service attacks and for generating new types of DoS attacks. The framework shows potentially serious discrepancies between virtual and physical environments. We initiate a discussion on hidden caveats of experimenting in virtual environment testbeds.

Acknowledgment. Authors would like to express gratitude to the members of Centre for Research on Cryptography and Security of Masaryk University for their valuable ideas and feedback. Special thanks go to Andriy Stetsko, Zdenek Riha and Marek Sys. Petr Svenda and Vashek Matyas were supported by the Czech Science Foundation project GBP202/12/G061.

References

1. Chertov, R., Fahmy, S., Shroff, N.B.: Emulation versus simulation: a case study of TCP-targeted denial of service attacks. In: Testbeds and Research Infrastructures for the Development of Networks and Communities. TRIDENTCOM 2006, p. 10. IEEE (2006)
2. Mirkovic, J., Benzel, T., Faber, T., Braden, R., Wroclawski, J., Schwab, S.: The DETER project: advancing the science of cyber security experimentation and test. In: Proceedings of IEEE International Conference Technology HST, p. 17. IEEE, November 2010
3. Schmidt, D., Suriadi, S., Tickle, A., Clark, A., Mohay, G., Ahmed, E., Mackie, J.: A distributed denial of service testbed. In: Berleur, J., Hercheui, M.D., Hilty, L.M. (eds.) HCC9/CIP 2010. IFIP AICT, vol. 328, pp. 338–349. Springer, Heidelberg (2010)
4. Eddington, M.: Peach fuzzing platform (2011). 30/11/2014. http://peachfuzzer.com

Challenges of Fiction in Network Security – Perspective of Virtualised Environments (Transcript of Discussion)

Radim Ostadal[(✉)]

Masaryk University, Brno, Czech Republic
255508@mail.muni.cz

Good morning, my name is Radim Ostadal, and today I would like to provide you with a brief overview of our research about the GANET project, particularly about the issues and difficulties we faced regarding the virtualized environment. GANET is an abbreviation for Genetic Algorithms in Networks. It is a framework for rapid evolution of denial-of-service attacks. Its core components are virtualization and genetic programming. Why are we using virtualization? Because it's quite easy to restore the whole environment into some kind of pre-defined initial state. It's easy to distribute the computation to different hosts and to repeat the experiments. We use a very modular system; it's able to employ different applications, different crypto libraries, and even different operating systems. For output we are interested in enhancement of current denial-of-service attacks, fine-tuning of its parameters, and in the identification of new vulnerabilities in tested components. We are using VirtualBox as our virtualization platform, Python as a scripting language, and pyvbox libraries as an API to VirtualBox. So far we run two scenarios that I will be speaking about later. The first is about the modification of HTTP headers, and the second is about the slow SSL attack. Before I start speaking about the virtualization issues, I would like to spend several minutes on the genetic programming as one of our core concepts, and on the GANET framework itself. The genetic programming is evolution-based methodology inspired by biological evolution. Its main target is to find a program or an algorithm that performs some specified objective. It is a generate-and-test approach that starts with a generation of a random population of candidate solutions. Each of those candidate solutions is evaluated using a fitness function that assigns a fitness value. Based on those fitness values, the worst part of a solution is discarded. We employ genetically inspired operators like mutation or crossover on the better part. Through these operations we prepare the next generation (the next population of candidate solutions), and we evaluate them again by a fitness function. We repeat the process until we find a sufficiently good solution. For GANET project we've defined several fitness functions that we can use. For example, the total processor time used by the application or the total length of connection establishment in case of slow SSL attacks. We also considered the usage of random access memory and the total volume of transmitted data. It's possible to use any application-specific performance counters and I am sure you would be able to think about several others regarding the denial-of-service attacks.

© Springer International Publishing Switzerland 2015
B. Christianson et al. (Eds.): Security Protocols 2015, LNCS 9379, pp. 152–157, 2015.
DOI: 10.1007/978-3-319-26096-9_16

Arash Atashpendar: You compare all the fitness values of all the individuals in the population with each other. You don't do any sort of selection? For instance a binary tournament?

Reply: Yes, you compare the fitness value; let's say we are using the total processor time.

Arash Atashpendar: But that's for two individuals. For two individuals, you assign this fitness value according to the criteria that you have there.

Reply: We take the better part from all individuals, and based on those individuals we prepare the next generation. The framework itself consists of two main parts. It's the management host and the computation host. The management host is responsible for distribution of particular sub-tasks to computation hosts and for the genetic programming itself. The computation host consists of two virtual machines. One is for the attacker, and one is for the victim. Some data is changed and we perform the measurements. From the beginning, the whole process starts with this generation of population of candidate solutions, that are distributed to multiple computation hosts. At the computation host side we restore the environment to the pre-defined state, we execute the attack itself, and perform the measurements. Those measurements are returned back to the management host where they are evaluated, and the process continues. The first scenario that was evaluated on GANET project was the HTTP request header scenario. Main target was to enhance the HTTP GET flooding attack by modifying the HTTP request headers. At the beginning we used 31 most commonly accepted header fields with six corresponding values each. One value was generated as completely random, one value had a wrong syntax, and four of them should have been accepted by most of the current web servers. For the evaluation we used the total processor time consumed by the application web server. And to get some reasonable data, we had to repeat every request by 10,000 times.

Keith Irwin: So you only used the processor though, you didn't look at the network bandwidth?

Reply: In this case we used the processor time. Regarding the results, the measurements were OK, and they were acceptable even for the evolution. The distribution of values was also good; there were even some clusters that you will see in a second. On the other hand, unfortunately, we weren't able to find any request header combination that consumes significantly more processor time than our baseline presented by an Internet Explorer request. In the end, the scenario was cancelled. We also observed a lot of issues regarding the virtualization. The first one was the relation of our results between virtualization and the physical world. In fact, we were able to find the requests that consume more CPU time than the baseline. Here you can see Best 1, 2, 3 on the graph. The baseline is presented by an Internet Explorer request in blue color. Those requests consume constantly more CPU time than the baseline request. Also, you can see some random requests. You can see those clusters that I was talking about. The cluster between 0 and 10 is formed by malformed requests that were answered with code 400. The key problem was that we tried to move from the virtualized environment to the physical world. We performed the same experiment on two physical computers, and the result was that the Best 1 and the Best 3 consumed a very similar CPU time as the baseline. The Best 2 consumed even a little less CPU time than the baseline. So this was kind of a problem. The fact that the values changed the order was really the problem. There are issues, I would say, we could have expected. It's a problem with the measurement precision that is much better in the physical world than in the virtualization. It also depends on the size of the website we have requested. Also, we had incomparable results running the virtualisation on the different hardware configurations. It was sometimes very hard to interpret some results, some anomalies, because we had to find what the key influencers were. Was it a configuration of the virtualization, a hardware configuration, a configuration of the host machine or networking on the host machine? What's even more interesting is the interpretation of the data. This is something we really didn't expect. You can see three cases: A, B, C. In case A, we were interested in the communication between the physical machines that host one virtual machine. In case B, we were interested in communication between two virtual machines running on one physical computer. Finally in case C, we were interested in the communication between two separate virtual machines running on two separate physical computers. We installed all of those systems with the same operating system, and with the same version of Wireshark application. We executed our experiment and we captured all the traffic into the Wireshark. Then we compared the results and the interpreted the data by the Wireshark. The fact is, it was quite different. For example, in the case B we had identical clones of the same virtual machine, on the same hardware, but the traffic looked very different. There were different packet and segment sizes; there were missing HTTP respond packets, missing response codes, and so on and so on. When we dug deeper, we realized that the underlying data was the same, but the interpretation of the Wireshark was very different.

Alastair Beresford: I could see why the packet sizes and the segment sizes would be different, but I dont understand what HTTP response codes are different, because its at the application layer.

Reply: Yes. It was really strange, and when you make some, lets say, observations, or if you conclude some results based on those interpretations of the data, they could be wrong, they could be very wrong. And it highly depends on which machine you will choose to interpret the data. Another interesting issue. Again, you can see several cases. In the case 1 we connected two physical computers through the WiFi. In the case 2, we connected the same computers with a cable. In the case 3, we had two virtual machines running on two physical computers connected through the WiFi. And the same is in the case 4 with the only change of connection with the cable. We were interested in two values. One was the CPU time used by the application, like the web server, and the second value was the duration of the experiment how long it took to send and receive those 10,000 HTTP requests and responses. There are the results. I might say that we were not able to interpret those results and to decide what the key influencer was.

Just the simple comparison: if you look at cases 2 and 4, the CPU time is 15 times bigger. Yes, this might be acceptable, because we are moving from the physical world into virtualization. We would expect the same in cases 1 and 3, simply because the only change is using a different physical connection. But you can see that the duration is completely different, and the CPU time is bigger only three times. The same comparison is in cases 1 and 2 where the duration was bigger with the WiFi, but it's significantly bigger in the case when we were using the virtualization. Even in case 3 we observed that the web server created around 10 additional sub-processes to handle the HTTP requests. Those are the measured values. Unfortunately, I cannot give you the interpretation of this behavior. Based on our experiments, we are more or less sure that those issues are connected to the high volume of transmitted data between those machines. During this experiment, it was 2 to 3 GB, so it was quite a lot. When we moved to the second scenario (the slow SSL scenario), there are no such big volumes of data transmitted, and we didn't observe those issues again.

Keith Irwin: On the previous slide in scenario 3, were the virtual machines communicating with, say, a USB WiFi LAN card?

Reply: No.

Keith Irwin: Or were they communicating with virtual networking in the host machine?

Reply: In the case of WiFi it was two physical computers and an access point, and it was a virtual card directly on the machine. The aim of the slow SSL scenario is to find as long SSL handshake as possible. What we are doing is to simply open a layer 4 socket and take the SSL handshake client messages. Then we break those messages into several parts, and introduce a different delay for every part. The target is to have as long handshake as possible. So far, there were no issues like in the previous example. This was the main part of the presentation. About the further development, we've spent most of our time on the application level. We've tested mostly web servers. We would like to move to other protocols and move from the application level to test the crypt libraries or even some operating system features. We are considering an implementation of the whole concept as a man-in-the-middle between a legitimate client and a server. Also, we are considering using the evolution for intrusion detection systems evasion techniques of similar attacks. During the slow SSL scenario we found some vulnerable applications, and we would like to test how they will react on a certain volume of open connections, even without sending any data. There are three parts to questions open for discussion. The first part is about the scenarios themselves. In the first scenario, we are interested if you are aware of any list of HTTP request header fields and corresponding values. It is quite easy to find a list of the possible field names, but to find legitimate values for those field names is not an easy task. For SSL scenario, do you know about any other applications that might be interesting from the viewpoint of a slow SSL attack? The second part is about the framework itself. Are you aware of any similar frameworks? We are considering the use of the generic fuzzers for our goal.

The third part is about the virtualization itself. What are your experiences with some other virtualization issues? What are your experiences with running the virtualization on different hardware configurations to get some consistent results that would be comparable? That's all from my side and I would be happy for any questions or any answers for those questions.

Tom Sutcliffe: We do a lot of work with hypervisors and we've observed that you're very dependent on effectively how good your hypervisor is at emulating network connections. I mean, it's a very intensive thing to do, and it very much depends on the implementation, for one of our products we switched from using a generic emulator E1000 network interface with JL virtual environment would give you to a custom para-virtualised driver, and we saw that throughput go through the roofs by making that change, it had a dramatic effect on a lot of different things. And we use that for some of our files for file access between host and guest, and it made huge differences to performance. And so it's, this type of thing is very sensitive to exactly how good your virtualisation system is. So yes, it's, you're kind of confirming, yes, you're seeing the same sorts of problems there, and possibly Virtualbox is not one of the greatest. I mean, they might be kind of slow, and steady, and reliable, in their emulation, but they're probably not designed for performance in a free product.

Petr Svenda: So the main problem with the hypervisor is the amount of data bits?

Tom Sutcliffe: That fits.

Reply: And in the new approach, is it so much better?

Tom Sutcliffe: We were generally looking for sort of throughput performance, we weren't tracking any other particular characteristics, I can't think of any offhand. We weren't interested specifically in anything like that, other than just latency went down as well, but yes.

Mark Lomas: Earlier on in your talk you were talking about choosing between algorithms by sort of comparing the fitness function. If you do that you're likely to find a local maximum rather than a global maximum. There may be several different virtualisations and one of them might only cause a small increase, but a combination of them might cause a different increase, and you might actually be willing to suffer a decrease in order to find a subsequent larger increase.

Reply: Yes, I understand. But even when stuck in local maximum, random mutation and crossing with other candidate solutions should be able to get us out of it.

Petr Svenda: Your result is based on the way how you make progress in one population. There are many different ways how you can progress it. For example, you can have multiple different populations that are independently probing the current search space in parallel, and only from time to time they are exchanging their knowledge. So there are ways how we can prevent to stay in local maximum.

Olgierd Pieczul: So the actual values of HTTP headers and their impact, you would have much different result depending on what actual server you're running, and what you're running behind the server. With Apache and HTML page behind it there may be not that much effect as with Flash and PHP behind it, because there would be much more processing those headers.

Reply: Yes, we ran, for this first scenario, Apache with a very default installation. For the second scenario, we are using many different web servers with many different configurations.

Petr Svenda: Can you give us some preliminary results on the slow SSL scenario?

Reply: Yes. For the slow SSL it seems that a lot of web servers enforce no timeout, or they enforce a for every particular SSL segment. So if you break one SSL handshake message into 100 parts, and you introduce a five minute delay for every part, the server still handles the connection without sending RST or FIN segments. It turns out that for the Apache case, the vulnerability was actually fixed in some previous version, but with a newer version, this vulnerability is back again. There are a lot of web servers that do not present basically any timeout for the whole handshake.

Daniel Thomas: How many concurrent handshakes can a server cope with before it experiences problems?

Reply: Unfortunately, I don't have any answer for this now because we are not that far. This is what we plan to do in the following weeks.

Device Attacker Models: Fact and Fiction

Jiangshan Yu and Mark D. Ryan[✉]

School of Computer Science, University of Birmingham, Birmingham, UK
{jxy223,m.d.ryan}@cs.bham.ac.uk

Abstract. According to standard fiction, a user is able to securely keep long term keys on his device. However, in fact his device may become infected with malware, and an adversary may obtain a copy of his key. We propose an attacker model in which devices are "periodically trustworthy" — they may become infected by malware, and then later become trustworthy again after software patches and malware scans have been applied, in an ongoing cycle. This paper proposes a solution to make the usage of private keys by attackers detectable by using public transparently-maintained logs to monitor the usage of long-term secret keys.

Keywords: Attacker model · Key compromise detection · Key usage monitoring

1 Introduction

Encryption is an important way to ensure the confidentiality of digital messages exchanged between a sender and recipient. However, there is a gap between the assumption that a secret decryption key is only known by the owner, and the fact that some party (e.g. an attacker) may have a way to gain access to the secret key. The security of existing systems cannot be guaranteed if the secret key is abused after being exposed to other parties.

Currently there are no effective methods to detect improper usage of a decryption key. In the scenario where symmetric key encryption is used, the communication parties share the same secret key for encryption and decryption, and the key owners cannot detect the condition that the key is compromised. Similarly, in the scenario where public key encryption is used, the key owner who has a pair of public key and private key for message encryption and decryption, respectively, cannot detect when his private key has been compromised. So, in both cases, the secret key owner is not prompted to revoke the compromised secret key or take other actions. Hence, the security that the system guarantees is broken until the secret key has expired. However even when a key is expired or revoked, the new key may also become compromised.

For example, if a user Alice wants to send a private message to a domain server Bob through the transport layer security (TLS) protocol, then Alice needs to obtain Bob's public key certificate, and encrypt and send a session key establishment message to Bob to establish a session key. Here, even if Alice has

© Springer International Publishing Switzerland 2015
B. Christianson et al. (Eds.): Security Protocols 2015, LNCS 9379, pp. 158–167, 2015.
DOI: 10.1007/978-3-319-26096-9_17

obtained an authentic copy of Bob's TLS certificate, if attacker Eve can somehow compromise Bob's private key corresponding to the certificate Alice obtained, then Eve is able to block and decrypt the cipher text from Alice, and play man-in-the-middle attacks by providing her Diffie-Hellman (DH) key establishment contributions to both Alice and Bob, without being detected.

Detection of private key usage when the private key is a signing key rather than a decryption key is easier, because security can be leveraged from the party that needs to verify and accept the signature. Such a party is a witness who saw the usage of the compromised signing key. Certificate transparency (CT) [1], accountable key infrastructure (AKI) [2], enhanced certificate transparency (ECT) [3], and distributed transparent key infrastructure (DTKI) [4] are existing key infrastructures that can audit such key usage by recording signatures (i.e. certificates) into the log.

Inspired by the above mentioned systems, we propose a mechanism to convert systems that use long-term symmetric or asymmetric keys for encryption to systems that can detect unauthorized usage of long-term secret keys, thus providing a better security guarantee.

2   Overview

The Problem. Suppose that Alice wants to send a confidential message m to Bob. Suppose Bob has a public/private key pair for encryption; that is, he has a decryption key dk_B which is kept private, and an encryption key ek_B which is published. According to the common practice, Alice encrypts the message m using Bob's encryption key ek_B, creating a ciphertext. If only Bob has possession of dk_B, then only Bob can decrypt the ciphertext (Fig. 1). However, if dk_B has become exposed to an attacker, then the attacker can decrypt the ciphertext. Bob has no reliable way to be aware that this has happened. Similarly, when Alice and Bob want to use symmetric key encryption for exchanging sensitive messages, the same problem would occur.

Adversary Model. Almost all systems (e.g. Windows or Mac OS) and protocols (e.g. TLS) suffer from an undesired life cycle of security:

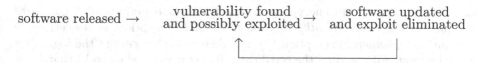

Based on the above life cycle of security, we consider an adversary who can get all (long-term and short-term) secrets of victims. The attacker can repeatedly fully control the victim's device, but each time only for a limited period.

For example, after the implementation of a system (e.g. Windows) or a protocol (e.g. SSL) has been released, there are always some undiscovered security flaws. During the time that the system has not been patched, an attacker is able to get some credential (e.g. a secret key) out from a victim's device. However,

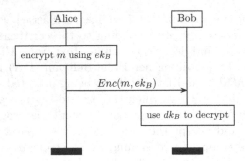

Fig. 1. An abstract representation of the original protocol. In this protocol, Alice encrypts message m by using Bob's public key ek_B, and sends the cipher-text $Enc(m, ek_B)$ to Bob who can decrypt it by using his private key dk_B.

some time later, the security flaw is discovered and fixed, and the attacker's ability to control the device is removed.

The security properties we want to guarantee are *forward secrecy* and *auditable-backward secrecy*. *Forward secrecy* is a property ensuring that the plaintext of transmitted messages will not be exposed if the associated long-term secret is compromised in the future; and *auditable-backward secrecy* is a property ensuring that if a compromised long-term secret will have exposed future messages, then the genuine owner of the long-term secret can detect the fact of the compromised secret.

The Solution. The basic idea is that the commitments about the usage of long-term private keys are recorded in a log. This enables a key owner to monitor the usage of a key. For a long-term asymmetric secret key, the commitment could be a signature, or a proof of knowledge. For a long-term symmetric key, the commitment can be done by using symmetric key encryption, or by using hash-based message authentication code (HMAC). In this paper, we focus on the asymmetric key case. (The protocol for symmetric key case is similar to the protocol for asymmetric key case.)

In more detail (as shown in Fig. 2), Bob uses a long-term public/private key pair (sk_B, vk_B) for signature generation and verification rather than for message decryption and encryption, respectively. Bob periodically[1] generates an ephemeral key pair (ek, dk) for encryption and decryption, issues certificate *cert* on the ephemeral encryption key ek, then publishes *cert* in the log. After receiving *cert*, Alice verifies the certificate. If *cert* is valid, she checks that (a) it is present in the log; (b) it is not revoked; and (c) the log is maintained in an append-only manner. If all checks succeed, she encrypts sensitive message[2] m using ek, and sends the ciphertext to Bob encrypted with ek. Bob should check

---

[1] The period is the lifetime of the generated S. It will be denoted as δ in the security discussion section. The smaller the δ, the more secure the system is.

[2] Note that m could be any sensitive data, such as a session key which will be used to encrypt messages in this communication.

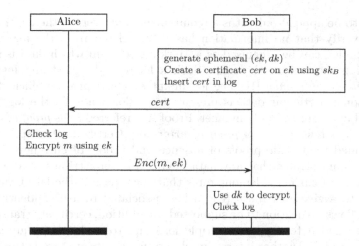

Fig. 2. The basic idea of our proposed system. In this abstract protocol, Bob has a pair (sk_B, vk_B) of long term keys for signature generation and verification, and Alice is assumed to have the verification key vk_B. Bob generates an ephemeral key pair (ek, dk) for encryption and decryption, issues certificate $cert$ on the ephemeral encryption key ek, then inserts the certificate into his associated log. After receiving $cert$, Alice checks that it is present in the log, then sends a message m to Bob encrypted with ek. Bob checks in the log whether there are certificates for his keys not generated by him.

in the log whether there are certificates for his keys not generated by him. Bob also keeps his own record of generated certificates, and periodically, he verifies that the certificates published in the log agree with his own record of published information.

Remark. Alice and Bob can be simultaneously online (synchronous) or the receiver may be offline at the time the sender sends a message (asynchronous). In the case they are synchronous, Alice can get the ephemeral certificate from Bob directly. In the other case, Bob can upload a pre-generated ephemeral certificate into a third party where Alice will get the ephemeral certificate from. Since Alice can verify the log, the third party is not required to be trusted. In addition, it is not necessary for Bob to be the log maintainer. He can ask some third party to maintain his log. The log maintainer is also not required to be trusted. Moreover, instead of generating a single key pair and putting it in the log each time, Bob can generate a sequence of keys, and publish the digest (with constant size) of the sequence into the log. The digest can be a hash chain of the sequence, or the root value of a hash tree that records the sequence. In this case, Alice needs to ask an additional proof that the obtained certificate is an element of the sequence that is presented by the digest. The proof is with size $O(\log n)$ if a hash tree is used, where n is the size of the tree (so the size of the sequence).

Properties of the Log. The security of the method requires that an attacker cannot remove information from the log. To achieve this, the log is typically stipulated to be append-only. It is a requirement that users of the log (including Bob) can verify that no information has been deleted from the log. For this purpose, the log can be organised as a Merkle tree [5] in which data is inserted by extending the tree to the right. Such a log was designed and introduced in *certificate transparency* [1]. The log maintainer can provide efficient proofs that (A) some particular data is present in the log, and (B) the log is being maintained in an append-only manner. Proof A is referred to as *proof of presence* and proof B is referred to as *proof of extension*. Certificate transparency has been extended to provide proofs of absence and proofs of currency [3]. Proof of absence demonstrates that any data having a given attribute is absent from the log. Proof of currency demonstrates that some data is the latest valid data associated to a given attribute (e.g. a key associated to a user identity). The extension allows revocation to be supported. In addition, certificate transparency has been extended to support multiple logs and to avoid the requirement of trusted parties [4]. Another interesting design for certificate logs is through the checks-and-balances proposed in AKI [2] and its enhancement (ARPKI [6]).

It is also a requirement that the log maintainer cannot maintain different versions of the log which it shows to different sets of users. Gossip protocols are a known technique to ensure that.

On the other side, user privacy is a concern. This can be solved by letting the log maintainer sign each user identity, then put the hash value of the signature into the log (rather than putting the user identity directly into the log). The signature scheme used should be deterministic and unforgeable, as suggested in a previous work [7]. Hence, users that have the recipient's identity can request the signed user identity from the log maintainer, and verify it; but an attacker who has downloaded the entire log cannot recover the identity of users, based on the unforgeability of the chosen signature scheme.

In addition, it would be difficult to maintain and sync all logs in real-time when they become huge, as any delay of receiving new update queries would make logs inconsistent. One countermeasure is to update the log periodically rather than update it in real-time. In this arrangement, log maintainers collect all new log update queries, synchronise with each other, then update the log when all log maintainers have agreed the same set of data for update.

Security Discussion. We assume that all sets of pre-generated ephemeral keys of the same user have the same lifetime, denoted δ. In addition, according to our adversary model, we know that Bob's system can be compromised repeatedly, but not continuously.

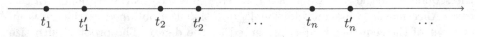

Fig. 3. An example time-line. In this time-line, for all $i \in \{1, 2, 3, \ldots\}$, the security of Bob's system is broken between time t_i and t'_i.

Suppose Bob's system is compromised at time t_i and fixed at time t'_i, for $i \in \{1, 2, 3, \ldots\}$ (see Fig. 3). If the attacker recovers the plain-text of messages exchanged at a time outside of the period $(t_i - \delta, t'_i + \delta)$, then the attacker has to leave some evidence in the log, which can be readily detected by Bob.

3   Application to SSH

Key usage detection can be applied to many scenarios where the secret keys might be compromised or escrowed by other parties.

For example, in existing identity based signature [8] systems, the identity provider can derive any of its client's signing key, and therefore can sign on behalf of any of its client. Similarly, in existing identity based encryption [9] systems, the identity provider can derive any of its client's decryption key, and therefore can decrypt a ciphertext sent to the client without informing the client [10]. One way to solve the above key escrow problem is adopting multiple private key generators to perform the secret generation process. So, no single party can derive the client secret. However, this solution is hard to achieve in practice.

In the case of identity based signature, key usage detection mitigates the problem in another way by recording all signatures in the public log, and allows a member to detect that an unauthorised signature (e.g. one made by the identity provider) has been issued. Key usage detection cannot be directly used to solve the key escrow problem in identity based encryption; however, it can solve the problem indirectly — instead of using identity-based encryption, the client obtains an identity based signing key from the identity provider, generates an ephemeral key pair for decryption and encryption, signs the ephemeral encryption key by using the obtained signing key, and publishes the signature into the log.

Each time when a sender wants to send a message, the sender downloads the signed encryption key of the recipient, verifies the signature according to the recipient's identity, and encrypts and sends the message if the verification succeeds. Note that the log does not need to be universal. Depending on the scenario, logs can be maintained by identity providers, by clients, or by third parties.

In this way, clients can use the user identity to verify the signed encryption key, can detect the un-authorised usages of the long-term signing key, and are still be able to do encryption.

Another example is to detect un-authorised key usage in the Secure Shell (SSH) protocol. Secure Shell (SSH) is an industry-standard cryptographic network protocol for securing data communication, and is one of the most popular cryptographic protocols on the Internet. It aims to establish a secure channel over an insecure network in a client-server architecture, connecting an SSH client application with an SSH server. SSH users can easily setup (or connect to) an SSH server on (resp. by using) their devices, e.g. a desktop or laptop, for secure communication and data sharing. The server authentication is done by using public-key cryptography, and the client authentication can be done by either using public-key cryptography-based authentication, or using password-based authentication.

We explain the problem and illustrate how to apply key usage detection to SSH as follows.

3.1   The Problem

The encryption used by SSH is intended to provide confidentiality and integrity of data over an unsecured network, such as the Internet. However, if the private key of a server (or a client) is exposed to an attacker (e.g. because the presence of security bugs [11] or malware), then the security is broken. In practice, the server operator or the client may periodically perform malware scans, operating system upgrades, and software updates. These actions will bring their devices back into a trustworthy state again. Unfortunately, since all secret keys are already exposed to the attacker, the regained trustworthy state will not help victims to regain the security.

To regain the security, victims need to revoke their keys and generate new ones; however, since they do not know when compromises take place, they are not motivated to revoke their keys. In practice, it is impractical to ask users to revoke their keys and distribute new ones after every security update. So, the security is broken from the time that a server or client device is compromised onwards.

3.2   The Solution

usage detection (KUD) can be applied to SSH to reduce the damage of a compromised long-term secret key. It could be applied to the client side, or the server side, or both. We present an abstract protocol to show how to apply KUD to the server authentication of SSH. In the modified protocol, the server has a pair of long-term signing key and verification key. The modified protocol has the same assumption as SSH, namely the clients have an authenticate copy of the server's long-term public key.

The server creates a public log, then periodically (e.g. every δ-long period)

Step 1. generates a pair of ephemeral decryption key and encryption key;
Step 2. issues a certificate on the newly generated decryption key;
Step 3. inserts the certificate into the log; the new certificate will revoke previous ones;
Step 4. verifies that all certificates in the log are generated by itself.

For server authentication, the user sends to the server a request for establishing a new communication session, together with a digest of the log that s/he has observed in the last session. The server sends to the user the currently valid certificate together with the following proofs:

– (**Proof of currency**) the received certificate is present in the log and is the latest valid certificate of the server; and

– (**Proof of extension**) the current log is an extension of the log that he has previously observed.

The user verifies the above proofs, then uses the obtained certificate to authenticate the server. All participants of the protocol should also run gossip protocols to detect inconsistent logs.

3.3   The Public Log Structure and Proofs

Similar to CT [1], the public log in this example is simply organised as an append-only Merkle tree. However, we do not have the problem that CT faces — namely, to efficiently prove that a given certificate in the log is not revoked. This is due to the fact that our log only contains one valid certificate, which is stored in the rightmost leaf of the Merkle tree. This design allows a log maintainer to efficiently generate the proof that a certificate is the latest one in the log (by proving the certificate is located on the rightmost leaf of the Merkle tree), and this proof can be efficiently verified by users. (We will detail it later.)

Log Structure. The public log is organised as an append-only Merkle tree. A Merkle tree (a.k.a. hash tree) [5], is a binary tree where each non-leaf node is labelled with the hash of the labels of its children; and where each leaf is labelled with some data. Suppose a node has two children labelled with hash values h_1 and h_2. Then the label of this node is $h(h_1, h_2)$. Relying on the properties of the hash function, a Merkle tree allows one to provide cryptographic proofs of the existence of some data in a Merkle tree; the size of those proofs is logarithmic in the size of the tree.

An append-only Merkle tree is a Merkle tree where the only allowed operation is appending a new data by extending the tree to the right side. Append-only Merkle trees allow one to provide cryptographic proofs that one version of the tree is an extension of a previous version; the size of those proofs is also logarithmic in the size of the tree. Note that an append-only Merkle tree is a not necessarily a balanced tree. The two trees in Figs. 4 and 5 are examples of append-only Merkle trees. Figure 4 shows a Merkle tree containing data items $d_1, \ldots, d_5$ stored at the leaf nodes. Figure 5 shows a larger Merkle tree containing data items $d_1, \ldots, d_7$.

Proof of Presence. To demonstrate that a hashed certificate d_3 is present in the tree T, it is sufficient to provide the additional data $d_4, h(d_1, d_2), d_5$, i.e. one data item per layer of the tree. The verifier can then verify the correctness of the root hash $h(h(h(d_1, d_2), h(d_3, d_4)), d_5)$.

Proof of Currency. To prove that a hashed certificate d_7 is the latest one in the tree T', the prover issues the proof of presence of d_7 in T'. The verifier verifies the proof, and additionally verifies that the path of d_7 is of the form $r \cdot r \ldots r$, where r is the path from a parent node to the right child node.

Proof of Extension. Proving that one Merkle tree extends another can also be done in logarithmic space and time, by providing at most one hash value per layer. For example, to demonstrate that T' in Fig. 5 is an extension of the one in Fig. 4, it is sufficient to provide the data $d_5, d_6, \mathsf{h}(\mathsf{h}(d_1, d_2), \mathsf{h}(d_3, d_4)), d_7$.

For user authentication, we can use a protocol similar to the protocol for server authentication. One difference is that rather than only recording the server's key usage (i.e. the ephemeral certificate) in the log, the usages of all clients' secret key should also be recorded. Since the log will contain one current valid ephemeral certificate for each user, we need to use a log structure that supports efficient proof of currency when the log contains multiple valid certificates of different clients. One possible log structure is proposed in ECT [3].

3.4 Security Discussion

Let's assume that an attacker has compromised the server at time t such that $t_i \leq t \leq t'_i$ for some i, has obtained secrets stored on the server, is remaining in possession of the obtained secrets, and wants to attack at time t' such that $[t'_i + \delta \leq t' \leq t_{i+1} - \delta]$ (see Fig. 3).

Let δ be the lifetime of ephemeral key pairs. We have that in a time period $[t'_i + \delta, t_{i+1} - \delta]$, all server authentication messages are protected by using an ephemeral encryption key that is generated when the device is secure. So, the attacker does not have the possession of the corresponding ephemeral decryption key, and the previously compromised decryption key does not help with the decryption.

Since clients will only accept an ephemeral certificate if it is accompanied by proofs of presence in the log, the attacker has to either sign a key and put it in the log, or generate a fake log and fool the user. The former will be readily detected by the server, and the later will eventually be detected by gossip protocols, as the inconsistent logs will be detected by users.

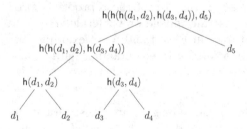

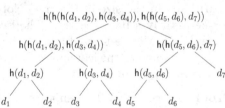

Fig. 4. Append-only Merkle tree T containing 5 leaves.

Fig. 5. Append-only Merkle tree T' containing 7 leaves. It is obtained after appending d_6 and d_7 into T by extending T to the right.

4   Conclusion

Unauthorized usage of secret keys may occur if computer systems are attacked and keys are compromised, or if backup keys or escrowed keys are abused. This paper proposes a direction in which we aim to make the usage of private keys detectable. This is achieved by using public transparent logs to monitor the usage of long-term secret keys.

We consider an attacker able to periodically compromise secret keys, for example by introducing malware onto a device. We assume that the legitimate user will eventually gain control of the device again, by applying software patches and malware scans and clean-ups.

Acknowledgements. The authors thank Ross Anderson, Daniel Thomas, and all other attendees of International Workshop on Security Protocols for their comments and discussions. Jiangshan Yu is supported by the EPSRC project EP/H005501/1.

References

1. Laurie, B., Langley, A., Kasper, E.: Certificate Transparency. RFC 6962 (Experimental) (2013)
2. Kim, T.H.J., Huang, L.S., Perrig, A., Jackson, C., Gligor, V.: Accountable key infrastructure (AKI): a proposal for a public-key validation infrastructure. In: The 22nd International World Wide Web Conference (WWW 2013) (2013)
3. Ryan, M.D.: Enhanced certificate transparency and end-to-end encrypted mail. In: Network and Distributed System Security (NDSS) (2014)
4. Yu, J., Cheval, V., Ryan, M.: DTKI: a new formalized PKI with no trusted parties. CoRR abs/1408.1023 (2014)
5. Merkle, R.C.: A digital signature based on a conventional encryption function. In: Pomerance, C. (ed.) CRYPTO 1987. LNCS, vol. 293, pp. 369–378. Springer, Heidelberg (1988)
6. Kim, T.H., Gupta, P., Han, J., Owusu, E., Hong, J.I., Perrig, A., Gao, D.: ARPKI: attack resilient public-key infrastructure. In: ACM CCS (2014)
7. Melara, M.S., Blankstein, A., Bonneau, J., Freedman, M.J., Felten, E.W.: CONIKS: A privacy-preserving consistent key service for secure end-to-end communication. IACR Cryptology ePrint Archive (2014)
8. Shamir, A.: Identity-based cryptosystems and signature schemes. In: Blakely, G.R., Chaum, D. (eds.) CRYPTO 1984. LNCS, vol. 196, pp. 47–53. Springer, Heidelberg (1985)
9. Boneh, D., Franklin, M.: Identity-based encryption from the weil pairing. In: Kilian, J. (ed.) CRYPTO 2001. LNCS, vol. 2139, pp. 213–229. Springer, Heidelberg (2001)
10. Al-Riyami, S.S., Paterson, K.G.: Certificateless public key cryptography. In: Laih, C.-S. (ed.) ASIACRYPT 2003. LNCS, vol. 2894, pp. 452–473. Springer, Heidelberg (2003)
11. CVE: Common vulnerabilities and exposures list. https://cve.mitre.org/cve/index.html. Accessed on Feb 2015

Device Attacker Models: Fact and Fiction (Transcript of Discussion)

Mark Ryan[✉]

University of Birmingham, Birmingham, UK
m.d.ryan@cs.bham.ac.uk

Good morning everyone, this talk is about the question of what happens when your device gets contaminated by malware and becomes under the control of adversaries. Is there anything that you can still do in the way of security functionality, for example, could you still make use of cryptographic keys that are stored on the device. Now that sounds a bit hopeless, because clearly if the device is controlled by an adversary then the adversary also has those keys and can make copies of them and so on. But I hope to convince you that there's a few weak results that you can get in that space. So the assumption that we make, the kind of fiction in this space is that we have a device that's capable of long-term storage of crypto keys, and of course that's the underlying assumption of cryptography. Crypto systems assume that you have a secure private key, but as we know, this is difficult to achieve in the face of security, vulnerability and malware. So I'm not going to spend much time convincing you that there is a lot of malware out there, and a lot of security vulnerabilities, here is a recent graph of security vulnerabilities in 2014, and as you can see, all of the major systems are affected. And then in the mobile space the amount of malware is of course increasing as mobiles become more penetrating, and more vulnerable.

So what options do you have if you're a user, well, one of the most common things that you do of course is apply security patches, and there are standard ways to do that on all the major operating systems of course. But applying security patches is of course not enough, because if an adversary has exploited a vulnerability he or she may have inserted a backdoor on your system, and then merely applying patches may not get rid of backdoors or malware that you already have there, and you may have to do some scanning in order to remove malware. And all of the major operating systems, including the phone based ones, do have products for scanning for malware. Now I'm not sure how widely they are used, or how effective they are, as we've seen several times in this workshop, there is malware that can avoid such things of course, and it's just a kind of arms race, and malware can be persistent, rootkits and so on can avoid that. But anyway, as we know, there is this kind of game in which people try to apply patches, and try to remove malware, in the hope that they will restore their device into a secure state.

So that's what I just want to look at for a moment, the kinds of state your device can be in. So the fiction, if you like, is that your device is secure all the time, and that's the fiction that you have to, to some extent, believe in at the moment if you store private keys, and cryptographic keys, on your device,

B. Christianson et al. (Eds.): Security Protocols 2015, LNCS 9379, pp. 168–177, 2015.
DOI: 10.1007/978-3-319-26096-9_18

you have to believe that it is secure all the time, otherwise there's no point in having keys on it. The effect may be as bad as this one, that it starts off secure, and then at some point some vulnerability is exploited and some malware is inserted, and then it remains broken, from a security point of view, indefinitely. So that's the kind of worst case. But it may be that you can actually achieve this case, and this is the case I want to focus on in this talk, where it starts off secure, then some vulnerability is exploited, so it's in a broken state. But then you do apply patches, and you do malware scans, and other things like that, and you do succeed in restoring it to its secure state for some time, until another vulnerability is exploited and it's in a broken state again. And you have this cycle of fixed/broken, fixed/broken, and the question then, the question for this talk is, is there anything that you can say about this kind of situation where you have keys stored on this device.

Now one assumption that I want to make is that you do not regenerate keys each time, because that's the reality, we do software patches, but we do not regenerate SSH keys, or the other keys, or passwords, or other secrets that we store on the device. So once it becomes broken we have to assume that the attacker now has those keys, even though you restore it to a secure state, so you're in control of the device again, but the attacker still has the keys that he stole from the last time it was broken. Is there anything you can do with such a device, is there any security guarantee that you can get? So, well that's why we call this key usage detection, because the idea is, could you detect that some adversary is using your key, is there some way in which you could detect that your key is being used because it got compromised by some adversary in the past, under the assumption that your device is now back into a secure state, or what we might call periodically secure, because as I showed you on that picture, it's secure/insecure, secure/insecure.

So here's this sort of goal that we have, but this is this situation in which Sally, a sender Sally, is sending a message to Robert, I'm not going to explain the protocol first, I'll show you that in just a moment, but Sally is S for sender, is sending a message to Robert, and she's using public key cryptography so Robert has some kind of public key. I'm not explaining how that works just in this slide, that's in the next slide. The goal that we're looking for is that Robert's device is periodically compromised in the way that I've described in this way down here, and suppose a message is sent by Sally at time t, then what we would like is that Robert can detect the attack, so suppose that plaintext is obtained by the attacker, so something has gone wrong, and we want to know when Robert could detect it. So Robert could detect this attack provided his device, at the time that the message was sent, was well within a trustworthy state, by which we mean that it's within the trustworthy state bound by t'_j and $t_j + 1, -$ and $+\zeta$ on each side, and in fact ζ is going to be the lifetime of an ephemeral key, so it's, ζ is a parameter that you can define as part of the protocol. So that's the kind of goal that we want to have, in other words, when you are in a secure state, even though the attacker may have your long-term keys and may use them, you are able to detect that has happened in a way that I'm about to make precise here, because I'm going to explain the protocol.

So just to set out the protocol, let me just remind you of the normal situation that we have. When a sender, Sally here, sends a message to a receiver, Robert, here, using a long-term key of Robert, so let's suppose that's an encryption key, namely Robert has an encryption key pair, then what Sally does is she takes her message and she encrypts it with Robert's public key, she sends that to Robert, Robert can decrypt it with the corresponding private key, the decryption key, and that's how things normally work. So for comparison, this is how we want things to work here. Robert will still have a long-term key, which I'm going to, his secret path is sk_r, and his public path is vk_r, so it's a signing key, this is the signing part, then there's a corresponding verification key. So what he does is, he generates an ephemeral encryption and decryption key, certifies the public part of the ephemeral key with his long-term key, and then sends this certificate to a log maintainer. So I'm assuming that there is a log maintainer who is offering certain kinds of services, and those are going to become clear, but roughly speaking, it's based on the idea of certificate transparency, which you may know, it's an idea in which certificate maintainers can be transparent about the way they are handling certificates, because they have a log, it's based on a Merkle tree, and they are able to prove the presence of certificates in that log.

So here Robert sends the certificate to a log maintainer for insertion into the log, and then sends the certificate to Sally. Sally requests from the log maintainer a proof that this certificate is present in the log, and is able to verify this proof, then encrypts the message using ek, sends that to Robert, and he is able to decrypt that. He also periodically checks the log to make sure that all the certificates that are in there are ones that he put there. Now one question is, is he able to do that, because he has to rely on his own record of what certificates he has put in there, and that's where the assumption that his device is back in a secure state. So if he's back in a secure state, and if previous keys have expired, because all these ephemeral keys have a lifetime, then he does have an accurate record of what is in the log that really is his, and he's able to detect keys that he did not put there, that maybe were put there by an adversary who compromised his key in the past.

So that's the kind of basic protocol, and now what we want to describe is a bit more, there's many applications you can put there, I mean, any situation in which you use public key cryptography. The one thing that we've been working on is a message system, a multiple device, multi user message system, then there are other applications like SSH and so on, we'll talk a bit more about some of those. Let me hand over to Jiangshan.

Jiangshan Yu: One of the most important things here is the log maintainer, he's not required to be trusted because in this system, as you can see, Robert, the key owner, actually needs to verify the log to see if his local copy is the same as what the log has recorded, to detect any unauthorised key usage in the log. And if the log maintainer is able to tamper with the log, to modify the log, then the key owner won't be able to detect any misusage of that key, right. So the question we need to make sure is the log maintainer can't tamper with the log, or if the log maintainer has modified the log then the key owner, or other clients, is able to detect this kind of misbehaviour. And another thing worth mentioning is, from this protocol it looks like the sender and the recipient have to be online at the same time, actually it's not, because all you need to do is to put some commitment, like a certificate into the log, and the log maintainer is always online, so they can be asynchronous online, such that the sender can ask the log maintainer for the certificate and use that certificate to send a message, which would be useful for the messaging protocol like email.

We are going to look at how can we construct the log in such a way that the behaviour of the log maintainer will be transparent. And also for the log structure, we will introduce two parts, two different parts. The first part is, how can we build a log for a single customer, which could be useful, in some scenario like for SSH, each server could maintain it's own log, so there is only one customer, that's the server itself. And in some scenarios like email applications, or messaging applications, you might want a log maintainer, like an email service provider, which can actually maintain the log for all email users, so that everyone can send secure emails, and will still be able to detect the usage of his key, like PGP key. And in that case we need a log for multiple users, so we will introduce these two different structures for these two purposes. And one main component of the log, is what we call ChronTree, which is actually a Merkle tree, also known as hash tree, and all data items in the tree are ordered chronologically, and stored only in the leaves.

So in this case let's assume that data item C_i is the certificate, and what do we want from this structure is, we want to have a few different proofs, so the log maintainer can give the client several proofs. The first proof we want to give is some data is in the log, so when the client asks the log maintainer, hey, how about this certificate, whether it's in the log, the log maintainer should be able to prove it. And the second thing we want to prove is the log is append-only, so the log maintainer is not able to tamper with the log, to modify the log, so it should be append-only, only extended to the future. And to give also the third proof, the data you obtain is the latest one in the log, because you might want to have certificate revocation, or some updates, and you want to make sure the data, the certificate you have from the log maintainer is indeed the latest valid one of the target domain or the user. And to give the proof of what we call proof of presence, namely a certificate is present in the log, and you can simply give the proof like, let's make an example of C_7, let's say the 7th certificate, by the way this is the log structured for only one client, we only have this tree, and what you do is, you take the certificate C_7 and you pick one data item, one value, in each layer, like C_8, $h_{5,6}$ $h_{1,4}$, and $h_{9,10}$, to reconstruct the root value of the tree. So one assumption is the root value of the tree is known by the clients, and that's what we need to verify later to verify it is append-only, so you can only extend the tree, and the client needs to know this value to get the proof.

For one client this will be an update of his certificate, and you only extend the tree to the right side, so the log only grows, and the log maintainer is able to prove something is inside of the log with size $O(\log n)$, and to prove the log is append-only, namely give you a later version you can prove that this version is extended from a previous version you have observed. And let's take the example here, so you've got a log with only six certificates here, and the log here has 10 certificates, so if you want to prove the second one is an extension of the first log, then all you need to give is very similar to the proof of presence, you give several hash values which are able to prove, to reconstruct the root value of the first version, of the earlier version, and several hash values to reconstruct the later version, so have several overlaps. And as our example here, all we need to give is just two hash values here so that you can reconstruct the first log. And we have these two values that would be here that you need to give several more values to reconstruct the second log, and there would be $h_{7,8}$. So you are able to go back to here, and you already know $h_{1,4}$ so you can all the way go up until the root value of the latest log, and you can prove it is append-only, so it's only extended from the previous version, and all certificates in the previous tree have been really included in the later version.

So, that is the extension proof. Another thing we want to prove is some data is the latest one for the client, and because this is the case for only one client, that means all certificates are belonging to the same client, let's say to an SSH server, so all we need to do is ask, what is the size of the log with the hash value. Then you ask the proof that, the certificate you got is the right most leaf of the tree, so that's the latest one. To verify it, you only need to verify the path to reconstruct the tree, and the path should only contain like R for right. So the path would be from the root all the way going down only to the right, and that is the latest certificate for this client in the log, because there is only one client in this case.

Keith Irwin: The proof of append-only is not really proving the log is append-only, it's proving something has been appended since the last time that person asked for a copy of the log.

Jiangshan Yu: Yes. If you have the first version and you have the latest version you can prove all the way through and it's only in O(log n).

Keith Irwin: Right, if you have all the versions along the way. But if your device is bad some of the time wouldn't you not be able to get it during those time periods?

Jiangshan Yu: What we can guarantee is that if the device is in a trustworthy state then you are able to detect it, but if the device is compromised then you cannot detect it, and the proofs are not reliable. In fact, you don't even need to get the proofs because we assume the attacker can get everything from your device, including all keys, so the attacker don't even need to tamper with the log because she can just take the ephemeral secret key and decrypt everything.

Bruce Christianson: Are you assuming that the log isn't kept by the attacker? I know you're saying the log doesn't have to be completely trustworthy.

Reply: We're assuming that the log maintainer is, if you like, malicious but cautious, so it's somebody who might be an attacker, but also has an interest in convincing you that he's not the attacker.

Bruce Christianson: He wishes to be honest seeming.

Reply: He wishes to be seen to be honest, that's right, yes.

Patrick McCorry: I was just wondering as well, does the public key need to remain private, or can anybody use public keys. If the public key is being public, maybe we do expect something like block chains like in Bitcoin.

Reply: I don't see what advantage you'd have by using the Bitcoin log there.

Patrick McCorry: Well I was assuming you have a trusted third party, and the block chain might help.

Reply: We have no trusted third party, we have a party whose malice can be detected, whose bad actions can be detected. Think of that like Google, you're a customer, and they've got an interest in doing what they say they're doing, because you're going to be able to detect if they don't. So, I think the Bitcoin log solves the problem of how can you have a log maintainer who has no secret, there's no private key, who just has proof of work, but we don't need that in this case, because you can assume that the log maintainer is willing to take responsibility for the log and be accountable to you for any deviations.

Jiangshan Yu: Here we are going to introduce the multiple clients case, for which you need the ChronTree as explained before while we also need another data structure, which we call LexTree, and which is also a Merkle tree, but everything is ordered in the lexicographic order. In this way you can still give the proof like the proof of presence, so something is inside of the log because of the hash tree, but you cannot give the proof of extension, because if you modified the tree then you cannot get the extension with $O(\log n)$ proof. But a different proof you can get is that you can actually prove something that is not in the log, something is absent from the log.

Ross Anderson: Yes, but that comes at a cost of scaling difficulty. Now the initial idea is great, and if you have got Alice and Bob having a tree maintained for the two of them, then you could clearly detect any, if Charlie pretends to be Alice to Bob, or whatever. But if you want a tree that encompasses everybody in the known universe so that you can assure yourself that for all values of Willy, for example, Willy hasn't probably communicated with Alice, then you need to have everybody, which means that the tree will be constantly growing, it's an engineering nightmare. What your interval will be, how do you replicate it, how do you deal with people joining, and so on and so forth. So I can see this working in clubs, I can see this working at a corporate scale, but not at a global scale.

Reply: I'm sure you're absolutely right, there are lots of difficulties to worry about that. We did look at the kind of sizes of proofs you would get with a very large number of users, 10^9, with a log having been run for a very long period, like 100 years, and it seemed reasonable. Now I know that those calculations can be a bit deceptive, and of course there will be loads of engineering problems.

Ross Anderson: I'm thinking about that if I'm working for Google and trying to engineer this. I've got 10^9 active users and every body's sending 10^3 messages a day, that's awful and there are a lot of stuff I've got to manage, and I've got to replicate it across three data centres, and so on and so forth.

Reply: I guess Google does seem to be capable of doing that sort of thing, if you look at the staff they have, I don't know if there were any particular challenges here.

Ross Anderson: Well the particular challenge is, if I'm running the live copy in a data centre in Finland, which goes down, and I backup in, and I recover from Oregon 40 s later, what happens if I was suddenly missing 40 s worth of the world's traffic. There's some very interesting challenges here if you want to actually build this.

My point is this is brilliant for a fair or a small conspiracy. Alice and I could use this to communicate with each other with easy certainty that we would detect if you filched one of my keys and pretended to me to be Alice or vice versa. But scaling this up is not just a matter of proof size.

Reply: Well it's a good point, but maybe we could find a niche application. I mean, I guess it's going to be niche anyway.

Bruce Christianson: There's a second latency parameter, which is how long or how quickly you've got to agree what the canonical version of updates was. And so the question, on the one hand you've got the threshold, how far inside the safe period was the protocol run, but the requirement that Bob becomes aware that he's been spoofed, the question is, how quickly does that have to happen, is there also a restriction on how rapidly Bob has to discover that. And that's a very different engineering practice.

Reply: Yes, that comes back to your question about who is actually maintaining the log, and on what kind of guarantee do you want. You might be willing to tolerate that you will discover attacks within a number of days. Now normally we would regard that as a far too long period, but if you think about my Gmail account, which I've had for 10 years now, and if I could be sure that everything up to the last 10 days was secure, and that this 10-day window was advancing all the time, that would be quite a reasonable guarantee.

Audience: So is there a trade-off here between sort of security or integrity and privacy in the sense that this is a public log that anyone could read, and therefore all the communications between all parties are all authorable or similar from this log.

Ross Anderson: The log is certainly coercible.

Reply: We're not aiming to protect metadata. Your communications provider can already hand over all this communications data, and we're not able to protect that with this system. I don't think it makes it any worse, and in particular it doesn't expose it to third parties, I think you can arrange the logs so that third parties can't to see what your communication data is. But of course the log maintainer and the communications provider can, but can anyway.

Bruce Christianson: You're alright for the actual, the data itself, because you can just store hashes and the log keeper never needs to know the real thing, but your proof that there isn't anybody between Alice and Bob relies on Alice and Bob being, if you like, plaintext metadata.

Reply: Not necessarily, no, they could be the hashes of Alice and Bob and I just show there's nothing between the hashes.

Bruce Christianson: Yes, and show the lexicographically closest hashes.

Daniel Thomas: But the problem with that is that the thing you're hashing hasn't a very high entropy so you can now brute force that there is no Charlie because you know what the hash of Charlie is.

Reply: Yes, we looked at kind of salted hashes, but I think essentially you're right.

Daniel Thomas: I don't think there is any way of doing that.

Reply: Yes, so there is a privacy leak there possibly.

Audience: If Ross and Alice have got some conspiracy, how would Ross know I had taken his key and used it to send a message to Alice?

Ross Anderson: Well because Alice's log would have an instance of somebody communicating to Alice using my key, it would not be present on my version of the log, and if our versions of the log are unified by being in the same Merkle tree then Alice and I see different sizes of Merkle tree, which is an instant alarm. Alternatively, we could have our own Merkle trees, and another meta protocol that compares them from time to time. So you can see this is a public key version of the key update.

There's another approach to this, which is instead of wanting to put everything in a Merkle tree you simply have counters, so every time I certify a new transient key, that is my key number X, then if you have one central authority, all it's doing is keeping types of the number of times that my signature key has been used to sign a transient key, and all I then have to do is to ensure that my version of the counter is in sync with its version of the counter, and you can arrange the thing so that the log would break otherwise. That means that you could then have multiple central authorities, and I could use multiple keys and multiple central authorities, which gives me some of the privacy, and this perhaps breaks the scaling problem bottle-neck.

Reply: But I'm not sure how, I mean, just counters alone doesn't sound fine grained enough to get the security property that you want.

Ross Anderson: My intuition is it would be enough for me, if I know that here's my signing key, 567 times. Google agrees, because he's only ever seen it 567 times, then we're sorted, and then you don't have the fine-grained time dependency. It's OK if a data centre goes away for a few hours and then comes back.

Keith Irwin: If the attacker is the one maintaining the counter, don't they just not implement the counter when they signing your keys.

Bruce Christianson: No, what the attacker would have to do is to substitute his use of, he'd make one use of the certificate, and he'd make sure that the log never saw one of your uses.

Ross Anderson: So you then have to have another protocol for why the person who had been spoofed by interacting with me, thinking it was me when it wasn't, would have to have some means of going at sometime and checking to see whether his, certificate number 460 was actually certificate 460.

Bruce Christianson: Yes, although a hash chain would do that. Does Bob have any way of knowing that the message is from Alice?

Jiangshan Yu: No, not in this protocol. The idea is that the sender only accepts a certificate if it's really in the log, and the log can be proved to be an extension of the one the sender previous observed. So that everything is only going forward, and the thing the sender actually uses is indeed in the log, hence the recipient can verify it.

Bruce Christianson: Sure, but what I'm thinking of is that the ephemeral public key really is public, anybody can see it.

Jiangshan Yu: Yes. This is the point.

Ross Anderson: So perhaps one wants to compare this with two other existing systems, your bog standard Diffie-Hellman, where your signing keys used to sign an ephemeral public key, which gives you the recoverability, but not the proof that your key wasn't abused. And then there's something like the defence messaging system, where you generate a number of signed ephemeral keys and you put them in a central government server, and then anybody wanting to send you a message goes and fetches one, so there the government has the counter saying, Virgil was sent 167 messages last month, and if one of them goes astray you've then got relative, you've got mechanisms local to your unit which enable you to at least sound the alarm. So what this is doing is pointing out whether there are neat ways to generalise this and scale up the protocol.

Jiangshan Yu: Actually the log, it isn't just this LexTree. The log is a Chron-Tree that recalls the whole update, and each update is a new LexTree, which recalls the latest keys of the user.

Ross Anderson: So from the security economics point of view what you want is for everybody to maintain their own log, because the incentive is that I want to make sure that if my laptop suffers a transient compromise, and my signing key is used to sign a transient key that somebody then uses for some nefarious purpose, then I get to find out about it. So I have the incentive to maintain my ChronTree, and to help the LexTree to be quite honest, and then have some check-pointing mechanism whereby anybody who thinks that they have communicated with me can come and verify that against the value regularly published by the server.

Reply: But the problem is how can you maintain your own ChronTree when your device has been compromised for your device.

Ross Anderson: Well exactly so, if I recover and I then find that my device has been compromised.

Smearing Fingerprints: Changing the Game of Web Tracking with Composite Privacy

Sandy Clark[✉], Matt Blaze, and Jonathan M. Smith

University of Pennsylvania, Philadelphia, USA
{saender,mab,jms}@cis.upenn.edu

Abstract. As web browsers have become more sophisticated at blocking unauthorized attempts to track users' online activities (incognito mode, Do Not Track), so too have trackers evolved to trump those protections. In many cases, these new forms of tracking have turned features designed to improve the web experience against user privacy. We focus on browser fingerprinting as a testbed for proposing a novel approach to fighting back for user privacy. By intercepting and obfuscating the information generated by browser fingerprinting scripts, the user not only frustrates the attempt to track their movements, but, more importantly, wider usage degrades the quality of trackers' databases, reducing the effective entropy of their metrics, thereby yielding privacy gains for all users, not just those employing this method of obfuscation.

1 Introduction

Successful tracking of users on the web yields significant financial upside for advertisers. Not only can advertising be specifically targeted for individual users or groups, but tracking information is a gold mine when sold to data brokers.

In the face of ubiquitous tracking (evercookies, flash cookies, misuse of HTML5 localStorage, cookie syncing, and canvas fingerprinting being among the current crop of offenders), methodologies designed to provide countermeasures like browser privacy modes and Do Not Track have proliferated, putting users on the defensive in maintaining online privacy. Today's approaches to unwanted web tracking require users to disable browser features, or install browser extensions that do the same.

Blocking degrades user experience and, what's more, it does little to hamper advertiser's data collection; in the case of canvas fingerprinting, there is little that can be done to block the practice, since the element is part of the HTML5 specification and a feature of many interactive, responsive websites. Indeed, two of the largest players in the browser privacy extension field, AdBlock Plus and the EFF's Privacy Badger don't, at time of writing, offer any countermeasures at all to canvas fingerprinting [1,2]. Acar et al. [3] noted that by far the most pervasive deployment of canvas fingerprinting comes from media web-tracking firm AddThis, making up 95 % of canvas fingerprinting scripts on websites in the top Alexa 100K.

© Springer International Publishing Switzerland 2015
B. Christianson et al. (Eds.): Security Protocols 2015, LNCS 9379, pp. 178–182, 2015.
DOI: 10.1007/978-3-319-26096-9_19

Fingerprint Characteristic usage			Screen				Navigator									HTML element		
Alexa Rank	Domain	colorDepth	height	pixelDepth	width	mimeType	platform	language	userAgent	appName	vendor	appCodeName	appVersion	plugins	getBoundingClientRect	offsetWidth	offsetHeight
6,444	bunte.de	0	1	0	1	0	0	2	8	0	0	0	0	1	2	205,115	202,909
8,039	nzz.ch	3	34	1	34	4	4	4	176	5	0	0	5	4	248	187881	187,349
191	spiegel.de	2	4	0	4	0	0	0	15	3	0	0	1	4	7	154,265	149,293
4,037	wistia.com	1	2	0	2	0	0	3	81	0	0	0	0	0	0	109,347	109,299
1,369	zeit.de	0	4	1	4	0	0	2	8	3	2	0	0	5	1,318	70,025	72,268
8,894	menards.com	0	0	0	0	0	0	0	3,783	0	0	0	0	0	37	43,847	38,715
4,754	groupon.fr	0	0	0	0	0	0	0	1	0	0	0	0	0	15	150,717	36,627
7,488	xinmin.cn	0	0	0	1	0	0	0	70,380	0	0	0	3	0	4,426	34,229	31,996
2,320	celebuzz.com	2	55	0	55	4	2	0	23	0	0	0	0	4	326	27,831	27,779
1,370	wetter.com	4	30	0	30	6	1	8	18	5	0	0	1	7	212	22,578	21,764

Fig. 1. The most common characteristics used to fingerprint browsers from [4].

Nikiforakis et al. [4] observed that the key value behind fingerprinting methodologies is linkability, denoting the ability to connect the same fingerprint across multiple visits. They explored the effectiveness of a set of randomization policies concerning "DOM properties of interest" to trackers, such as plugin configurations, screen sizes, color depth, and available fonts.

Figure 1, from Nikiforakis et al., shows the usage of various common fingerprinting characteristics in the wild. Experiments using their tool PriVaricator proved that it is possible to deceive several fingerprinting providers with regard to plugins. From our own observations, browser plugins and system fonts are the two characteristics that appear to convey the most fingerprinting information, with user-agent strings next, conveying about half as much information.

EFF's Panopticlick browser fingerprinting tool gives insight into the number of bits of entropy provided by each of the most commonly used identifying characteristics (notably not including canvas fingerprinting). At the time of this writing, they have collected 5.06 MM unique browser fingerprints, corresponding to 22.27 bits of entropy across all the attributes measured. Browsers with large numbers of plugins or system fonts appear to provide 22+ bits of entropy from those single characteristics alone. With a larger sample size, the combination of these largely independent characteristics should provide even more identifying resolution. Indeed, Nikiforakis et al. experienced a significantly lower level of success deceiving one fingerprinting provider whom they believe relied on system fonts more than plugins.

2 Discussion

The results from these experiments make it clear that focusing on a single characteristic is insufficient to disrupt linkability in all cases. We observe that AddThis' fingerprinting script uses more indicators than those proposed by Mowery and Shacham [5] for canvas fingerprinting (see Related Works), and combines this with a range of other fingerprinting attributes, yielding far more entropic differentiation.

It is well understood, that fingerprint uniqueness is a requirement to yield linkability, and that obfuscating enough information should remove the ability to distinguish one user from another. We propose subverting linkability by providing false information not only as a means to hinder tracking, as Nikiforakis et al. suggest, but also claim that this will force the advertisers to shoulder the cost burden of developing countermeasures.

By intercepting certain calls and replacing the output with an equivalent composed of random data, we generate two effects: firstly, we avoid the need to block elements altogether by simply obfuscating the signal generated by a user's unique browser configuration with a plausible-yet-false replacement signal; secondly, injecting plausible fake data into trackers' databases degrades the value of these repositories by reducing the entropy of data gathered. Reducing the number of bits of information available to the tracker to identify users offers composite privacy even for those not employing our proposed strategy. Since some combinations of fingerprinting attributes deliver more information than others, we propose choosing a group of attributes which combined provide sufficient obfuscation, composing that set anew at each tracking instance and varying its members to further interfere with attempts to correlate any tracking information received.

However, the key insight of our approach is not merely to enhance user privacy, but to shift the cost of developing new tracking methods to the 'attacker', without the user incurring the cost of a degraded experience. We are proposing disrupting fingerprint linkability as a first experiment for changing the rules of the game when it comes to users' control over their internet footprints.

We hypothesize that trackers are in the 'honeymoon' of data collection right now. Currently there's no way to feed them false data: as noted, the existing methods of evading tracking only use blocking. Trackers likely are not expending the extra effort to validate incoming data, but they are likely to use more than one browser characteristic for their fingerprinting, which makes them more prone to the methodology we propose.

3   Related Work

Mowery and Shacham's 2012 paper on canvas fingerprinting [5], written before the HTML5 specification was finalized, outlines the practice of canvas fingerprinting from a theoretical point of view, detailing the method of examining rendered text and WebGL scenes. They noted the consistency and high-entropy of the results from canvas rendering in identifying users. Moreover, they realize the potential difficulty of blocking canvas fingerprinting, noting that "any website that runs JavaScript on the user's browser can fingerprint its rendering behavior."

In a paper presented at ACM CCS 2014, Acar et al. [3] outlined a study of advanced web tracking mechanisms, which formed the inspiration for this work. They detail the practices employed by advertisers using canvas fingerprinting and some possible mitigation strategies. They note that only the Tor Browser offers successful defenses against canvas fingerprinting by prompting the user on each canvas read attempt and returning an empty image when the user denies the request. This doesn't much hinder trackers' efforts, but rather limits their data collection to a set of sites trusted by the user. Our approach differs in that, rather than simply decreasing the volume of data trackers are able to collect, we are instead proposing a methodology to actively devalue the information gathered.

Eckersley's paper introducing the EFF's Panopticlick 'device fingerprinting tool' [6] finds that when fingerprinting a standard set of browser measurements, the distribution contains over 18 bits of entropy. Notably, Eckersley finds that many of the common technologies intended to be privacy-enhancing have the unexpected side-effect of making fingerprinting easier (e.g. User Agent spoofing and Flash blocking browser extensions). This finding validates our assertion: defences against browser tracking have thus far had the goal of enhancing privacy on a user-by-user basis. This fails because use of these defences is itself an identifying factor.

Besson et al. [7] approach the mitigation of fingerprinting with a similar definition of privacy: bounding the probability that a tracker is able to identify a given user. They examine algorithms for randomizing the output of fingerprinting scripts through the tradeoff between efficiency and usability. However, their approach explicitly declines to consider the effects on the trackers' databases; their definition of quantitative information flow (QIF) concerns the information distance between probability distributions of attackers' beliefs before and after an observation. We instead chose to examine the large-scale phenomena associated with polluting trackers' information collection.

4   Conclusion

The single-user approach to defending user privacy fails to account for the ongoing game-like nature of the interaction between the tracker and users. Only by disrupting linkability in the trackers' databases, can users change the dynamics of the game and force the tracker to shoulder the cost of developing countermeasures to reestablishing linkability. The corollary to this that inserting phoney data into trackers' stores yields a defence analogous to herd immunity. A composite privacy, instead of hiding in the noise, like 'Where's Waldo' [8], one becomes a 'Master of disguise' generating lots of different noise each time one is viewed. By decreasing the entropy of the information gathered by canvas fingerprinting for a large enough segment of browsers, and by combining this technique with other forms of deception, trackers will be forced to abandon data for all users gathered this way: the difficulty in discerning which entries are valid and which are spoofed will exceed the expected value of those bits of information. Since trackers are still in their 'honeymoon' phase, we hypothesize that a large-scale, rapid adoption of these techniques would force trackers to react in response to the users' 'move' putting the users ahead in the game.

The immediate follow-up to this paper will be to attempt to quantify the financial impact of pursuing this approach to user privacy on the bottom line of trackers. We are seeking to answer: what does it take to put an economic value on each of these tracking indicators? In what combinations the loss of individual details the most costly for the trackers?

References

1. Privacybadger. Found at: https://www.eff.org/privacybadger/#does_it_prevent_fingerprinting
2. Adblockplus. Found at: https://adblockplus.org/blog
3. Acar, G., Eubank, C., Englehardt, S., Juarez, M., Narayanan, A., Diaz, C.: The web never forgets: persistent tracking mechanisms in the wild. In: CCS 2014, 3–7 Nov 2014
4. PriVaricator: deceiving fingerprinters with little white lies. Found at: http://research.microsoft.com/pubs/209989/tr1.pdf
5. Mowery, K., Shacham, H.: Pixel perfect: fingerprinting canvas in HTML5. In: Proceedings of the Workshop on Web 2.0 Security and Privacy (W2SP) (2012)
6. Eckersley, P.: How unique is your web browser? In: Atallah, M.J., Hopper, N.J. (eds.) PETS 2010. LNCS, vol. 6205, pp. 1–18. Springer, Heidelberg (2010)
7. Besson, F., Bielova, N., Jensen, T.: Enforcing browser anonymity with quantitative information flow. In: Research Report (2014). https://hal-univ-rennes1.archives-ouvertes.fr/file/index/docid/984654/filename/enforcing.pdf
8. Handford, M.: Where's Waldo, US edn. Little Brown & Co., New York (1987). ISBN #978-0316342933

Smearing Fingerprints: Changing the Game of Web Tracking and Differential Privacy (Transcript of Discussion)

Sandy Clark(✉)

University of Pennsylvania, Philadelphia, USA
saender@cis.upenn.edu

So we're calling this one composite privacy, and we want to talk about shifting costs for web tracking or for user tracking. In previous years at this workshop we've presented ideas on a variety of subjects. We've talked about what we can learn from locks and from safecracking, we've talked about eVoting systems, we talked about the benefit you get from the attackers learning curve early in a vulnerability lifecycle, we've talked about the P25 radio systems and the problems with those, and we've also presented information on the lessons you can learn from casino security, and from military strategy. And to the casual observer it might seem that as we jump from topic to topic that we've got the researcher equivalent of ADHD, but we can discuss the truth of that over lunch. But I claim that all of the things that we've been researching, we've been actually looking at the same problem, exploring the same idea, and trying to answer the same questions in every ecosystem we can find.

What we're trying to do is, we're trying to understand the parameters and the rules that control how actors in systems move. And thinking about security as a system, and particularly as an ecosystem, has led us to some interesting insights. For example, an action on the part of one actor in a system, whether that action is deliberate, accidental, or reactive to some other action, results in the other actors in the system doing something, making some move. There is co-evolution in these systems. Second, the systems are changing, and they're changing all the time, and in particular the members and the actors change. Competition for things like 0-days has never, never been fiercer than it is right now, and you only have to look at last week's pwn2own, to see the amount of permutation and convolution that an attacker had to go through to get through Chrome's protections, and yet it still worked. But Chrome had evolved these protections because of other attacks. There are different stressors in these ecosystems, and the amount of resources, and the types of resources, and the competitors are all changing.

Thirdly, these systems always have a blood in the water attack, or at least a blood in the water effect. Every time that someone finds something new other people begin looking in that area. Heartbleed led to Shellshock, which led to a complete renaissance in the way that, in people examining old code, old libraries, to look for new weaknesses. Fourth, all of these new systems, every single device we've got, the iPod that's in my case, and the iPad that's in my satchel, and the phone that I'm wearing, the other two phones that are in my hotel room,

B. Christianson et al. (Eds.): Security Protocols 2015, LNCS 9379, pp. 183–194, 2015.
DOI: 10.1007/978-3-319-26096-9_20

my laptop, all have to communicate with each other, and they all have to communicate with every other device that you're carrying, and they've got to communicate with my smart meter at home, and they've got to communicate with my smart fridge, and they're going to have to communicate with my smart car, which is going to communicate with a smart traffic light, which are going to communicate with the police force, etc., etc. Everything interoperates, everything has to be compatible with everything else, everything is always backwardly compatible with everything else, and that complexity is only increasing. So in terms of an ecosystem we're talking about an ever-expanding universe, and we're talking about a system that is dynamic, it is never static.

And so that leads us to the first of our fictions. This is not a software engineering problem. It can't be solved with software engineering. Software engineering has worked for 30 years to make sure that our planes stay up in the air, they don't fall out of the sky. If we want to do purchasing, we can send our money in little bits all over the world, and that all works. If we want reliability, and we want functionality, software engineering is the way to go. But there aren't software engineering models that account for living, intelligent actors in the system, for that we're going to have to look somewhere else. And we think that this is best thought of by looking at game theoretic models, in particular evolutionary game theoretic models. And when you start thinking about things and trying to understand them as a game, you realize that there may be some security scenarios, and some privacy scenarios, where this is the only reasonable approach.

So let's get to the first, the one that I want to consider today, which is, browser fingerprinting and user tracking. This is so phenomenally easy to do, and there are so many different methods to do it, that everybody is doing it. Companies like AddThis, which is not the biggest, but it's a quite popular one, or Axicon, which is the biggest, have, AddThis in their last financial report, claimed that they get more than 1.8 billion unique customers monthly. They have 14 million websites, and this allows them not only to collect data but to link it from person to person to person. Each individual company that's doing this is sharing with other companies, or partnering with other companies. Axicon partners with the Guardian, with the New York Times, with Yahoo, with BlueKai, with Cisco, with Facebook, and this allows them not only to get the information from their own trackers, but to build a database of information from everybody else's trackers, and then figure out how to do that. And once they do that they they categorise it. Let's see, if we take a second and show this to you, this is a 242 page sales brochure of the different categories, and the different classifications, and sub-classifications, and sub-sub-classifications that Axicon will put your people into. And just their package for advertising to GameDay is six pages long. And the problem with what they're doing, their secret source that they sell, is this ability to uniquely identify their users, their customers, in such a way, that they can then classify them so deeply, and then sell that classification.

So an interesting question is, how much information do you need to actually uniquely identify a person. And there are 7 billion people in the world, so that's 33 bits of entropy that you need. So in DefCon 18, which was six years ago, EFF presented Panopticlick, and one of the, this is their table, at that time they found that the most useful of the eight characteristics that they looked at were things that plugins and fonts. At that time you got about 15 bits of entropy from plugins and about 14 from fonts. That's changed, six years later you now get 22 bits from plugins. And when you combine that within something like postal code, it's pretty easy to uniquely identify somebody. But it's worse than that, you don't have to use

Audience: Quick question, does this problem gets better or worse for mobile devices?

Reply: If you're using Android it gets worse, if you're using iPhone it gets better. It's because iPhone is not customizable, you can't put Flash on your iPhone, and because there are a hell of a lot of iPhones out there you get a form of herd immunity, but there are other ways to track you on your phone, and if you don't manage your cookies you're screwed anyway on whatever phone. But you don't even have to use just browsers fingerprinting, you can use things like hardware, the clock skew is another way to do this, and on CCS history and font lists. And if you want to play around with this go to browserspy.dk, there are 50 different tests you can run on your own browser to see how you're fingerprinted, and a lot of it is downloadable. And then it gets even worse than that. You can do your best to try and manage your privacy online, you can delete your cookies, and you can block JavaScript, and you can not install Flash, but there are evercookies, or super cookies, which use your own local storage methods to save whatever cookies someone has managed to create in such a way that even when you delete them as frequently as you can, they can rebuild themselves, they re-spawn, they're like zombies. And then, when they re-spawn, if third parties are cookie syncing, then they're sharing the user ID from one cookie to another, so you've deleted your cookie but it's re-spawned it, and someone who had your old cookie can then coordinate that with a new cookie and keep an entire history of what you've been doing. And then it gets worse than that.

There were two papers at TCS last winter about canvas fingerprinting and the consensus from both of them is that you can't block this. You can do what Tor does, which is send back a blank page, but you can't block it. It's fundamental to the specification of HTML5. And then it gets worse than that. EFF found that those people who were trying to do everything to block tracking tended to be highly technical people and really understand how the system worked, and that made them fingerprintable. So the very thing that you're using to defend yourself might be the things that set you apart from the crowd. And then of course anything that you do to protect yourself breaks your interwebs. You lose your ability to use the web with all this design function. So we don't want to do that, we can't do that. So what's the game that we want to play here. Maybe we can't block them, can we fool them instead? And when you think about security this way, not just for web privacy, but you can think about a lot of problems like this. There are a lot of new strategies and tactics that you can come up with, so let's see if you can.

Well it turns out, yes. Sending misinformation actually does work. Microsoft Research created a tool they called Prevaricator, and they loaded it on top of

Chrome, they found that doing it as a plugin, it didn't work as easily because there are so many different browser setups. So for their experiment, Prevaricator is an interceptor that intercepts the fingerprinting JavaScript calls, and then sent back misinformation according to a randomized strategy. Sometimes they would send back this much, and other times they would send back another, and it did work, they were successful much of the time. And we did the same thing for canvas in a very rough, not ready for primetime and not well-tested fashion, so please don't ask to borrow it, but yes, it also works for canvass.

The thing is, this is a game, right, and if it were this easy it wouldn't be any fun to play. There are problems. One of the problems that Prevaricator had was that you could lie, but how much you lied, and how often you lied, determined things. If you sent back too little misinformation, of course they could link you to something else. If you sent back too much information, it still might set you apart in a way, you might lie that you had more fonts than you did, which then makes you uniquely identifiable. So there's some balance in here that has to be found. And EFF found that when people were trying to play with Panopticlick, and see what different setups would result in, that they would get different fingerprints, but they could guess 66 % of the time, and their guesses were right 99 % of the time. So if not enough changed, or if the wrong things changed, then you were still uniquely identifiable. So these are the rules of the game we're going to have to mess around with. The other thing is that we have to make sure that in the game we play we don't cost the user too much. They can't have a lot of technical knowledge, and we don't want to destroy their experience on the internet. So these are all the things we're going to have to think about in this game that we develop.

Now the reason we changed the title is because it's, in the written proceedings we referred to this as differential privacy, and that isn't technically correct. In differential privacy you add noise to your outliers so that they don't stick out as much, and essentially do this, and that's not what we're proposing here. The game we want to play here is this kind of privacy. We want to make you an outlier every single time you return to a site. We want to make you a different outlier each time you return to a site. We want to break the linkability in such a way that it destroys the usefulness of the information that you get. You may end up with this kind of herd immunity eventually, but this is how you go about it. So we call it a different kind of differential privacy, we think of this as a composite sort of privacy. And this game we want to play, we have yet to define and formalise it, but it looks to be a particularly and evolutionary game theoretic model that would work here, and this confusion, this misinformation, deception, seems to be a valid technique we can have in our toolbox. It breaks or removes linkability.

So our game. What do we want to ultimately get out of this? It's not going to stop tracking, as was stated so nicely in the talk right before me, this is a game that you can't win, you have to play it over and over and over again. But you can win it for a little while, you can shift the cost in such a way that you're on top for a while, and that's good enough. What this sort of misinformation and deception would do to browser tracking is that it would slowly and eventually poison their datasets in such a way that the information that they've been storing for a long time, and that they've been using for their characterisations, is now useless to them. And that means it's going to cost them more to figure out another way to do this, or they're going to have to combine with more companies that do it in different ways, and they're going to have pay somebody to figure out something else, or it's going to slow them down, any sort of costs in their resources. And it won't cost the users much.

Certain of the issues that can be tracked, Mozilla, and reluctantly Chrome, are building some of this out of the browser, there's no reason for us to spew so much information about ourselves like black smoke across the internet highway. A lot of this was done for debugging reasons, and that's why it's in there, and that's why we shouldn't be responding to every single query that

Ross Anderson: Well there's one question here, which is whether we're trying to give privacy to all the people or to some of the people. Now if you could persuade Mozilla to give privacy to all the people by making every instance of Mozilla look the same and by causing or cookies to evaporate at midnight, then this would so badly effect the marketing ecosystem that there would be a large-scale and violent response, perhaps even a legislative one, or perhaps it simply wouldn't show you your copy of the Guardian if you weren't there using Firefox. If on the other hand you simply want to privacy to the 1 % of people who care, then that's a very different ballgame, but there you're not poisoning datasets and pushing up search costs across the board, you've got a different strategy surely.

Reply: And that might give those who care sufficient herd immunity essentially. But the game we're, that is part of the game we're playing because these marketers have a, as controversial as this is, they have a valid place in this system.

Ross Anderson: Yes, they pay for the internet.

Reply: Exactly, and we pay for the tools, or we're paying for the tools that they give us for free, for the toys, and the games, and whatever it is we want to use, with our information. And that is valid in our little, in the trifecta of privacy, which is user, marketing and government, right. The problem is that right now it doesn't cost them anything to do this, and it costs us everything in order to slow them down, or to make it harder.

Ross Anderson: There is something you can do, which is always a new PC and a different one everyday.

Reply: That's a cost isn't it.

Ross Anderson: Well let me give you an example. Until this week it was possible to read the Economist, there were five free articles at a time by simply deleting cookies. They somehow fixed that, but goodness knows which of these mechanisms they used. So if you want to read 15 articles in the Economist, you read five now with Firefox, five with Chrome, and five with Opera.

Reply: We should go and check because that ought to be available if you find the JavaScript they're sending at you, you have to see what it is they're using.

Ross Anderson: I haven't had time to look but that in principle be fixed, that in principle will be fixed by simply walking into the student computing lab, sitting down at a new machine, logging on, reading 5 articles, logging off, and then going to the next machine.

Reply: Except that only fixes it for you. What about the student, or the person after you who wants to do the same thing.

Ross Anderson: We have this thing called virtualisation.

Audience: So what you describe is a very combative approach, is there a sort of coordinated thing you could do with the advertisers so say, OK, we know you pay for the internet, maybe instead we will now give you some of the demographic data that you perhaps need to ship us ads, and in return you promise not to do some of the other bad things that you're doing at the moment.

Reply: There have been a couple of proposals for that, I read a few when I was looking at this. I think the game is very complex and that we can play it in a number of different ways, but the idea behind the game, whatever game we decide to play, and that game doesn't have to be a static one either, because you can play it one way one time and one way another. But whatever game we play we've got to figure out how, who pays the costs, because right now we're paying all of them. For any form of privacy we want, the individual user has to pay them, there's no other way to get privacy.

Frank Stajano: But the evidence seems to me that the advertisers will not do anything that they don't like, just even something as basic as Do Not Track bit they didn't support, so how can you expect them to cooperate on something?

Keith Irwin: Yes, and several of them sort of said they would support it as long as it was an official standard and so forth, and then a lot of them went back on that immediately, they took Do Not Track out of being, well we'll stop tracking you in an easily detectable way, and start tracking you in less easily detectable way. So it's clear that when they have been involved in negotiations their main goal in the negotiations seems to be to slow the process down so as not to create any kind of legal regime that they could be violating. That seemed to be their only interest.

Audience: Spread this information.

Reply: Well yes, and they're good at that.

Audience: So you know you talk about kind of spoiling the datasets of the companies by trying to break the linkability, but would another possible and like maybe much easier method just for you to like break it by, they are still able to identify you but like there's just a lot of noise in what you're like tracked doing. So if you randomly, like just for every page you went to just randomly visited like 10 more at random, or like 10 more samples from like pages that other people in the network have viewed, that basically makes their data worthless because they can't identify anything like

Reply: That seems to be harder to do in real life Someone, there was a talk where someone proposed that, and it's possible but it requires a lot more effort, and it seems to be that they can eventually, the 10 random don't end up being random, and you have to figure out how many of those would actually work, 10 seems like it wouldn't be enough, and particularly because you're still going back to those same sites.

Bruce Christianson: Another approach you could take is to randomly aggregate with other people and practice it first.

Reply: Yes, a mixed master approach.

Audience: Yes, that's more what I mean, I mean like, so say 10 million people installed some browser add-on and every address they visit gets like written to some blog, so like every get request they make goes and takes like 10 out of the last 10 in the log, and then you're basically averaging your traffic pattern with like some random set of people.

Reply: Some K out of N, yes, I like that, I think that's a possibility.

Virgil Gligor: So ultimately it seems like you have to be able to randomise behaviour, user behaviour, not just information about some fixed parameters characterising the user. So in other words, if I can check my identity and my location very frequently, but I don't change my behaviour, people are going to correlate these different kind of graphs they get into one, and they still can tell it's me, they might not know my name, but

Reply: Is that enough?

Virgil Gligor: So the question is, is that enough?

Reply: Yes, and that, so we're only really beginning to think about this, and I think there's a lot of research potential here. We need to figure out how much, we need to figure out what works best, we need to figure out what trade-offs we can make, and then we need to measure the cost of all of that. And it's hard, by the way, to get advertisers costs, I've been trying to do that for a while.

Audience: Could you use some other strategy like, I use a very aggressive ad blocker on my machine, so even if I'm leaking all sorts of data I don't really see the ads, at least 90 % of them.

Reply: So what's your goal then, just not to see the ads or not to be tracked?

Audience: Well I like to disrupt the ecosystem if I can in some way.

Reply: There's an interesting young adult book called Feed, and in it everyone is wired into the world net at birth, and whoever, everything you do is paid for and subsidised by the ads that they can send you. So you go to a particular school because those advertisers think that they can send you stuff and you'll buy their stuff. And the conceit of the story is, what happens when a couple of teenagers decide to cheat the system by doing something similar to what you suggested, going to a bunch of random places. And then one of them gets sick and they can't get any of the medical advertisers to pay for their stuff because no-one can classify them into one thing.

Bruce Christianson: My problem is that I don't want to be tracked, but on the other hand I quite like the target of advertisers.

Audience: So maybe my suggestion of, you know, you provide your demographics that you want to get the ads for would fit your use case.

Bruce Christianson: Yes.

Reply: Yes.

Audience: So have you looked at the possibility people might do things like certain creative roots where they periodically, when they receive a request from a website they forward it along to someone else and say, what would you say to this, and then return that one to them.

Reply: I like that.

Audience: So that when they're trying to leak based on their unique thing they wind up leaking all these different things together, and they think that 20 different people are actually one person.

Reply: But going back to Virgil's randomising behaviour, you'd have to make sure that the groups that you contact were not the groups that you were comfortable with.

Audience: So I think, didn't Avi Rubin have a paper on this kind of thing? I can have a look through.

Reply: Something sounds familiar, well let's go find that.

Audience: Where the idea is somebody's web request would be sent off to other local machines that would make the request for you, and then the result would come back.

Reply: Yes, as long as we're out of our comfort zone so that we don't keep going into the same places. So I don't know how to do this yet. I just know that the key point we have to make here is that it's got to cost us less than it costs them, right. Every game that we play, if we're going to stay on top most of the time, we have to make sure that we never do more than the minimum required, whether it's parrying the punch, or turning into a chameleon, or making sure it hits your neighbour and not you, whatever it is you have to do you do the least amount of it possible. And that's why I think that evolutionary game theoretic models are the things to do. And, you know, I'm not the first person to look at this, Ross suggested this, I think you may have been one of the earliest, years and years ago. But as was mentioned in the talk before, the really important new thing here is that we have to think of computer security as a game we can't win, you cannot play this game to win, there will never be a final solution. The way to play this game is not to lose, and that requires that you adapt, that requires that you change quickly, and that you understand that change is an essential part of this game. And that's pretty much all I have to say.

Changyu Dong: My question is, what if the companies to play hard ball in the game, like if they can't make money then they just make it mandatory, you have to give me your data otherwise you can't use free products, or whatever. And then, well customers they might not seem equal placed to play with the companies?

Reply: But that might be an acceptable trade-off because then you actually want the thing that they're doing. Most of the tracking that's being done is being done without your knowledge for stuff that you're never going to use, it's just trying to build information about you that they can sell to somebody else who might advertise to you. It's called onboarding, and there was a New York Times article on this a couple of months ago that interviewed some of the companies that do this onboarding, collecting this information, and they're doing things like trying to sell particular health care just to the wealthy. And they're also going to do it to deny certain people things. This is going to, being able to characterise people so closely, and categorise them in such ways, is going to be used for discrimination, and that's what we need to be careful about.

Ross Anderson: That's the whole purpose of the internet, is to enable you to discriminate between customers who are rich and customers who are poor, customers who are healthy and customers who are not. This is economics 101, and that means that some people will have an incentive to be truthful, like healthy people looking for health insurance, and other people will have an incentive to lie, and so it cannot be static, of course it's going to the adversarial.

Reply: Good point.

Audience: So I think the game is kind of break here, the one you're trying to play comes to what Virgil said earlier, if we don't change this social behaviour, what we're doing right now, is this is an argument for mass surveillance, I will collect everything now in case you use Tor in the future, and then you're not likely to change your routine, if you visit Light Blue Touchpaper and blog at 3 pm, that's definitely you, I don't care?

Reply: It depends on the use case, right. How about, if this is a court case do you have plausible deniability.

Audience: You do, but does NSA care about the court or plausible deniability.

Reply: Fair enough, but if that is your threat model then you're better off using Tor, which at present is the best thing you can use to be untrackable, it really does work against most of these things, and they had anticipated a lot of the fingerprinting problems and built protections against them into it.

Audience: There has been quite a bit of mention of sites might not allow them to access them if you don't give the data. Equally though people may choose not to access a particular site because it demands the data. So I think when you've got that option it sort of, we'll be talking, the dialogue, the company might be prepared to let you access it for less data because they know there's a chance that you're not going to access it at all.

Reply: That's a good point because company B over on the other side doesn't require the data to shop there. Maybe that will be an outcome of this.

Audience: I have some problems with the fundamental assumption of this model and all these things that we get, like google etc., because at the end of the day they are paid for by advertising, advertising is budgeted into our groceries, and everything, and the only thing free would be something like Wikipedia, which is donations it's not, we're paying for advertising.

Reply: Well a couple of things are changing, right, because certainly in Europe, having internet access is now considered a human right, so some of the things that advertisers are paying for may become things that we get through taxes, or whatever. Others, all we're doing is shifting the costs, right, we're not stopping it, we're trying to figure out a way that they don't get all of this for free. Maybe we're going to put some competitors out of the market, but that's what happens in ecosystems.

Audience: Well my point was that if like right now I might get the Guardian for free, but as a result my groceries are slightly more expensive.

Bruce Christianson: Yes, but so are mine, and that's the point.

Audience: Yes, and later on I wouldn't mind if I had to pay a small amount to access the Guardian if the price of everything else were to go down comparatively.

Bruce Christianson: Yes.

Audience: That would be alright.

Bruce Christianson: If we make everybody read the Guardian whether they want to or not, that's a good first

Keith Irwin: Well the other consideration to that too is that the price, the value of their advertising and the value of the service provider are, really they're kind of separate markets of supply and demand, right, and it's only as long as one exceeds the other that they can make profit, but you know, bandwidth has gotten a lot cheaper, and this doesn't means they've started showing us less ads, so really they're showing us the ads and doing the tracking that they can do that we're willing to accept.

Bruce Christianson: But you're right that the information arbitrage is where the action is, that's where Sandy came in.

Audience: It may be worth pointing out that last week Google lost a court case in the UK Court of Appeal, because they asserted they were allowed to track users, and the Court of Appeal ruled that, you may not track users without their consent.

Reply: Fair enough, so that makes the game much more possible.

Audience: Another interesting application of this tracking capability is like, well there's a technical in things like, something like that so on Facebook for example the content that you see is determined by like your browser which can say, for example, if you have a history of reading only like left-wing political articles, then you content like whereas the opposite would be kind of filtered out, which leads to a sort of non-web and you just live in a kind of bubble where they're not exposed to ideas outside of what they're comfortable with.

Reply: And, I've actually been afraid of that, because if you only learn things that you're comfortable learning, you are

Audience: The reason I think it's interesting is that like this idea is that you can just kind of defeat it by it costing a little bit more doesn't necessarily apply, because while obviously there's still a cost element to this, not just like this great relationship between my selling stuff and making a profit, I don't know, the advertising work, well?

Reply: But one result of this if it's done well should be that you are then introduced to things that you wouldn't have been introduced to otherwise, that they think you fit in a different category, or they can't categorise you, so they send you a generic, or a different type of advertisement.

Audience: US political candidates have been doing this for a while in that they target, they profile the people they are trying to attract votes from, and they do not tell those people about policies which they think that they would disapprove of, such that, you know, and that's just being outrageous.

Reply: Yes, and this control of information frightens me.

Audience: Yes, it's politics.

Audience: I know, but it's particularly greedy politics.

Audience: Yes, I keep getting all these flyers for things that, you know, it's like, this person is threatening such and such, it's like, well yes...

Reply: Yes but admittedly you live in a rather conservative state.

Audience: I do, but I live in a fairly balanced town.

Reply: If anyone by the way wants these characteristics, tell me and I'll let you have them, it's just ridiculous, they have 70 categories, and then they have a bunch of the clusters, and you can fit in multiple different ones, and it just goes on and on.

Ross Anderson: Well I'm reminded of something Mike Reiter did about 20 years ago, crowds, and the idea there was that you have privacy for your web browsing by pooling your resources with perhaps a hundred other people, so he was then at Bell Labs, and you find 99 other people at Bell Labs, you put in a plugin, and then whenever you browse, your browser session goes at random from the machine of one of your 99 colleagues or perhaps 1 % of the time from your own. So you've got a pool of machines in effect that are sharing all the cookies. It's like a scaled up version of what happens with a laptop on our kitchen table, which I use, and my wife uses, my daughter uses, visitors use, you just smear it so that people can't be sure anymore. And if you're a crowd it includes people who have, you know, views supporting all the main political parties, and come from different demographics and so on, then you largely defeat this stuff, you can do it locally by means of doing a plugin that's shared with a few dozen people.

Reply: So we need to do this with extremely powerful, we need to make sure that we share our stuff with the most powerful people of the world, so that there's no chance of us being picked up, because you certainly don't want to do that with people who are part of, like a dissident group that's being monitored.

Audience: You want to do it with as different people as possible.

Audience: More locations.

Audience: So if you're into child pornography, putting it onto other people's machine is great.

Reply: They're already trying to do that.

Pico Without Public Keys

Frank Stajano[1]([✉]), Bruce Christianson[2], Mark Lomas[3], Graeme Jenkinson[1],
Jeunese Payne[1], Max Spencer[1], and Quentin Stafford-Fraser[1]

[1] University of Cambridge, Cambridge, UK
frank.stajano@cl.cam.ac.uk
[2] University of Hertfordshire, Hatfield, UK
[3] Capgemini, London, UK

Abstract. Pico is a user authentication system that does not require
remembering secrets. It is based on a personal handheld token that holds
the user's credentials and that is unlocked by a "personal aura" generated
by digital accessories worn by the owner. The token, acting as prover,
engages in a public-key-based authentication protocol with the verifier.
What would happen to Pico if success of the mythical quantum computer meant secure public key primitives were no longer available, or if
for other reasons such as energy consumption we preferred not to deploy
them? More generally, what would happen under those circumstances to
user authentication on the web, which relies heavily on public key cryptography through HTTPS/TLS?

Although the symmetric-key-vs-public-key debate dates back to the
1990s, we note that the problematic aspects of public key deployment
that were identified back then are still ubiquitous today. In particular,
although public key cryptography is widely deployed on the web, revocation still doesn't work.

We discuss ways of providing desirable properties of public-key-based
user authentication systems using symmetric-key primitives and tamper-
evident tokens. In particular, we present a protocol through which a compromise of the user credentials file at one website does not require users
to change their credentials at that website or any other.

We also note that the current prototype of Pico, when working in
compatibility mode through the Pico Lens (i.e. with websites that are
unaware of the Pico protocols), doesn't actually use public key cryptography, other than that implicit in TLS. With minor tweaks we adopt this as
the native mode for Pico, dropping public key cryptography and achieving much greater deployability without any noteworthy loss in security.

1 Introduction: A Motivating Story

In 2013, an Adobe authentication server was famously broken into [1]. Consequently, every one of the 150+ million customers whose credentials were leaked
was forced to change their password. Why? There are several reasons, some
resulting from Adobe's carelessness and others that are more fundamental.

© Springer International Publishing Switzerland 2015
B. Christianson et al. (Eds.): Security Protocols 2015, LNCS 9379, pp. 195–211, 2015.
DOI: 10.1007/978-3-319-26096-9_21

Adobe's sins in this affair are numerous and have been widely publicized. To begin with, although the passwords were encrypted[1], password hints were stored in plaintext next to each password. The fields stored in the database for each password included the following:

- User ID
- Username
- Email
- Password (*the only encrypted field*)
- Password hint.

If I chose an especially stupid hint (such as "try qwerty123", which actually occurs in the leaked data), my password would now be known to the attackers. But, with an easy password (such as "12345678", which also occurs many times in the leaked data), even if my own hint wasn't totally stupid I would probably be in trouble: if my password was insufficiently original, so that several other people among those 150 millions of victims also happened to choose it, then chances are that *someone else* provided a stupid hint for it. If so, because the passwords were encrypted with ECB and without salt, the attacker could read off the stupid hint from one of them and apply it to all the other passwords that encrypted to the same ciphertext. Moreover, even if no hint obviously exposed the group of people who shared my easy password, if thousands of others share my "12345678" stroke of genius, chances are it's one of the handful of popular passwords[2] that are well known from many other leaks and that attackers try before all others.

So let's stop flogging the Adobe dead horse. Assume that some imaginary site, say `bettersite.com`, had hashed and salted its passwords, as should be best practice ever since Morris and Thompson's 1979 landmark paper [2], and that they imposed a password policy requesting uppercase, lowercase, digits and so forth in order to enforce diversity and prevent those easily guessed common passwords. Then, first of all the policy does not even let you use a really terrible password such as "12345678"; second, even if you do pick an easily guessed password that is chosen by thousands of other clueless users, thanks to the salt it will appear in the credentials database as thousands of *different* salted hashes, so that the attackers can't tell that thousands of people share that same password, nor which ones of them do. It is true, however, that the attackers can still try the most likely guesses that fit the policy. Chances are they'll find that user John chose his dog's name and birth year: "Bella2008" complies with the policy but can be guessed relatively easily in an offline search. So, when their credentials file is compromised, the operators of `bettersite.com` still have to ask each of their customers to change their password. This is not merely because the attacker

---

[1] Reversibly encrypted with 3DES, not salted and hashed as they should have been. To add the insult to the injury, the encryption was performed by treating each block independently, in ECB mode.

[2] Splashdata publish an annual list: the most recent one at the time of writing is http://splashdata.com/press/worst-passwords-of-2014.htm.

could otherwise log into John's account at `bettersite.com`, but also because, knowing many people's propensity for reusing the same memorable password on several sites, the attacker will now try "Bella2008" at John's accounts on Amazon, Ebay, Google and so forth. So John had better change that password on all the other sites where he used it[3].

But perhaps the most annoyed user of `bettersite.com` would be Emily the Geek, who diligently took all the password recommendations very seriously and went to the trouble of composing and memorizing a strong password along the lines of "caeF@#qSFQH?T!@$YF". Since `bettersite.com` salted and hashed it, she is quite safe from guessing attacks, even if the bad guys have a basement full of graphics cards to devote to their cracking. And yet, when `bettersite.com` is hacked, the site operators will still ask Emily to change her password, because they can't tell that she had a strong one and shouldn't have to change it[4]. That's really unfair towards her, after she went to so much trouble, and more so because we know it's quite unnecessary.

Would life not be so much better if websites accepted public keys instead of passwords? Neither John nor Emily would have to change their credential at the compromised website nor at any other, even if they gave their same public key to every site. By stealing a file of public keys, the attackers would not be in a position to impersonate any of the users anywhere—neither at the attacked site nor, a fortiori, elsewhere. This alone looks like a strong incentive for websites to accept public keys instead of passwords.

So let's imagine moving to public keys instead of passwords for user authentication. That was Pico's original plan [3]. With that strategy, stealing the credentials file does not in itself compromise any accounts. The website does not have to force any password (or private key) resets in the event of a breach and, perhaps more importantly, doesn't make front page news of the Financial Times with the consequent drop in share price.

There is one additional benefit of adopting public keys instead of passwords for user authentication: assuming (as is common practice with, for example, PGP) that Emily encrypted her private key with a passphrase, then even an attacker who got her public key by hacking into `bettersite.com` would not be

---

[3] This may not be part of the advice John receives from `bettersite.com` when they ask him to change his password there, since they have no incentive about protecting his other accounts, despite the fact that it is the leak at their site that has made John vulnerable to fraud elsewhere. But they might argue that it was John's reuse of his password that put him at risk and that, since he contravened their advice against it, it was his fault. We do not condone this buck-passing, since demanding that users remember complex and distinct passwords for each site is unreasonable in the first place.

[4] A better designed password mechanism should blacklist all passwords that have appeared in a document, at least as far as the maintainers of the system are able to figure out. If they knew about this paper, for example, then even Emily's password would no longer be acceptable. VAX/VMS, developed in the 1970s, rejected all of the password examples that appeared in its own documentation.

in a position to verify any guesses of her passphrase (unless he also obtained her encrypted private key from her computer). But this is an aside.

Another aside is that Pico's unconventional strategy of using a *different* public key for each website that Emily visits, rather than the same one for all, gives Emily an extra privacy advantage: even colluding websites cannot correlate her visits[5].

Someone might however object that these benefits (no accounts compromised if credentials file stolen, etc. etc.) don't really derive from public key cryptography but from the fact that we're now using unguessable credentials. The core of this objection[6] is that, if one could assume the availability of the same mechanisms on which Pico relies, namely tamper-evident tokens to hold the principals' secrets, then one could offer the same benefits without using public keys at all.

This paper explores this alternative and its accompanying trade-offs.

2   Objective

We like the crucial property, which Pico has, that a compromise of the credentials file at Adobe does not expose the accounts at Facebook; or, more strongly, that the compromise of one website does not expose any credentials that could be used for future login, whether at that same website or at any others. We wish to offer this property without using public key cryptography. Why? Perhaps because the mythical quantum computer might one day break public key cryptography. Or perhaps, less dramatically, because in mobile and wearable computing we want to conserve battery energy while performing user authentication. Or maybe for yet another practical reason related to deployability, as we shall see in Sect. 5.

We assume that users (and websites) have tamper-evident tokens that can securely remember as many high-entropy secrets as needed.

3   The Core Idea

The basic idea is very simple. Assume the website has the decency of salting and hashing the passwords properly[7]. For each website, the user's token picks a different, strong and totally random password of generous length[8] and remembers it. The user never has to type it or even see it[9]. The strong password

---

[5] This corresponds to having different passwords for the different site, but without Emily having to remember them because the Pico does that for her.

[6] Which was the germ of the discussion among the first three authors that eventually resulted in this paper.

[7] Although we know that this often doesn't happen, as documented by Bonneau and Preibusch [4].

[8] Unfortunately inconsistency between password policies may frustrate this. Some websites reject strong passwords on spurious grounds such as suggesting that they are too long. Our PMF specification [5] addresses this issue, as briefly summarized in "Level 2" in Sect. 5.1.

[9] Some people, but not us, no longer call this a password, because users can't remember it. Note that, if the attacker can perform any industrial-sized number of guessing attempts offline, most passwords that the average user will actually remember are vulnerable.

is only stored in salted and hashed form, so it can't feasibly be guessed: even though the attacker could verify a correct guess, the search space is too large. The compromise of the credentials file therefore does not expose any passwords and does not affect the attacked site nor any other sites. If "legacy users" (with human-remembered and thus guessable passwords) coexist with "secure users" (with strong random passwords that are too long and complex to remember in a brain, but which a tamper-evident token remembers for them), then, so long as the website can tell which is which, in case of compromise only the legacy users need be required to reset their password.

In fact we have already taken this route with Pico when we implemented the compatibility mode we presented at this workshop last year [6], which essentially transforms Pico into a password manager in your pocket. Since then, we have enhanced our system with the "Password Manager Friendly" (PMF) specification for websites [5]. The changes at the website side to achieve PMF compliance are minimal[10] but they allow Pico (as well as any other password manager, whether stand-alone or embedded in a browser) to reliably create and submit a strong uncrackable password for the website without user intervention, and of course to adopt a different one for every website. PMF almost[11] removes the need for the public-key protocol (Sigma-I [7]) originally used by Pico, so long as the Pico has a secure channel[12] over which to send the password to the website.

3.1 A Small Leftover Problem

The last point we just mentioned needs further attention. How can the user, or the user's tamper-evident token, send the strong password to the website? In Pico, even in compatibility mode, that's done using the TLS channel that

---

[10] They consist essentially of a set of semantic labels for the HTML of the login form, saying in a machine-readable format that this is a login form, this field is the username, this field is the password and so on. The HTML5 specification contains something similar and some web browsers recognise this. For example, you may specify a policy that when web forms are cached any password fields are omitted from the data that is cached.

[11] Why "almost"? Because, with public key, there is the additional benefit that the website cannot impersonate the user. This does not affect accounts at other sites if the user adopts a different password for each, but it does affect logins at the site itself. Without public key, the website, which on exit from the TLS tunnel receives the user's password in plaintext even though it is not supposed to store it other than salted and hashed, could pretend to a third party that the user authenticated at other times. With public key, it would not be able to produce evidence of any other logins than the ones in which the user actually replied correctly to the challenge. As with other arguments in favour of public key, this one too becomes problematic once the possibility of revocation is accounted for. It should also be noted that a better web login scheme would allow the prover to demonstrate knowledge of the shared secret without revealing it—cfr "Level 3" in Sect. 5.1.

[12] In this context, secure means offering confidentiality, freshness and authenticity of source and destination.

protects the HTTPS login page. But that itself uses public key cryptography. If we want a solution that completely avoids public key, we must use an alternative.

This is not a problem specific to Pico: the scope is much broader. If we assume we can't use public key crypto, how does the web work? How do we do HTTPS? How can a user communicate securely with (let alone log into) a website that they have never seen before?[13]

The rest of the paper will pursue two threads. First (Sect. 4) we revisit the problem of web login without public key technology, which will become topical again if quantum computers become capable of factoring numbers a little larger than 3*5. Next (Sect. 5) we sketch an alternative architecture for Pico that uses as little public key technology as possible, pointing out its advantages and disadvantages compared to the previous design.

4   Web Login Without Public Keys

The technology for establishing secure connections with unknown principals without using public key cryptography is well-known (Needham-Schroeder [8], then upgraded to Kerberos [9]). Whereas, with public key, the client can contact the website directly and check the validity of the site's public key certificate, with symmetric key you need an introducer (the Key Distribution Centre, or KDC) with whom both parties share (separate) secrets.

The symmetric key faction will be quick to point out that this requirement is no worse than with public key, because there you need an introducer too: the Certification Authority that signed the website's public key.

The opposite faction will now object that, without public key, the introducer (Kerberos authentication server) must be online, so public key is better because it does not require that of its introducer (the Certification Authority).

The symmetric key faction will then ask how their opponents deal with the case in which a private key has been compromised and a public key must therefore be revoked. If you need to check for revocation online at every login, that's no better than having to talk to the Kerberos KDC at every login. And, if you don't do that, you only have the *illusion* of superiority while instead you're vulnerable for a time window whose length depends on the expiration frequency of the issued certificates.

These issues and trade-offs were extensively discussed in the 1990s, mostly as debates at crypto conferences, but remarkably little of this discussion seems to have been published for posterity in the open literature, if we except a

---

[13] Note that we are not even beginning to address the even more complex human factors problem that the average user can't understand the difference between the HTTPS padlock in the address bar (whose appearance changes between browsers and between versions of the same browser anyway) and a bitmap of a padlock in the client area of the page, and can therefore be phished.

discussion by Christianson, Crispo and Malcolm [10] in a previous Security Protocols Workshop[14].

So let's have a closer look at how revocation is handled on the web today, twenty years later.

4.1   Revocation on the Web Today

Once credentials are suspected (or known) to have been compromised, they must be revoked and replaced with new ones. This tends to be a weak point in many systems. Even deployed ones. Even on the web as we know it today.

In the original Pico system [3], each Pico token follows the unconventional strategy of using a separate key pair for each website it talks to, which makes it relatively easy for the Pico to know whom to contact if revocation is needed. On the TLS-based web, instead, in which a website offers a public key to all its correspondents (the traditional way of using a public key), it is this widespread sharing of the public key that makes revocation hard. When a principal uses the same public key for all correspondents, and this public key is distributed promiscuously[15], then, when this public key is revoked, the principal can never be sure of having warned all correspondents that the previously used public key should no longer be used. This is particularly true for *future* correspondents, who might begin to use a previously known-good public key without awareness that it has meanwhile been revoked.

In today's web, it's usually only the website that offers a public key to the client, and not vice versa, because client certificates are not commonly used. As we noted, the website's public key is hard to revoke because many correspondents use it, whereas the Pico uses a different credential for every website (regardless of whether it is a public key, in native mode, or a strong password, in compatibility mode) and that makes credentials relatively easy to revoke. If you lose (or discover evidence of tampering on) the tamper-evident device, rather than the individual credential, then you need to revoke *all* the keys (or

---

[14] It was a common discussion theme at conferences such as Oakland in the mid-1990s, and the subject was also discussed by the Internet Research Task Force (IRTF) Privacy Task Force in the late 1980's/early 1990's. It was widely understood that both symmetric key set-up cost and public key revocation cost were of order $k \log N$ with N counterparties in the case of hierarchical servers. Possibly for economic reasons the early CAs pushed for short certificate life, rather than effective revocation mechanisms, contributing to the rather unsatisfactory situation that we have today. Interestingly, version 1 of the SWIFT protocol used a trusted logger in conjunction with symmetric keys to prevent message forgery, and 3GPP has a current Generic Authentication Architecture that is based on symmetric-key. The authors would be delighted to hear from any readers who are aware of other publications that address in a measured way the trade-offs between symmetric and public key in the presence of revocation.

[15] For example via public key certificates propagating in an uncontrolled way.

passwords) it contained and that's a pain[16]. But at least you have the exact list of the correspondents you should contact. The website doesn't even have that luxury, because the same public key is used by all clients—including the future clients that the website doesn't even know about.

In today's web, for the website, revocation essentially doesn't work. What happens? A site gets hacked, as happened to Adobe. It had a public key certificate valid until next year, but it makes itself a new key pair because the hackers, who exfiltrated the passwords file, might have done the same with the private key. If the website does not revoke its public key then the attackers, who have grabbed the old key pair and have a still valid CA-signed certificate for the public key, can impersonate the website to any client whose connection they can man-in-the-middle[17].

There are essentially two alternatives to prevent this attack, essentially corresponding to client pull and server push respectively.

The first alternative is for the client to check every certificate with the CA to see if this is still valid, as per the Online Certificate Status Protocol (OCSP) [11]. This adds latency and introduces brittleness: what should the client do if it can't contact the CA, either because of non-malicious network errors or because of a purposeful denial of service? If the client is paranoid and rejects the connection to Adobe whenever it can't contact the CA, essentially the web stops working, as per Leslie Lamport's old adage that "a distributed system is one in which the failure of a computer you didn't even know existed can render your own computer unusable"; if instead the client accepts the connection anyway, then impersonation attacks go through[18].

The second alternative is for the Certification Authority to regularly push a certificate revocation list to all clients; but, to reduce the vulnerability window, this requires frequent updates (say daily), which are costly in terms of bandwidth and downtime regardless of whether any impersonation attacks are taking place, and it creates an incentive for attackers to DDOS the CA.

---

[16] As well as a privacy concern—because a global observer can now link your interactions with the various websites to which your Pico issues revocation requests by their timing and network origin.

[17] Note also that there are often more than two parties involved in a session. I may authenticate Amazon when I buy a book, but the part of the transaction I really care about is the payment via my bank. Unfortunately the current protocol requires Amazon to protect my credit card details so I should check the revocation status of Amazon's certificate. A better protocol would allow me to send an encrypted bundle to Amazon (running the risk that it isn't Amazon) which instructs my bank to pay Amazon (say) £20. Only the bank, not Amazon, should be able to decrypt that bundle.

[18] There is an alternative that is used in many financial networks. The decision to check for revocation might depend upon the value of the transaction. When buying a coffee I might neglect to check revocation status, accepting the risk. When ordering a new television I might insist on checking the status because the value at risk is higher. However this assumes a protocol that prevents the coffee shop from reusing my credentials to buy a television.

Neither of these options is desirable and therefore, in practice, with TLS, invalid certificates are not revoked[19]. New certificates are served but compromised keys have certificates that still appear as valid; therefore impersonation attacks remain possible[20].

4.2   TLS Without Public Key, but with Revocation

If we used symmetric key technologies to implement TLS, how would it work? And how would it deal with revocation? We need a Key Distribution Centre, that is to say an authentication server that can do introductions. In the e-commerce context, payment organizations such as Visa or Paypal are third parties known to and (of necessity) trusted by both the user and the website, so we might imagine that they could serve as introducers. Why would they? If the web transaction involved a payment, they might ask for a small percentage. If it didn't, they might ask for a micropayment—perhaps merely the ability to display an advertisement—or, maybe better, they might request a small fee from the website (which probably profits indirectly from the visit even when it does not charge the user). The first time a user visits a website, Visa or equivalent provides an introduction and an initial session key. On subsequent visits, the user and the website already have a shared secret and they can bootstrap further security from that[21].

How could revocation work in this architecture? After the very first contact between client and website via the third-party introduction, the client and the website should negotiate and agree two revocation codes (one each for the client and the website) to be used when needed, as part of an emergency transaction initiated by either party that revokes the current shared key and ideally installs a replacement one. For convenience of exposition, we primarily describe revocation initiated from the website side in what follows.

To set a baseline for comparison, we first outline what occurs in the public key case[22]. The revocation code for the website could consist of $S_{K_w^-}[\text{Revoke}, K_w^+]$ or

---

[19] It is interesting to note that browser makers can decide individually on the policy they choose, though they compete against each other on security, features and especially performance.

[20] We don't hear much about such attacks. Is it because they don't happen and we shouldn't worry or because they happen so effectively that we are not aware of them?

[21] This design is architecturally plausible but has the potentially undesirable property that now the client and the website must trust Visa (or equivalent) not just with their money, but also with the confidentiality and authenticity of all their subsequent communications with the website. This problem is shared by all KDS mechanisms; one solution is to combine several keys distributed by mutually mistrusting authentication servers, at the expense of further complexity, latency and potential failure points.

[22] Notation: K^+ is a public key and K^- is the matching private key. A K without exponent is a symmetric key. $E_{K^+}[m]$ or $E_K[m]$ is the encryption of message m under key K^+ or K respectively, whereas $D_{K^-}[m]$ or $S_{K^-}[m]$ is the decryption or signature, respectively, of message m with key K^-. Finally, $h(m)$ is the one-way hash of message m.

204 F. Stajano et al.

even just of K_w^- itself. Ideally the original key certificate for K_w^+ would contain $h(K'^+_w)$, a hash of the replacement public key. Note that website revocation is global, i.e. only one public message is required in order to inform all clients, whereas client key revocation has to be done individually with each website, because of our Pico-specific assumption that websites send the same public key to all their clients, but clients send a different public key to every website.

The revocation transaction does not intrinsically require interaction with any third party, but (in the shadow of a denial of service attack) it does rely upon the website having the ability to post the revocation code securely[23] in a place where the client cannot be prevented from looking, and vice versa.

In the symmetric key case, where the shared secret between client C and website W is K_{cw} after the introduction brokered by the Key Distribution Centre, website W immediately gives client C the string

$$R = E_{K_{cw}}[E_{K_w}[\text{Revoke}, W, K'_{cw}]]$$

where K_w is a master key known only to the website[24]. As soon as the revocation string[25] R has been passed to the client, website and client immediately replace K_{cw} by a new shared secret K_0 (constructed by each of them applying a one-way hash to K_{cw}) and destroy their copies of K_{cw}[26]. The revocation process is for W to publish K_w, which allows the client to obtain K'_{cw} and also provokes the client to cease using all keys based on K_0 and replace them with keys derived from $K'_0 = h(K'_{cw})$. As before, K'_{cw} can be used to share its successor, K''_{cw} encrypted under K'_w, before K'_{cw} is deleted. Note that, just as with the public key case, website revocation is global.

---

[23] The security requirements for posting revocations are surprisingly subtle. Clearly public visibility, persistence, and integrity of the revocation string all need to be assured by the publisher, to prevent the attacker from overwriting it. But what about a denial of service attack where the attacker publishes a bogus revocation string to prevent the correct principal from publishing the real one? We can't require the principal that is revoking their keys to authenticate themselves to the publisher in any conventional way: after all, the keys are being revoked precisely because they may have been stolen. One possibility is for the principal to pre-reserve space with the publisher at an "address" corresponding to a hash of the revocation string, with the agreement that the publisher will allow only the corresponding pre-image to be published at that address. Notice that we needn't care *who* it is that posts the legitimate revocation string: revocation strings are supposed to be kept secret from attackers, so if a revocation string has been stolen then a tamper-evident device has been compromised, and the corresponding keys therefore need to be revoked anyway.

[24] Thus, at that stage, the client cannot decrypt the inner set of brackets $E_{K_w}[\text{Revoke}, W, K'_{cw}]$ which appears as a blob of gibberish.

[25] To avoid confusion: even though we call R a revocation string, this string is necessary but not sufficient to cause a revocation. It behaves like an inert component until activated by primer K_w, mentioned next, which is the trigger for the revocation.

[26] In the client case, after first decrypting R using K_{cw}. Forgetting K_{cw} gives forward security: a subsequent leak of $K_0 = h(K_{cw})$ does not reveal K_{cw}, so even knowing K_w the attacker still cannot obtain K'_{cw} from R.

We need to ensure that the new secret (or private) keys are not themselves compromised by the same attack on secure storage that triggered the revocation[27]. For the sake of conceptual clarity, we shall assume in what follows that the entire website (or at least the authentication and login component) consists of a single tamper-evident device, which may periodically lose confidentiality and/or integrity, and then (following detection of the security breach) be restored to a known secure state on a "new" tamper-evident device prepared (possibly in advance) offline[28]. In practice, a multi-layered security architecture at the website is probably more realistic. For example, we could assume the existence at the website of an even more secure, but less convenient, storage medium that it would not be practicable to involve in routine transactions. In extremis, this medium could even be a USB stick in a safe, or hard copy output from a physically secure logging printer that requires to be typed manually back in as part of the recovery process.

4.3   Avoiding Unnecessary Re-Registration

Remember that the client's first step in establishing a fresh session with the website is to build a leak-proof end-to-end pipe (TLS or its symmetric-key replacement), as described in the previous section. Establishing that this pipe has the correct website at the far end entails an online check by the client that the website has not been compromised since the previous session[29].

The second step (the actual login) is for the website and client to authenticate to one another, and agree a fresh session key. This process requires the client to reveal their identity to the website, and so must take place inside a leak-proof pipe in order to preserve client anonymity. In the public key case, this can be done using protocols such as Sigma-I [7]. How might we implement these steps using only symmetric keys?

Let us suppose that the Pico client Alice has generated a root secret x_n where n is a suitably large number, and computed the reversed Lamport hash chain $x_i = h(x_{i+1})$. The element x_i of this chain is the login credential that will be used in round i to authenticate client Alice to the website[30]. Some time ago,

---

[27] In contrast, we don't need to worry about the attacker learning the revocation codes as a result of the attack, but we do need to ensure that the principals can still get access to these codes after the attack has happened.

[28] This is similar to the threat model of Yu and Ryan [12].

[29] This involves checking for the absence of the appropriate revocation string, both in the public key and in the symmetric key case. When a key is revoked, the replacement key is used to share the latest time guaranteed to be before the breach, that is, the latest time at which the tamper-evident hardware was known to be intact. Sessions between then and the new pipe build are assumed to be compromised.

[30] Prover Alice sends the verifier a succession of x_i with increasing i. The verifying website holds x_i from the previous round and cannot derive x_{i+1} from it, but if it receives x_{i+1} it can verify it's genuine by checking whether $h(x_{i+1}) = x_i$. The number n is the length of the chain and determines the number of logins that Alice can perform before having to reload the chain. A version of the Guy Fawkes protocol [13] can be used to refresh x_0 when n is exhausted.

during her initial contact with the website W, Alice privately shared x_0 with W. It is now several sessions later, and the website currently has the value x_i stored in a table, together with a symmetric key K_i and a randomly chosen number t_i. The value t_i is the current pseudonym for Alice, and is used as a key (in the database sense) to access the authentication table entry corresponding to Alice. This table entry may contain, or link to, Alice's actual (persistent) identity, but need not[31].

In the course of the previous session, Alice pre-agreed the new symmetric key K_i with the website, and this key will be used to establish a leak-proof pipe for negotiating the new login session that is about to be established, thus concealing the "password" x_{i+1} from third parties, including man-in-the-middle attackers. At the time when K_i was agreed, the website W privately gave Alice the revocation string $E_{K_w}[t_i]$ where K_w is a master key known only to W.

Here is the session establishment protocol:

$$A \longrightarrow W : E_{K_w}[t_i]; E_{K_i}[x_{i+1}] \tag{1}$$

W first recovers K_i using t_i, and then verifies that $h(x_{i+1}) = x_i$. W next chooses two random strings t_{i+1} and s_i, then sets $K_{i+1} = h(K_i)$. Now W replies to Alice with the following message:

$$W \longrightarrow A : E_{K_i}[E_{K_w}[t_{i+1}], s_i, x_{i+1}] \tag{2}$$

W replaces x_i with x_{i+1}, t_i with t_{i+1}, K_i with K_{i+1}, and deletes t_i and K_i. The shared keys for the new session between Alice and W are derived from s_i, and are deleted on logout when the session ends.

W can work out which client message 1 is from, by decrypting the first part with K_w, but the attacker can't do this without first breaching the website to obtain K_w. The second part of message 1 can only be decrypted using the key K_i obtained by decrypting the first part. This ensures that only the correct website can obtain the pre-image x_{i+1} of the current authentication credential x_i. The fact that this pre-image is correct authenticates the client to the website, and assures the freshness of both parts of message 1. Message 2 shows knowledge of K_i and x_{i+1}, thus authenticating the website to the client and proving freshness of message 2[32]. Authentication is thus mutual, however the identity of the client is revealed only to the correct website. Upon receiving the second message, the client simply replaces K_i with $K_{i+1} = h(K_i)$ and deletes K_i.

After the website breach, we cannot prevent the attacker mounting a man-in-the-middle attack to obtain client session credentials to spoof individual sessions, any more than we can prevent this in the public key case. Just as in the public

---

[31] The table entry accessed by t_i will include $h(T_A)$, where T_A is the revocation string for Alice. Alice initiates the revocation protocol with W by revealing T_A.

[32] To allow for the possibility that the two parties might get out of sync, for example through non-malicious communication errors, we might relax the verification slightly. If the pre-image check fails, the verifier should hash again for a configurable number of times. If a match is found, they will have both authenticated and resynchronized.

key case, the credentials for the leak-proof pipe (i.e. $E_{K_w}[t_i]$) will have to change to the fall-back credentials, using the revocation protocol described in Sect. 4.2. But, just as in the public key case, the attacker gains nothing from the client that they can use in the longer term. In particular, once the website is re-secured the client can continue to use the same Lamport hash chain[33] without the risk that the attacker can impersonate her.

We therefore have the property that we wanted to preserve from the public-key scenario, namely that a compromise of the credentials file at the website does not require revocation of the client credentials at that site or any other in order to prevent masquerade attacks subsequent to website recovery[34].

5   Pico Without Public Keys

With Pico, we are much more concerned about offering a viable alternative to remembering and typing passwords than we are about guarding against the cryptanalitic threat of quantum computers. We assume that, at least in the short and medium term, password login on the web will continue to rely on TLS. We are, however, interested in maximizing adoption of Pico. In that spirit, using login credentials that look like passwords rather than public keys is potentially a worthy optimization[35] because it minimizes the changes required of a website to achieve Pico compliance.

5.1   Levels of Pico Compliance

We define the following scale of possible levels of Pico compliance, with higher levels promising higher security but requiring greater disruption at the website end and thus greater difficulty for wide-scale adoption and deployment [14].

Level 0. The Pico compatibility mode we presented last year [6] requires no changes whatsoever to the website: the client sees a Pico-friendly login page, rewritten by the Pico lens browser plugin, but the website still receives a traditional username and password and need not even know that a Pico was used to log in. This option would in theory provide maximum deployability, if not for the fact that many websites mess around with Javascript on their login page and as a result cannot be reliably operated upon by a password manager (or by Pico) other than by writing ad-hoc heuristics that cater for special cases.

---

[33] Note that the hash chains x_i and K_i run in opposite directions. The Lamport hash chain is x_i.

[34] Of course, following a second break-in to the website, the attacker will be able to correlate client identities from the second attack with those stolen from the first. Just as in the public-key case, clients who wish to prevent this will need to update their login credentials (x_0 or K^- in the symmetric and public key cases respectively) before the second attack. However no third-party mediated authentication is required for this.

[35] Hopefully not merely a Needham optimization: replacing something that works with something that almost works but is cheaper.

Level 1. To address this problem we developed the previously-mentioned PMF specification [5]: concise semantic annotations on the login page allow any password manager to submit username and password to the website accurately and reliably, without any guesswork[36]. The website only needs to annotate the HTML of its login page, without changing any of its back-end logic; in return, by becoming password-manager friendly, the website improves its security. There is still the security problem, though, that the password is generated by the user (even though the user no longer needs to remember it) and therefore is probably vulnerable to a guessing attack.

Level 2. To counter that additional problem we specified an extra step in PMF whereby the website allows password-manager-created passwords without imposing its customary composition policy on them (uppercase, lowercase, symbols, digits etc.) provided that they are at least t characters long[37], on the basis that only software agents, not humans, will ever use such extravagantly long and hard-to-retype passwords. This strategy allows password managers, including Pico, to generate for each account a distinct random password that will be many orders of magnitude stronger than anything a human could reliably memorize. This strategy requires a small change in the back-end logic of the website (changing the password definition policy to consider any passwords of length t and above as acceptable without checking what classes of characters they contain) but enables security that effectively stops any offline guessing attacks. It is assumed that the website salts and hashes the passwords and that therefore an increase the length of the supplied password does not affect the per-account storage cost of the credentials at the website.

Level 3. Architecturally, from the security viewpoint, it would be preferable not to send the shared secret from client to website at every login but instead to use a challenge-response protocol, as suggested for example by Bonneau [15]. Level 3 would allow for that. While not using public key cryptography per se, it would require changing the back-end logic of the website from verifying a password (salt, then hash, then compare against stored hash) to challenging the client and verifying the response. Challenge-response may add an additional message in the protocol, and thus additional communication delays; with care one might try to optimize away the delays by serving the challenge at the same time as the web page, but this might amount to an even more disruptive change for websites.

Level 4. This level would provide mutual authentication, with the user only supplying their own credentials after having verified the authenticity of the website. In the previous "native Pico" implementation this was achieved with Sigma-I [7], which uses public key cryptography. Using public keys as credentials and a mutual authentication protocol was the original design of Pico [3], but this is clearly the most disruptive solution of all for the website and therefore it is the most damaging in terms of deployability for Pico.

---

[36] As we said, HTML5 also supports similar annotations.

[37] We suggested $t = 64$ characters taken at random from the `base64` alphabet.

5.2   And When the Token Is Not Available?

Unfortunately tamper-evident tokens may be lost or temporarily unavailable. Imagine I receive a phone call while sailing on my yacht. My broker advises me of a business opportunity that requires my digital signature. My signing token is at home in a safe because I didn't want to lose it at sea. There is insufficient time either to collect the token or to deliver a replacement token before the opportunity expires. This suggests that we want a mechanism that temporarily relaxes the requirement for a tamper-evident token.

Fortunately my bank realises this may happen and values my custom. It can establish a proxy service—a remote tamper-evident box—that I may use in such circumstances. Having established my identity by phone they create a temporary account for me on the proxy server which I use to authenticate the transaction. There is a raised level of risk since I am now relying upon the security of my phone which I use to access the proxy server, which is why I revert to using the more secure physical token after I return home.

Since I know that my token is unattended while I am on holiday, I might even ask the bank to disable it temporarily while I am away to reduce the impact if it is stolen.

The research question for Pico is now how to offer this alternative while respecting the primary directive of "you shall not be required to remember any secrets in order to authenticate".

5.3   How Should Pico Evolve?

The discussion that brought us to write this paper suggests that the security gain from level 3 to level 4 is not significant, and that level 2 is more than strong enough against the threat of offline guessing. Level 2 is also sufficient to offer the desired property that a compromise of the credentials file at the website does not require revocation of the client credentials[38].

We therefore argue that levels 1 and 2 are the sweet spot that offers adequately strong security at acceptable costs in deployability. We won't be pushing for levels 3 or 4 any more: we take level 2 as our new "native mode" for Pico and support levels 0 and 1 as "compatibility mode".

In summary, the Pico login credentials are no longer public/private keys[39] but we continue to use public key technology implicitly insofar as the web relies on TLS.

---

[38] The website is able to distinguish machine-generated passwords by their length and flag them as such in the hashed credentials file. The website is therefore in a position not to bother those users with a password reset, since their password cannot be realistically brute-forced from the hash even by an arbitrarily powerful offline adversary.

[39] They are instead t-character-long random sequences of `base64` characters. With $t = 64$ they are equivalent to 384-bit symmetric keys.

6   Conclusions

Although our investigation started by looking at whether Pico really needed to rely on public key cryptography to offer its desirable properties, we then broadened the scope to investigate what web authentication might look like if it had to work without public key technologies.

Reviving a discussion that was popular in the last decade of the past millennium, we noted once again that the alleged advantages of public key over symmetric key for authentication don't seem overwhelming when the operational need for revocation is taken into account. We also noted a posteriori that, in the current TLS-based (and thus public-key based) web authentication scenario, revocation essentially doesn't work. Public key may have won on the web in terms of deployment, but hasn't really solved the problem. We argue that, should quantum computers succeed in breaking public key cryptography[40], we could implement alternatives based on symmetric key technology that, though imperfect, would offer comparable benefits and trade-offs when deployed in conjunction with tamper-evident tokens such as Pico.

In particular, one desirable property of a public-key-based authentication system is that users do not need to change their credentials, there or elsewhere, if the website is compromised and its credentials file is stolen. We showed how to achieve this result without using public key primitives.

Coming back to Pico, we had already gradually introduced a compatibility mode that did not require public key cryptography (save for that implicit in TLS). The above investigation prompted us to consider its trade-offs against those of the public-key-based solution. We concluded that, given the ability of the token to generate and define a strong random password for every account (as enabled by PMF), the solution without public key offers comparable security but much greater deployability, because it requires almost no changes on the backend. We have therefore made it our new native mode for Pico.

Acknowledgements. We thank Ross Anderson, Bruno Crispo, Michael Roe and Alf Zugenmaier for their comments on the history of the public key vs symmetric key user authentication debate. Thanks also to Steven Murdoch for his comments on revocation on the web today. The authors with a Cambridge affiliation are grateful to the European Research Council for funding this research through grant StG 307224 (Pico).

References

1. Hern, A.: Did your adobe password leak? now you and 150m others can check. http://www.theguardian.com/technology/2013/nov/07/adobe-password-leak-can-check (2013). Accessed 28 May 2015
2. Morris, R., Thompson, K.: Password security: a case history. Commun. ACM **22**(11), 594–597 (1979)

---

[40] In the sense of allowing an adversary to derive the private key from the public key, for key sizes that are today considered secure against the strongest classical computers.

3. Stajano, F.: Pico: no more passwords!. In: Christianson, B., Crispo, B., Malcolm, J., Stajano, F. (eds.) Security Protocols 2011. LNCS, vol. 7114, pp. 49–81. Springer, Heidelberg (2011)

4. Bonneau, J., Preibusch, S.: The password thicket: technical and market failures in human authentication on the web. In: Proceedings of the Ninth Workshop on the Economics of Information Security (WEIS), June 2010

5. Stajano, F., Spencer, M., Jenkinson, G., Stafford-Fraser, Q.: Password-manager friendly (PMF): Semantic annotations to improve the effectiveness of password managers. In: Proceedings of the Passwords 2014. Springer, Heidelberg (2014, to appear). http://mypico.org/documents/2014-StaSpeJen-pmf.pdf

6. Stajano, F., Jenkinson, G., Payne, J., Spencer, M., Stafford-Fraser, Q., Warrington, C.: Bootstrapping adoption of the pico password replacement system. In: Christianson, B., Malcolm, J., Matyáš, V., Švenda, P., Stajano, F., Anderson, J. (eds.) Security Protocols 2014. LNCS, vol. 8809, pp. 172–186. Springer, Heidelberg (2014)

7. Krawczyk, H.: SIGMA: the 'SIGn-and-MAc' approach to authenticated Diffie-Hellman and its use in the IKE protocols. In: Boneh, D. (ed.) CRYPTO 2003. LNCS, vol. 2729, pp. 400–425. Springer, Heidelberg (2003). http://www.ee.technion.ac.il/hugo/sigma.html

8. Needham, R.M., Schroeder, M.D.: Using encryption for authentication in large networks of computers. Commun. ACM 21(12), 993–999 (1978)

9. Kohl, J., Neuman, C.: The kerberos network authentication service (v5) (1993)

10. Christianson, B., Crispo, B., Malcolm, J.A.: Public-key crypto-systems using symmetric-key crypto-algorithms. In: Christianson, B., Crispo, B., Malcolm, J.A., Roe, M. (eds.) Security Protocols 2000. LNCS, vol. 2133, pp. 182–183. Springer, Heidelberg (2001)

11. Myers, M., Ankney, R., Malpani, A., Galperin, S., Adams, C.: RFC 2560, X. 509 internet public key infrastructure online certificate status protocol OCSP. Internet Engineering Task Force (1999)

12. Yu, J., Ryan, M.D.: Device attacker models: fact and fiction. In: Christianson, B., et al. (eds.) Security Protocols 2015. LNCS, vol. 9379, pp. 155–164. Springer, Switzerland (2015)

13. Anderson, R., Bergadano, F., Crispo, B., Lee, J.H., Manifavas, C., Needham, R.: A new family of authentication protocols (1998)

14. Bonneau, J., Herley, C., van Oorschot, P.C.v., Stajano, F.: The quest to replace passwords: a framework for comparative evaluation of web authentication schemes. In: Proceedings of the 2012 IEEE Symposium on Security and Privacy, SP 2012, pp. 553–567. IEEE Computer Society, Washington, DC (2012)

15. Bonneau, J.: Getting web authentication right: a best-case protocol for the remaining life of passwords. In: Christianson, B., Crispo, B., Malcolm, J., Stajano, F. (eds.) Security Protocols 2011. LNCS, vol. 7114, pp. 98–104. Springer, Heidelberg (2011)

Pico Without Public Keys
(Transcript of Discussion)

Frank Stajano[✉]

University of Cambridge, Cambridge, UK
frank.stajano@cl.cam.ac.uk

I will start with a motivating story. This is a true story, one of the latest in a long series of similar stories. Once upon a time, in a certain land, in the year of Our Lord 2013, Adobe lost 153 million passwords. Adobe was broken into and every one of their 153 million customers had to change their password. Why? Because Adobe was especially stupid and, instead of using salting and hashing, they used 3DES (reversible encryption). Never mind the fact that, if Adobe lost this encrypted file, then maybe the bad guys also got the key to decrypt this file, which was probably nearby. Let's just look at the file itself, of which Fig. 1 shows a short portion, reproduced courtesy of Sophos.

In the file you have the user ID, the user name, the email address of the person and the password data, which is the outcome of encrypting the data with 3DES and then base64-encoding it (note: base64 encoding of 3DES *in ECB mode*–yuck!). And then you have a password hint, helpfully in plaintext! So, for example, this first person had this password, "g2B6Ph...", and this hint: "try: qwerty123". *(Laughter from audience)*. So, if I choose a stupid hint, then my password is most likely exposed. If I choose a stupid enough password that a thousand other people also choose the same password, even if *my own* hint is not that stupid, maybe someone else with the same password has a naïve hint. But even in the unlikely case that none of the thousand people with the same stupid password as me have an immediately crackable hint, then the attacker can still say: "what passwords are stupid enough that over a thousand people have the same one?" And you just look for a popularity list like the one in Fig. 2 and these are all good things for an attacker to try. So the credentials file in the format leaked from the Adobe site was a treasure trove of passwords that you could recover. So that didn't go very well.

So let's imagine a better site, bettersite.com, and bettersite.com has read the Morris Thompson paper from 1979, and therefore their passwords are salted and hashed, and they also tell you that if you invent a password you have to have an uppercase, and a lowercase, and a digit, and all that stuff, so you cannot have things like 12345678, nor can you have trivial keyboard patterns like qwerty. You can however still have a number of slightly less stupid passwords that still are easy to guess; but even if they are guessed, the bad guy cannot compile a dictionary of them because they are salted and hashed. He has to try every one individually with its own salt, and if you do enough key stretching then you force him to pay some non-trivial amount of time for each one of these attempts.

© Springer International Publishing Switzerland 2015
B. Christianson et al. (Eds.): Security Protocols 2015, LNCS 9379, pp. 212–223, 2015.
DOI: 10.1007/978-3-319-26096-9_22

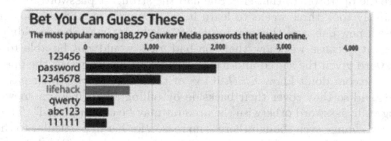

Fig. 1. The passwords file lost by Adobe (courtesy of Sophos)

Bet You Can Guess These

The most popular among 188,279 Gawker Media passwords that leaked online.

Fig. 2. Popular online passwords (courtesy of Sophos).

Still, nowadays we have GPUs and all that stuff. If someone thinks of the bad guy having the job of finding a particular individual's password, that's going to be a hard thing. But the bad guy finding *some* passwords (any passwords) out of the pool, that's not going to be that hard: if they just try likely guesses they will hit someone who had a stupid enough password. If someone chooses the name of their dog and the year they got the dog (Bella is the most popular dog name, apparently), then they are going to be found by someone who tries the possible guesses, even if the passwords are salted and hashed. Now, if this "Bella2008" password is used not just at bettersite.com but also at other sites that this person visits, like for example at Amazon, then it is exposed: the Amazon account is exposed as well the account on bettersite.com. When the bad guy attacks bettersite.com, the bettersite.com operator says "you have to change your password" to everyone on that site. But since people do recycle the same passwords on several sites, the people who had an account on bettersite.com had better also change that password on all the other sites where they recycled it.

Wouldn't it be better if websites accepted public keys instead of passwords? Then the person would not have to change their credential when the website was compromised. The website loses a file of credentials used for verifying (in this case public keys) and it's no longer a big deal, because a public key cannot help the bad guy impersonate me, it can only help the bad guy verify that I am me if I ever did an authentication with him. So, even if all the other sites hold the same public key for me, once the first site loses the credentials, including mine, I am not worried that I should change anything for the other sites. This alone would be a strong incentive for websites to accept public keys instead of passwords for the purpose of user authentication.

Now there's a twist in the tale, which is the reason why Bruce, Mark and I started discussing this. Imagine you have a user who, with respect to passwords, is especially disciplined, and especially motivated for high security: call her Emily the Geek. She has a password like `caeF@#qSFQH?T!@$YF`, which not only complies with those policies[1] but is completely impossible to brute-force or guess with current resources. Despite that, if bettersite.com loses their password file, they would ask *all* their users to change their passwords, *including* Emily the Geek! And she didn't do anything bad; the guys who had poor security were the operators of that site. She had the strongest password imaginable. She probably took three weeks to learn it, to memorise it, and she now has to memorise a new one, and this is totally unfair: why is that? She shouldn't have to change it because we know that the bad guys would *not* be able to crack her password given the salted and hashed password file. However the operators of bettersite.com don't know *which* 0.1 % of their users have strong passwords like that, and so they cover their backside by telling all their users "now we're resetting your password otherwise the account may be compromised". They will force her to change even though there is no reason for her in particular to change. This is quite unfair towards her; they put a heavy burden on her, and it's not even necessary! With public keys, Emily the Geek would be better off because she would not be subjected to this abuse by the website operators.

So let's consider the idea of using public keys instead of passwords for user authentication. This is what the Pico system does. Then, if the credentials file is stolen at the verifier, we don't care: no account gets actually compromised by this action, the operators don't force any of their users to reset their passwords, and the website itself doesn't make the front-page of the Financial Times with a title that says "Shame, shame, they lost 153 million passwords". That's nice.

And what is it, this Pico thing that I mentioned? Regular attendees of this workshop will have seen me present it for the first time in 2011[2], and we have made various enhancements since then. If you haven't been at the previous workshops, then scan this QR code[3] or go to http://mypico.org, and there is a short video (with some of the people here as actors) that will tell you what Pico is about. For the purpose of this discussion, you can consider Pico simply to be a device that replaces passwords with a system where you (the client) have a different public key pair for every verifier, and you have some tamper-evident token that acts as a memory prosthesis so you don't have to remember any of these secrets because the token remembers them for you. Never mind that in the current prototype version it is an app on a smartphone, as opposed

---

[1] Actually it might not, because it doesn't contain a digit; but that just shows the inflexible stupidity of such policies.

[2] LNCS 7114, pp 49–97.

[3]

to being a tamper-resistant or tamper-evident token: the one in the video is the envisionment version where we have our own dedicated hardware that does nothing else. And if you're going to say the word Pico then say "peeko" and not "pike-o", because it's the name of a person—Pico della Mirandola.

Bruce Christianson: Bruce Christianson It might be worth saying why there's a different public key pair for each counterpart, because that's not the standard use of public key.

Reply: Reply OK, thanks for the hint. The reason is because Pico was designed with privacy protection in mind. If you have a different public key for every verifier they cannot track your accesses to the various sites, even if they collude, because you use a different identity every time. Pico does mutual authentication, with the other service going first to protect user privacy. Before revealing my identity to Amazon.com I first say: "Are you really Amazon.com? Prove to me you are Amazon.com." And then, if the proof is satisfactory, I reply: "OK, then I'm Frank"—or rather "OK, then I'm the client known to you as Stetson" if I prefer not to reveal my actual identity. You could say this is equivalent to first checking that I am on https://amazon.com and that the lock is there, and then typing my username and password only after having done that check.

So, "Objection your honour", says a voice from the back, "these benefits you mentioned don't really come from public key cryptography, they come from the fact that you are now using unguessable credentials. And if I could use the same mechanisms that you're playing for Pico, namely the tamper-evident tokens, to hold the secrets that the principals have, then I could offer the same properties without using public key at all." Whoaaa, everybody speaks at the same time, session is adjourned.

OK, then, let's start again. This is the next hearing. Please state exactly what it is that you want to do. All right... We like some properties of Pico, chief among them the fact that the compromise of the credentials file at Adobe does not expose the accounts at Facebook. Or, more strongly than that, that

---

Benefit: the compromise of the credentials file at Adobe does not expose *any* login credentials, whether at Adobe or anywhere else, because they are only usable for verifying, and not for impersonating.

So we want to offer this benefit. Pico currently offers it using public key, but imagine that quantum computing works and succeeds in making current public key cryptosystems unusable: could we offer the same benefit without public key crypto? Less dramatically, another reason for eliminating public key might be because in a mobile and wearable computing environment we want to conserve energy and public key is considered too expensive. We keep the assumption we had previously from Pico that we may use tamper evident tokens (whether we are storing private keys in them, or symmetric keys, or other kinds of secrets). We have a way of freeing the user's mind from having to work as a storage place for secrets: we can dump any required secrets into a physical token where it doesn't matter how many there are and how complicated they are. The token can securely remember as many high entropy secrets as we need.

Could Pico do all that without public key crypto? Well, it (almost) already does, you'd be surprised to hear. The idea is very easy: instead of having a different key pair for every verifier, you have a different strong random password for every verifier. Because the token remembers them, it's OK: there's no penalty for users because they never have to remember, type or even see those passwords. We have already implemented this. If you were there last year and you remember what we said[4], we had the problem of bootstrapping the Pico system. No users had a Pico because we were just developing it. Therefore, if we had asked a website to support Pico, they would have said no, because nobody has one. So, if we had then approached people to ask if they would be interested in trying Pico, they'd answer no, because no websites support it, so what could they use it for? To break this vicious circle we made a system where, to the user, the website would look as if it supported Pico, while to the website it would like the user is typing a password. And this two-headed Janus in the middle was the Pico Lens, an add-on in the browser that transformed any website you viewed. When viewed through the Lens, it would look as if the website were Pico compatible and had a QR code to scan, while behind the scenes the Pico Lens would instead send a password to the website. With the Pico system you may use passwords that are strong, randomly generated, complicated, much harder than the ones that you would actually remember, and you can have a different one for every website without imposing a memory burden on the user.

The trouble is that, if the Pico stores the password that the person already used for that website before adopting Pico, then it is still potentially a crackable password. So we said: wouldn't it be nice if, on account setup, the Pico also generated a *strong* password every time, and registered *that* with the website, instead of the human-generated password, which is probably much weaker? But there was a practical problem: websites don't actually offer a machine-friendly interface for entering a password, whether it's the one that you already registered (login), or, even worse, a new one you are registering (account creation or update). Also, websites may have a password policy but they don't expose it in a machine readable way. If you enter a password like the one that Emily the Geek had, they might still complain that it doesn't have a digit. But Emily's password manager had no way of knowing from the website that a digit was required in there before randomly generating the password. So we've also come up with a new scheme called "Password Manager Friendly", which is a simple specification that websites can obey to be friendly to password managers and any other software agents that manage your passwords. That way, without guesswork, a password manager (like the one you already have in your browser, or like the Pico one that you hold in your hand) can then enter passwords on your behalf.

In summary, with these two steps (Pico Lens + PMF) Pico already more or less[5] offers the desired benefit without using public key primitives. It does this

---

[4] LNCS 8809 172–196.

[5] More or less because this depends on websites offering PMF compliance.

by having a strong, uncrackable, unguessable password for every site, that the website stores with salting and hashing.

Tavish Vaidya: Tavish Vaidya How is it different from software-based password managers that we currently use like 1Password, LastPass and so forth?

Reply: Reply It's quite similar, but different in two respects. First, our Password Manager Friendly specification takes out the guesswork when entering passwords on behalf of the user. Without PMF, even with the commercial password managers you mentioned you would see unavoidable problems. For example, imagine you already have an account with Amazon.com, but you have not entered it into your password manager. So you login manually. The password manager notices that you're logging into a site it doesn't have a password for and very helpfully says: "would you like me to remember that?", because it's one you might re-use in the future. But it says so *even if you made a mistake* while typing the password, because the password manager has no way to know whether the login succeeded or failed, because the website will always return 200 OK to signify that it correctly served the page. And if the page has red text that says "sorry you entered the wrong password" or "there was a problem with your user ID or password", the password manager has no clue about that, and it will still offer you to remember the *wrong* password. So that is one issue that we solved with PMF.

The other thing is that the Pico has secure storage for your credentials (in this case passwords) that is independent of your computer. So we run on the assumption that it's easier to have lots of malware on your computer than to have it on the Pico, which ideally is this dedicated single-purpose device. When Pico is implemented as an app on a smartphone, this is not quite as true as it would be, but this is the direction we're going in[6].

We were saying: Pico offers that benefit without using public key, but there is still a little problem. There is a place where Pico still uses public keys, and that's while establishing a secure channel to the website. On which occasion? Well, when I am interacting with a TLS-enabled website (Fig. 3 is a screenshot of me going to https://www.amazon.co.uk), from the `https` prefix and the padlock I see that it's the genuine amazon.co.uk; at least the certificate verifies as genuine, according to my browser, so this login page is OK for me to use because TLS gives me a secure pipe between my computer and Amazon's computer. So if I say "Yes, I have a password" and I type it in here, then it cannot be overheard because it's protected by this pipe that TLS provides. If we didn't have public key we wouldn't have this armoured pipe from TLS, but that wouldn't be a big deal because we already share a secret, namely this password, so we could use it: instead of transmitting the password we could have some kind of challenge-response based on the password where whoever first acts as the verifier[7] sends a challenge, and then the prover computes a response based on the known shared

---

[6] Sandboxing technologies such as TrustZone may help secure the phone.

[7] If we do mutual authentication the roles will reverse at some point.

Fig. 3. Amazon login.

secret and sends that, and it's different every time so it isn't a problem if we don't have the pipe from TLS.

The problem instead comes when I am not using the "Yes, I have a password" radio button but this other one, "No, I am a new customer". In that case, how do I open an account? I will have to type that my name is X, my email address is Y, my chosen password is Z, type the password again... and this time, *without* TLS, this is not going to be protected by an encrypted pipe. So how do I first communicate this secret (the newly-invented password) from me to the website at the other end in the absence of public key? And that's a problem we need to solve before solving the much harder human factors problem that, even with a public key and with the icon of a padlock, users don't really understand HTTPS and they can still be phished and fooled in about a million ways even with technical security in place.

There is a traditional solution for that, which is Needham-Schroeder (which later morphed into Kerberos). If we wanted to apply that solution to this case we would need some kind of introducer with whom both parties already shared some secret. If we compare the two alternatives for transferring the initial secret (in this case the password) between me and Amazon, then in the case of the public key system the client talks to the website directly whereas, in the case of the symmetric key system with the Kerberos style arrangement, the client must first talk to some authentication server that acts as the introducer. So the defender of the symmetric key solution would say: "Why do you penalise me for that? You have a third party in the public key solution as well, that's the certificate authority who signed the public key of the website. So you need a third party with public key crypto as well." But then the public key guy would reply: "but in my case the client can talk to the website without having to talk to that third party", and then the symmetric key guy would object: "but wait a minute: if you don't talk to that third party, then what happens on revocation?"

When Adobe loses 153 million passwords, probably one of the next things it must do to recover from this mess is to say: "My website's public key is no longer valid. Even though it was due to expire in 2017, you had better not use that in the intervening time. Please use this new one I made after recovering from this attack.". If the client visiting Adobe's website doesn't check with the CA (says the symmetric key guy), then how is she going to know that the public key she receives is not the old one whose private key had already been hacked out of Adobe? How does she know that she's not talking to some Adobe impersonator? On the other hand, if she instead checks every time that the CA is validating that key, then she is no better off[8] with public key than she is with symmetric key, i.e. with Kerberos.

So let's have a closer look at what happens with revocation on the web. Once the credentials are suspected (or known) to have been compromised, they must be revoked and replaced with new ones. This activity, like most of the clean-up, deletion and so on, tends to be a weak point in many systems: if you look at object oriented systems, for example, there's a higher chance of bugs hiding in the destructor rather than in the constructor. This is a common pattern. We don't put as much care into cleaning up as we do into doing the thing in the first place. Even on the web as we know it today, revocation is somewhat of a mess. So let's consider a few aspects of this problem.

First, *revoking for public key* versus *revoking for symmetric key*. What makes revocation hard is the sharing of public keys. When I share a public key among many parties then I have to talk to all these parties in order to revoke it. But the problem is that, since it's a public key, people can look it up in a directory. I don't know who has looked it up; worse, I don't know who will look it up in the future. Pico doesn't suffer from this problem because it doesn't share a public key with many parties (it sends a different public key to every correspondent), but this approach is unconventional. It does mean a proliferation of public keys for Pico, but at least it will know whom to contact when it needs to revoke. With the traditional approach, instead, when a principal uses the same public key for all his correspondents, then it can never be sure that it has warned all of them when it needs to revoke, especially future ones who may dig out an old stale copy from somewhere.

Second, *revoking for a client* versus *revoking for a server*. In today's web, the problem is only there for the server who may have to revoke its public key. Nobody uses client certificates, so it's just the website that has to say "sorry, I have changed the key", and the clients don't have long-lived private and public keys at all. In the case of Pico, instead, it may happen that the Pico needs to do a revocation, because the public key authentication is mutual and both the website and Pico have private keys. Note that, if I lose the whole token, then

---

[8] In terms of communication costs and dependencies on external infrastructure.

all the credentials will need to be revoked, which means I have talk to all the correspondents.

Mark Lomas: Mark Lomas When you said nobody uses client certificates, did you mean very few people?

Reply: Reply Yes, nobody *in practice.*

Mark Lomas: Mark Lomas Some of us do.

Reply: Reply My hat off to you.

Mark Lomas: Mark Lomas Some organisations do as a matter of policy, and it's an important safeguard.

Reply: Reply That's interesting. Is it actually supported by the software that is normally used, or is it such a tiny edge case that you end up having to fix things on your own?

Bruce Christianson: Bruce Christianson I'm assuming this is in a closed corporate context rather than buying stuff off the web.

Mark Lomas: Mark Lomas That's the only place I've seen it, yes. But, I mean, properly designed web servers do support client side SSL certificates and it's a very good idea to use them if you've got the opportunity to use them, for much of the reasons you're exactly saying.

Bruce Christianson: Bruce Christianson But in a corporate environment you can enforce a sensible revocation authority policy for public key.

Reply: Reply Yes, and the interesting thing I'm wondering about is that if you use commercial off-the-shelf software, and the commercial off-the-shelf software never encounters the case of clients having certificates, then is it going to be likely to work? Or will it have bugs in that area that is never exercised? Or do you have to develop your own software for that?

Mark Lomas: Mark Lomas Let's put it this way: Microsoft SharePoint servers supports it.

Daniel Thomas: Daniel Thomas If you get an SSL certificate from startssl.com they issue you with a client certificate, and then you must use that for authentication. This appears to work on most web browsers.

Keith Irwin: Keith Irwin The Roku streaming video boxes actually use client certificates for the default authentication for some of the streaming services. So it's being used in a very controlled way; not by J. Random User but by somebody who's taken the time to set it up for their Roku streaming service. Still, it is in use.

Reply: Reply OK, thanks. Now let's rewind a bit. In the context of revocation on the web as it happens today, what is Adobe supposed to do when it loses its credentials file (and presumably, in the same incident, its private key)? There are essentially two options. One is to have a certificate revocation list repeatedly issued by the CA all the time. This means the CA would have to give its clients a list of certificates that have been revoked since the last time (or "ever", if one wanted a self-contained list) and this may have to be distributed hierarchically through the makers of the browsers. That would mean daily updates of lots of megabytes of data, and this is not done by many certificate authorities; plus there are over a hundred certificate authorities inside the browser, and each one of them would have to do that in parallel. This is not what is currently happening. The other option is for the client to always check with the certificate authority whether the certificate that is being provided by the website is still valid, using the Online Certificate Status Protocol, and that would add an extra call to another party on the net at every login[9]. Plus all the issues of whether either of these two solutions puts any incentive on the attackers to take down the CA, or take down some links. There's more of an incentive to attack the CA if, by attacking the CA, the bad guys can now carry out an attack on clients.

Bruce Christianson: Bruce Christianson The CA has got to come more and more online in order for this to work.

Reply: Reply Yes, and every transaction pays the penalty of extra overhead whether there was going to be an attack or not. So yes, all very nice but in practice it isn't used much. If instead we did the revocation without the public keys then the secure but inefficient alternative would be that the client contacts the third party (the Kerberos server) at every login, and after a website compromise the Kerberos server is told by the website that they should no longer use that credential (which is not a public key anymore: it is the key that the user shares with the website), and the website would have to change the credential for every one of its clients. Every one of the correspondents, when they got to the Kerberos server, would be given a new one. But this assumes that the client talks to the Kerberos server not just the first time when setting up the password, but also whenever she accesses the website, which is not the story that we told earlier. And this is perfectly equivalent to the asymmetric key case of every certificate being rechecked with the certification authority.

Now the "optimisation" (in the Roger Needham sense of "replacing something that works with something that almost works but is cheaper") is where the client only contacts the third party the first time, as we suggested earlier. But then we have exactly the same problem as the public key: when the website wants to revoke its certificate it can tell the Kerberos server, but the client is only going to figure out that the key is revoked the next time she decides for some reason to talk to the Kerberos server, which she doesn't need to do because she already shares a key with the website. Of course, when she talks to the genuine website, she would get a warning that she should change the credential. But, if she talks to the impersonating website, then she has no way of telling that they are impersonating. So she would be vulnerable to misuse of the unexpired credentials exactly in the same way as with public keys. In the contrapuntal discussion we had earlier between public and symmetric key

---

[9] Worse: at every request of a TLS-protected page.

authentication systems, it first seemed like they had different properties, but in fact they both have the same properties. The two systems end up having exactly the same trade-offs.

And so, to conclude this much less controversial talk than we all originally thought it was going to be... The issue here, despite the original title, has a much broader scope than just Pico, and it's basically "can we do web authentication if public key cryptography doesn't work anymore?". And the answer is: yes, it's even fairly straightforward, except for that part of replacing TLS. Pico shows the way, by using tamper-evident tokens as a memory prosthesis, which is necessary if the client is going to have to remember credentials more complicated than human-generated secrets that can be easily guessed or brute-forced. Pico uses public keys unconventionally, giving a different one to each verifier; this paves the way for our new compatibility mode where we give a different credential to every verifier, but now it's not a public key anymore. This alternative can be essentially as secure as with public key, but more easily deployable, so that's what we'll adopt in the future for Pico, making this the default. The problem of using public key is that it forces us to make a lot of changes to the backend, and so it's harder to convince the operator of the website to adopt Pico than if we say "just make yourself PMF compatible", which is a change they could technically do in an afternoon, as opposed to having to support public keys, and the Sigma-I protocol, and changing the backend database and so on and so forth. The new compatibility mode without public keys makes our life much easier, while not losing much of the security.

However, for Pico we still rely on the TLS that exists today on the web, which is based on public key. That is not a public key protocol that *we* introduced: it's one that's already there and we do rely on it in this compatibility mode. Now, as for the separate hypothetical business of replacing TLS with a Kerberos-inspired alternative, we argue that has comparable costs and trade-offs, when we consider all the costs that are normally hidden.

Vashek Matyas: Vashek Matyas I've seen that you argue for that. I would be inclined to believe that, but can you provide more arguments than you provide in the talk? Is it a general statement that replacing TLS with Kerberos as an alternative would have the same costs and trade-offs, or is it for this particular purpose?

Ross Anderson: Ross Anderson This is all a discussion people had 20 years ago between shared key and public key, and there's nothing to add. It's all engineering detail.

Bruce Christianson: Bruce Christianson Yes: the final twist of the knife is to say that you need tamper-evident hardware to make a public key work, because if you haven't got tamper-evident hardware I can either read your private key or substitute mine for it. But Ross is exactly right.

Paul Wernick: Paul Wernick Another quick question. I notice in the paper you referred to the aura that ensures that the Pico device is actually held by you and not by the bad guy. Is there any more progress on that? Because obviously that's a key part of it, to make sure that the device is with the right person.

Reply: Reply Yes. Unlocking the token with the aura is another important part of the Pico project, and it is quite orthogonal to what we discussed here, which is how Pico interacts with the verifier. Other systems, like smartphones or second-factor-gadgets for banking, lock their tokens with a PIN, or with a squiggle, or with a fingerprint, something like that. We didn't want user-chosen secrets and we wanted the user not to have to do anything other than using the device naturally: if their Pico is not with them, it just stops working. My coauthor Graeme, over there, is working on a prototype of this aura, using Bluetooth LE. Ideally we would do everything from zero, with an ad-hoc physical layer for the radio so that we can prevent relay attacks through distance bounding. We cannot do that with Bluetooth LE but we can simulate most of the things we want. He has built some devices that we plan to embed into wearable items of clothing, jewellery, and things like that. When the Pico device (or in the case of the prototype, the smartphone) feels that it's in the proximity of enough of them, then it unlocks itself.

Paul Wernick: Paul Wernick So it's no longer the right person, it's the person wearing the right clothes.

Bruce Christianson: Bruce Christianson Well it's the person wearing my large earring, with my glasses and my Prince Albert[10], yes.

---

[10] Discovering whether the speaker meant the coat or the piercing is left as an exercise for the reader.

Do You Believe in Tinker Bell?
The Social Externalities of Trust

Khaled Baqer and Ross Anderson[✉]

Computer Laboratory, University of Cambridge, Cambridge, UK
{khaled.baqer,ross.anderson}@cl.cam.ac.uk

Abstract. In the play Peter Pan, the fairy Tinker Bell is about to fade away and die because nobody believes in her any more, but is saved by the belief of the audience. This is a very old meme; the gods in Ancient Greece became less or more powerful depending on how many mortals sacrificed to them. On the face of it, this seems a democratic model of trust; it follows social consensus and crumbles when that is lost. However, the world of trust online is different. People trust CAs because they have to; Verisign and Comodo are dominant not because users trust them, but because merchants do. Two-sided market effects are bolstered by the hope that the large CAs are too big to fail. Proposed remedies from governments are little better; they declare themselves to be trusted and appoint favoured contractors as their bishops. Academics have proposed, for example in SPKI/SDSI, that trust should flow from individual users' decisions; but how can that be aggregated in ways compatible with incentives? The final part of the problem is that current CAs are not just powerful but all-powerful: a compromise can let a hostile actor not just take over your session or impersonate your bank, but 'upgrade' the software on your computer. Omnipotent CAs with invisible failure modes are better seen as demons rather than as gods.

Inspired by Tinker Bell, we propose a new approach: a trust service whose power arises directly from the number of users who decide to rely on it. Its power is limited to the provision of a single service, and failures to deliver this service should fairly rapidly become evident. As a proof of concept, we present a privacy-preserving reputation system to enhance quality of service in Tor, or a similar proxy network, with built-in incentives for correct behaviour. Tokens enable a node to interact directly with other nodes and are regulated by a distributed authority. Reputation is directly proportional to the number of tokens a node accumulates. By using blind signatures, we prevent the authority learning which entity has which tokens, so it cannot compromise privacy. Tokens lose value exponentially over time; this negative interest rate discourages hoarding. We demotivate costly system operations using taxes. We propose this reputation system not just as a concrete mechanism for systems requiring robust and privacy-preserving reputation metrics, but also as a thought experiment in how to fix the security economics of emergent trust.

Keywords: Trust · Reputation · Metrics · Unlinkability · Anonymity

© Springer International Publishing Switzerland 2015
B. Christianson et al. (Eds.): Security Protocols 2015, LNCS 9379, pp. 224–236, 2015.
DOI: 10.1007/978-3-319-26096-9_23

1   Introduction

Children know the story of Tinker Bell from JM Barrie's 1904 play 'Peter Pan; or, the boy who wouldn't grow up'. She is a fairy who is about to fade away and die, but is revived when the actors get the audience to declare their belief in her. The underlying idea goes back at least to ancient Greek mythology: the Greek gods' power waxed and waned depending on the number of men who sacrificed to them. More modern references include Jean Ray's 1943 novel *Malpertuis* [21] puts it as (translation from French): "Men are not born of the whim or will of the gods, on the contrary, gods owe their existence to the belief of men. Should this belief wither, the gods will die." The same concept was used recently in the 2012 movie *Wrath of the Titans.*

The idea that authority emerges by consensus and evaporates when the consensus does is not restricted to mythology; democratic institutions perform a similar function. In the context of a nation state, or even a professional society, they are developed into a governance framework optimised for a combination of stability, responsiveness and the maintenance of trust.

How are things online? The honest answer is 'not good'. When talking of trust online the first port of call is the Certification Authority (CA) infrastructure, which has many known failings. A typical machine trusts several hundred CAs, and trusts them for just about everything; if the Iranian secret police manage to hack Comodo, they can not only impersonate your bank, or take over your online banking session, they can also upgrade your software. Since an Iranian compromise caused the browser vendors to close down Diginotar, we have seen corporates moving their certificate business to the two largest players, Verisign and Comodo, in the belief that these firms are 'too big to fail' (or perhaps 'too interconnected to fail'). Firms hope that even if these CAs are hacked (as both have been), the browser vendors would never dare remove their root certs because of the collateral damage this would cause. As for ordinary users, we trust Verisign not because we decided to, but because the merchants who operate websites we use decided to. This is a classic two-sided market failure.

Can we expect salvation from governments? Probably not any time soon. Governments have tried to assume divine powers of their own, first during the crypto wars by attempting to mandate that they have master keys for all trust services operating in their jurisdiction, and second by trying to control authentication services. Such initiatives tend to come from the more secret parts of states rather than the most accountable parts.

Can we users ourselves do better? The SPKI/SDSI proposal from Ellison, Rivest and Lampson attracted some research effort in the late 1990s and showed how every individual user could act as their own trust anchor, but the question is how to deploy such a system and scale it up; the one user-based system actually deployed in the 1990s, PGP, remains widely used in niche applications such as CERTs and anti-virus researchers, but never scaled up to mass use. The application of encrypting email suffers from strong network externalities in that I need my counterparties to encrypt their email too. This has become the norm in specific communities but did not happen for the general population.

Can we scale up deployment in other applications from a club that provides a small initial user base? One case where this happens is in the Internet interconnection ecosystem, where trust among some 50,000 ASes is founded on the relationships between about a dozen Tier-1 providers, who form in effect a club; their chief engineers meet regularly at Nanog conferences and know each other well. But how could a service scale up from a few dozen users?

2   Motivation

In this paper we present another example for discussion. We propose an anonymous online reputation system whose goal is to let people get better quality of service from a distributed proxy service such as Tor. Our proposed new trust service has limited scope; if it works, it can provide faster network access, while if it fails its failure should be evident. The more people trust it, the more effective it becomes; if people observe that it's not working and lose faith in it, then it will fade away and die. What's more, multiple such trust services can compete as overlays on the same network.

The Tor network [9] consists of volunteer relays mixing users' traffic to provide anonymity. The list of relays is disseminated through a consensus file which includes the IP addresses of all relays. IP addresses are required to allow a user's client (Tor software) to locally decide which relays to use to route traffic. However, an attacker (say a *censor*) can also download the consensus file, extract relay addresses, and block traffic by cooperating with local ISPs or using a nation-wide firewall. Thus, *victims* of a technically competent censor need private relays to connect to one of the publicly known relays. The private relay must not be known to the censor, or it too will be blocked. These private relays, called *bridges*, act as transient proxies helping victims to connect to the Tor network. Bridges are a scarce resource, yet play a critical role in connecting censorship victims to the Tor network. Therefore we want to incentivise Tor users to run more bridges.

The system proposed in this paper was originally designed to motivate nonmalicious node interaction in anonymous remailer networks. We then realised that the design fits into the literary theme for the Twenty-third International Security Protocols Workshop, "Information Security in Fiction and in Fact".

3   System Design

The system consists of competing *clubs*; each is managed by a club *secretary*. This is a major design difference from using a quorum of Directory Authorities (DAs) organised as a failover cluster, as currently implemented in Tor. The club secretaries, acting as Bridge Authorities (BAs), are responsible for disseminating information regarding club *members*. Each secretary is supported by a community of members who use its tokens as a currency to prioritise service. Members help censored users (*victims*) to circumvent censorship by volunteering their resources to act as bridges, and can claim token rewards for their help. To the secretaries, the performance of members is visible and measurable.

Secretaries clear each others' tokens, just as banks clear each others' notes. Through private token payments, we can analyse the behaviour of nodes and determine which are actively and correctly participating in the network. Tokens are blindly-signed objects used to request services from other nodes. Tokens lose value over time, to demotivate hoarding. We discuss now the details of operation.

3.1 Member Registration

Members can join any club they choose; loyalty to a club is determined by the incentives and performance it offers. Members can participate in one club or many, volunteering for whoever provides reliable services. Members offer service to a club by broadcasting their services: "this is my key, address, etc. and I'll be available for contact between 11:00 and 11:30; send victims my way". This process can be automated using an uncensored and trusted means of communication. We assume that most members are outside the censor's jurisdiction, though some will have ties of family or friendship to the censor's victims. Thus some members may be motivated by the wish to help loved ones while others are altruistic and others are revenue maximisers. Some members will be within the censored jurisdiction.

We assume that keys can be exchanged successfully between members and secretaries: either the secretary publishes public keys somehow, or passes them on to new members as part of the recruitment process (about which we are agnostic). Within the censored jurisdiction, one or more designated *scouts* communicate with victims: we assume these are existing members. We assume the existence of innocuous store-and-forward communications channels such as email or chat; only a handful of censored jurisdictions ban Gmail and encrypted chat completely.

3.2 A Simple Threat Model

Suppose that Alice and Bob belong to a club organised by Samantha to provide bridge services. Alice volunteers her IP address at time t to Samantha; a victim, Victor, contacts Sam to ask for a bridge; Sam gives him Alice's IP address and a short one-time password N_A; Victor contacts Alice and presents N_A; Alice shows N_A to Sam, who checks it, and Alice connects Victor to the Tor network. The protocol runs

$$A \rightarrow S : IP$$
$$S \rightarrow V : IP, N_A$$
$$V \rightarrow A : N_A$$
$$A \rightarrow S : N_A$$
$$S \rightarrow A : OK$$

The first problem with this simple protocol is that Samantha has to be online all the time; as she's a bottleneck, the censor can take down the system by running a distributed denial of service attack on her, and even without that we have two messages more in the protocol than we probably need. Our first attempt at improvement is to make the nonce N_A one that Alice can check; Alice shares a key K_{AS} with Samantha and we construct the nonce N_A by encrypting a counter k with it. The protocol is now

$$A \to S : IP$$
$$S \to V : IP, \{k\}_{K_{AS}}$$
$$V \to A : \{k\}_{K_{AS}}$$

Alice can now check the nonce directly, so Samantha doesn't have to be online.

The next problem is harder; it's that the censor's shill, Vlad, can also ask for an IP address, and if Samantha gives him one, the censor will block it. This is the real attack right now on Tor bridges; the censors pretend to be victims, find the bridges and block them. Various mechanisms are used from restricting the number of IP addresses given to any inquirer, and trying to detect Sybil inquirers using analytics; but if you have a repressed population where one percent have been coopted into working for the secret police, then telling Vlad apart from Victor is hard (at least for Samantha who is sitting safely in New York).

3.3   A More Realistic Threat Model

In what follows we assume that of the two representative club members, Alice is in the repressed country, while Bob is sitting safely in exile. Alice, if honest and competent, is better than average at telling Victor from Vlad, perhaps because of family ties, friends, or ethnic or religious affiliations. Alice might be undercover, or might have some form of immunity; she might be a diplomat, or religious official, or sports star. She might hand over bridge contact details to victims written on pieces of paper, or on private Twitter messages to fans. The full gamut of human communications, both online and offline, are available for members who act as scouts to get in touch with victims.

We now introduce another layer of indirection into the protocol. After Bob volunteers to be a bridge, Samantha gives the scout Alice a token for her to give to a victim Victor, constructed as $\{k, N_{AS}\}_{K_{BS}}$. When this is presented to Bob, he can decrypt it and recognise the counter, so he knows Samantha generated it for him, and grants bridge service to the victim. He sends it to Samantha, who can recognise it as having been generated for Alice, and can thus note that Alice managed to recruit Victor (or alternatively, if Bob's IP address then ended up on the blacklist, that Alice recruited Vlad by mistake). Formally

$$B \to S : IP$$
$$S \to A : IP, \{k, N_{AS}\}_{K_{BS}}$$
$$V \to B : \{k, N_{AS}\}_{K_{BS}}$$
$$B \to S : N_{AS}$$

N_{AS} can of course be constructed in turn by encrypting a counter; but once we start encrypting a block cipher output and a counter under a wider block cipher, we are starting to get to the usability limit of what can be done with groups of digits written on a piece of paper. As AES ciphertext plus an IP address is about 50 decimal digits. In some applications, this may be all that's possible. In others, we might assume that both scouts and victims can cut and paste short strings, so that digital coins and other public-key mechanisms can be used.

In a more general design, we have to think not just about running scouts to contact victims and tell victims apart from censors, but also about scouts who are eventually turned, and about clubs that fail because the club organiser is turned, or has their computer hacked by the censor, or is just incompetent. We also have to think about dishonesty: about a bridge operator or scout who cheats by inflating his score by helping nonexistent or Sybil victims. How far can we get with reasonably simple mechanisms?

3.4   Payment System

We avoid using external payments, as offering cash payments as incentives to volunteers risks trashing the volunteer spirit (this is why the Tor project has always been reluctant to adopt any form of digital cash mechanism for service provision; volunteering is crucial for Tor's operation). Furthermore, we avoid using complicated zero-knowledge protocols or creating huge log files to protect against double-spending; large audit trails cannot scale very well. We prefer a lightweight mechanism that uses blind signatures made with regularly changing keys and member pseudonyms to provide privacy and unlinkability, as well as symmetric cryptography to create data blobs verifiable by the secretary or bridge. The token reward can then be used to pay for other services in Tor. For example, club members who run successful bridge services might enjoy better quality of service by using service tokens to get priority.

We now sketch a design using blind signatures rather than just shared-key mechanisms.

3.4.1   Member Identifier

After registering a member, the secretary creates a series of data blobs as the member's *identifiers*. An identifier can be the result of encrypting the member's name plus a counter or random salt with a symmetric encryption algorithm and a key known to the secretary; identifiers change constantly, and the secretary alone can link them to members other than by context. As well as knowing which members correspond to which identifiers, the secretary also notes which victims are introduced to which identifiers as possible bridges. This is to make it hard for a member to generate fake victims and claim rewards without providing them with service. It does mean the secretary is completely trusted, but secretaries compete with each other to provide effective service. We discuss all this in more detail later.

3.4.2 Victim Accounts

Secretaries maintain reputation scores not just for members but also for victims. Upon being introduced by a scout, a victim gets a default score of 1 allowing them to make a single bridge request. After a successful initial request, the victim's account is reduced to zero for the current period. This is one of a number of rate-limiting mechanisms to prevent Vlad from draining the IP pool.

Secretaries use victim accounts to mitigate a few possible attacks, which we explore in more detail in the discussion section. One purpose is Vlad detection: if the members a victim learns about are not censored after a period of time – the IP addresses are not blacklisted and the scout is not turned – the victim's account is increased; the opposite is true if a scout is arrested. Eventually, a diligent secretary should be able to identify fake victims by intersecting groups of victims and groups of censored members. It follows that the censor would have to refrain from blocking members if he wants to learn about new members. If he blocks members immediately, he betrays his shills. The conventional law-enforcement approach would be to block immediately, while the intelligence approach would be to merely observe quietly until all or most of the members are identified. Forcing the censor to make a strategic choice opens up all sorts of possibilities.

Secretaries have a clear incentive to protect their members' identities; if the censor can spot and arrest the scouts and block the bridge IP addresses, the club will be ineffective and volunteers will help other clubs instead. Some volunteers will be picky, as if they join a badly-run club their IP address will be quickly blocked in that club's country of interest. Other volunteers may be happy to help victims in fifty countries and consider it a badge of honour to be blocked in a dozen of them. And if participation is rewarded not just with honour but with improved quality of service, then this will mostly be forthcoming from the jurisdictions in which you are not blocked.

3.4.3 Token Creation

Account payment mechanisms can be replaced by blind tokens at one or more stages in the process. In the simplest implementation, we can reward Bob for providing bridge services with tokens that offer better quality of service from Tor nodes. Given the way Tor works, this requires some form of anonymous payment or certification. So when Bob services a request from Victor, Bob can now use Alice's nonce N_{AS} to request an anonymous token from Samantha rather than just banking the credit. He does this by generating a well-formed token C_B, blinds it with a multiplier, and sends it to Samantha, who generates a blind signature [4] and returns it. With simple RSA blinding, where e is the public signature verification exponent, d the private signing exponent and n the public modulus, we have

$$B \rightarrow S : N_{AS}, r^e C_B \quad (\text{mod } n)$$
$$S \rightarrow B : r C_B^d \quad (\text{mod } n)$$

Bob now unblinds C_B by dividing out the blinding factor r. This token is unlinkable and can be used for interacting with Tor nodes. The token C_B includes a random number, generated by Bob, to detect double-spending. Unlinkable tokens can now be used to request other services by embedding them in the request; for example, if victims can handle public-key mechanisms, Victor might use such a token to request bridge service from Bob. However, it's in prioritising anonymous service requests that blind tokens really come into their own.

3.4.4 Defining Time Using Key Rotation

As noted earlier, we assume that new public signature verification keys are announced for each future epoch. (It is possible to use an identity-based signature scheme by setting the public key for epoch i to be the value of i). We can simplify matters if we define a time interval as an epoch; this enables us to avoid using timestamps in token protocols (we'd prefer to avoid the complexity of using partially blinded signatures that contain timestamps). Changing public keys frequently also greatly reduces the amount of state that must be retained to detect double spending, a known problem with blind payment systems. If tokens are used only by members such as Tor nodes with high-quality network service, this is probably a reasonable simplifying measure. We note in passing that nodes have an incentive to pay attention to the stream of signature traffic, to ensure they are not cheated by being passed a stale token.

3.4.5 Validation and Value of Tokens

Tokens expire if they were issued using a signing key that was retired or revoked; for example, a signing key may be deemed retired if it was first used a certain number of epochs ago. We propose that the number of epochs since the token's signing key was first used is a deflator, which will decrease the value of a token. The formula used might be exponential, to represent a negative rate of interest; it is not clear that it matters all that much whether deflation is exponential or linear. Club secretaries can refresh tokens with new ones of an appropriately lower value, according to rules we will discuss later, and will reject double spend attempts. Expired tokens will also be recognised and rejected by all nodes, limiting the volume of data needed to detect double-spending.

3.5 Generating Trust and Reputation Metrics

Each secretary acts as a bank and keeps members' accounts: each member's balance is the amount of correctly performed identifiable services plus the number of tokens claimed or refreshed in each epoch. These balances act as a proxy for reputation. The balances also deflate over time, but significantly less quickly than tokens in circulation. For example, if a token loses 20 % of its value at each epoch when in circulation, it might lose only 5 % when banked. Thus a member wanting to maximise its reputation has to do useful work and bank tokens promptly. The history of members' bank balances may also be made available to other members; there are second-order issues here about the potential identifiability of members involved in particular campaigns, so whether the secretary publishes member account history or smoothed metrics derived from it would depend on the application.

The overall effect is that the network as a whole can take a view on how much it trusts particular members. The more tokens Bob has in the bank, the higher his reputation. Note that there is little incentive for a group of colluding nodes to manipulate the reputation system by trading among themselves; they achieve nothing except to decrease their original endowment of tokens by the amount of time these tokens are not in a bank.

Another advantage of using a rapidly depreciating currency is that we can use the reputation system itself as an indicator of member liveness. We want to avoid sending requests to offline nodes; yet if we contact each node directly to request proof of liveness (for example with an ICMP packet), we open up a denial-of-service attack where a malicious node saturates the system with liveness checks. A real-time reputation system may help us avoid this.

4   Discussion

The system proposed in this paper is mainly concerned with enabling a group of users to maintain situational awareness in a censorship avoidance system. Each club of users can set up their own bridge authority maintained by a club secretary; an authority trusted by more users will become larger. In equilibrium we hope that clubs would settle each others' tokens, just as banks clear each others' notes. It can happen of course the community supporting a particular club fails. Our system is designed to enable social externalities to determine the level of trust in the system. If nodes believe in Tinker Bell, then they can bank their tokens with her bank; but if trust and belief fade, then tokens for Tinker Bell deplete, her reputation metrics decrease, and her bank eventually goes bust. The mechanisms to deal with this are a matter for the implementation.

4.1   Mitigating Collusions and Malicious Members

There are a number of possible ways in which members might behave improperly. Alice and Bob might collude, so that Bob pretends to service Sybil victims invented by Alice; Samantha can mitigate the risks of this to some extent by randomising the allocation of IP addresses to scouts, and running appropriate analytics. The worst case is if the target country's intelligence service manages to hack Samantha's computer; then it's game over. (For that reason we posit multiple competing clubs.) The next most severe attack might be if the target country's intelligence service manages to subvert Alice and most of her fellow in-country members, and uses their bridge resources to make innocuous network connections, rather than blacklisting them, thereby denying the resources to censorship victims and denying both Bob and Samantha knowledge that Alice has been subverted[1]. While a normal censor will act as a policeman and block bridge IP addresses, a more strategic adversary might prefer to leave them be

---

[1] Such subversion might involve a national-scale malware implementation programme; see for example Gamma's 'Project Turkmenistan' disclosed on wikileaks.

and exhaust the resource. Detecting and defeating such attacks requires further channels of information. Ultimately we rely once more on the facts that there are multiple clubs, and multiple channels of communication between censorship victims and their family, friends or co-religionists in exile.

4.2 Mitigating Sybil Attacks

Members can claim tokens by fabricating victims, but those members end up 'burning' their victims' account balances (and their email identities) if they don't use the identifiers. Recall that victims are assigned to members randomly, and Samantha can run analytics to determine which scouts and which bridges have outlying patterns of victims. Diagnosis is not always going to be straightforward; Samantha might suspect that some victims are bogus, or that some members refuse to service victims, but it may in fact be the case that some victim group cannot contact members due to censorship or DoS attacks.

It does little good if multiple members collude to exchange each others' identifiers; they end up burning their fabricated victims' identities, as long as there are honest members acting correctly serving genuine victims. Members are better off acting correctly.

4.3 Security Economics

In this proposal, we attempt to incentivise correct behaviour, to generate metrics to identify which nodes are most interconnected, and empower nodes to shift trust to other nodes. In other words, we facilitate the mechanisms required to democratise trust and power, by empowering participating nodes to vote (transact using tokens) for the node that deserves their trust. Moreover, by creating a system to generate useful metrics, this design can be used to facilitate research on the security economics of users' interactions, inspired by [1, 8].

5 Related Work

In their paper *On the economics of anonymity* [1], the authors argue that the actions of interacting nodes in the network must be visible for informative decision-making about malicious behaviour. Through the trust and reputation metrics introduced in this paper, we can now understand node interactions better while preserving privacy. A thorough and insightful discussion based on practical experience is provided in [8], whose authors state that in order to provide the mechanisms for verifiable transactions and reputation ratings in anonymity systems, they needed to retrofit appropriate metrics. In fact, those authors already wondered whether it might be possible to create a reputation currency that might "expire, or slowly lose value over time". The redesigns that the authors discuss in [8] were originally introduced in [6,10]. In [6], the authors integrate into Mix networks (anonymous remailers such as Mixmaster [17]) the role of witnesses: semi-trusted nodes that act as referees to service rejection or abnormal behaviour (but this introduces multiple trust bottlenecks and can be abused if the witnesses are compromised). In [10], the authors decided to drop the witness construction. Network paths are constructed in cascades; if one node in the path fails, every node in the path is rated negatively. Without proof of service failure to pinpoint the node responsible, this design is vulnerable to an adversary joining multiple correctly-operating cascades, perhaps in order to route traffic to other adversary-owned cascades (which would de-anonymise users). Similarly, Free Haven [7] uses reputation to reward correctly-operating servers that store data and fulfil their contracts. The reward is a higher reputation that allows a server to store its own data with other servers (so long as no issues occur when validating service contracts). In fact, Free Haven is one of the first designs to use reputation as a form of currency. Moreover, the stamp-trading system discussed in [18] suggested that reputation built through proofs of providing services can be used as a currency to facilitate node interaction.

In the context of anonymity networks, there have been many proposals to rate and incentivise service-providing nodes (Tor relays). Most of these designs rely on bandwidth verification. For example, in [11], the authors suggest granting priority to the traffic of high-bandwidth nodes using gold stars. However, this can profile relays that also run clients by isolating the gold star traffic from the ordinary variety. More traditional approaches include XPay [5] and PAR [2] which use digital cash to reward relays. A more novel approach is discussed in BRAIDS[2] [13] which employs a similar architecture to the one proposed in this paper; but BRAIDS uses partially blind signatures to embed timestamps in tickets. This allows the Directory Authority (DA) in a BRAIDS-enabled system to expire tickets based on timestamps. In contrast, we expire tokens by key rotation, which enables tokens to be unlinkable. BRAIDS nodes create relay-bound tickets that can be verified by the relay; this increases efficiency, but limits the freedom to transact, as a relay has to contact a DA to issue new tickets for other relays. If a Tor path includes a relay that refuses service, the node must create new relay-bound tickets (generating another request to DA), since the original tickets will not be accepted by another relay. In LIRA [14], the authors attempt to increase efficiency by introducing a probabilistic micropayment protocol into their design (in fact, the authors use a similar construction to MicroMint [22]). In rBridge [23], the authors aimed to solve a different problem: rewarding users using a credit system based on how long information about a Tor bridge remains secret from an adversary (measured by its reachability and non-censorship). This credit system can then be used to obtain information about another bridge if the original bridge is censored.

Other authors were inspired by cryptocurrencies: In [15], high-bandwidth relays are awarded with *Shallots* which are redeemable for *PriorityPasses* that can be used to classify and prioritise Tor traffic. In TorCoin [12], TorPaths are used to verify paths constructed in Tor, and can be viewed as an enhancement for Tor's bandwidth verification. Another approach that aims to preserve users'

---

[2] We initially designed our system without knowledge of BRAIDS then amended this paper to refer to it, but did not set out to design an improvement to BRAIDS.

privacy was proposed in [3] that uses Proof-of-Work shares as micropayments for relays. Relays can then submit those shares to a mining pool and claim rewards in Bitcoin [19]. This provides anonymity for users but not for relays if they use the pure Bitcoin protocol.

Trust and reputation metrics are used for various reasons. For example, Advogato [16] was used to create attack-resistant metrics to correctly rate user-generated content. Another prominent example is Google's PageRank [20], which rates web pages based on how many other pages point to it and creates a reputation rating for how reliable a page is (essentially, the pointers to a page are votes for that particular page but are weighted recursively by their own reputation).

A common problem with most proposals for incentivising Tor relays by using bandwidth verification schemes, or user-generated feedback, is that the authors do not discuss Sybil attacks which involve the adversary creating many circuits to her own relays to game the system. We attempt to solve this through key rotation which provides token expiry and decay.

A further issue is that an overlay on Tor that enables some club of users to enjoy priority service would risk a substantial decrease in the size of the anonymity set. In our proposal, a large number of clubs can each have a secretary acting as their own DA, and the secretaries can clear each others' tokens.

6 Conclusion

In this paper, we sketched a design for an anonymous reputation system that can provide a quality-of-service overlay for an anonymity system like Tor or Mixminion. Unlike most electronic trust services today, it has the right incentives for local and democratic trust management. Groups of users can each establish their own token currency to pay for forwarding services, and the nodes that work hardest can acquire the highest reputation, enabling them to get still more work. Groups can clear each others' tokens. And finally, any group that fails to compete will find that its failure becomes evident; its users can desert it for other groups and it can just fade away.

Acknowledgements. The first author thanks colleagues Laurent Simon and Stephan Kollmann for discussions regarding anonymity networks.

References

1. Acquisti, A., Dingledine, R., Syverson, P.F.: On the economics of anonymity. In: Wright, R.N. (ed.) FC 2003. LNCS, vol. 2742, pp. 84–102. Springer, Heidelberg (2003)
2. Androulaki, E., Raykova, M., Srivatsan, S., Stavrou, A., Bellovin, S.M.: PAR: payment for anonymous routing. In: Borisov, N., Goldberg, I. (eds.) PETS 2008. LNCS, vol. 5134, pp. 219–236. Springer, Heidelberg (2008)
3. Biryukov, A., Pustogarov, I.: Proof-of-work as anonymous micropayment: rewarding a tor relay. In: Böhme, R., Okamoto, T. (eds.) FC 2015. LNCS, vol. 8975, pp. 445–455. Springer, Heidelberg (2015)

4. Chaum, D.: Blind signatures for untraceable payments. In: Chaum, D., Rivest, R.L., Sherman, A.T. (eds.) Advances in Cryptology, pp. 199–203. Springer, New York (1983)
5. Chen, Y., Sion, R., Carbunar, B.: XPay: practical anonymous payments for Tor routing and other networked services. In: Proceedings of the 8th ACM workshop on Privacy in the electronic society, pp. 41–50, ACM (2009)
6. Dingledine, R., Freedman, M.J., Hopwood, D., Molnar, D.: A reputation system to increase MIX-Net reliability. In: Moskowitz, I.S. (ed.) IH 2001. LNCS, vol. 2137, pp. 126–141. Springer, Heidelberg (2001)
7. Dingledine, R., Freedman, M.J., Molnar, D.: The free haven project: distributed anonymous storage service. In: Federrath, H. (ed.) Designing Privacy Enhancing Technologies. LNCS, vol. 2009, pp. 67–95. Springer, Heidelberg (2001)
8. Dingledine, R., Mathewson, N., Syverson, P.: Reputation in P2P anonymity systems. In: Workshop on Economics of Peer-to-Peer Systems, vol. 92 (2003)
9. Dingledine, R., Mathewson, N., Syverson, P.: Tor: the second-generation onion router. Technical report, DTIC Document (2004)
10. Dingledine, R., Syverson, P.: Reliable mix cascade networks through reputation. In: Blaze, M. (ed.) Financial Cryptography. LNCS, vol. 2357, pp. 253–268. Springer, Heidelberg (2003)
11. "Johnny" Ngan, T.-W., Dingledine, R., Wallach, D.S.: Building incentives into Tor. In: Sion, R. (ed.) FC 2010. LNCS, vol. 6052, pp. 238–256. Springer, Heidelberg (2010)
12. Ghosh, M., Richardson, M., Ford, B., Jansen, R.: A TorPath to TorCoin: proof-of-bandwidth altcoins for compensating relays. In: Workshop on Hot Topics in Privacy Enhancing Technologies (HotPETs) (2014)
13. Jansen, R., Hopper, N., Kim, Y.: Recruiting new Tor relays with BRAIDS. In: Proceedings of the 17th ACM Conference on Computer and Communications Security, pp. 319–328, ACM (2010)
14. Jansen, R., Johnson, A., Syverson, P.: LIRA: lightweight incentivized routing for anonymity. Technical report, DTIC Document (2013)
15. Jansen, R., Miller, A., Syverson, P., Ford, B.: From onions to shallots: rewarding Tor relays with TEARS. HotPETS, July 2014
16. Levien, R.: Attack-resistant trust metrics. In: Golbeck, J. (ed.) Computing with Social Trust. Human–Computer Interaction Series, pp. 121–132. Springer, London (2009)
17. Möller, U., Cottrell, L., Palfrader, P., Sassaman, L.: Mixmaster protocol-version 2. Draft, July 2003
18. Moreton, T., Twigg, A.: Trading in trust, tokens, and stamps. In: Proceedings of the First Workshop on Economics of Peer-to-Peer Systems (2003)
19. Nakamoto, S.: Bitcoin: a peer-to-peer electronic cash system. Consulted 1(2012), 28 (2008)
20. Page, L., Brin, S., Motwani, R., Winograd, T.: The PageRank citation ranking: bringing order to the web (1999)
21. Ray, J.: Malpertuis, vol. 142. Marabout, Brussel (1943)
22. Rivest, R.L., Shamir, A.: PayWord and MicroMint: two simple micropayment schemes. In: Lomas, M. (ed.) Security Protocols. LNCS, vol. 1189, pp. 69–87. Springer, Heidelberg (1997)
23. Wang, Q., Lin, Z., Borisov, N., Hopper, N.: rBridge: user reputation based Tor bridge distribution with privacy preservation. In: NDSS (2013)

Do You Believe in Tinker Bell? The Social Externalities of Trust (Transcript of Discussion)

Khaled Baqer and Ross Anderson[⊠]

University of Cambridge, Cambridge, UK
Ross.Anderson@cl.cam.ac.uk

Ross: OK, we've heard from previous talks about how TLS certificates are all or nothing. It's particularly annoying that if I trust a certificate because I want to read a website, then in many systems that certificate can now update my operating system. But I'm not talking so much about the technology as about the incentives, and certification is about as thoroughly broken as you can get because certification is a two-sided market, like payments and like operating systems. People don't decide to trust VeriSign or Comodo, we have to – because if you don't trust Comodo you can't book a flight with EasyJet. Why do people trust, why do merchants trust VeriSign and Comodo? Because they are reckoned too big to fail. Ever since DigiNotar got put to death, merchants have been rushing to the biggest two or three CAs because they reckon that will prevent them suffering something unpleasant. And we know that two-sided markets create an awful lot of security economics problems.

So how can we fix this? Well 20 years ago Ellison, Rivest, Lampson and some others worked on SPKI/SDSI as an alternative to X509. So instead of having a view rooted in 'Britain's .uk's' whatever, you start from user and you say, 'my view of Simon', or 'my view of Vashek', or whatever. This was an attempt to systematise the kind of web of trust that we'd seen with PGP and make it scale. Now you still ended up having to trust one or two outliers, such as VeriSign for '.com', but this still left us with the idea whether it's possible to build a bottom up trust mechanism that's scalable and incentive compatible.

So 20 years later we come back to it and we get the idea that trust in a CA should arise from the trust exercised by the people who use it. It should not be the government or the NSA; it should not be Mozilla or Microsoft; it should be the people who actually use the thing.

So how do you start this? Well let's start off by considering CAs that are trusted for a limited scope, and the idea is that this then arises naturally. Now you may recall J. M. Barrie's play, 'Tinker Bell' where Tinker Bell the fairy is about to expire because kids don't believe in fairies anymore, and so you get all the kids in the theatre to say, 'Yes we believe in you!' and she gets up off her deathbed. And we see the similar things in many cultures, Greek gods, for example, got strength – their strength waxed and waned according to the number of people that sacrificed to them. And we find many literary references: 'Men are not born of the whim or will of the gods, on the contrary gods owe their existence to the belief of men. Should this belief wither the gods will die.'

© Springer International Publishing Switzerland 2015
B. Christianson et al. (Eds.): Security Protocols 2015, LNCS 9379, pp. 237–246, 2015.
DOI: 10.1007/978-3-319-26096-9_24

That's a 1943 reference, but there are many, many others all the way backwards and forwards through culture.

So let's remind ourselves of Tor basics. Your Tor client goes to an entry guard through a middle relay and an exit relay to a destination, and this service enables victims of censorship to escape censorship and browse websites like the BBC or Cambridge University, or for that matter, Light Blue Touchpaper, our blog. I just learned this morning that LBT is now blocked in China, presumably because of that post back in 2009 about the Dalai Lama.

The problem is that if you are in China, the Chinese government knows where the entry guards are, and so you need to have a private entry guard, a bridge, in order to get into the Tor network, and that's the point that we'll come to later.

So here's our worked example for local trust, for scalable trust. It starts off with a discussion about half a dozen years ago about whether a subset of Tor users could set up a club with particular properties. You could have a low-latency club, for example, for time-critical communications, or you could have a high-bandwidth club if you want to share very, very large movies that are banned in your country. And so the first idea that came along was Jansen, Hopper and Kim in 2010, the BRAIDS system. The idea was that if you were to run a Tor relay you could get paid in bandwidth credits, so the more stuff that went through your relay, the more tokens you would have to spend to make your own movies download faster. And the beauty about this is that here performance is visible and measurable – unlike for example, DigiNotar, which quietly betrayed its customers to the Iranian secret police.

The next paper that we pick up on – Jansen, Miller, Syverson and Ford last year – came up with TEARS, which is a variant of BRAIDS, but using e-cash for auditability, so that you can get slightly stronger privacy, confidentiality, anonymity guarantees, but at the cost of using a fair bit more cryptographic mechanism.

So as we're thinking in terms of social mechanisms, is it possible to organise Tor helpers as clubs? And one of the reasons that we're thinking this way is because of a paper that George Danezis and I wrote a decade ago about the Economics of Censorship Resistance, and there we pointed out that the people who resist censorship tend to be quite diverse. You have got Tibetans who want to escape the Chinese secret police; you've got critics of Scientology, who don't want to get injunctions; you have people who view sadomasochistic pornography that's legal in California but not in Tennessee. And groups like this don't really have anything in common. I mean, if you're a Tibetan monk you quite possibly don't approve of sadomasochistic pornography any more than a churchman in Tennessee does. And so the problem is that as soon as such a system comes under stress it tends to fragment.

So a natural way to organise something like this is as clubs where people can cooperate when times are smooth, but which can perhaps stand on their own when times get tough. What's more, if you organise people in clubs they can compete; they can compete within the club – you know, which batsman in the club has got the highest average of runs – and they can compete within clubs, and between clubs, you know, which cricket team is at the top of the league this year. So that gives us potentially some useful resilience mechanisms.

The next thing is what are we trying to do. Now previous work has focused on how you get more people to run Tor relays. Now there's 60–100 users for every relay, and more relays would be good, but the problem is that to run a relay you need high bandwidth upstream as well as downstream, and if you're sitting at the end of my DSL line out in the sticks, you ain't going to get that! You know, you might be able to help one or two people, but you definitely can't run a hundred sessions through there without noticeable degradation.

However, don't despair, because the real short resource is bridges! There's actually quite a lot of relays, but the difficulty is we've only got half as many. Last time we looked it was what, 3000 bridges for 6000 relays, were active a couple of days ago. So there's half as many bridges, and the problem is the bridges get used up because the Chinese secret police pretend to be Tibetan dissidents, they get the addresses of bridges, and they then add their IP addresses to the Great Firewall. But it would be great to have a very, very large numbers of bridges, and a very diverse way of getting these bridge addresses to people who want to use them to escape censorship. And if you've got a DSL link you can help, because if someone is desperate to escape censorship then they're prepared to put up with their traffic going through a DSL link the wrong way. OK, they wait a few seconds more for a page to load, if that's the price of getting on the Internet, people will pay it.

So here's the outline. Clubs compete to provide bridges; we've got a club secretary whom the club members elect, who acts as the bridge authority, and also as the bank; members run bridges, or/and introduce victims to them, and you can have great diversity here. The members who run bridges are probably going to be outside the area of censorship, whereas the members who introduce victims to them might be citizens in the area of censorship, or somehow in contact with members outside. Members claim rewards. You make bridge performance visible and measurable. Payment history provides reputation, which gives you the incentive. And also you get feedback, because you can see whether or not a particular club, and the set of bridges that it operates, is being effective in helping victims to communicate with the real world. And Khaled will take over at this point.

Khaled: So what can you do with bridges right now? I mean, we have a couple of scenarios, and you might have a lot more than this, but bridge members can be in the UK, but the introducer can be a family member in Damascus trying to help a censored victim contact the internet or the Tor network. You can have other scenarios where you have an Iranian preacher going around visiting and preaching in different Gulf countries, for example, giving a Shia in Saudi Arabia a piece of paper that has relay information on the bridges, the private bridges. Note that the relays, as Ross mentioned, are publicly known, so they can be blocked easily. You get a list of IPs, block them, and on a good day there are like 8000 relays, so it's not really hard to block. Bridges, however, are private, we don't know about them. You can actually choose not to broadcast your bridge information, so you keep them private and you can disseminate the information to people you know. Or you can go to the British Council and get the information, attend a class, whatever, and then pick up two bridges there.

Khaled: As for a US Naval Intelligence agent: the NSA has its tailored access unit who can hack into a machine. You want a proxy or a bridge for 15 min? Sure, why not? We can create an NSA botnet for that. What we're thinking is maybe 'data mule as a service'. Can there be a black market for bridges? Essentially just proxies to connect you to the Tor network. You can meet some sketchy guy who says, 'Boy do I have a bridge for you!' (laughter) I mean, there's a lot of possibilities here that you can do. What we don't want is an external payment system; we don't want to trash the volunteer spirit of the Tor network right now. We don't want a heavyweight e-cash mechanism where we have huge logs, or zero knowledge, and so on, to make it too prohibitive and easy to mess up when we implement. What we want though is a simple blinded signature. For those of you who don't know blinded signatures, you sign something, you don't know what you're signing. Why would you ever have something like that, because we want your signature, but we don't want you to know what you signed. We want transient tokens that expire and lose value based on the signing key. We rotate keys frequently, and whenever we rotate a key we declare a new epoch (epoch is just a fancy word for a time segment). For example, you can have the tokens lose value every epoch by 10 % unless you bank them with your club.

Khaled: So to dissect how this might work: we start with the first one. Point 1 and 2 can be a single registration, so the club member would contact the secretary saying "hey I volunteer my PC for like 15 min from 12 to 15", and the victim would contact the secretary, but this dashed line represents an out-of-band communication. Obviously the victim is censored, they can't contact the Tor network directly so what they need is, we assume that they have an email communication that's not being censored, they can communicate with the Tor world. So the secretary would reply with blobs, a blob is just a random number encrypted with the secretary's master key. The victim would choose a bridge, and contact that bridge with the blob. So at that point the bridge would forward the traffic to the Tor world. So the bridge will try to claim the reward after that. What they do is, have that blob and the blinded token. If the blob matches the bridge the club secretary approves the blinded token, signs it, and returns the token.

Tavish Vaidya: I have a question. What prevents the club member to just falsify all that information, let's say, he claims to give Alice some routes, and he thinks up 99 victims so you can claim that I gave Alice 99 bridges so give me the money for those 99 victims?

Khaled: So if the bridge creates a lot of Sybils?

Tavish Vaidya: Yes.

Khaled: OK, well we've thought about that too. See this point here, the bridge cannot create the victim because these bridges and blobs are assigned by the secretary, right, so you can't choose which blob you're going to get signed. And you can do a lot of fancy things here, but we're trying to avoid crypto, we're trying to do incentives. So, for example, you get a blob that's not yours, you don't want it, if you don't use it this victim will not be issued new blobs. Does that kind of make sense? You're getting three randomly chosen blobs, if you don't use them for the bridges that we just gave you we decrease your account, so we keep an account for the victim.

Tavish Vaidya: So there is no way that I'm a club member, and I can just pop up, make up 99 victims, even though they're not like real victims, but I just happen to say that, I have clients who just happen to request bridges?

Khaled: Right, but there is a probability here that you will not get the bridge that you are, you will not get assigned the bridge that you want, right, to increase your credit. So if you don't use the blobs that we give you, you end up burning the email accounts that you just signed up with.

Changyu Dong: How can the victim find the, where is the club secretary? How can the victim first time contact him?

Khaled: Ross, do you want to answer that.

Ross: Well we give you a number of different examples, and the whole point here is that you use human mechanisms, you use diversity, and you let the clubs compete with each other. There is no way using cryptologic mathematics you can distinguish between a victim and a secret policeman, right? They're both Syrian citizens, they're both standing there on the street corner in Damascus, and one of them happens to harbour nice thoughts towards President Assad, and the other happens to harbour nasty thoughts. And if you have a way of telling who harbour nice thoughts and nasty thoughts, then the secret police would use them to drag away all the people that harbour nasty thoughts. So you cannot assume the existence of a mind-reading ray for this exercise. But what you can assume is that people have human contacts. You can assume that people have social context. You can assume that there are some people who can travel around with some impunity, like Iranian preachers who travel around in Saudi Arabia, and are allowed to preach at least in peacetime, who might have their visas revoked if you start having a shooting war between Iran and Saudi Arabia and in the Gulf, and so on and so forth. By having a diversity of clubs that can compete with each other, and by keeping score within clubs and between clubs, it's possible to incentivise behaviour, that will up the cost, and reduce the effectiveness of civil attacks. And finally, if a civil attack does start making bridges less available that becomes immediately obvious.

Bruce Christianson: The key point is you can't do it without it being obvious.

Ross: The key point is that you can't solve a civil war problem with cryptology. And people who have tried to do that, as I think you've understood, are completely barking up the wrong tree. It is not capable of being done. So you have to build mechanisms that support human action, and that means in our first pass setting up clubs.

Khaled: So essentially, instead of penalising Sybil attacks, or malicious behaviour, we reward correct behaviour, that's incentives, aligned incentives. So if you're wondering why, you know, we talk about Greek gods, and decaying power, and all that stuff, if the bridge screws over the victim, so the other way from what you said, or maybe they're not colluding together, right? – so they take a blob but they don't provide a service, the victim will never use that bridge again, even if they randomly assign that bridge. So they don't use the bridge, reputation goes down, and nobody ends up using it. This is the cycle: bridge, club, victim, and so on. You get more tokens, you get more reputation, and you can get more victims, and you can start adding to your reputation.

Ross: And there's something that we didn't put in here which is that your club members, who are also in the business of taking blobs from the secretary to the victims, right, the Iranian preacher, the librarian at the British Library.

Michael Roe: An observation on that: so Tor is a mechanism where you're keeping very much to communications between the server and the client at the computer level. There's anonymisation but it's interesting that you're bootstrapping from something that has to be fundamentally very much not anonymous. You're a member of some revolutionary group who has contact with another member of the revolutionary group, who therefore knows you're not a policeman. And all this stuff you're bootstrapping from is kind of the absolute opposite property from what Tor is providing, which is the property that the web server has absolutely no idea who you are. It's kind of interesting.

Ross: Well in many real life scenarios this would be bootstrapped off family ties, clan ties, religious ties, you know, good old-fashioned human interaction.

Khaled: But here's an important point though: your first step (goal) when you're censored is different than being de-anonymised. What you want, what your main target is, is to avoid the local adversary, not a global one, not a powerful one, right? The adversary here is the Iranian government, your local ISP; you really want to get out of the country to contact the Tor world by any means necessary. And this means that use meek, which is a pluggable transport, using Google and Amazon. You know, they will be your antidote. If Google and Amazon are in your threat model, you have bigger problems here.

Ross: It's also important that we're not solving all the world's trust problems with this, because there's an attack on this you can't stop with these mechanisms. Suppose for example, you're reaching out to the Shiite minority in Saudi Arabia, the Saudi Arabian council intelligence police, if they're really smart, would set up a very highly functional bridge simply in order to find out who all the dissidents are, so that if there does start to be a shooting war they can go and knock on all their doors. So this is not all of the solution, but part of the solution for people in such a situation is that Tor provides strong anonymity, and hopefully that other people will be using Tor for other purposes so there's some deniability. So this is just part of the solution, and the threat model is very, very much bigger than just sybils.

Khaled: Right, so what's the point of having tokens at all, instead of having a big ledger, and people buy for honour. Well we have touched on most of these points briefly. You want to enable, or have the option to create a 'quality of service'. When people can mine for tokens maybe you can have Tor enable quality of service in the sense that do you want to prioritise your service? Fine, use a token. Do you want high bandwidth? Use a token. You want low latency? You can spend whatever you want. Another point is you can have different club facilities where they provide different services, and you can have inter-commerce between the clubs. Maybe they have a better service; usually clubs have different services. The inter-commerce between them should be cleared by the club secretaries just like banks clear each other's payments. We also want the blinded-signature aspect of the tokens just because we want to provide anonymity against downstream relays where the token that you obtained does not link you to the victim that you helped, or your secretary; it's absolutely unlinkable from any other activity that you have. There are probably other possibilities that we haven't thought about yet, but that's limited by our imagination and everyone's in this room.

Audience: Have you thought about using flashproxy [Tor pluggable transports], I don't know if you're familiar with this...

Khaled: Sure I know about pluggable passwords, but I'm not really an authority, I guess, on pluggable transports I know about meek, I know about obfsproxy, but not really flashproxy.

Micah Sherr: Well what we do is we map website operators who you're...

Khaled: I see we have this point here, so maybe you can enlighten us...

Micah Sherr: Well I don't think, it's not a pluggable transport though, so it's, you know, can you go back one slide? Club manager... the website update essentially makes the website the club secretary. So if you're going to the services you could, you know, choose that Facebook have a botnet that says 'click here' to increase your anonymity...

Khaled: This is a really good idea, but it's probably like an engineering aspect of where do we put this.

Micah Sherr: It is, but I think you can map this model easily on to this...

Khaled: I would rather use something existing like transports, rather than having another external binary that people have to trust.

Micah Sherr: Right, I mean, the advantage of this is it makes the club member bridges, you know, when people go on to bridges, people who are blocked go on to one of the club browsers, so it makes things easier.

Ross: Well there's also the path to deployment; if you want to be able to deploy stuff without having all the Tor community involved from the word go, and if you can field this by using credible transports that are optional, well there's a market in that too.

Khaled: So how can we start gathering early adopters here, how can we convince them? Can take a snapshot of the system right now and reward top performing relays, for example, give them tokens and say, hey tell a friend, let's join this party? Can then say, set up a club, and say, hey guys we have excellent relays here, sponsored by the NSA, sanctioned, everything is good, so use them? But this is not saying much really because the NSA can have high performance, high bandwidth relays, and after a while they get updated to guard nodes, or guard status, so they can already perform this, they probably are performing it right now. Point is either you have a victim or you not; you either provide a bridge for censored victims, or you just maintain the status quo, and not worry about helping the system at all. We already talked about the Tor pluggable transports, so I'm just going to skip that.

Khaled: So the conclusion was demonstrated that, you know, certifications are OK in between a monopoly and dictatorship where you can't do anything to change that as a user, you can't change the trust that you're already given. What we want is an incentive compatible certification mechanism where it scales for more users than we already have, in the previous attempts that Ross explained earlier. And we suggest two ideas. Mainly can we get this via clubs, and align incentives so people have more incentives to help users and censored victims contact the Tor world. And we suggest that we use these multiple bridge authorities, which we call clubs, as a test-bed to experiment with the social aspects of introducing a payment system to a voluntary network like Tor. That's it, I can take questions now.

Keith Irwin: Is there any incentive to make sure that if you're operating a bridge you don't only provide service to someone until you get their blob, and then you just stop providing service to that person?

Ross: We don't really think about a fair exchange protocol here, we don't want to complicate things. Cryptography doesn't really solve many of the things, we think about the cost of maintaining the system, right? We try to align the incentives that if you screw someone over your reputation goes down, you have to burn another ID to join the system again, right? Aligning incentives rather than penalising malicious behaviour.

Keith Irwin: I guess, but is that true if someone does admit their decision is like, I will want to try and get the most good reputation possible, but with using as few resources as possible.

Ross: I'm not considering that, or think that's a realistic threat, because there's no marginal cost to me in running my bridge for three hours rather than one hour. But what there maybe is an attack where somebody sets up bridges that cooperate for the first minute or two and then pull the plug. In that case what you do is that particular club gets screwed – because the reputation it has with victims goes plummeting and nobody uses it anymore.

Khaled: It affects the member and the club itself, so the club secretary has an incentive to monitor the behaviour of its club members.

Ross: So if the tickets that you get from the travelling Iranian preacher are only good for 90 s of connectivity then people will stop using them – and they'll also stop listening to the preacher, which is the real pain if you're a preaching man and your job is to get people to listen to you, right? So what we're doing here is we're pooling the social mechanisms in A. Similarly, if you get your token off your brother who was lucky enough to emigrate to Britain, and things start breaking after 90 s, well hey, that's a family issue.

Audience: The system looks very similar to a trusted revocation management system in wireless sensor networks, where their role is to gain some trust to join the system, and then they earn their credit to transfer data, and if they serve the relay then to other nodes then they can pay it, if they pay they can transfer their own data.

Ross: Yes, there's a whole literature on what happens in wireless sensor networks: Eschnerauer and Gligor, our suicide bombing protocol, and there's some papers here over the past 10 or 15 protocols workshops, and yes there are some similarities. But here the threat model is different and the need to get the incentives right is almost paramount. At least if you deploy a sensor network you assume that all those nodes that are still behaving will be running the same software image.

Jeunese Payne: Are you basing this any psychological research that suggests that people do things just to have positive reputation, and you don't even have to give all that much; is this based on anything other than a hunch?

Ross: Well we're very grateful to you for your suggestion that we think in terms of reputation rather than just in terms of tokens, and money.

Khaled: Ross, maybe you want to mention the Israeli nursery example.

Ross: Yes, there's the Israeli nursery example where this is mentioned by Yochai Benkler when he writes about this problem. There's a nursery brought in a late fee for parents that turned up to collect their kids late, and all of a sudden all the parents started turning up late because it was no longer a matter of good behaviour, but simply something that you could pay for. And so the Tor community is very, very nervous about the idea of bringing in incentives that are linked to any kind of external monetary stuff, a digital cash that could turn into Bitcoin, for example, because they're terrified that would undermine the volunteer nature of the Tor network in a way that would not be repaired again once you stopped paying people. So insofar as you use a payment mechanism you're careful to say that it's a token rather than a coin, right, you certainly would not call this a coin, and we prefer to call the organiser, the multiple bridge authorities, 'club secretaries' rather than 'authorities' for the same reason.

Khaled: In fact this is the biggest criticism even from the Tor team, and Steven Murdoch also, when they said, you have to be careful what the social aspect of trashing the volunteer spirit.

Keith Irwin: Yes there's also, there's a study that was done where they looked at, they went around and asked people, we have a landfill that needs to be put somewhere, this is really important to the country, you know, are you willing to make the sacrifice and have it be put near your house. And when they couched it in those terms 85 % of people said, well yes, I guess I'm alright with that. And then they, the alternative was they had them say exactly the same thing except it ended with, and we'll pay you $50, and they found that only 30 % of the people said they were OK with it.

Ross: Exactly so.

Security is Beautiful

Giampaolo Bella[1] and Luca Viganò[2]([⊠])

[1] Dipartimento di Matematica e Informatica, Università di Catania, Catania, Italy
[2] Department of Informatics, King's College London, London, UK
luca.vigano@kcl.ac.uk

Abstract. In the movie "Life is Beautiful", Guido Orefice, the character interpreted by Roberto Benigni, convinces his son Giosuè that they have been interned in a nazi concentration camp not because they are Jews but because they are actually taking part in a long and complex game in which they, and in particular Giosuè, must perform the tasks that the guards give them. A ghastly experience is turned into a livable, at times even almost enjoyable, one.

In this position paper, we advocate that, in the same spirit as Guido's ingenious trick of turning a nazi camp into a sort of playground for his child, security should be beautiful; and if it isn't so yet, it should then be made beautiful, so that the users experience it in that way. This is, of course, an extremely challenging objective, and we will discuss through further scenarios a few ways in which it could be made possible in the future. It turns out that the Peppa Pig cartoon may also be inspiring.

1 Introduction

In "Life is Beautiful"[1], Guido, who does not speak German, transforms into a game the instructions of the guards for setting up the concentration camp. He explains in a way that suits his purpose features of the camp that would otherwise be scary for his young child. Time and again he convinces his son Giosuè to endure the extreme hardships of the camp in order to go along with the game. His fatherly love is so profound that even when he walks to his sure death, knowing that Giosuè is peaking at him from his hideaway, Guido walks a funny walk to reassure his child and make him laugh. The just reward will come at the end when Giosuè is rescued by an American tank: the prize he has earned. With this position paper, we want to argue that this and other fictions may teach security folks a great deal.

If we analysed the information security arena as it looks nowadays, it would emerge that a number of clever technologies are in place to (attempt to) achieve

L. Viganò— Supported by the EU FP7 Project no. 257876, "SPaCIoS: Secure Provision and Consumption in the Internet of Services" (www.spacios.eu) and the PRIN 2010-11 project "Security Horizons". This work began while Luca Viganò was at the Dipartimento di Informatica, Università di Verona, Italy.

[1] *Life is Beautiful (La vita è bella)*, Italy 1997, directed by Roberto Benigni, written by Roberto Benigni and Vincenzo Cerami.

B. Christianson et al. (Eds.): Security Protocols 2015, LNCS 9379, pp. 247–250, 2015.
DOI: 10.1007/978-3-319-26096-9_25

security. While security is there to ultimately *help* the user consumption of services, it is very often not perceived quite so. With security interpreted as a fastidious burden, it cannot be made clear enough that the biggest security threats are often the users themselves. Although this may look like a macroscopic contradiction, there is supporting evidence that users often perceive security as too limiting upon their normal operations, and hence try to circumvent it [4]. It must be remarked that, even if bypassing password-authentication is perhaps most common routine, the layman customarily facilitates hacking, for instance by ignoring security warnings that modern browsers make, or by granting superfluous permissions to mobile applications.

It has become clear to everyone that the security of any system should be established *in the presence* of the system users. The question remains open, however, on how to achieve this, with only a few attempts being advanced thus far [6,10]. This position paper advocates a significant step forward by means of beautiful security.

2 Position

We advocate that computer security should be twisted the way Guido twisted life in the camp, namely it should be (made) beautiful. In this vein, the ideas of incentives or rewards for users who secure their systems are very valuable and there already exists some work in this area [3,12] along with extensive work on security economics [1,2,5]. We believe that these are fundamental but still incomplete steps in the right direction. Rather, we advocate a more fundamental approach, which can be outlined by its requirements for security:

- security should become a primary, inherent feature of the system; at the same time,
- security should not be disjoint from the system functionalities; at the same time,
- security should contribute to the very positive experience that the user has of the system, ultimately making that experience beautiful.

We believe that, if security meets these requirements, fathers (the sys-admins) will teach their children (the users) not only to watch out and be secure, but simply to experience the system and the security it comprises — without more appealing or useful alternatives, or alternatives at all. One could argue that if Guido managed such an enormous twist over a concentration camp, then we really should be able to twist the experience that users make of system security into a beautiful one. The example of Guido and Giosuè is, of course, just an extreme case and we are not advocating that one should outright lie to the system users. Rather, it is the experience of the system users that must be modified.

Remarkably, the three requirements advocated here should be met at the same time. The first requirement alone already receives sufficient attention at present, for example by the adoption of the security-by-design principle. The second has been raising increasing attention, for example by web sites offering HTTPS access only.

We argue that the last requirement is innovative as it stands and, as such, yet to be explored. Its underlying question is: *what is a beautiful user experience of a secure system?* Not only is the answer subjective, but also vast. Here, we only outline a couple of connotations of what users could find beautiful while they engage with technologies.

An obvious connotation is simplicity and ease of use. This is already understood, and the vast amount of work in the area of usability addresses precisely this form of beauty. It is widely accepted that technologies should be usable [7,8].

Here, we want to point out a second connotation of the beautiful adjective. This is again inspired by fiction, and by kids' cartoons in particular. Episode 38 of the third season of the "Peppa Pig" cartoon series [9] teaches us another element of beauty. In this episode, aptly titled "The Secret Club", Peppa's friend Suzy is building a secret club whose membership is identified by wearing a mask. Joining the club demands uttering a one-time password. The opening excerpt goes like this:

Peppa has come to play with Suzy Sheep.

- *Peppa: Hello, Suzy.*
- *Suzy: Hello, Peppa.*
- *Peppa: Why have you got that mask on your face?*
- *Suzy: So people don't know it's me. I'm in a secret club.*
- *Peppa: Wow! Can I be in your secret club?*
- *Suzy: Shh! It's not easy to get into. You have to say the secret word.*
- *Peppa: What word?*
- *Suzy: Blaba double!*
- *Peppa: Blaba double!*
- *Suzy: Right, you're in.*

This is obviously an insecure protocol but it is remarkable that Peppa and Suzy are already familiar with one-time passwords as in fact Suzy will state later about the password that *It changes all the time to keep it secret!*

Our attention goes to the exclamation of excitement by Peppa at the sheer news of a secret club. She immediately wants to join in. We speculate that solving the security problem of today's society, with its pervasive use of mobile devices and the amount of sensitive data that are handled, may require answering this question: how can we make security desirable, engaging and exciting? Notably, Peppa's excitement is sudden at the news of a secret club. It would appear that anything related to secrecy is received as an enjoyable game, even before the rules are set, and perhaps this is the direction that should be taken with information security. It is all the more clear that the security problem is inherently an inter-disciplinary one, demanding collaboration of computer scientists with researchers from the Humanities.

A third connotation of a beautiful user experience can be supported. "Life is Beautiful" teaches us that even horror can be made somewhat similar to a game, ultimately making life still beautiful. "The Secret Club" makes the case that a form of secrecy can be presented and well received as an exciting game, producing a beautiful adventure. Hence, it would seem that playing a game could be one of the facets of a beautiful experience, although an in-depth study would be required to confirm this.

3   Conclusions

If technicists still think that information security is a matter of preventing insecure interactions with the technology, hence forcing the user to specific paths, we believe they are fundamentally wrong. The biggest mistake is a purely architectural one: the enemy is not the user, rather, the technology should enable the user to engage securely with it.

If users are repeatedly compelled to interactions that are orthogonal to their paths of practice, they will sooner or later start reducing their use of the system or attempt to subvert it. This statement is supported, for example, by recent research of a British inter-disciplinary team [11] concluding that technology should engage users, not enslave them.

With the supporting tales derived from fiction, we argued that, if security is beautiful, users will then engage with the technology refraining from looking for insecure deviations. We attempted to elaborate a few reasonable connotations of beautiful security — we believe that establishing the main connotations of beautiful security in fact is the route to address the information security problem.

References

1. Acquisti, A.: The Economics of Privacy. http://www.heinz.cmu.edu/~acquisti/economics-privacy.htm
2. Anderson, R.: Economics and Security Resource Page. http://www.cl.cam.ac.uk/~rja14/econsec.html
3. August, T., August, R., Shin, H.: Designing user incentives for cybersecurity. Commun. ACM **57**(11), 43–46 (2014)
4. Blythe, J., Koppel, R., Smith, S.W.: Circumvention of security: good users do bad things. IEEE Secur. Priv. **11**(5), 80–83 (2013)
5. Böhme, R. (ed.): The Economics of Information Security and Privacy. Springer, Heidelberg (2013)
6. Karlof, C., Tygar, J.D., Wagner, D.: Conditioned-safe ceremonies and a user study of an application to web authentication. In: SOUPS 2009: Proceedings of the 5th Symposium on Usable Privacy and Security. ACM Press (2009)
7. Lampson, B.: Usable security: how to get it. Commun. ACM **52**(11), 25–27 (2009)
8. Payne, B.D., Edwards, W.K.: A brief introduction to usable security. IEEE Internet Comput. **12**(3), 13–21 (2008)
9. Peppa Pig, Series 3, Episode 38, "The Secret Club" (2010)
10. Radke, K., Boyd, C., Gonzalez Nieto, J., Brereton, M.: Ceremony analysis: strengths and weaknesses. In: Camenisch, J., Fischer-Hübner, S., Murayama, Y., Portmann, A., Rieder, C. (eds.) SEC 2011. IFIP AICT, vol. 354, pp. 104–115. Springer, Heidelberg (2011)
11. Visualisation and Other Methods of Expression (2012). http://vome.org.uk/
12. Wash, R., Mackie-Mason, J.K.: Incentive-centered design for information security. In: HOTSEC 2006: Proceedings of the 1st Conference on USENIX Workshop on Hot Topics in Security. USENIX Association (2006)

Security is Beautiful (Transcript of Discussion)

Luca Viganò[✉]

King's College London, London, UK
luca.vigano@kcl.ac.uk

Let me start by saying this is joint work with Giampaolo Bella, and that what we have actually written, and that you can find in the proceedings, is not just a position paper, but actually a pro-position paper, where we are using the word pro-position not with the meaning of a true statement or false statement, but rather as something that we state for discussion and/or illustration. That is, I won't give you answers, rather I will ask a few questions and propose what is perhaps a slightly different state of mind than the one that we are used to. Let me also say there are many connections to the talks that we've heard today and also yesterday, and I will try to make references as much as I can.

The subtitle of this year's workshop is "Information Security in Fiction and Fact", and I'll try in the talk to mix up the two a bit, and use fiction to motivate fact, and use fact to somehow introduce fiction. Let me start with something that is, in my opinion, both a fact but unfortunately also kind of a fiction, namely the notion that security is there to help, meaning that we have a number of clever technologies that achieve security, that in some cases attempt to achieve security, and that therefore help the consumption of services by the users. Now, some of these do indeed work and are incredibly effective, and have much potential (like we just heard in the previous talk) to actually make the world a better place. But in many other cases, security, from the point of view of the user, is perceived as a burden. For instance, I tested this with my family: I have four cousins who are between 20 and 30 years old, they all live in the same city, not in the same house anymore, they're siblings, and they use Facebook to set up meeting points and appointments to have an aperitif, or a beer or something like that, but they do it publicly, so everybody can read what they write. I asked them why they're doing that and they replied something along the lines "we don't really care that it is secure or not, it would be too complex to make it secure (you know, send an email and everything), so we just post here so every one of us can see it, and if somebody else sees it, who cares?"

This is often a state of mind, that leads to the point that I am trying to make, and indeed we have heard many talks about this, not only this year, but also in the previous years of the Security Protocols Workshops, where it was discussed that actually one of the biggest threats to security are the users themselves. Not just the attackers, not users who make mistakes, but actually users who refuse to take part in the system. And sometimes they have good reasons to do so. I'm going to use passwords as an example because it's a very easy example, but what I'm going to say is more general than passwords, and indeed, say, if and when Pico works, then we will scratch this as an example and look at other scenarios, so I'm just using it here for the sake of illustration. What I want to say

© Springer International Publishing Switzerland 2015
B. Christianson et al. (Eds.): Security Protocols 2015, LNCS 9379, pp. 251–260, 2015.
DOI: 10.1007/978-3-319-26096-9_26

is that users often tend to choose the path of least resistance, which sometimes is erroneously attributed to electricity, but which you can attribute, for instance, to raindrops falling on a window: they do fall on the window by searching for the path of least resistance, and sometimes users do that as well.

I mean, if you have an over-prescriptive use of technology... let me make a very concrete example: I used to work at the University of Verona, and a few years ago the Head of IT Security of the University decided that every university staff member had to change their password every three months. And of course this created an immediate rebellion by people saying "hey, six months is already too much, why three months?" and so on. But this is something that happens, and indeed it might lead to bad user experiences. It might lead actually to users trying to circumvent security, and try to find ways to make the system more usable. I'm using the word "usable", but actually what I want to say goes beyond passwords, and goes beyond usability, because there are a lot of solutions actually for usability.

The message is that we really make it tough for the users. I mean, we have passwords since authentication is a problem; we might have solutions like Pico, we might have other solutions, we might use 2 or even 3 way authentication, which in many, many cases is perceived as a burden. We have the Mastercard secure code versus 1 click purchase, to give you another example, which users do find extremely annoying. Let me tell you about another experience from my personal life: at some point my bank in Italy decided to change the credit card from Visa to Mastercard, and Mastercard introduced the secure code. I had a friendly relationship with one of the people working in the bank, who told me that a lot of customers complained, not because they cared about whether it was Visa or Mastercard, they didn't care about that, but because now they had to type in a password whenever they wanted to buy something online, because Mastercard introduced an additional level of security. In fact, people are extremely annoyed, I certainly am, that whenever you have a new device, a new mobile device such as a smartphone or tablet, in many cases you have to go through a very long registration ceremony at the beginning when you turn it on before you can actually use it. And many of the things that you are being asked are important for your future use, but many others could really wait. There are many more examples. I will try not to lose too much time in talking about examples, but let me generalize a bit more and attempt to explain why I don't think it is just a matter of usability or of authentication.

So imagine that somebody stole your laptop, which for me would be a disaster because my laptop is my office. Of course, you could think "how am I going to protect it?" Well in addition to my normal user password, I could, for instance, protect the laptop with additional passwords, for instance, like one to encode the disk, or a bios password to make the laptop unusable, and so on. Now this of course would do the trick in making sure that your laptop is much more protected, but you would have to remember three passwords, people choose passwords badly, and so on. There was until a while ago, I've been told, I don't have an Android phone, but there was until a while ago an app on Google play that was called App Ops, which was an application permission manager, to check the permissions that the apps on your smartphone had, and reduce them, control them, and make sure that they were not getting too much information. It worked, but apparently at some point it was discontinued because people got bored, users got bored with it.

Daniel Thomas: It was never actually released, it was a hidden feature and they took it away again. There's a nice paper where they did stuff with this feature.[1] While they took it away again they have since taken steps towards reintroducing it for apps which explicitly support it through runtime permissions.

Reply: Thanks, actually, that's a very good point.

Audience: Also, I understood that the reason why they took it out was because there were a lot of applications which broke, not just the applications, but Android itself.

Reply: The point that I'm trying to say is that we do end up with the layman facilitating hacking, and not the layman who is careless, just a layman who doesn't want to go through all these things, who ignores password authentication, who does set his password to "incorrect" (so that whenever he types in the wrong password, the system will answer "your password is incorrect"), who ignores security warnings of browsers, who grants superfluous permissions to mobile applications. I mean, let's be honest, even though I work in security I don't really always check what the apps on my iPhone are actually doing, I do in some cases but not always. So to paraphrase a quote by Shakespeare, we could say that security is "mortals' chiefest enemy" (it's in the Scottish Play, Act 3, Scene 5). Shakespeare meant it in a slightly different way, but there are two ways we could interpret this sentence. On the one hand we could say: well security is expensive, difficult, in some cases impossible, but in particular tedious, and you could summarise the state of mind by saying, "well, breaches will occur so my computer cannot be protected so why bother?" And if you studied psychology and philosophy, this is a form of Nietzsche's Turkish fatalism meaning, saying, briefly put, "whatever! It will happen, so who cares". Alternatively you could actually interpret it as security in terms of over confidence. By the way, if you're interested, it is the only occurrence of the word security in any play by Shakespeare, and it is not really the meaning of the word that we consider today. So here it's over confidence, it's mortals' chiefest enemy, which is "well, it won't happen to me, so why should I bother with security", which is actually

---

[1] The paper is Almuhimedi, H., Schaub, F., Sadeh, N., Adjerid, I., Acquisti, A., Gluck, J., Faith Cranor, L. and Agarwal, Y. (2015). Your Location has been Shared 5,398 Times! A Field Study on Mobile App Privacy Nudging. In Proceedings of the 2015 ACM conference on Human factors in computing systems (CHI) (pp. 787796). Seoul, Republic of Korea: ACM. doi:10.1145/2702123.2702210.

Also relevant is the paper: Ferreira, D., Kostakos, V., Beresford, A. R., Lindqvist, J., and Dey, A. K. (2015). Securacy: An Empirical Investigation of Android Applications Network Usage, Privacy and Security. In WiSec. New York: ACM. doi:10.1145/2766498.2766506.

the point that I'm trying to make, meaning "my computer needs no protection", or in other words, a form of Freud's fiction of omnipotence: "it won't happen to me, it happens to everybody else". But actually we know that history is full of security breaches due to poor screening.

Sandy Clark: There's a really good example of this in writings from the Peloponnesian war.

Reply: Thanks for pointing this out. Let me make my point, and explain why we're talking about beautiful security, or actually why we say that security is or should be beautiful. Many of the talks today, and many of our works in general, have shown that we cannot really deal with security unless we involve the user, unless we really focus on establishing security in the presence of the user. Of course the question is still fairly open, I mean, there are a number of attempts on how to achieve it, but in many cases, even if you look at the literature on socio-technical security, for instance, there is still quite a long way to go. And our point, or our pro-position is that security should be made beautiful, even though, as I said, we don't really know how to do it, but we have some ideas.

And now I'll tell you why we picked this title. We picked this title because we think that security should be made beautiful in the same way that life is made beautiful in the eponymous movie "Life is beautiful" by Roberto Benigni, which won a couple of Oscars actually, and not that I really liked the movie so much, I think it's OK, but it makes a very good point by saying "well, if you're going through an ugly experience", which is what I advocated users of our systems in many cases do, "then you could try to turn it around and make it more livable, more enjoyable, as much as life in a concentration camp can be made enjoyable, by looking for the beautiful things". Let me try and make this a bit more interactive by showing a clip of the movie. In case you haven't watched the movie, then I'll explain: this is Roberto Benigni's character, Guido Orefice, and he has been sent to a concentration camp in Germany along with his child who's called Giosuè, who is extremely scared. Actually his biggest desire in life is to own a tank, a toy tank. And this is the setting.

> *A clip of the movie "Life is beautiful" is shown in which, as described in the accompanying paper, Guido Orefice mistranslates what the nazi guards are saying and transforms the concentration camp experience into a game for his son, a game in which the winner wins a tank.*

Now, this is a very cool trick to make life in a concentration camp more bearable, and indeed if you watch the movie it will actually make sense; if you haven't watched it, watch it, it's actually quite a good move, not so great, but quite good. Guido takes the point up to the very end of the movie where he walks this funny walk, while his child is hidden somewhere, just to reassure him and make the whole thing more livable.

So, this was the starting point that we took, this is actually the reason for the title of the talk. Our paper was called "Beautiful Security" at the beginning, but we changed it to "Security is Beautiful" to properly show the transformation that we are advocating. Now, there are many steps in this direction that have been taken, and of course usability is one of them. OK, typing two or three passwords, yes, it's certainly usable, but it is not beautiful in the sense that users will get bored. We have heard about incentives and rewards, which are extremely important in some cases, especially in situations like in the previous talk, and there is much literature on security economics (and Ross Anderson, for instance, maintains a page on security economics), where all these forms of making security more attractive and more present from the point of view of the user are described. What we are saying is that we are trying to make an additional step. And let me say why we can do that by outlining three requirements for security.

First of all security should be a primary inherent feature of any system and, second, at the same time it should not be disjoint from the system functionalities, and (OK, this we already know) third, it should contribute to the positive experience of the user when using the system. This third point is in our opinion the crucial point. Let me stress again: the three points should be satisfied at the same time.

Joan Feigenbaum: Do you think you have more of a chance of making that true of computer security than the character Guido Orefice had of making it true of a concentration camp? Or do you have less of a chance?

Reply: Well, actually the character had quite a success.

Joan Feigenbaum: I know.

Reply: In the movie, of course.

Joan Feigenbaum: Yes. So, have you set a harder task for yourself or an easier task?

Reply: That's a very good question.

Jeunese Payne: In the movie, he's outright just lying to the kid, are you suggesting that you just outright lie to users? Because outright lying is arguably easier to do.

Reply: No, I'm suggesting to transform the experience, without lying, possibly.

Jeunese Payne: Transform the experience without lying, but yes, I don't think he really transformed the experience, he just lied.

Reply: Well, I was saying lying as a consequence that he transformed the experience.

Jeunese Payne: The security guys are saying, have this many bits in your password, do it uniquely for every account, and then you're saying, you don't need to have this many bits in your password, you don't need to...

Reply: No, this is not what I'm saying, what I'm saying is, I'm going to give you other motivations for why you should have them. I'm not saying you should not have them. But let me go on, because I think I have a point, and then we can discuss it again at the end, because I'm going to show you another movie. So the first point, security inherent in the system, well yes, we have the "security by design" principle, we know how to do it, but it is often looked at as a standalone thing. What we're advocating is satisfying it at the same time with the second point, which has also received quite some attention, for instance, a number of websites that you can only access with HTTPS, and then good luck if you are in China, or in some other countries where it is not really possible to do that. The third point is the point that we want to stress. And the third point really requires us to say what is a good definition of something beautiful, and the problem is that beauty is in the eye of the beholder, it's subjective, or to quote again Shakespeare, it is bought by judgement of the eye, meaning it really depends on the kind of user that you're trying to capture.

Now, of course simplicity and ease of use are often perceived as characteristics of beauty (not always, if we look at the history of the arts), but there is more, and let me play you another movie.

> A clip of an episode of Peppa Pig is shown (see the paper for more details).

Beside the fact that they're using one-time passwords and that the protocol is not really secure, there are a number of things that we can learn from this. And this is...

Audience: Everybody gets in the club.

Reply: Exactly, so membership is identified by wearing a mask, and by knowing the secret word, which changes all the time, and it is very interesting because it is trying to make security more desirable, more engaging, and exciting.

Ross Anderson: But this is what many websites do, they abuse security to make the website desirable, engaging and exciting, because they give you a password, not for any engineering reason, but to make you feel that you belong. So, Peppa Pig is actually much more inline with the web's real practice than you might think.

Reply: True, true, but I think you said exactly the right words, they abuse it, whereas what we're trying to say is that perhaps we could try to use it instead of abusing it. I don't really know how to do it, we have some ideas, and the point is that in the clip everybody is excited at just the news of a secret club and being able to belong to it. And you're perfectly right, this is a good stepping stone for abusing the whole security. But it is perceived as enjoyable, it is perhaps the direction that we should take, of course without the abusers, without the lies, making it enjoyable, and obviously it will require to work with not just economics, but psychology, humanities, to talk about security as one of the inherent features that contribute to the beautiful experience. And let me go towards the conclusion by using the immortal words of General Melchett: "Security is not a dirty word, Blackadder!"

> A clip of "Blackadder Goes Forth" is shown.

That's precisely the point: we should try and make sure that security is not perceived as a dirty word. So, concluding, we believe that we should think about security in a slightly different way: it should not just be a matter of preventing insecure interactions with the technology, forcing the user to take some particular paths, because the user will find other paths. And it should engage the users and not enslave them. Sometimes when I look at some of the security features that are implemented, well, sometimes I think that they're really there to punish the users, to really make them feel the pain, you know, like when you're doing abs training and you should feel the pain since that's when you know that your exercise is good. Trying to make it more enjoyable, trying to make it more engaging, should be, or could be, a route to address one of the principal problems of information security: users tend to find paths of least resistance.

How we can do that? We don't have a final solution. We have a few ideas, some of which are briefly outlined in the paper, but it would make sense that we all think a bit about it more. Let me conclude with the third and final quote of Shakespeare, this time from "Loves Labour's Lost": security... "she's beautiful and therefore to be wooed", and in this case I really mean woo in the sense of gaining the favour of someone to move him/her to do something. And that's all I have to say.

Virgil Gligor: I read a paper by Butler Lampson published in the *Communications of ACM*, in November 2009[2], and one of the points he makes is that security has always been inconvenient. So in view of this, how could one make security beautiful, since almost by definition inconvenience is not that beautiful?

Bruce Christianson: I can give you a counter example. There was a pub chain that introduced a new requirement that bar staff had to sign into the till every time they used it by using a physical token, and all the managers thought this was going to be like a lead balloon, and that people were just going to sellotape their tokens to the till, and all this sort of thing. And it was very, very popular for a reason that no-one had foreseen, which was that if your session had timed out and you locked into another till the transaction that you were doing pulled up instantly on that till. So, if you were preparing a big order of drinks for lots of people you had to move around, you could always just walk up to the nearest till, put your token on the till, and have your transaction recovered to that point immediately. So because the security feature came, or enabled as a side effect something that improved the user experience, the users thought it was wonderful.

Audience: It also allowed several bar staff to use the same till without overlapping your orders.

Bruce Christianson: Several bar staff could use the same till, like so there were some groups at one end of the bar, and there were some at the other end. It's a token on a spring-loaded attachment to your belt.

Virgil Gligor: And when one doesn't wear a belt? One would have to wear some physical device that one would not forget. Right? Otherwise, whenever

---

[2] We added a reference to this paper in the camera-ready version of our paper.

one changes one's belt one would have to change the device from one belt to the other.

Bruce Christianson: The point was, because they saw this device as making their job easier they were very happy to put up with all the infrastructure they needed to support it. If they had understood that it was just a security feature, they'd have immediately started looking for a way around it.

Sandy Clark: Apparently it wasn't just a security feature, like you just said, so there was a trade-off between inconvenience and benefit that really didn't include security at all.

Bruce Christianson: That's right, and it was security that they perceived as the side effect.

Sandy Clark: But when you want to teach people about the problems with weak passwords, for example, one of the things that you can use to teach them is something like a regular padlock, right. A padlock is so easy to open that you can do it with a beer can. And the reason why it's easy to open is because it's convenient to lock, it's spring loaded, and as long as you can get something in-between the spring and the shackle the lock will just pop right open. Convenience is never security. So one of the things that I think you've demonstrated with your clips is that a possible incentive to that is to turn this into a game, or as I suggested, dance to your password. But any silly thing, anything that takes it out of the strain or adds some other benefit, would fix that.

Audience: So does it mean you literally lie to the user that, OK, this is not a security product, it's something fun so you should use it, but the side effect will be security.

Audience: There's a difference between lying and downplay.

Reply: But it's not only that, I mean, sometimes we are designing products really in a bad way. I don't know if you've ever used the Oyster card in the London underground: nowadays you get all these warnings "beware of double touching because you will be double billed". That's a poorly designed system where you are demanding the user to take care of his own security. They said they designed it that way because it would have been too difficult actually to change everything. But that is a poor security experience from the point of view of the user because you have to take care as a user of your own security.

Virgil Gligor: So we're just trading inconvenience, from their inconvenience to the user's, but it's still inconvenience.

Reply: No, what I'm saying is we should make sure that we don't design it as an inconvenience, we should not hide under the presumption that it has to be inconvenient.

Virgil Gligor: However, the authority could have undertaken the inconvenience and expense of changing all this. Instead they passed it on to the user... It is still inconvenience... one just pushes it around, but it's inconvenience.

Reply: Yes, but here I'm talking about the user who should perceive it, not about the system. I think the problem, or the burden, should lie not on the user but on the system designer.

Audience: Part of the problem is that if Oyster was the only card you had there wouldn't be any inconvenience, so the system works as long as you don't have to use any other systems, and the same is true of your passwords, and if you only had one password to remember it would be fine, it's the fact that you have 20 and they're all different where it becomes a terrible problem.

Reply: Here it's however slightly different. The point is that they're transitioning to not having the Oyster at all. And in the meantime they have just done a business analysis and realised that it is more proficient to repay the people who claim the double billing than to really re-implement the system.

Audience: In fairness though when Oyster was being planned I don't think they had necessarily an entirely card free plan in there.

Reply: Exactly, yes, but they could have done it, or they could have done it differently.

Audience: Maybe, but I think that the bigger thing is that you can't solve that. They solved the problem with isolation but the problem was actually bigger in that it involved everybody else's cards, and security is very similar in that you have to solve the problem by looking at the whole overall thing of, for instance, too many passwords, and try and solve that rather than, well I have a new service, my service needs to be secure, I will add a new password, a simple, small, box solution, but bigger picture.

Reply: But isn't asking the user to take care of their own security and warning them really the opposite of what I'm trying to say? And saying, we don't care, we told you. This is their attitude.

Audience: Yes, basically that is the same one as you have to remember a new password.

Audience: It's kind of one-sided to say they're just pushing the problem to the users, because if they took on the costs of changing their system, I don't know what they have to do, but certainly if it involved changing all the card readers, or anything like that, it's going to be fairly expensive and disruptive to all those people. So maybe they just decided that on balance it would be better to put up some posters and warn people of the problem that maybe doesn't actually affect many users. Whereas it's like having to have like half the turnstiles in all the tube stations not working for however long while they repair them, and then, you know, it's just a trade-off, right? And users are paying for the service after all, so if they have to pay a lot of money to change the system for a new way, then that's negatively impacting the users as well in their pocket.

Reply: True, I would agree with that, I mean, it's just one of the many examples, and there are good reasons why they did that. For them it is also a matter of reputation because it's not good for their reputation that there are these problems. They probably did an analysis and it's much cheaper in that way.

Bruce Christianson: But the issue is seeing security as a separate thing, and a problem for the rest of the user experience.

Reply: It's like saying "you can use your debit card now if it is contactless, but security is your business" and that, I think, is the wrong message. Security should be beautiful.

On the Use of Security and Privacy Technology as a Plot Device

Joan Feigenbaum[✉] and Brad Rosen

Yale University, New Haven, CT 06520-8285, USA
{joan.feigenbaum,brad.rosen}@yale.edu

Abstract. We believe that the handling of information security in fiction is, in general, neither technically realistic nor dramatically interesting. Furthermore, we believe that technically realistic treatment of information security *could* be an effective plot device. We provide examples (and one counterexample) from well regarded television shows to support our beliefs. We conclude with a short fictional work of our own creation that attempts to use information security in a technically realistic and dramatically interesting manner.

1 Introduction

In answer to the question "how is information security handled in fiction?," we are tempted to say that there doesn't seem to be much information security in fiction. Intelligence and law-enforcement protagonists generally seem to be able to break into computer systems almost effortlessly whenever they need to in order to catch villains, and their break-ins generally don't leave any tracks or have any negative consequences. Ironically, the one thing that fictional good guys sometimes have a hard time doing is something that real-world intelligence and law-enforcement agencies do pretty well, namely locate sources of incoming phone calls and messages.

There are some notable exceptions to this general state of affairs – fictional episodes in which the technical difficulty of achieving information security is apparent and in which attempts to circumvent security measures either succeed or fail in realistic and dramatically effective ways. It is our thesis that such prolonged and nuanced treatment of information-security challenges can be a great plot device and that it is underutilized by novelists and screenwriters.

2 Talk Summary

Break-ins are Easy and have No Consequences. To support our claim that information security is often treated unrealistically in fiction, we showed three clips from well regarded TV shows. In each, a white-hat hacker manages to break into an ostensibly well defended enterprise database in less than one minute while his colleagues or friends stand around making small talk. The three targets were

B. Christianson et al. (Eds.): Security Protocols 2015, LNCS 9379, pp. 261–275, 2015.
DOI: 10.1007/978-3-319-26096-9_27

a CIA personnel database [1], a Mossad personnel database [2], and a phone-company operations database [3]. In none of these episodes did the hacker suffer any consequences for his blatantly illegal act; nor did the organization that was broken into demonstrate any awareness of the break-in.

Tracing Phone Calls is Hard. The *trace race* [4] is a police-procedural trope in which the police try to determine a calling number or to locate a (criminal) caller. They need the caller to stay on the line for a certain amount of time. The amount of time needed varies. Even if the person talking to the criminal is told to "keep him talking," and the criminal obliges by blabbing on forever, it never seems to work. Sometimes, the criminal seems to know exactly when to hang up in order to defeat a trace.

To illustrate this trope, we showed two clips from a **Law and Order: SVU** episode in which the detectives spend more than an hour (of elapsed time, not screen time, obviously) trying to locate a cell-phone caller [5].

In fact, tracing a calling number was nontrivial when "telephone switches" were actually mechanical racks of switches. Now, however, telephone switches are software systems. One can go to a console during a call, enter the number, and get the other number(s) on the call. Phones can also be located; phone companies locate them all the time, and so do police departments.

A Counterexample: Pacemaker Hacking. One compelling exception to the weak treatment of information security in fiction is the pacemaker attack on Vice President Waldron in **Homeland** [6]. Responding to a terrorist's threat to kill his beloved Carrie Mathison, protagonist Nicholas Brody breaks into Waldron's office and finds the serial number of the pacemaker. Armed with the serial number, an unnamed, apparently highly skilled hacker (in the employ of the terrorist who has threatened to kill Carrie) gains wireless access to Waldron's pacemaker and kills him.

One of the reasons this attack is so utterly gripping is that it goes on for almost six minutes of screen time; viewers are not misled into thinking that even a skilled hacker could pull it off in a matter of seconds or that even a successful attack would kill the victim instantaneously. In the talk, we were able to show just three short cuts from the 6-min scene.

The scene is technically realistic. Wireless-networked, implanted medical devices *are* insecure, and patients are at risk [7,8].

A Story Idea: Car Hacking. Just as wireless access to implanted medical devices is a real threat, so is wireless access to *electronic control units* of automobiles [9]. Our talk concluded with the question of whether a good espionage story could be based on the idea of a "black operative" who uses car hacking to disguise an assassination as an accident. We solicited plot suggestions from the audience and received many good ones (unsurprisingly, given that this was a Cambridge workshop audience); they can be found in the transcript that appears in this volume.

After the workshop, we wrote a story that features both car hacking and intelligence operatives. It can be found in the appendix.

Drive Me Crazy

Friday, June 19, 2015, early evening. David's apartment

Arriving home after another humdrum day at work, David hung his windbreaker on a peg in the hall, left his shoes directly under it, and flopped onto the bed. It was hard to believe there were so many allegedly smart people who enjoyed these god-awful boring tech jobs. They must have no idea what kind of adventures the internet offered.

After 10 min of staring at the ceiling, he gave in and went to the closet to retrieve the photo from the dress-shirt pocket. It had been almost a week since he'd looked at this photo of Ari and himself on the crowded beach in Tel Aviv. Progress, perhaps. But he still thought about Ari constantly and still longed for him. He'd never loved anyone so intensely, before or since. More to the point, he'd never found anyone else nearly as interesting. It was hard to believe he ever would.

They'd met by chance at the Apple Store in New York's Grand Central Station. Ari was on vacation, and David was working for a hapless start-up in Silicon Alley, long since defunct. By the time Ari was scheduled to return to Israel, David had quit his boring job, packed the few of his belongings that he needed, and sold or discarded the rest. For the next 18 months, he was happy. Increasingly worried, yeah, as it gradually dawned on him what a lunatic Ari was, but he'd mostly been happy. There were always more technical challenges, more financial rewards, and more great sex.

He put the photo back into the pocket of the dress shirt. He'd been told to erase all remnants of his life with Ari, but he figured that no one would expect him to value an old-fashioned snapshot – or anything else that wasn't just bits. So he'd kept only this one, pocket-sized print. Still, it was an addiction at this point, not a source of real pleasure. He knew that he needed to move on.

He turned on the evening news and opened the refrigerator, thinking about what to have for dinner. He'd not yet decided what to cook when he heard the news from Vienna.

"The Iran-deal negotiations were thrown into chaos today in Vienna by a fatal car crash. Iranian Deputy Foreign Minister Abbas Araghchi was en route to a meeting with representatives of all of the P5-plus-one nations when the chauffeured sedan, a 2014 Chrysler 300, in which he was travelling turned suddenly into oncoming traffic. The crash killed Araghchi, his driver, and the driver of one of the three other cars involved. Four other people were injured, two of them seriously."

David closed the refrigerator and listened intently to the rest of the news report. Of course, the most anti-western members of the Iranian delegation were accusing the other parties to the negotiation of tampering with the car. Of course, the other parties were saying that they wanted nothing more than to conclude the deal successfully at this point and that, moreover, the car, which had been in fine working order the day before, had been in a locked garage under both armed guard and video surveillance all night. Of course, it was evident that no one had tampered with the car. Perhaps the Iranian chauffeur was the one who wanted to blow up the negotiations, even at the expense of his own life.

This was Ari's handiwork. David knew it as soon as he heard the phrases "Iran-deal negotiations" and "fatal car crash" in the same news story. Ari had perfected car hacking years ago and had been waiting for an opportunity to use it. At the time he'd demoed his car-hacking skills in the parking lot, he'd told David that there didn't seem to be any suitable targets. Ari was ambitious and amoral, but he wasn't bloodthirsty. He wouldn't cause a fatal crash just to show he could do it; there had to be something important at stake.

David turned off the TV and called his CIA handler. He wasn't without ambition himself.

Saturday, June 20, 2015, mid-afternoon. Mitchell Park, Palo Alto

Joe Dunant stared at David across the picnic table. He was extremely unhappy about the crazy story that he'd just heard, but he stayed calm. He'd dealt with erratic assets before – even seriously neurotic ones – and managed to get some good stuff out of them, at least for a while. David had never flaked out on him before, but Joe would cope with flakiness if it was the price to pay for David's technical expertise and first-hand knowledge of the global hacker underworld.

"Let's go over this again, ok?" Joe said. "First of all, how is this supposed to work exactly?"

David knew better than to take that question literally. He gave Joe a quizzical look.

"OK, not *exactly*," Joe admitted. "In high-level terms, what the hell do you think he did?"

"He exploited what's known in the computer-security world as a 'remote automotive attack surface' to get control of the car. Cars, as you probably know, are full of computers these days. For just about every essential function (steering, acceleration, braking, and so on), there's an ECU. Stands for 'electronic control unit.' There are ECUs for inessential functions, too – power windows, for example."

This was one of the great things about David, Joe thought. Unlike almost all of the genius geeks he'd run since jumping on the cyber-espionage bandwagon, David really knew how to explain things. Joe had learned a huge amount from him about what kinds of attacks were feasible, what kinds of damage they could do, and what might be done to prevent them. Of course, Joe still didn't know *how* people got computers to do all of this scary stuff, but he really didn't need to; he wasn't in the business of writing code. He listened carefully as David went on with his explanation of car hacking.

"The ECUs are connected by an internal network. A group of related components that need to coordinate with each other is usually connected by a 'bus,' which a very simple kind of data network. So far, so good; having an internal bus connect the doors and the dome light so that the light goes on when someone opens the door to get in makes perfect sense and needn't cause insecurity. But there are problems. For example, these separate buses are 'bridged' so that different groups of components can communicate."

"Why?," Joe asked. "That sounds like a bad idea. It also sounds like something that would make the whole network more complicated and more expensive to build."

"Good," David said. "You're right that cost is a factor. I'll get to that. As far as bridging goes, it turns out to be necessary in some important cases. The ECU that controls the door locks, for example, has to receive messages from at least two other ECUs that are usually on different buses. The powertrain-control module has a sensor that determines a car's speed. It broadcasts the speed on the car's internal network. If you've ever gotten onto the highway and suddenly your doors auto-locked, it was because the ECU that controls the door locks got the message that you'd gone above the speed for auto-lock. But the same ECU also needs to get messages from the crash-detection ECUs that control the airbags ... so when a crash is detected, the doors are unlocked and survivors can get out – or be pulled out."

"Got it," Joe said. "But all this is still going on inside the car. How does someone hack in from the outside?"

"Just about every car has components that have to communicate with the outside world. Think of OnStar, for example. GM aggressively advertises the fact that OnStar can track cars and make emergency phone calls. Even in cars that are not supposed to be communicating with the outside world while their owners are driving around, dealers and mechanics want wireless access to do diagnostics – they need to replace an ECU if they determine that it's faulty."

Joe was getting used to the idea of car hacking as a way to kill someone. He wondered whether the agency had ever used it. But he was still having trouble swallowing David's theory that Ari had hacked into this car at this time.

"David, wouldn't someone need to know a lot about a particular make and model of car in order to break into it? You said that Ari was seriously into car hacking years before you hooked up with him. How would he know what kind of car an Iranian diplomat would be in 2015? How would he even know there would be negotiations with Iran in 2015?"

David smiled. "Good. Again. You asked about the cost of designing and developing automotive networks. You're absolutely right that, if every car manufacturer had to start from scratch for every model of car, it would be too expensive. Not to mention too time-consuming. But there are a lot of industry standards, notably CAN buses and OBD-II ports that ..."

"OK, stop." Joe was reaching his limit on the amount of new technical information he could absorb in one sitting. "Since you mentioned 'standards,' I'm assuming your point is that, once a super hacker like Ari figures out how to hack into one kind of car, it's not that hard for him to hack into other kinds."

"Right. Besides, at this point, there are some good survey papers about vulnerabilities in popular makes and models. All he'd need is for someone in Vienna to tell him what the Iranian was being driven around in; that kind of information is for sale everywhere. Then he could find most of the technical information he needs in one of the papers."

These survey papers raised another red flag. "Wait a minute. If this information is widely available, then why do you think Ari did this? Couldn't lots of skilled hackers have pulled off this attack on Araghchi's car?"

David shook his head. "No, not really. The deep magic here is bridging between buses."

Joe listened with rapt attention. Most assets have verbal tells – expressions with which they build up to something that shows why their intel is valuable. David's was "the deep magic here is ..."

"Any hacker worth his salt can figure out how to get onto one of the less privileged buses in a standard, modern automobile without having physical access to the car. It's not all that different from hacking into any supposedly private network that's connected to the internet. Bridging from a less privileged bus to a more privileged one is much harder. A few academic researchers have done it, but their papers don't say exactly how they did it. No one can just read up on how to bridge to an ECU that will steer a car into oncoming traffic. It takes many months of work to figure out how to do that, and Ari put in those months of work."

"You're sure of that?," Joe asked.

"Yeah, I'm sure. He did a demo for me in a parking lot. I was the driver."

Much as he wished he could dismiss it, Joe knew he had to take this bizarre story to his superiors and the rest of his team. If he ignored it, and it proved to be true, his relationship with David would be seriously damaged. Not to mention that Ari may strike again if the negotiations continued.

He flicked the ON-OFF switch on a device that looked like a USB stick but was actually an audio recorder. He would need to give the more technically oriented members of his team a fleshed out version of David's theory, and he didn't trust himself to render it accurately. This device could be shredded after he played the recording for his colleagues.

"Once more. What do you think he did?"

"He probably took over the car's built in telematics system, which is connected to the internet. Then ..."

"Wait. Telematics? What's that?"

"It's a catch-all term for the many ways in which cars collect data, process it, and send the results to various Big Brothers using wireless communication. Insurance companies use the data to reward good drivers and penalize bad ones. Car manufacturers use the data to keep track of how well various features are working – airbags, for instance. Dealers can keep track of when routine maintenance is performed and remind the owners if it's overdue. The most straightforward kind of telematics is simply vehicle tracking. If a car is stolen, and the thief doesn't disable the telematics system, the police should have an easy time catching him."

"OK, go on."

"Then he probably used the bridge to the parking system. Advanced models like this one have ECUs that let the car park itself; they're awesome in really tight spots in which drivers can't see well enough to maneuver in and out but sensors can. The parking ECU can turn the wheels as much as it needs to. It's not supposed to do anything when the car is driving at high speeds, but it's easy enough to bypass that by flooding the CAN bus with traffic. And then *WHAM*, your steering wheel is jerking hard to the left or right, and you're flying into oncoming traffic. And in the split second before you're splattered across the dash, the code is busy erasing itself so there's no trace."

Joe wasn't sure whether that would make sense to his colleagues and figured it wouldn't hurt to ask for some clarification.

"So what's 'flooding' exactly, and how does it make the wheels turn when they're not supposed to?"

David answered patiently. They went on like this for a little while longer and then parted. Joe said he would be in touch soon.

Sunday, June 21, 2015, mid-morning. David's apartment

Usually, he slept well after meeting with Joe but not last night. He could tell during the meeting yesterday that Joe didn't believe that Ari was trying to blow up the Iran deal.

Maybe that made sense. Joe knew that Ari was a brilliant and unscrupulous cyber criminal, but he didn't know him personally. All of the attacks by Ari that Joe knew about were motivated by profit or technical challenge or both. The idea that Ari would attack "the enemies of Israel" probably sounded ridiculous to Joe.

During the year and a half that they were together, David had delighted in the profit and technical challenge. It felt like a dream come true for a while: the best sex he'd ever had, the most interesting work he'd ever done, and more money than he knew what to do with. Plus Ari knew an amazing number of smart and crazy black hats from all over the world; David's "professional" network was expanding by the day.

And life wasn't all work. They talked about everything, including politics. Including Israel's "right to exist." David didn't know what to make of Ari's embattled, aggressive world view when he first heard it. He'd read about the rightward drift in Israeli society and in the American Jewish organizations that considered themselves "pro-Israel," but he'd never actually talked to anyone who believed that stuff. At first, he chose to ignore it – to concentrate on everything he loved about Ari. As time went on, it didn't sound so weird to him; they were living in Israel, and lots of people held similar views, including many whom he agreed with about everything else. He kept reminding himself that nobody was perfect and that his life with Ari really was closer than he'd ever been to the life he'd always dreamed about.

But dreams don't actually come true, do they? As time went on, he couldn't ignore the fact that much of what they were doing was not only illegal but dangerous. And that Ari could be reckless. In the middle of their second year together, recklessness caught up with them. Or at least it caught up with David.

They'd been part of a massive banking scam that Ari had spearheaded. It was not the first time that Ari had a brilliant idea, enough enthusiasm and charisma to enlist a lot of people, but not quite enough devotion to make sure that those people had all of the information they needed to cover their tracks. This time, David was one of the ones who got caught. End of dream.

That was when he met Joe Dunant. He'd been an emotional basket case at the time, but even then he'd had a hint that Joe was a no-bullshit guy. And a decent one. The US Treasury department had orchestrated the sting, and Joe had been read in very early. He'd arranged to meet with David shortly after he was arrested, rather than leaving him to grow increasingly terrified and disoriented in jail as time went by. And Joe had been completely straight about what he wanted: David's unqualified cooperation with the CIA and the rest of the US intelligence community in exchange for extradition to the US and a good job in Silicon Valley. Joe would be his handler; he'd be an "asset" with intimate knowledge of the cyber underworld. He'd known that he had no cards to play and had accepted the deal very quickly. But making the deal with Joe had been less disgusting than making it with someone else would have been.

That was a year ago. This "asset" business had gone pretty smoothly for the first year. Nothing Joe had asked him to do was particularly interesting, but none of it was particularly hard either. And Joe was an ok guy to have a cappuccino with from time to time.

This time was different. Joe hadn't asked. David had come to him with the best intel he'd ever received, and Joe didn't know what to make of it.

Sunday, June 21, 2015, mid-afternoon. David's apartment

David was desperate for something to happen. Joe hadn't called to report on his team's reaction. Did that mean that they were still considering it or that Joe was just being polite when he'd said that they would?

He'd resisted the temptation to search for evidence to support his theory. He wanted to know whether anyone had indeed purchased information recently about chauffeured sedans in Vienna, but he knew that such a search was bound to leave some breadcrumbs. Let Joe's CIA colleagues leave those breadcrumbs if they really needed the evidence.

He started reading his work email, figuring that he might find something to focus on. He opened the BBC World Service radio player in a browser window. It was more effective as background noise than music.

Just ten minutes later, he got the confirmation that he needed.

"Confusion and accusations continue to dominate the Iran-deal negotiations. Today in Geneva, the American Undersecretary of State Wendy Sherman failed to show up for a meeting with similarly high-placed members of the Iranian and other P5-plus-one delegations. A US State Department spokeswoman said that the Undersecretary's car had stalled out en route to the meeting, that she had tried to phone the meeting participants to explain that she would be late, but that the car was in a large cell-phone dead zone. Later, it was discovered that the driver had followed an incorrect route delivered by the car's GPS device."

"Coming hard on the heels of the fatal accident that killed Iranian negotiator Araghchi, this further disruption threatens to derail the negotiations entirely. Nonetheless, the leaders of Iran and the P5-plus-one nations have issued statements saying that they intend to press on and to meet the June 30 deadline if at all possible. 'We've come so far in these negotiations,' said US President Obama. 'We can't let a bizarre but innocent mishap stop us when we're so close to a deal that would benefit all of the parties.' "

David reached for the secure phone. "Joe, it's me. Did you hear about Wendy Sherman's car?"

"Yes, we got the call about 15 min ago. I was just going to call you. Is it on the news already?"

"I heard it on the BBC World Service. Do you want to meet?"

"6:00 in Foothills Park."

Sunday, June 21, 2015, 6 p.m. Foothills Park, Palo Alto

Joe had gotten right down to business. The agency had tipped Sherman's people in Geneva that a car hacker might have killed Araghchi in Vienna and advised them to disable external wireless access to Sherman's car.

David was one step ahead of him. "Ari could get access to that car's system through Bluetooth, even if the cellular network was disabled. They probably left Bluetooth on for hands-free calling, and that's enough. All it takes is a little patience and a brute-force attack to find the PIN. With a directional antenna, you don't even have to be that close if you start brute forcing a day in advance."

Joe had heard something similar from the geeks on his team. As usual, he didn't understand the technical details, but he got the general idea: Someone with Ari's skills and connections could hack into a car network with a Bluetooth connection. The purpose of this meeting was to verify that David had the same story as Joe's colleagues. David would have learned this stuff from Ari; it made his theory that Ari was the culprit very believable.

"So how did he fool the GPS system?," Joe asked, continuing the verification exercise.

"I doubt he needed to mess with the custom hardware that processes the GPS coordinates. The *maps* used by GPS systems are just regular data displayed by easily compromised software. The GPS screen in that car probably showed the right coordinates, but the map was fake, and it led them into the dead zone."

So far so good. Joe had one more question.

"The breakdown?"

"If he could spoof the dead-zone coordinates, he could also take the engine out. There are specific diagnostic messages used to control individual cylinders in the engine, but flooding the engine ECU can shut them all down."

David stopped walking. "Joe, listen to me." Joe stopped and turned around to face his companion. "The BBC said that the negotiations are continuing. Is that right?"

"Yes. They'd probably all have cut and run if Sherman had been driven off a cliff, but what happened today wasn't quite a show stopper."

"You have to stop him. Someone else is going to get killed. Maybe many more people. You saw what happened on Friday."

Joe nodded. Now wasn't the time to explain that his agency's primary concern was the successful completion of this Iran deal on which the Obama administration had staked so much. More casualties would only be problematic because they'd mean the end of negotiation.

"We're working on a plan to disconnect him from the internet."

"You need to mount a DDoS attack. It stands for 'Distributed Denial of Service.' Hit the internet connections through which he's contacting these cars with so much data from so many sources that they can't send anything. I'm sure your people know how to DDoS someone."

"So they tell me," Joe said. "We're probably going to need your input during the next two days. Stand by."

Tuesday, June 23, 2015, early afternoon. L'Acajou Bakery and Cafe, South of Market, San Francisco

Joe and Mary Lawson, his opposite number in MI6, were finishing lunch at Mary's favorite spot in SoMa. Once again, Joe marvelled at how the Brits had placed Mary in the city, surrounded by cutting-edge start ups and great food and coffee, while Joe's own fine country had placed him in Sunnyvale, a mature, boring suburb, near a bunch of mature, boring, incumbent tech companies.

Nonetheless, it was Joe's agency, his asset, and his connections at the National Security Agency who were going to salvage the Iran talks. This was a once-in-a-decade career booster – assuming everyone up the chain in Langley gave him credit for it. Time for him and Mary to go over the crucial points of their joint op. They couldn't have that conversation in L'Acajou. Joe asked for the check, and soon they were strolling on 9th toward Mission.

"Well, Dunant," said Mary. "I admit that I was pretty skeptical when you sprung this on me yesterday morning." They walked on, Mary looking straight ahead and Joe looking at her. "Skeptical! Hell, I was bloody incredulous."

"Yeah, I was incredulous, too, when it was sprung on me. But the intel is solid, and the op is pure cyber. There's really nothing to lose."

"And a lot to gain," said Mary. "Look, we can't assume that 'pure cyber' means non-lethal. We could wind up DDoS'ing a control system . . ."

"Oh come on," Joe interrupted. "You're not talking to a fresh recruit, Lawson. Of course there are risks. There always are. But this is probably the least risky op we'll ever run together."

Mary smiled, nodded, and turned toward Joe. She'd felt obliged to say that they needed to be cautious and acknowledge the risks. But, truth be told, she loved the idea of this multinational DDoS attack, and she was amped up.

"Right then. You're sure this lone wolf we're targeting could actually have hacked into both cars? And, more to the point, that he would want to?"

"Yes and yes. Our asset is his ex-boyfriend."

Mary raised her eyebrows, having just heard for the first time that there was a gay angle here. For that matter, she was hearing for the first time that there was a sex and romance angle at all. Oh well. Not worth interrupting Dunant's story – all sources of good intel were fair game, and ex-lovers of all orientations were the most tried and true of sources.

"Our target hates the idea of a deal with Iran that would bring the Iranians into the 'international community,' whatever the fuck that is. He's not for a pre-emptive strike on Iran . . ."

Mary snorted. "Nice of him, that. Especially since Israelis who are in favor of a pre-emptive strike usually mean a pre-emptive strike by the US, with the UK to follow."

Joe didn't need a lesson in geopolitics any more than he needed a lesson in cyber-physical risks. "As I was saying, the target just wants Israel, Saudi Arabia, and all of their allies to be in a permanent cold war with Iran. A deal that ends that cold war would 'upset the balance of power in the region.' So, yeah, he wants to blow up the negotiations."

They turned left on Mission. No one was following them. Hell, no one had noticed them. They blended perfectly into the neighborhood.

"More interestingly, he's studied car hacking seriously for years. The attacks used against Araghchi and Sherman are well documented in the open literature at this point, but he had them years ago, well before they were published."

"He knew them, or he did them?," Mary asked. Just as Joe had asked David. It was a crucial question.

"Did them. Our asset left no doubt about that."

"OK, Dunant. I'm not going to press you for those details."

Joe was happy to be working with a professional. Mary knew that she and her agency would benefit if this op worked and that Joe had done her a favor by bringing her into it. She didn't expect Joe to tell her everything about his asset, who had probably been up to his eyeballs in illegal activity during his affair with the target.

Joe continued. "I do want you to know how we got the target's IP address. Actually, his IPs, plural. He's not the type to use just one." Indeed, Mary needed this information. The IPs were the cyberspace addresses of the machines they'd be attacking, and those machines would be crippled for quite some time. They needed to aim carefully.

"One of the most useful things we've gotten from this asset is the fact that the target is a regular in the Gaybros Internet Relay Chat room, especially on Tech Thursdays. We've been chatting with him every week for a year now. Lots of different guys on our end; we don't want him to get too interested in any of them. But they're interesting enough to keep him chatting."

Stopped at a crowded intersection, they had to change the subject while waiting for the walk signal. A minute and a half on real-estate prices – currently the least remarkable topic of overheard conversation in San Francisco.

"Anyway, he uses Tor to connect to Gaybros IRC, and he's careful enough to use the version with stronger crypto. But a year is more than enough time for our NSA friends to crack a specific instance of even the stronger version, and we've given them all of the traffic we've collected. There are four IPs with high-bandwidth connections that he uses regularly. It stands to reason that he's using them for these car hacks."

Mary was impressed. Millions of people use Tor to connect anonymously with chat rooms and other online services; Tor protects the users' IPs with encryption, and even the NSA cannot break that encryption quickly or at scale. If Joe's asset had showed up when the first car hack was performed on Araghchi and said "That's my ex's work. Go find him on Gaybros IRC on Thursday," they'd have been out of luck. But Joe and his people had been tracking this target for a year, ever since they were tipped by their asset that the guy was bound to strike at some point and that he'd do so anonymously and in cyberspace. So they'd patiently collected the data that the NSA needed to deanonymize a specific user. Now that the strike had occurred, they were ready to strike back.

"It's a go, then, as far as I'm concerned. I assume you've got to clear it all the way up?"

"Yeah," Joe said. "I'm working on getting that done by noon on Thursday. How long do you need?"

"Thursday should work for me, too. I don't think I'm going to have to go all the way up. High-tech, no bloodshed, work with the cousins, . . ., this is exactly what we're supposed to be doing these days."

"Let's touch base on Thursday afternoon, then."

Mary nodded. "In the meantime, we need to get a bunch of our favorite geeks on stand-by, ready for activation. I'm assuming we're going to hit this target from everywhere on the planet that's home to a lot of black hats."

"Good assumption." Joe had been about to explain that part of his thinking, but Mary was already there. "Our Mossad friends will know that your agency and mine are involved. If there's DDoS traffic coming from everywhere, especially the other P5-plus-one countries, maybe they'll spread the blame around."

"France, Russia, China, US, UK, and Germany. A veritable 'permanent five plus one' club of fucked up geeks. We can spread the net even wider – include Ukraine, why not? Confuse the issue further."

"I agree," Joe said. "Talk to you Thursday."

Mary nodded and turned toward the nearby BART station. "I wouldn't worry too much about alienating Mossad," she said in parting. "They're not as paranoid about Iran as the Netanyahu government."

Few people are, Joe thought.

Thursday, June 25, 2015, 11 a.m. Secure videoconference room, Mountain View

Joe swirled the dregs of his second hit of coffee around in the styrofoam cup. He didn't mind waiting, really. It was only the second time in his 15 years with the agency that he'd met with the Director of National Intelligence and the first time he'd done so by videoconference from the Silicon Valley field office. The fact that the DNI wanted to talk to him directly could only mean good things for him and for SV station. But waiting was still a drag.

At last the station chief, Larry Stern, arrived with a late-20s guy Joe didn't know.

"Could you connect us with the DNI's office, Seth?," the chief asked.

Seth remained silent but got to work. Must be the videoconference guru.

"Hello, sir," Joe said to the division chief. "Good to see you again."

"Call me Larry, please. It's California. No one calls anyone 'sir.' Thanks, Seth. Stay by your phone in case we need help." Seth nodded and left without a word. "Ready, Joe?"

They sat facing the screen and watched the DNI's face come into focus.

"Morning, gentlemen."

Seth had turned the volume too high. Fortunately, that was something Stern didn't need a guru to fix. He pushed a button on a hand-held control. "Morning, sir," he said. Joe coughed quietly into his fist instead of chuckling.

"It's afternoon here. And there's a lot to do before close of business. So let's get down to it. This is a highly unusual operation you've proposed, Dunant. Are you sure it's our best option?"

Joe didn't hesitate. "It's our only reasonable option, sir. David knows more about Ari's m.o. than anyone else. We're as well positioned to DDoS him as it's possible to be at this point."

"I'm not asking whether you've got the best DDoS plan in place. I'm asking whether DDoS'ing Ari is the best option. Do we want to stay in the shadows on this? If we went to the President with this car-hacking story, he might be able to force the Israelis to arrest the son of a bitch."

This was a strategic question, not an operational one. Stern took over. "Taking this to the President is unlikely to work, sir. He would need time to convince the Israelis that Ari is behind these disruptions, and they would need more time to find him and put him out of commission. We're into the last week of negotiations, and Ari's almost certainly poised to strike again. If we want to spare the next victim, we either have to neutralize Ari or temporarily suspend the negotiations; the deal won't survive a suspension."

This DNI was a great listener, with a great poker face. He turned calmly to Joe. "What do you think, Dunant?"

"I think Mr. Stern is right, sir. Besides, reading in the President and the Israelis would mean burning David, who cost us quite a bit to acquire and who's been a superb asset. I'd hate to lose him."

Seven seconds of silence, which was an eternity in a videoconference. Any longer and people start wondering whether the link has gone down.

"OK, I can see your point," the DNI said at last. "And of course there might be leaks if the President confronted Netanyahu with your theory. 'Iran Nuclear Deal Taken Down by an Israeli Car Hacker.' Jesus. The public would think we're totally crazy."

He was clearly ready to move on to the next crisis. Easy peasy, Joe thought.

"You're working with the Brits on this?," the DNI asked.

"Yes, sir." Stern and Joe said in unison.

"OK, carry on." The screen blanked as the DNI was standing up to leave his own secure conference room.

Stern used the remote to power down on their end. "He didn't mention the real reason that the President can't ask Netanyahu to shut Ari down."

Joe just raised his eyebrows and waited for Stern to continue.

"Netanyahu wouldn't do it. The Israeli right wing hates this Iran deal. They'd probably view car hacking as a brilliant way to blow the whole thing up."

Tuesday, June 30, 2015, early evening. David's apartment

The BBC presenters were droning on about sports. David spooned coffee into the stove-top espresso maker, more because he needed something to do than because he really wanted coffee. There's always a soccer game on somewhere, and people actually seem to care, don't they? David forced himself to listen, even though he truly hated sports, especially soccer. The sports news finally ended as he was pouring his first espresso.

"Negotiations between the government of Iran and the P-5-plus-one powers have concluded successfully in Vienna. President Rouhani of Iran appeared with the leaders of the P-5-plus-one at 1:37 this morning Central European summer time to announce the signing of the agreement and the beginning of a new era in relations between Iran and the west.

"BBC News with Neil Nunez."

David sipped his espresso, listening with one ear as the terms of the agreement were presented yet again – for people who were tuning into the news for the first time in over a year, he guessed. He took the coffee over to his computer, turned the volume down, and started reading his work email. He wanted to look for news of the DDoS attack in the chat rooms, but he also wanted to avoid the whole thing. Dunant would probably fill him in.

Sure enough, the secure phone rang just as he hit send on the one message that his colleagues needed to read. He wasn't planning to go to the office tomorrow, and no doubt he'd get some grief for that, but the smartest and most conscientious guys in his group would stay busy all day with the information he'd just sent them. That would be the subject of conversation when he showed up on Thursday, not why he was out sick on Wednesday.

"Hi, Joe."

"Good evening. Looks like you were right."

David closed the BBC player window and sat in silence for a few seconds.

"David? You there?"

"Yeah, I'm here."

"Let's meet. How about 2 o'clock tomorrow in Mitchell Park?"

"OK." David disconnected, sipped some more coffee, and then closed the email client. He walked to the bedroom closet, pulled the photo out of the dress-shirt pocket, and flopped onto the bed. They were even now, sort of. He could stop being angry at Ari for not protecting him well enough in the banking scam. Maybe someday he'd stop thinking about him constantly. Not any time soon.

Wednesday, July 1, 2015, mid-afternoon. Mitchell Park, Palo Alto

"You did something great, David," Joe said. "For your country and for the whole world."

"You and your black-hat network did it, Joe. All I did was betray my friend."

They finished their second walk around the quarter-mile path and sat at a picnic table. Joe had been through this kind of thing with assets before. David now knew the full implications of the deal he'd made to avoid conviction and imprisonment in Israel. He'd now seen how unhesitatingly, even eagerly, the CIA would use the intimate details about Ari that he'd given them. He may or may not be able to go on with his second-chance life in Silicon Valley; if he couldn't live with himself and carry on without attracting attention, Joe would have to treat him as a threat.

"Do you know where he is now?," David asked.

"No. Nothing from any of his known pseudonyms or locations since we attacked. No contacts with any of his known associates."

David stared at the kids playing on the lawn and their helicopter moms. What the hell was he doing here? There was nothing to live for here. Nothing in the park, in the Valley, or in the whole damned country. How much longer was he supposed to pretend that working on data-center network security most of the time and meeting with his CIA handler every once in a while was anyone's idea of a life?

"What do you want me to do now?," he asked Joe.

"Take it easy for a while. I'm sure you'll be back in touch with us before too long. Or we'll be in touch with you."

"That's it? Ari's off the grid, and you people aren't even looking for him?"

"We'll find him, David, if there's a reason to. Maybe you'll point us to him, as you did this time. Try to focus on something else now. Maybe someone else."

David snorted and looked back at the lawn. "Yeah, sure," he said, "Someone else." What did Dunant mean, anyway? Find another boyfriend, or give them intel on another cyber wacko? Both, maybe. It was a pretty creepy way to live.

But he didn't walk away.

References

1. Royals and Loyals: NCIS, Season 8, Episode 4. Oct. **12**, (2010)
2. Berlin, NCIS, Season 10, Episode 21, 23 April 2013
3. Let's Get to Scooping, How to Get Away With Murder, Season 1, Episode 4, 16 October 2014
4. http://tvtropes.org/pmwiki/pmwiki.php/Main/PhoneTraceRace
5. 911, Law and Order SVU: Season 7, Episode 3, 4 October 2005
6. Broken Hearts, Homeland, Season 2, Episode 10, 2 December 2012
7. Halperin, D., Heydt-Benjamin, T.S., Ransford, B., Clark, S.S., Defend, B., Morgan, W., Fu, K., Kohno, T., Maisel, W.H.: Pacemakers and implantable cardiac defibrillators: software radio attacks and zero-power defenses. In: 29th Symposium on Security and Privacy, pp. 129–142. IEEE, Piscataway (2008)
8. Denning, T., Borning, A., Friedman, B., Gill, B.T., Kohno, T., Maisel, W.H.: Patients, pacemakers, and implantable defibrillators: human values and security for wireless implantable medical devices. In: 28th SIGCHI Conference on Human Factors in Computing Systems, pp. 917–926. ACM Press, New York (2010)
9. Valasek, C., Miller, C.: A Survey of Remote Automotive Attack Surfaces (2014). http://illmatics.com/remote%20attack%20surfaces.pdf

On the Use of Security and Privacy Technology as a Plot Device (Transcript of Discussion)

Joan Feigenbaum(✉)

Yale University, New Haven, CT 06520-8285, USA
joan.feigenbaum@yale.edu

My coauthor Brad Rosen is a former student of mine who took a course I gave in 2003 entitled *Sensitive Information in a Wired World*. It was sort of a sociotechnical treatment of information security. He decided to become a lawyer, and he started telling everybody in the computer science department that it was because of my course that he decided to become a lawyer. That didn't make me very happy, and it didn't make them very happy with me. Since then, things have changed. Nowadays many people say we actually *need* tech-savvy lawyers at least as much as we need more technologists. I agree with them.

I'm still friends with Brad, and I told him that I was going to a workshop on how information security is handled in fiction. After some discussion, he and I both concluded that, in our experience, there really *isn't* much information security in fiction: People who need to break into computer systems just do it, almost instantaneously, and then they never suffer any consequences for having done so.

So I'm going to give you some ... what?

Frank Stajano: It's the same for killing people – in movies.

Reply: Not quite. Anyway, I'll give you what Brad and I consider to be some very typical examples of this phenomenon. The first is an episode from NCIS. I don't know whether you watch NCIS, but the geek guy, whom you will recognize instantaneously for some reason, manages to hack into a CIA database in about 3 s.

[First NCIS clip]

OK, so that's our first example. Just to show that sometimes it's a little bit harder, in our second example, the same guy spends about 30 s hacking into a Mossad database.

[Second NCIS clip]

In that episode, Orli, who's the Mossad chief, actually *does* threaten the NCIS people for about 2 s that she's going to get them in trouble for hacking into the Mossad database. Then they point out that she lied and caused a lot of trouble for the US intelligence community; so she doesn't get them in trouble.

Now for one last example of this weird phenomenon. This one is from a different show, one I have never seen. It's Brad's example, from How to Get Away with Murder (HTGAWM).

© Springer International Publishing Switzerland 2015
B. Christianson et al. (Eds.): Security Protocols 2015, LNCS 9379, pp. 276–282, 2015.
DOI: 10.1007/978-3-319-26096-9_28

[HTGAWM clip]

So screenwriters seem to think you can easily break into databases of phone companies, intelligence agencies, whatever. However, there seems to be one thing that they have trouble with in cop shows and spook shows, and that's phone calls: tracing calls and locating phones. There are so many examples of this phenomenon that there's a whole page on the "TV Tropes" website devoted it: It's called "the trace race." The amount of time that the good guy is supposed to have to keep the bad guy on the phone varies, but, even if the police or intelligence officer tells the good guy to "keep him talking," and, even if the bad guy obliges by blabbing on indefinitely, somehow it never works. The authorities can never figure out what the calling number is or where exactly the phone is. Sometimes the bad guy seems to know exactly when to hang up, just before the trace is going to succeed.

Here's a scene in which they're trying locate a phone; it's from Law & Order SVU, and the episode is called "9-1-1."

[First Law & Order SVU clip]

Apparently, this kid is not just someone whose parents didn't pay for a babysitter. Now, for some reason, Olivia, who's New York's best when it comes to talking to special victims who are kids, can't get things to work. Here we are an hour later in time and about 10 min later in the show, and Olivia is still on the phone with the kid.

[Second Law & Order SVU clip]

OK, so again, information security in fact and information security in fiction seem to be completely at odds, because in practice calling numbers are easily traced, and phones are easily located. Phone companies, for example, locate phones everyday, and so do police departments. I read the TV-trope "trace-race" webpage, and it said that the race was once based in fact; when "telephone switches" were actually mechanical racks of switches, it was non-trivial for the called phone to determine what the calling number was. Nowadays, of course, telephone switches are computer programs, and you can go to a console, type in the called number, and find out what the calling number is.

So my general impression is that information-security fiction, at least in the TV shows and movies that I watch, is just completely off base; it does not correspond to information-security fact at all. A great counterexample, however, is the pacemaker attack in season 2 of Homeland. Has anyone seen this?

Audience: [yes/no]

Reply: Most of you haven't: Good, because I'm going to show it. Unfortunately, it's too long for me to show you the whole episode from the beginning of attack to the guy's actually dying, but I picked out 3 sub-episodes. They feature Nicholas Brody, one of the two main characters of the first 2 seasons. He is a US marine who was captured and imprisoned in Iraq, and he was "turned" by the enemy while in prison. Since the beginning of season 1, he has been turned back by the very beautiful, but also seriously bi-polar, CIA officer Carrie Mathison. (Unfortunately, Carrie didn't make it into these three clips I'm going to show.) The episode also features Abu Nazir, who's the charismatic terrorist who turned Brody; Nazir knows that Brody is lost to him, but he's trying to get Brody to abet this attack on Vice President Walden by threatening to kill Carrie. Walden is Dick Cheney – pacemaker included – except that Walden, unlike Cheney, is running for president; at this point in the story, he's trying to get Brody to be his running mate. The episode also features an unnamed Muslim hacker who does not look like a goofy geek at all; he looks like a serious, calm, mindful, techie, skilled guy.

In this first clip, Brody has just persuaded Nazir to let Carrie go, and he's going to text Nazir the serial number of the pacemaker.

[First Homeland clip]

Next, they get into a discussion. Brody is starting to reveal who he really is and why he's not actually going to be a vice-presidential candidate. (I think that's a rare case of Homeland's screen writers' making Brody out not to be very bright, by the way, because he starts spilling the beans *before* Walden starts having a heart attack.)

Here we see the continuation of the attack.

[Second Homeland clip]

And here we see the end of the attack and the last clip that I'm going to show you.

[Third Homeland clip]

So I don't know what that phrase (that the young hacker uttered at the end) means – probably something like "mission accomplished."

This Homeland episode got a huge amount of media attention, with viewers asking "could that really happen?" All the alleged experts who replied said, yes, that could really happen. Of course I didn't know whether that was an example of information security's being treated unrealistically by the news media instead of by the entertainment industry; so I Googled around a bit, and it turned out that, yes, that actually could happen. [Shows a PowerPoint slide[1] with some references to papers about remote attacks on implanted medical devices; one of the co-authors is S. Clark.] I think this is not our very own S. Clark, right?

Sandy Clark: That's a different S. Clark, but I've done some related stuff.

Reply: There have been quite a few papers on wirelessly networked, implanted medical devices. They do pose precisely that type of insecurity, and patients are at risk.

Sandy Clark: And often for the same reason that we touched on in a lot of other things: for debugging or for the doctors' convenience.

---

[1] Slide deck available at http://www.cs.yale.edu/homes/jf/JF-Cambridge2015.pptx.

Reply: Right, exactly.

Sandy Clark: Intel and Pomsar have said that the defibrillators that are just sitting on a wall for somebody to use are also this way.

Reply: Exactly. So that scene from Homeland was realistic. We had a job candidate this year who talked about a similar thing. [Shows a PowerPoint slide (See footnote 1) with some references to papers about remote car hacking.] Some of the authors of these papers are the same as the authors of the defibrillator and pacemaker papers. (I think this is not our very own Ross Anderson but rather Dave Anderson.) The thing that our job candidate talked about that gave me a story idea was automotive insecurity. In the same way that wirelessly networked implanted medical devices put patients at risk, it turns out that wirelessly networked car-computer networks put drivers and passengers at risk.

Sandy Clark: With the exception of Tesla right now.

Reply: I'm not saying that you could do this to every make and model of car. I'm just saying that there are commodity automobiles that can be hacked into remotely. In fact, these papers were written based on experiments that these authors did by simply purchasing two identical-make-and-model ordinary cars from a dealer, playing with them, and examining what they called the "external attack surfaces." It was already known that, if you actually have physical access to the car, you can tamper with its computer network and, you know, get it to misbehave drastically and wind up killing someone. So their question was, what if we're somewhere else, we don't have physical access to the car, but we have wireless-network access to it, and we've already reverse engineered an identical make and model? Could we actually take it over and render the driver incapable of driving properly? And the answer was yes.

In these papers, what they say is that they were not only able to come up with a hypothetical attack but to demonstrate to the manufacturer that they could put a car in an empty parking lot and, through the wireless network, gain complete control over its system. Of course, that was the only way to get the manufacturer to pay attention.

So I was listening to this interview talk and, towards the end, the candidate said that he and his collaborators had gotten a lot of attention and that they'd consulted with police departments, with the US military, and with the UK military. So I said, "This is interesting. Why don't we hear about this being done? Why aren't criminals and terrorists doing this? I mean, you've demonstrated that you could wreak havoc this way."

Sandy Clark: It's been in the hacker cons for years.

Reply: OK, hold on, I know that. I understand that people do it for fun and to impress their friends. I'm asking why military services and run-of-the-mill murderers aren't using this technique. His answer was basically "it's an inefficient way to kill people. The US military and the UK military were very interested in hearing about the technical aspects of what we did, but, if you're going to kill people on the scale that they kill people, you're going to use a bomb, not a car.

If you're an ordinary murderer, it's probably easier to buy a gun than it is to hack a car – at least in the US."

Here's my story idea: If not the military or an ordinary murderer, what about a CIA black operative? Would this be a good way for a black op to get an assassination target simply to drive off a cliff, drive into a brick wall, or drive across the highway divider into oncoming traffic and appear to have died in a car accident? He wouldn't cause an international incident, he wouldn't get in trouble, his cover wouldn't be blown, blah, blah, blah, as it might be if he just stabbed the guy or something. So Brad and I are talking about writing this story, and we've come up with the following potential problems.

I know that some of you might not believe this, but in fiction even a black operative might worry about killing someone or about collateral damage. What about the passengers? What about the innocent bystanders? If you create a highway pile up, you do more than just kill off your one target, right? So would a black op who hacked a car in order to kill a target and wound up killing others as well just say "oh you know, shit happens, ..., small bad in service to the greater good, ..., we're going to head off a nuclear war, ..., whatever"?

Another problem: What happens if the tampering is evident after the crash? Hacking a car in order to kill a target is supposed to be a way of not calling attention to yourself or to your agency; after all, the guy died in a car accident. But what if the car is actually examined forensically? So maybe if you get him to drive off a cliff, and the car bursts into flames and burns to a crisp, it doesn't matter, because there's not much to examine. Then we thought about whether there is a way to use car hacking to undermine a target without actually killing him. Can you neutralize this threat by just getting the target to be such an erratic driver that he is somehow disabled? He's no longer a threat, because he's so incompetent; people are so suspicious of him because of his driving problem that's enough, and you don't actually have to kill him.

Keith Irwin: Or you make his job more difficult by having his car drive away every night.

Sandy Clark: Or just not start.

Reply: Right, exactly! He's supposed to go off to a meeting with a king, or with his boss, or with ... who knows, and he can't find his car. Why? Because you drove it to the other parking lot.

Sandy Clark: When DARPA did a little car-hacking thing a year or two ago, one of the winning groups locked their victim in the car and then turned the heat on and the radio on full blast. So he couldn't start the engine, he couldn't get out of the car, and he couldn't stop the heat.

Reply: Before I take the next question, I should tell you that I really want to *write* this story.

Mark Lomas: Before you write it: You've reinvented the plot of "The Sontaran Stratagem," which was a Doctor Who episode.

Reply: OK. See, I knew this was going to happen. Is Doctor Who a science fiction show?

Audience: Yes.

Reply: I knew I was on thin ice here, because, when this crowd hears "information security in fiction," it thinks of science fiction, which I have never read (or consumed in any medium whatsoever). I'm a detective-fiction and spy-fiction kind of gal.

Keith Irwin: Actually, I have a book about car hacking that's detective fiction.

Reply: So you should email me the title and author.

Keith Irwin: I'll look it up; it was one of those little pulp detective novels.

Note (from a later email message to Feigenbaum from Irwin): I didn't forget, but I couldn't find the book in my house or my father-in-law's house. (He's the one who gave me the book and to whom I may have returned it.) I also tried a bunch of Googling, but I couldn't find it that way either. Sorry, I will say I didn't think it was a very good book. It was the sort of novel with a magic hacker who can take over any car anywhere with no special effort.

Reply: OK, so you [points at Irwin] should send me the title of that book, and you [points at Lomas] should send me the pointer to the Doctor Who episode, because I think there's more than one story to be written about this. If you put it into the intelligence context, you get a few more types of constraints.

Mark Lomas: Sontarans were a bit more ambitious. They decided to take over all of the cars in the world.

Reply: OK! That's exactly what our black op does not want to do.

Audience: This is done for planes as well.

Reply: Yes, that was something that our job candidate told us. Yes Sandy.

Sandy Clark: Well a couple of simple things. With the CAN Bus system, you could just take over the airbags and set one off. There was an entire Honda recall because of airbags. So this would be something that, realistically, could actually happen, and no one would ever check whether it was done deliberately. The same thing with brakes.

Reply: Right! The Toyota brake scandal.

Sandy Clark: Yes, the Toyota brake scandal. If you're using things for which there are precedents, no one is going to question it.

Reply: The problem that you would cause is something that is known to happen *without* hacking.

Sandy Clark: Exactly. Ancillary attacks would be to take over the electronically controlled lights, the traffic lights, or something like that, instead.

Reply: That was actually done in a Covert Affairs episode.

Tom Sutcliffe: So one of the other things that you could have as your goal, rather than simply to kill someone, is to attempt, say, manipulation of a company's stock price – perhaps by creating bugs that cause a massive recall, because lots of people's brakes start failing after you've hacked all the cars. Driving the stock price down undermines a particular company rather than a specific person.

Reply: Don't know really whether that's a CIA issue, but OK.

Ross Anderson: There's something I once actually suggested to a German foreign-policy person, and it's as follows. Zimbabwe is under EU sanctions. Mr. Mugabe pays off his thugs by buying them Mercedes motorcars; so what's to stop the EU from ordering Germany to order Mercedes in Stuttgart to remotely brick all the Mercedes cars in Zimbabwe? And when I put this suggestion to her, she kind of lost her temper and said, "That's you Brits; that's how you think with your post-imperial thing. Germany is a country governed by law, and we would never do something like that to a German company." But as an idea: Brick cars as a foreign-policy sanction.

Reply: Sanctioned by hacking. That's great!

Frank Stajano: Well, more interestingly, brick all the *guns* that we sell to them!

Vit Bukac: Maybe you could have a gang that specializes in stealing cars. Instead of going to the car location, moving them all to some ship, and keeping them outside, the gang could just sit in the location to which the cars will be delivered, remotely access the cars, and drive them to that location.

Reply: That's a somewhat different story, though.

Dylan Clark: So when the target is in the house, start flashing the lights on the car and honking the horn so that he comes out, drive the car down the road, and crash it into a wall. Do this on a night when he's been drinking, and then his excuse to the police is, "no I wasn't driving drunk! My car just drove itself into the wall."

Reply: Yes, that's OK unless he's protected by an intelligence agency. That's another TV trope: You have some ordinary crime that the police want to solve, but the intelligence community quashes the investigation.

Keith Irwin: In the crash scenario, where you want to hide the evidence of tampering, I think it would make the most sense to drive the car into a salt-water body, like an ocean or a sea, instead of hoping it catches fire. By the time it's pulled out of the salt water, the odds of anyone's trying to deal with badly corroded chips seems pretty small.

Reply: So, if Brad and I actually write this story, will you read it? If my proceedings paper is a short story, will you read it?

Audience: [Some head nods and yeses]

Sandy Clark: What about having him go slightly over the speed limit in a school zone so that he's inconvenienced by it?

Reply: I think that would have to be an American target. In the rest of the world, people aren't slayed for driving fast in a school zone.

Bitcoin: Perils of an Unregulated Global P2P Currency

Syed Taha Ali$^{(\boxtimes)}$, Dylan Clarke, and Patrick McCorry

School of Computing Science, Newcastle University, Newcastle upon Tyne, UK
{taha.ali,dylan.clarke,patrick.mccorry}@newcastle.ac.uk

Abstract. Bitcoin has, since 2009, become an increasingly popular online currency, in large part because it resists regulation and provides anonymity. We discuss how Bitcoin has become both a highly useful tool for criminals and a lucrative target for crime, and argue that this arises from the same essential ideological and design choices that have driven Bitcoin's success to date. In this paper, we survey the landscape of Bitcoin-related crime, such as dark markets and bitcoin theft, and speculate about possible future possibilities, including tax evasion and money laundering.

1 Introduction

Bitcoin emerged in 2009 with the aim to provide a secure and independent currency alternative to the global financial infrastructure, which has seen massive downturns and scandals in recent years. In the words of Bitcoin creator, Satoshi Nakamoto:

"The root problem with conventional currency is all the trust that's required to make it work. The central bank must be trusted not to debase the currency, but the history of fiat currencies is full of breaches of that trust. Banks must be trusted to hold our money and transfer it electronically, but they lend it out in waves of credit bubbles with barely a fraction in reserve. We have to trust them with our privacy, trust them not to let identity thieves drain our accounts. Their massive overhead costs make micropayments impossible." [1]

To realise this libertarian agenda, Bitcoin was envisaged as a trustless decentralized network where all transactions are cryptographically verified by users and recorded in a decentralized ledger. This ledger, the blockchain, is populated by miners who compete in a lottery-style contest. So far the Bitcoin experiment has been very successful in certain respects: users have ownership over their wealth, third parties cannot manipulate currency creation, transaction fees are very low, and users can achieve a certain measure of anonymity.

These factors contributed to a surge in Bitcoin's popularity after the Cyprus banking crisis where the government authorized banks to impose losses on shareholders and large depositors. Bitcoin, trading at US$40 rose to US$200 as a result, and shortly after, soaring Chinese demand pushed it up further, at one

B. Christianson et al. (Eds.): Security Protocols 2015, LNCS 9379, pp. 283–293, 2015.
DOI: 10.1007/978-3-319-26096-9_29

point past the US$1000 mark. Bitcoin prices now hover around the $350 mark [2], and the current market cap is at $4.7 billion [3]. Bitcoin is also gaining traction with vendors. Prominent brands such as Dell, WordPress, Paypal and Microsoft now offer Bitcoin payment options [4] and Bitcoin payment processors, such as Coinbase and BitPay, are seeing record growth and expansion. However, Bitcoin has also received substantial negative press due to its role in powering dark markets such as Silk Road. High-profile hacks of Bitcoin exchanges have resulted in thefts of hundreds of thousands of coins belonging to customers.

In this paper, we argue that these negatives should essentially be understood as the flip side of Bitcoin's key strengths, its ephemeral, trustless and distributed nature. We survey the range of Bitcoin-related criminal activity, such as dark markets, online extortion, malware, and theft, and highlight how these threats derive from the same fundamental qualities that have thus far also defined Bitcoin's success. We observe that this criminal activity is growing rapidly, becoming increasingly diverse and sophisticated, and presenting us with a variety of new ethical and legal dilemmas.

Many of these issues were not foreseen by the Bitcoin community, and we anticipate more will emerge as adoption increases. Visualizing these threats as a natural consequence of Bitcoin's ideology and design choices also allows us to speculate about future threats before they occur. We discuss distinct future possibilities such as tax evasion, money laundering, and esoteric scenarios where the Bitcoin P2P network itself may be exploited for criminal activity.

In conclusion, we observe that this ideological conflict within Bitcon is likely the reason that proposed solutions to these threats are falling short.

2   Bitcoin and Crime

We begin by describing how Bitcoin has triggered a boom in online black markets by effectively 'de-risking' illegal transactions.

2.1   Dark Markets

Silk Road: Silk Road was an anonymous online drug market, accessible to the general public from July 2011 [5]. A combination of technologies, including Bitcoin, were used to protect anonymity with the goal that the identity of sellers would be protected absolutely, whereas buyers would need to provide sellers with a physical shipping address for the product. If law enforcement officers infiltrated the site as sellers they may be able to obtain addresses for buyers, but no information about sellers (a higher value target) other than what may be leaked from the content of the seller's communications or the packaging of the shipment.

Silk Road was only accessible as a TOR hidden service [6], thereby preventing users from discovering the IP address of the site, and also preventing outside observers from discovering that a particular user had accessed the site. Payments were made using Bitcoin, thereby preserving anonymity of all parties, and an escrow service was provided to give buyers more confidence in their dealings [7]. The site also provided advice on how to package drugs to bypass common detection methods, and the site owners actively encouraged community discussion about the quality of sellers and related customer experiences. The website interface and user experience was modelled on the pattern of legitimate online marketplaces, such as eBay and Amazon. In testimony to its success, Silk Road was widely acknowledged as the 'eBay of drugs' [8], making it "easier and faster to order drugs than it is to order a pizza" [9], and raking in an estimated annual revenue of $1.2 billion.

Dark Markets Go Mainstream: Silk Road was shut down by the FBI in October 2013 after the arrest of the alleged owner of the site. Silk Road 2.0 was launched soon after and then shut down [10], and currently a Silk Road 3.0 site is available. However, there has been a massive surge in the number of sites selling drugs online using the Silk Road model, and the overall effect is that even the online drugs marketplace has now, in a sense, become decentralized. Researchers at the Digital Citizens Alliance [11] note that when Silk Road was taken down, there were four dark markets dominating the landscape and totalling about 18,000 drug listings. A year later, in October 2014, a dozen large markets accounted for some 32,000 drug listings, alongside a significant increase in advertisements for other illicit goods such as weapons. There is now even a dedicated Google-style search engine [12] which allows buyers to compare listings across multiple dark markets.

Since these sites exist as TOR hidden services, their addresses can be publicly posted. This not only makes them easy to find for the novice Internet user but also allows users to post reviews of suppliers on public message boards. This has bizarrely enough resulted in a situation where customer service and product quality are now key differentiators between drug suppliers. Customers openly discuss their experiences with different suppliers on public forums. Some even post results of chemical tests they have performed on the product they purchase.

This new phenomenon also raises complex new challenges for existing drug laws. Online customers are usually unaware of the location from which drugs will be shipped, and even when they are aware, this may be less of a consideration than testimonials of good customer service and drug purity. However, in many countries the laws prescribe harsher penalties for the import of prohibited drugs than they do for possession. Likewise, when buying drugs online with high packaging costs, it may be economical for suppliers to offer larger quantities at discounts, and for buyers to make larger and less frequent purchases. This may result in prosecution of those who buy drugs for personal use under laws intended to target suppliers [9].

De-risking Crime: Analyzing Silk Road in greater detail, researchers Aldridge and Dcary-Htu contend that these "cryptomarkets" are a "paradigm shifting criminal innovation" in that, by facilitating anonymous virtual transactions, they overcome the dangerous physical limitations of the drug trade, effectively de-risking the enterprise [7]. Physical drug deals are known to put the purchaser at an increased risk of violent crime [13], especially if they require the individual to deal with people from a culture where they do not understand cultural norms of behaviour [14]. Purchasing drugs online using Bitcoin as per the dark market business model and receiving them in the mail eliminates the need for users to visit drug dealers in person and is therefore much safer. This contrast is graphically highlighted if one considers the lifestyle of alleged Silk Road mastermind Ross Ulbricht [15]. Ulbricht was arrested at a local public library, in the science fiction section where he would oversee Silk Road's daily operations on his laptop using the library's public WiFi. This is a far cry from the stereotypical image of a typical drugs broker, running a billion dollar empire, and surrounded by bodyguards and hitmen.

Expanding on this theme, Infante speculates that the use of Silk Road may even have reduced incidences of death and other harm associated with cross-border drug smuggling . He estimates some 1,200 deaths potentially related to drug-violence may have been prevented over the course of the three years that Silk Road was in operation [16].

2.2   Theft and Malware

We next examine how Bitcoin's global reach has opened up new opportunities for online theft, extortion, and triggered a massive upsurge in malware.

Hacking Bitcoin Exchanges: Unlike traditional currencies, bitcoins exist exclusively as virtual assets and transactions, once made, are irreversible. This makes Bitcoin a fair target for hackers and scammers. Sophisticated attacks on Bitcoin exchanges, the cryptocurrency equivalent of bank heists, are now common. The MtGox saga has received significant media coverage. In February 2014, MtGox, the largest Bitcoin exchange in the world at the time, handling approximately 80 % of all Bitcoin transactions, was allegedly hacked (or the victim of some other kind of fraud) and shut down shortly after [17]. 850,000 bitcoins belonging to customers were stolen, with a value of more than half a billion dollars. This significantly impacted user confidence in Bitcoin, which was correlated with a drop in Bitcoin value.

The list of Bitcoin exchanges and wallet services that have been successfully hacked and driven to collapse also includes names such as Bitcoinca, BitFloor, Flexcoin, Poloniex and Bitcurex. In a paper on the topic, researchers Tyler Moore and Nicolas Christin quantify the risks and hazards associated with Bitcoin exchanges and note that of 40 Bitcoin exchanges established recently, 18 soon shut down [18]. Several hundreds of thousands of dollars worth of customers' coins were stolen or lost in these incidents. Some of these sites were guilty of poor security design and practices, but it is also believed that hacks are becoming increasingly sophisticated. At the time of writing another incident involving the BitStamp exchange has been announced with 5 million dollars in losses [19].

Malware: Researchers from Dell recently reported [20] that 146 strains of malware have thus far been discovered that are designed to steal bitcoins from victims' computers. Around 50 % of these successfully bypass most antiviruses. This count is up from 13 such strains discovered in 2012 and the rate of malware creation has loosely tracked the surge in Bitcoin exchange rate. These malware search victims' machines for common wallet formats to steal their private keys. Some advanced variants are equipped with keyloggers to target password-protected wallets. Yet another strain switches Bitcoin addresses on the fly when users' copy an address to the clipboard while making payments, replacing them with the malware owner's address, thereby diverting the payment to him [21].

Ransomware: In 2004, Young and Yung first suggested the idea of a virus that encrypts data on victims' computers using an asymmetric cipher and holds it hostage for ransom [22]. The decryption key is not embedded in the virus code-base, so the attack cannot be reverse-engineered. However, ransom payments had to traverse the traditional financial infrastructure which risked exposing the owner of the malware and therefore this scheme had limited appeal. However, Bitcoin's anonymity, independence of centralized authorities, and global accessibility makes it the ideal solution.

As a result, ransomware is now thriving. CryptoLocker, a ransomware trojan which demanded payment in bitcoins, was first observed in September 2013. CryptoLocker claimed 250,000 victims and earned an estimated $30 million in just 100 days [23]. It has since then spawned an entire family of malware. A variant, CryptoWall, infected over 600,000 systems in the past six months, holding 5 billion files hostage, earning attackers more than US $1 million. CryptoWall even infected the systems of official government departments. The office of the Dickson County Sheriff in the US paid the ransom in full to decrypt their archive of case files. Durham Constabulary in the UK has refused [24].

In a recent blogpost, researchers at McAfee Labs point out that this class of ransomware is now being crowdsourced. Tox [25] is a free and easy-to-deploy ransomware kit that 'customers' can download from a website and use to deliberately infect computers belonging to others. Tox uses TOR and Bitcoin, it resists typical malware detection tools, and can be customized, prior to installation, as to the amount of ransom the malware charges. The Tox website tracks all installations and charges 20 % of any claimed ransoms. The authors note that other classes of malware may soon incorporate this crowdsourcing and profit-sharing model.

Bitcoin Mining: Malware have also been discovered which covertly mine cryptocurrencies on victims' machines. These malware either mine independently or participate in public or dark mining pools, connecting either directly or through proxies [26]. Customized malware builds have also been found for smartphones, webcams, and even network storage devices. One botnet successfully utilized network attached storage devices over a two month period to mine $600,000 worth of Dogecoin, a Bitcoin inspired alt-currency [27].

However, in the case of Bitcoin, mining malware is no longer proving a profitable venture given the increased block difficulty level and the rise of mining pools, and some commercial botnets which offered mining services (such as ZeroAccess) have now stopped offering mining as a service.

3   Future Threats

Here, we briefly consider some hypothetical examples of criminal activity which derives directly from Bitcoin's anonymous and trustless nature. We observe that Bitcoin's lack of regulation facilitates tax evasion and money laundering. We also consider esoteric threats which use the Bitcoin P2P network.

Tax Evasion: In a panel discussion recently [28], when asked about Bitcoin enabling tax evasion, Princeton's Edward Felten commented: "You could argue that [Bitcoin] does [make it easier to avoid taxes] because it's a transaction that doesn't involve the banking system." However, he downplayed the risk: "The conspiracy to not report income has to be too large in a sizeable company, and the consequences of getting caught [for] the leaders are too large."

While this may be true for large corporations, it is not very difficult at the individual level to evade taxes. Due to the economic downturn, there is already a growing trend in underreporting taxes. Tens of millions of ordinary people, people who are not career criminals but instead nannies, fitness teachers, barbers, construction workers, etc. are increasingly participating in the shadow economy and working off the books. In 2013, economist Edgar Feige estimated that there was an estimated 2 trillion dollar gap in what Americans reported to the IRS - a huge sum when compared to a 385 billion dollar estimate by the IRS in 2006 [29]. This trend might increase: 30 % of Americans today are self-employed and some predict this figure will rise to 50 % by 2020 [30]). There is no way of knowing if income is taxable unless the recipient voluntarily reports it, and this growing freelance economy may prove very hard to track if they start transacting in Bitcoin.

Tax Havens and Money Laundering: There is also an ongoing discussion about Bitcoin functioning as a tax haven and its use in money laundering. Traditionally, tax evasion or money laundering would require criminals to divert funds through a complex financial maze involving multiple actors such as banks, shell companies, and offshore accounts. Governments in recent years have found it more effective not to target offshore tax havens directly, but to cooperate with foreign governments and attack links in the financial infrastructure, namely banks. A good example of this trend is the US Foreign Account Tax Compliance Act (FACTA) which targets tax cheats by requiring foreign banks to directly report to the US Internal Revenue Service about financial accounts held by US taxpayers [31]. Failure to do so exposes the bank to the risk of being penalized on its earnings from American investments.

However, Bitcoin, with its pseudonymity, its ephemerality, and its total independence of the banking infrastructure defeats this entire strategy. All that is required to successfully hide or launder funds with Bitcoin is a series of private anonymized transactions. There already exist 'laundry' services and tumblers which accept bitcoins from multiple sources and mix them in a way that the link between input and output addresses is broken.

Money laundering may not be an immediate threat due to Bitcoin's limited usage and high price volatility, but researchers have started to sound the alarm [32,33]. The US government has applied money laundering rules to virtual currencies [34] and Europol, the EU law enforcement agency handling criminal intelligence, has requested greater policing powers [35] to meet this challenge.

Exploiting the Bitcoin Network: New research has shown that it is possible to exploit Bitcoin for non-payment purposes, such as timestamping data [36,37] or building advanced financial services [38]. Likewise, we believe, threats will emerge which do not involve the currency but which use the underlying Bitcoin network. Some attacks have already been practically demonstrated.

Interpol has recently warned that the Bitcoin blockchain can serve as a vehicle for malware and illegal content [39]. In a demo at the Black Hat Asia conference, researcher Vitaly Kamluk, showed how a hacker may embed malicious payloads in the blockchain where it could be retrieved by malware on remote machines. In a similar vein, researchers have demonstrated that the Bitcoin P2P network can function as a reliable low-latency command-and-control (C&C) infrastructure to power botnets [40]. In existing botnets, C&C commands from the botmaster are typically delivered to bots over IRC networks, custom P2P protocols, or via HTTP sites. These communication channels are also therefore the botnet's key vulnerability, and allows security researchers and law enforcement to expose the botmaster and disrupt C&C communications.

In the case of Bitcoin-based C&C communications, the botmaster embeds commands in legitimate Bitcoin transactions using a variety of mechanisms (such as the transaction OP-RETURN field, subliminal channels, unspendable outputs, etc.) which are then dispatched over the Bitcoin network where bots may receive them. This has several advantages, most notably that it is far more robust and secure than current C&C methods. Disrupting C&C transactions in this case would not only violate the ideology Bitcoin was built upon, but it would likely impact legitimate Bitcoin users and significantly affect network usability as a whole. Botmasters also stand to benefit from greater anonymity and less risk using the Bitcoin network for C&C communications.

4   Discussion

As we observe from this brief overview of Bitcoin-related criminal activity, current and future, Bitcoin's strengths and weaknesses both derive from the same essential ideological and architectural design choices. For this reason, we believe there are no easy solutions to the problems we have discussed so far. Anonymity and lack of regulation which is meant to free users from central authorities also empowers drug dealers and money launderers. Denoting money as virtual assets to remove reliance on banks also opens the doors to hackers and malware. Setting up a global financial network exposes unwitting users to threats from all over the world and opens up a Pandora's box of ethical and legal issues.

This is akin to the Tor dilemma. Tor is much hyped as a platform providing Internet access to citizens living in the shadow of repressive regimes, but it is equally well known as the communication medium of choice for hackers and supports a thriving underground economy and trade in illicit pornography.

There is no technological mechanism to disentangle these two usage scenarios. In supporting Tor, we implicitly acknowledge that the positive applications of the network justify the negative. This deadlock leaves us with questions: What now? Is it worth trying to fix Bitcoin? Can it even be fixed?

Several solutions are being developed which try to address some of the currency's problems. Online wallet services (such as Coinbase) aim to protect and simplify management of users' Bitcoin credentials. Hardware wallets (such as Trezor and BTChip) are available which store user credentials in protected hardware which is mostly kept offline. Multi-signature escrow services have been proposed for consumer protection (such as Bitrated.com) which allow for arbitration over disputes. Multisignature wallet services (such as CryptoCorp) propose to use fraud detection algorithms to co-sign user transactions to protect them from scammers and malware. Researchers are working on 'coin-tainting' techniques [41] to identify and track illegal transactions and clustering techniques to identify single ownership of groups of Bitcoin addresses.

However, none of these solutions decisively solve our problems. Some, ironically, even suggest a return to the regulated centralized framework that Bitcoin originally rebelled against. As we have learnt from the experience of WiFi, it would be unrealistic to expect the majority of people today to protect Bitcoin addresses and wallets from sophisticated hackers and malware. Online wallet services and multisignature facilities, much like banks, take away the key elements of anonymity and privacy, as they are privy to all user transactions. Depending on which part of the world these services are based in, governments may even be able to regulate them via legislation. The same applies for companies like CoinBase and Bitpay which act as a conversion portal between Bitcoin users and traders/merchants who accept traditional currencies. These companies could be subject to regulation which might negatively interfere with the customer experience.

Researchers have also questioned the strategy of tainting suspect bitcoins as a crimefighting technique [42]. Blacklisting certain coins will reduce their value, making them harder to spend, and this ultimately stands to have a destabilizing effect on the currency as a whole.

5   Conclusion

We have shown that Bitcoin has become both a useful tool for criminals and a target for crime. Furthermore, the desirability of Bitcoin for criminals derives directly from its anonymity and freedom from central regulation, otherwise desirable properties that the Bitcoin network was designed to provide.

We believe this fundamental paradox at the heart of Bitcoin is the reason why Bitcoin-related crime is rapidly growing and diversifying. As we observe, the trends show a marked increase in the mainstream proliferation of dark markets, a surge in Bitcoin-related malware, and a growing number of attacks on Bitcoin exchanges. Our analysis also provides a useful perspective to reason about future criminal possibilities, such as tax evasion and money laundering. This may also include non-financial applications, such as hijacking the Bitcoin network for illicit communications.

References

1. Bustillos, M.: The bitcoin boom. The New Yorker, April 2013. http://www.newyorker.com/tech/elements/the-bitcoin-boom
2. Kitco news. 2013: Year of the Bitcoin. Forbes, 10 December 2013. http://www.forbes.com/sites/kitconews/2013/12/10/2013-year-of-the-bitcoin/
3. CoinMarketCap. Crypto-Currency Market Capitalizations. BitcoinTalk, 28 July 2014. https://coinmarketcap.com/
4. Langley, H.: Bitcoin value surges as microsoft starts accepting cryptocurrency. TechRadar, 11 December 2014. http://www.techradar.com/news/internet/bitcoin-value-surges-as-microsoft-starts-accepting-cryptocurrency-1276552
5. Barratt, M.J.: Silk road: ebay for drugs. Addiction (2012)
6. Dingledine, R., Mathewson, N., Syverson, P.: Tor: The second-generation onion router. In: Proceedings of the 13th Conference on USENIX Security Symposium - Volume 13, SSYM 2004, Berkeley. USENIX Association (2004)
7. Aldridge, J., Décary-Hétu, D.: Not an 'Ebay for Drugs': the cryptomarket 'Silk Road' as a paradigm shifting criminal innovation. In: Social Science Research Network Working Paper Series, May 2014
8. Mail, D.: Mastermind behind $180M 'eBay of drugs' silk road convicted after jury deliberates just three hours, 4 February 2015
9. Stuff. Silk Road Drug Buyers in Court, 3 December 2014. http://www.stuff.co.nz/auckland/63779228/Silk-Road-drug-buyers-in-court
10. FBI. Operator of Silk Road 2.0 Website Charged in Manhattan Federal Court, 6 November 2014. http://www.fbi.gov/newyork/press-releases/2014/operator-of-silk-road-2.0-website-charged-in-manhattan-federal-court
11. Wong, J.I.: Dark markets grow bigger and bolder in year since silk road bust. CoinDesk, 6 October 2014. http://www.coindesk.com/dark-markets-grow-bigger-bolder-year-since-silk-road-bust/
12. DeepDotWeb. Interview with Grams Search Engine Admin: Exciting Features Ahead!, 3 May 2014. http://www.deepdotweb.com/2014/05/03/interview-with-grams-search-engine-admin-exciting-features-ahead/
13. Macyoung, M., Pfouts, C.: Safe in the City. Paladin Press, USA (1994)
14. Macyoung, M.: Violence, Blunders and Fractured Jaws: Advanced Awareness Techniques and Street Etiquette. Paladin Press, USA (1992)
15. Olson, P.: The man behind silk road - the internet's biggest market for illegal drugs. The Guardian, 10 November 2013. http://www.theguardian.com/technology/2013/nov/10/silk-road-internet-market-illegal-drugs-ross-ulbricht
16. Infante, A.: Coin report: how many lives did silk road save. CoinReport, 26 June 2014. https://coinreport.net/many-lives-silk-road-save/
17. Decker, Christian, Wattenhofer, Roger: Bitcoin transaction malleability and MtGox. In: Kutyłowski, Mirosław, Vaidya, Jaideep (eds.) ICAIS 2014, Part II. LNCS, vol. 8713, pp. 313–326. Springer, Heidelberg (2014)
18. Moore, T., Christin, N.: Beware the middleman: empirical analysis of bitcoin-exchange risk. In: Sadeghi, A.-R. (ed.) FC 2013. LNCS, vol. 7859, pp. 25–33. Springer, Heidelberg (2013)
19. Higgins, S.: Bitstamp claims $5 million lost in hot wallet hack. CoinDesk, 5 January 2015. http://www.coindesk.com/bitstamp-claims-roughly-19000-btc-lost-hot-wallet-hack/

20. Greenberg, A.: Nearly 150 Breeds of Bitcoin-stealing Malware in The Wild, Researchers Say, Forbes, 26 February 2014. http://www.forbes.com/sites/andygreenberg/2014/02/26/nearly-150-breeds-of-bitcoin-stealing-malware-in-the-wild-researchers-say/

21. Hern, A.: A history of bitcoin hacks. The Guardian, 18 March 2014. http://www.theguardian.com/technology/2014/mar/18/history-of-bitcoin-hacks-alternative-currency

22. Young, A., Yung, M.: Malicious Cryptography: Exposing Cryptovirology. Wiley, New York (2004)

23. Blue, V.: CryptoLocker's crimewave: a trail of millions in laundered bitcoin. ZDnet, 22 December 2013. http://www.zdnet.com/article/cryptolockers-crimewave-a-trail-of-millions-in-laundered-bitcoin/

24. Goodin, D.: We "will be paying no ransom," vows town hit by Cryptowall ransom malware. Ars Technica, 7 June 2014. http://arstechnica.com/security/2014/06/we-will-be-paying-no-ransom-vows-town-hit-by-cryptowall-ransom-malware/

25. Walter, J.: Meet 'Tox': ransomware for the rest of us. McAfee Labs - Blog Central, 23 May 2015. https://blogs.mcafee.com/mcafee-labs/meet-tox-ransomware-for-the-rest-of-us

26. Huang, D.Y., Dharmdasani, H., Meiklejohn, S., Dave, V., Grier, C., McCoy, D., Savage, S., Weaver, N., Snoeren, A.C., Levchenko, K.: Botcoin: monetizing stolen cycles. In: Proceedings of the Network and Distributed System Security Symposium (NDSS) (2014)

27. Tung, L.: NAS device botnet mined $600,000 in dogecoin over two months. ZDnet, 18 June 2014. http://www.zdnet.com/article/nas-device-botnet-mined-600000-in-dogecoin-over-two-months/

28. Torpey, K.: Bitcoin and tax evasion: are the possibilities overstated? Inside Bitcoins, 28 October 2014. http://insidebitcoins.com/news/bitcoin-and-tax-evasion-are-the-possibilities-overstated/25805

29. Surowiecki, J.: The underground recovery. The New Yorker, 29 April 2013. http://www.newyorker.com/magazine/2013/04/29/the-underground-recovery

30. Wald, J.: How an exploding freelance economy will drive change in 2014. Forbes, 25 November 2013. http://www.forbes.com/sites/groupthink/2013/11/25/how-an-exploding-freelance-economy-will-drive-change-in-2014/

31. Palmer, K.: FACTA: new federal law causes swiss banks to reject american investors. Watchdog Wire, 23 October 2012. http://watchdogwire.com/blog/2012/10/23/facta-new-federal-law-causes-swiss-banks-to-reject-american-investors/

32. Stokes, R.: Virtual money laundering: the case of bitcoin and the linden dollar. Inf. Commun. Technol. Law 21(3), 221–236 (2012)

33. Moser, M., Bohme, R., Breuker, D.: An inquiry into money laundering tools in the bitcoin ecosystem. In: eCrime Researchers Summit (eCRS). IEEE (2013)

34. Sparshott, J.: Web money gets laundering rule. Wall Street J. 21 March 2013. http://www.wsj.com/articles/SB10001424127887324373204578374611351125202

35. McCallion, J.: Europol calls for greater bitcoin policing powers. ITPro, 25 March 2014. http://www.itpro.co.uk/public-sector/21903/europol-calls-for-greater-bitcoin-policing-powers

36. Kirk, J.: Could the bitcoin network be used as an ultrasecure notary service? PCWorld, 24 May 2013. http://www.pcworld.com/article/2039705/could-the-bitcoin-network-be-used-as-an-ultrasecure-notary-service.html

37. Bradbury, D.: BlockSign utilises block chain to verify signed contracts. CoinDesk, 27 August 2014. http://www.coindesk.com/blocksign-utilises-block-chain-verify-signed-contracts/

38. Counterparty: Pioneering Peer-to-Peer Finance. Accessed 22 July 2014
39. Fox-Brewster, T.: Bitcoin's blockchain offers safe haven for malware and child abuse, warns interpol. Forbes, 27 March 2015. http://www.forbes.com/sites/thomasbrewster/2015/03/27/bitcoin-blockchain-pollution-a-criminal-opportunity/
40. Ali, S.T., McCorry, P., Lee, P.H.-J., Hao, F.: ZombieCoin: powering next-generation botnets with bitcoin. In: 2nd Workshop on Bitcoin Research (2015)
41. Gervais, A., Karame, G.O., Capkun, V., Capkun, S.: Is bitcoin a decentralized currency? IEEE Secur. Priv. **12**(3), 54–60 (2014)
42. Möser, M., Böhme, R., Breuker, D.: Towards risk scoring of bitcoin transactions. In: Böhme, R., Brenner, M., Moore, T., Smith, M. (eds.) FC 2014 Workshops. LNCS, vol. 8438, pp. 16–32. Springer, Heidelberg (2014)

Bitcoin: Perils of an Unregulated Global P2P Currency (Transcript of Discussion)

Syed Taha Ali[✉]

Newcastle University, Tyne and Wear, UK
`taha.ali@newcastle.ac.uk`

So our topic is "Bitcoin: Perils of an Unregulated Global P2P Currency". Before I start, just a quick introduction: I'm not going to talk much about the technical aspects of Bitcoin, this is more of a holistic perspective, but there will be a discussion of some relevant technical concerns. So if anyone has any questions about how Bitcoin works in the course of this talk you can just ask me, that's not a problem. Bitcoin was first launched in 2009, so we're in its sixth year, and there have been a lot of positive steps so far. The value of Bitcoin has gone up and down quite a bit, but it's still considerably up compared to where it was six years ago, and market cap is about $3.6 billion, and it is gaining traction with vendors, and so far the kind of legislation that we're seeing is relatively positive; people aren't outright condemning Bitcoin. There are some bills in America in the works, which are actually supportive of Bitcoin. So there's a lot of positives, and there are also negatives. If any of you checked the news in the last two days, Silk Road is back in the news, every two or three weeks there's some Bitcoin scandal or the other happening, some exchange crashes, or someone runs off with someone's coins. So you have the positives and you have the negatives, and we're going to talk a lot more about that, but first I'll sort of lay out the focus of what we're saying.

This slide is something of a mission statement for Bitcoin, it's from the main man himself, Satoshi Nakamoto, and if you appreciate what's laid out here you sort of get the spirit of Bitcoin even if the technical aspects don't really make sense. There are four things here. First central banks are really bad, because they debase the currency. Second, the banks hold the money but then they do all sorts of weird stuff with it, so in that sense the banks are also bad. And then banks also compromise our privacy and our identity. And of course banks are also very expensive at the end of the day.

So this slide is a very, very high-level technical description of Bitcoin. Essentially what you have is a global unregulated network, and then you have these 'coins', which are really virtual assets, which are created and traded on this network. And these virtual assets, their ownership is denoted by pseudonymous credentials. So this is Bitcoin in a nutshell. And when you look at these facts, the four policy decisions, in a sense, that we discussed earlier, are that you want to remove reliance on central banks, you want self ownership of your wealth, you want user privacy, and you want to keep it all low cost. And you can see that there is a clear correspondence between these properties, and Bitcoin's technical design choices. For instance, you want privacy, that derives directly from the

© Springer International Publishing Switzerland 2015
B. Christianson et al. (Eds.): Security Protocols 2015, LNCS 9379, pp. 294–306, 2015.
DOI: 10.1007/978-3-319-26096-9_30

fact that the system has pseudonymous credentials, you want to remove your reliance on central banks, you bring about virtual assets which trade on a global unregulated network. So there's a clear correspondence between what we want and the technical choices that have gone into Bitcoin.

Now, what we're claiming is that the negatives that I just mentioned two minutes ago, like dark markets and exchanges that are getting hacked, and even malware, which steals your bitcoins, all of these also derive directly from these same technical design choices. They are sort of like the flipside derived from the same fundamental ideological and design choices. And why is that important? We have something of a dilemma here. It's like Tor, you have a network, which empowers activists and free speech, but you can also have hate speech on it, and all sorts of illegal pornography. And you can't really do anything about it one way or the other, it is a trade-off at the end of the day. So what that means is that these problems with Bitcoin are probably here to stay. There has been a general perception of sorts that if I tweak the code a bit, if I build this fancy app, or do this or that with Bitcoin, then somehow these negatives can be neutralised while still maintaining those advantages. What we argue here is that it is probably not going to happen, these things are here to stay as long as Bitcoin is, and if anything is done to regulate these aspects, then you will correspondingly have some sort of diminishing in Bitcoin's strengths as well.

So what we do in this paper is, we survey criminal activity. We give you an update on what's new, and you will see that all of these negatives are thriving, the dark markets are really big, malware is thriving, and hacking attacks are evolving. And the perspective we take in this paper explains why. Plus, not only are criminal practices thriving, but we are also coming up with new dilemmas. This is another very interesting thing about Bitcoin, that when it came about people thought that it's just a replacement for money, sort of like virtual money. But it turns out that it's actually a very different creature in a way, and it has its own problems as well, which we're only now realising. So we'll discuss a few of these cases as well. Another advantage of thinking in this way is that you can also reason about future threats before they actually occur, it's a way to sort of incorporate them into a framework. We'll discuss a few of those, a quick glance at the fact that Bitcoin is probably great for tax evasion, for money laundering, and there are emerging attacks which exploit the underlying P2P network. So that's the talk in a nutshell, and I'll get started now.

Dark markets, very quickly: Silk Road came about in July 2011, and it was shut down in October 2013, so it's a little over two years. And the model is really simple. You have a Tor hidden service, and, using Tor, you enter in an onion address, and you access a market which is based on the appearance of sites like eBay and Amazon. This is a screenshot of Agora, it's not really Silk Road, but it's pretty much the same template, and you've got these categories of things that you can buy, and here you have the items, the attractions and pretty pictures. Anonymity is paramount. The sellers and the buyers don't need to give any personal information at all, all they need to give are Bitcoin addresses, and the buyer needs to send a delivery address, or an address where everything gets shipped to eventually, and that's it. And to improve trust in this model, Silk Road also came with an escrow service: if I were to go online and buy drugs from a certain seller, the seller could just take my money and run away with it, and not send me anything. But what happens instead is that I make a payment to Silk Road, and then Silk Road holds that money until I get the delivery, and then it forwards it on. So this has two positive aspects. Everyone starts to trust the system, which is great, and on the other hand there is a disconnect between the buyer and seller. Since everything gets routed through Silk Road, you can't really tell who the buyer and the seller are by looking at the blockchain. So that's another positive aspect.

Frank Stajano: In the interaction with the world of physical artifacts, and with all the participants being mutually mistrustful so much so that they want to have an escrow party, if I try to buy something from the third picture and they send something and I get it but I pretend that I never got it so I could get it for free, and I don't pay, how is this redressed by the escrow agent?

Reply: I don't know the specific process in place, but they are evolving policies all the time. I can tell you about one or two policies of theirs, which might give you an idea. So one possibility is that, suppose I was to make a large payment for a shipment, and it gets put into escrow, and over the weekend there's a massive price fluctuation in Bitcoin, so suddenly that payment is meaningless, but I have already made that payment in good faith, and I should not be expected to pay more. In that case what the Silk Road administrators say is, that they personally guarantee that we will make up the shortfall. So they're making up the rules as they go along.

Ross Anderson: I expect this is stateful, right, if you think about the discussion yesterday, there are some things you cannot fix with cryptography that you can fix with humans. Now if you're Ross Ulbricht, and you see that one particular customer repeatedly complains that he didn't get the drugs, you may come to the conclusion that he's a thief, and you just blow him away.

Frank Stajano: But everything is anonymous, so I can always do it with another identity.

Ross Anderson: It doesn't matter.

Frank Stajano: You might have to limit: if you're a first timer you can only do it for a small amount.

Ross Anderson: It doesn't matter, so I don't care.

Reply: Well, you do give a delivery address, so there may be a process in place.

Dylan Clarke: There was a lot I know with Silk Road to do with the reputation of the sellers as well. Sellers were keeping certain domains and the reputation was what was getting them the sales. So a seller wouldn't want to rip off a first-time buyer generally.

Frank Stajano: But in this case it's the first-time buyer who would be ripping off the seller as per my example.

Dylan Clarke: So if lots of first time buyers kept appearing and all saying on their first time, I've been ripped off, the chances are they wouldn't be believed.

Ross Anderson: But this is stateful, it relies on an intelligent, profit-seeking human being sitting at the centre of the web, and if a scam like that emerges he's got to decide how to deal with this. Does he find the guy and kill him, does he close down his business, does he start another business? What does he do?

Frank Stajano: The point is, all of these don't have a reputation the first time round; they're protected by the anonymity of the system anyway.

Dylan Clarke: The other thing with first-time buyers as well is they do still have to give an address to the seller, so they are traceable on a human level in some ways.

Ross Anderson: So what you're saying in effect, there's an FBI attack on the new Silk Road where the FBI sybils a very, very large number of first-time buyers who complained that they haven't got the drugs. And the completely convincing response to this Sybil attack is to say, "Screw you".

Frank Stajano: Well, the buyer has to decide whether to ship the goods or not, and in fact he has already shipped the goods.

Ross Anderson: Exactly so. So the response of the markets operators is to say to all the falsely complaining FBI agents, who have actually received their hashish, "Sorry, we don't believe you, go boil your head". That is a completely convincing answer to that denial of service attack, and it's one the person operating the network has got no choice but to take.

Paul Wernick: But how does he know that it's an attack, or just some just bad luck. So there is in fact no protection.

Ross Anderson: There is no answer within the framework of cryptologic mathematics to this objection, but there is an entirely trivial answer in brutal, street operational terms. If you suddenly got a large wave of complaints, you just ignore them. And you continue operating your business and see if it continues to run, and if that was an attack by the FBI and you ignore it, then your business will continue to run.

Paul Wernick: So as a buyer you've really got no protection at all, because you might just get hit on a day when a lot of people are conducting that attack.

Reply: As a seller you don't, as a buyer you do.

Dylan Clarke: And also people who buy illegal drugs are quite used to that.

Reply: Plus I think a lot of these people they have a certain percentage of fraud built into their prices as well, so it's assumed that something like this may happen.

Bruce Christianson: But there's a general rule that says, don't buy on a day when the FBI are staking your seller out

Reply: Does anyone here have any personal experience of buying drugs on Silk Road because we can talk about it, and then we can edit it out of the transcripts later on.

Keith Irwin: I was going to say, that is, do you kill them, or you call a hit on them, there is evidence that he actually attempted to do that to someone who was committing enough fraud.

Reply: Well, apparently he tried to call a hit on a fellow administrator of the site.

Khaled Baqer: Yes, but the reason they use this is because you're not going to stabbed in a dark alley because you're buying drugs.

Reply: Yes, exactly.

Khaled Baqer: This is why this is popular.

Bruce Christianson: And then you get a whole lot of hit men complaining that they haven't been paid.

Reply: There's a thriving community discussion here. This is another typical posting, 28 grams of Blue Dream - I don't even know what that is. There's a lot of feedback, people posting reviews, "Oh, I got the drugs in X amount of days, great service," and "Oh, I did a chemical test, and here are the results". You have all sorts of things: "Superior product, five business days, my favourite vendor," etc. And there's even advice on how to package the drugs in a way so that you can escape postal detection by customs. And there's advice on what to do, which seller to target. And the thing about this is that since these are onion addresses you can have these conversations on the actual World Wide Web as well, you don't need to go on Tor all the time because you can post onion URLs in plain sight out here, and that is happening. And the annual revenue for Silk Road, according to the FBI is $1.2 billion.

So Silk Road got taken down, and within a few days we had Silk Road 2.0, started by some of the ex-Silk Road administrators. And here is a snapshot of what the situation was when Silk Road was seized, and these were the other dark markets, and you can see that originally Silk Road had the overwhelming majority of drug listings, 13,000 out of 18,000. Now after Silk Road went down, and these are figures from last year, you have 32,000 total drug listings, which is almost double the amount, and now you've also got weapons showing up in many of these places. So we're seeing a decentralisation of this phenomenon, which means that if one or two of these sites get taken down, there's plenty of others to fill in the gaps.

Audience: Is there any sense in which listings is the right metric for the size of the market? I don't know whether that's a good or a bad metric.

Reply: The best metric would be the reviews. I suppose, if you want to buy a certain product.

Audience: Well, there's a whole bunch of metrics you could pick, reviews, volume of sales, cash.

Reply: Perhaps, yes.

Audience: Well, this is easily measurable at least.

Ross Anderson: Well, in the blockchain, you can use part of the blockchain and look at the volumes. That would be your current source of data in that respect, some groups have been doing that.

Audience: So it might be worth having more than one dimension.

Audience: Is there enough information in the blockchain to work out if the transaction went through Silk Road, when it was operational?

Ross Anderson: Yes, there was a paper by Adi Shamir at last year's Financial Cryptography, which showed how to parse the blockchain to spot the laundry that Silk Road was using, where large numbers of bitcoins went in and then came out of a series of linked transactions, and with that you could track down various previously hidden deposit accounts that Ulbricht was using.

Reply: When Silk Road wrapped up, by that time it had serviced over a million successful orders, so that's something. Now, more on decentralisation: here we have something called OpenBazaar, which we're probably going to see in another few months. This is a project from some folks within the Bitcoin community. Right now, the model for these markets is still a centralised server. It's hidden behind Tor, but it's still centralised, and can be seized, and you can identify location, and make an arrest. It's not easy to do, but that's what they did with Silk Road. With OpenBazaar, they're using BitTorrent to distribute the site itself. So there's no centralised location, there's no person to go after, it could be a thousand people who shared bits and pieces of the site, and it is still behind Tor. This project was originally called Dark Market, but then they rebranded it to Open Bazaar, to give it a more positive spin. A basic open-source version has been released, and we will probably see something coming up very soon.

And here's something called Grams, the slide speaks for itself. You type in an onion address and you can search multiple darknet markets. It's updated twice a day. And then there is the fact that, as Khaled mentioned, that you're de-risking crime using Bitcoin. This is a picture of a San Francisco Library, and this is the science fiction section. And this is apparently where Dread Pirate Roberts used to sit and manage Silk Road. He used to go into the library, connect to the Wi-Fi there, and he'd to sit in one of those chairs, and just talk to his administrators, take complaints from customers, and delegate operations, etc. Normally you'd expect a drug lord, or some such person, to have a lot of bodyguards, and people outside the door, and a lot of security, but this, no-one would have guessed, this is actually where he was arrested. And it's really fascinating, I was going over this again last night and it struck me that, if any of you have read, there's a lot of drone warfare happening in the Middle East, US drones go around shooting everyone, but the pilots who actually manage the drones, they sit in places like these, they have nice offices, air-conditioning and everything, and just relax, and they probably have a game room as well.

There was a paper on this phenomenon called "Silk Road, not just an eBay for drugs". It's a 'paradigm shifting criminal innovation'. Essentially what's happening is that if two people do not meet face-to-face that means that they do not shoot each other and you're de-risking crime. With these sites it's now as easy to buy drugs as to buy pizza. You just place an order. And this study, done by Judith Aldridge at Manchester, she does an estimate of how many lives Silk Road might have saved, and it's very interesting. Apparently there is some $10 billion in drug money which flows from the US to Canada every year, and they calculated that because of that $10 billion, as it traverses the whole chain going all the way up to Mexico and the cartels, there are about 10,000 Mexican lives lost. When Silk Road came in it had about $1.2 billion in monetary flows - and they also pointed out that a lot of people who used Silk Road were also suppliers talking to other suppliers, making sales to other suppliers, raw materials - and they estimated that thanks to Silk Road we might have saved about 1200 Mexican lives last year.

Ross Anderson: Sorry, who is this?

Reply: This is Judith Aldridge, her paper is under submission, she's from the University of Manchester. I believe she has a legal background. The paper is called "Not an eBay for Drugs: The Cryptomarket Silk Road as a Paradigm Shifting Criminal Innovation". According to Dread Pirate Roberts, Bitcoin is the secret ingredient that makes this whole chain work. Things like these dark marketplaces have been talked about since the 90s, they showed up on the cypherpunks mailing lists. And the missing ingredient - well, already had Tor for quite a few years, we had access to censored information, but we did not have a anonymous financial network, which was impervious to any sort of takedown. And thanks to Bitcoin, this is now here.

Another question is, how do you legislate this? You're getting all sorts of legal dilemmas showing up now. There was this case from New Zealand last year, where a couple used Silk Road to order drugs. Typically what one would do is that you go down to the local gang hangouts and just get five or six pills of something. But because of Bitcoin, the economics of it all, how it's done on Silk Road is that they ordered 200 pills in bulk, since that made the whole process economical. Now because they had 200 pills they got charged with something else, it wasn't possession of drugs, they got charged with importation, and the punishment is about thirty times worse. And the lawyer argued that the importing charge would only have been a possession charge if his client had not used modern methods of drug purchase. And one of the reasons they used the modern methods, apart from the fact it's convenient and you don't have to go to dangerous areas, is the fact that the drugs were more likely to be unadulterated as per the ratings of sellers by past purchasers on the website. So we're getting all sorts of funny, funny situations.

Khaled Baqer: You said Dread Private Roberts said that this is the missing ingredient, but he just got convicted because they proved that he made a profit out of this, based on Bitcoin.

Reply: Well yes, there's two things here: he made that statement in an interview before he got arrested when he said that.

Khaled Baqer: Right, that's kind of naïve though, I mean, the Bitcoin ledger is open for everyone to see, and all they needed was an address.

Reply: Yes, but he did not get arrested because of that. You do know how they traced him, right? It wasn't via the blockchain.

Khaled Baqer: It was the Tor malfunction, but they proved it through Bitcoin.

Reply: Yes, but the proof is still very iffy. I mean, yes, there is suspicion, but did you go through his legal defence? He says that, I did build Silk Road, but I was not the one who ran it.

Khaled Baqer: He would say that.

Reply: Yes, but he does have a point in the sense that the Feds identified him by certain posts he made on forums saying, "I want to build this, how do I do this, how do I do that?" and he used his original email address, which the actual Dread Pirate Roberts would probably not do. And then, a year or two before the arrest, in the interview that I'm talking about, Dread Pirate Roberts himself says that, "I had someone else build the site, I took over later on." So there are some discrepancies here and there in the story.

Patrick McCorry: And in some of the reports they also mentioned that there's a third person who hasn't been found yet. He's known as Mr Wonderful, so he could be the real operator of this site.

Reply: Moving on: stealing virtual assets. So you've probably heard of the MtGox, it was very big a while back. 80 % of all Bitcoin transactions used to go through MtGox, we're still not sure how the coins got hacked, but one day it just turned out that 83,000 coins were missing. Well not over one day per se, it was over an extended period of time that revealed the exact amount. But this is very common, exchanges are getting hacked a lot, very regularly, and it's a long list. People thought that after MtGox there would be some sort of wake-up moment where people would get serious about security. But these incidents are still happening. And the thing about Bitcoin is that it's a virtual asset which is stored online in many cases. With a regular bank you would expect that robbers would come in through the door with guns, but in this case you have hackers sitting at the other corner of the world trying to break in, and they do succeed. And we should expect this to happen in this case, it's really not very surprising.

The case with malware is the same except in a more compressed dimension, a micro-version of the same phenomenon. In 2012 there were 13 strains of malware that stole your bitcoins from your computer, just hijacking the wallets. In 2014 there were 146 discovered strains, which is an order of magnitude larger. And, of total amount of financial attacks detected by Symantec in 2013, about 20 % were related to Bitcoin wallets. And some of them were very ingenious: suppose your wallet is protected by a key with a password, in that case the malware comes with a keylogger so it records your password when you type it in. Or sometimes when you copy and paste a Bitcoin address, you copy the address onto your clipboard and paste it into a transaction, so between Control+C and Control+V the malware switches the addresses, so it's pretty nifty. And the rate of growth in malware is growing alongside the rate of Bitcoin's exchange rate, so when Bitcoin prices go up, apparently malware goes up too. And the problem is, 50 % of malware bypass most anti-viruses, according to Dell from last year. So this is again another problem that we don't seem to have an easy fix to.

Audience: So with this hacking, I'm not really au fait with it but I thought the suspicion was that the owners of MtGox went off with everyone's money and they just said, "Oh yes, we were hacked". So I mean, didn't they say that they'd used that 'mutability', I don't know what it's called, and said, "Oh no, that's how we lost the money," and then someone did some analysis and it turned out they didn't.

Patrick McCorry: Yes, there was a paper released that said that it's very unlikely that transaction malleability that was the cause the coins getting lost.

Audience: But were they actually lost?

Patrick McCorry: Well they don't know, it could be.

Reply: There are multiple theories. One of the theories is that it's malleability, basically attackers managed to exploit that and take off with the Bitcoins.

Audience: Presumably the Bitcoin addresses that MtGox had those Bitcoins sitting in are known, so they'll be seen when any of them are sent anywhere else. Has that happened?

Reply: True, but apparently there were a lot of internal addresses as well. There was one instance where after they had reported that, "We've lost so many bitcoins," a few months later they suddenly said, "Oh, we checked this random wallet, and we suddenly found X amount of bitcoins". So it seems to be ad hoc, it's not something you can just view on the blockchain and audit I think, they have internal systems in place as well. And, whereas there's a bit of doubt about what actually happened at MtGox still, in many of the other incidents it was clearly hackers. And even in cases where it's not hackers there have been cases where the people themselves just said, "Oh, we have so many coins in reserves, let's just take off while we can". Last week there was the case of Evolution Marketplace, which was all over the news as well. Evolution was basically like Silk Road, where people would put money into escrow and then wait for their order to come. So for one week they just didn't clear the escrow account, and they estimated they had between $12 million and $34 million dollars, and said to the customers, "So we're going to take off while we're still ahead, and we're going to the Bahamas. Hope you folks understand". They actually put that statement up.

There's also a trend in ransomware, I'll just walk you through the cycle. You get an email saying that this is an attachment, please download me, and once you do that it's a malware which encrypts all your files, and it says that you have to pay a ransom, you have 96 hours, there's a counter here, and these are the instructions for how to make a Bitcoin payment if you want to ever decrypt your files. And you can access these instructions in multiple languages. Once you close that window your desktop wallpaper has been changed as well, and your files are thoroughly encrypted. These seem to be very successful if you look at the figures, $30 million in 100 days, and then $1 million in six months. And then, if you're not sure that the malware actually does what it claims to do, that is, if you will ever be able to get your files back again, this facility allows you to randomly decrypt five files, so you can be confident that once you make the payment you will get your data back. When the time expires you basically lose all your files. This practice is also booming. The original idea for this came out in academic research in 2004, courtesy of Adam Young and Moti Yung, termed 'cryptovirology', using asymmetric cryptography to build something like this. Why was it not built for so many years? Pretty much because Bitcoin was not there. Any ransom that a person paid had to traverse traditional financial networks, and there could be checks. But with Bitcoin, it's a new market that's opened up. So again, Bitcoin is the secret ingredient.

A quick word on possible future issues. There is an argument saying that tax evasion will likely not happen using Bitcoin. It's by Ed Felten, comments he made at a panel discussion, and he's probably right, the conspiracy to not report income in sizeable companies is a pretty large. But at an individual level it's a completely different ball game. And if you look at trends there's already a lot of under-reporting in taxes happening in the US at least. In 2006, the IRS estimate was that there were $385 billion in taxes that had not been paid. In 2013, the figure is approximately $2 trillion, and much of it has to do with the fact that there's a global financial crisis and people just decided to not report their money. And these are not career criminals, these are ordinary people, people like hairdressers, people who mow lawns, handymen, in fact the largest increase in jobs since the recession has been in hospitality and bartending.

Ross Anderson: Well, those figures are about an order of magnitude higher than the figures claimed by Inland Revenue in the UK who reckon that the tax evasion is costing them in the high hundreds of pounds per person.

Reply: Could be. I am not aware of the UK figures.

Ross Anderson: But that's in the high thousands of dollars per person.

Reply: It could be something that differs from place to place. I've got an info-graphic here, which is from Latin America, and here it appears to be 50/50. For every tax dollar collected, one dollar is lost to evasion, only 3 % of returns are mass audited, only 0.2 % are in-depth audited. So trends differ a lot from place to place because of the cultural aspects.

Paul Wernick: There's also a another interesting thing with tax evasion which is that if you're conducting an entirely legitimate business via Bitcoin it might be quite difficult for the authorities to audit exactly what your income was.

Reply: Exactly, it relies entirely on the fact that you keep diligent records and you report everything honestly. If I'm walking along the street and someone asks me to mow a lawn and pays me in bitcoins, there's no way an observer can differentiate it from a drug transaction on the other side of the world. So that's something that may happen, it's something that we should actually expect in the Bitcoin universe.

Ross Anderson: You would expect that payments in physical cash is still as easy to conceal as payments in Bitcoin given that most Bitcoin users use a service to hold their wallet for them, and even if you have your own wallet it wouldn't have it's own audit trail unless you deliberately deleted it, which would lead forensic traces.

Paul Wernick: So you'd actually have to organise your Bitcoin world to enable that.

Ross Anderson: My point is that it's not, that it's not as straightforward to be dishonest with Bitcoin as it is with controlling banknotes.

Paul Wernick: I was thinking more in terms of trying to prove you are honest with the Internal Revenue Service.

Ross Anderson: If you want to try to prove you are honest you just run a wallet that's properly backed up so that you can show the revenue snapshots of your laptop everyday going back over the last tax year.

Reply: Yes, but that sort of defeats the main thrust of Bitcoin which is anonymity and freedom from regulation.

Ross Anderson: Not necessarily.

Reply: Well, if I were to get a large payment in cash, it would still show up in the banking system, I'd probably put it in the bank, and then even if I don't report it, there would be some signs. Like, for instance legislation like FACTA, that is, overseas banks are required to disclose the funds an American holds. So stuff like this is, even if I don't report it, the bank might.

Paul Wernick: If I want to be honest I'd just produce my bank statements, which are from a third party, as opposed to my screenshots, which are from me and could be anything.

Ross Anderson: Or use a Bitcoin wallet provider, like MtGox, only honest, and they provide you with statements which you can then show to the revenue services.

Reply: But again, if I were to reveal that then they'd also see my Silk Road purchases, right, if I gave them some information?

Daniel Thomas: If you want the tax man to be happy with your accounts, you do also need to obey other aspects of the law.

Reply: Yes, but in this case, if I don't obey the law it is much harder for the law to catch me, and Bitcoin makes that possible in a sense. This slide sort of speaks for itself, Bitcoin makes an ideal tax haven. Essentially earlier on for tax havens you need a whole infrastructure, you put money into the banks, and then you have shell companies, and a whole set of layering, and then it would be clean money, but with Bitcoin you can just make a series of anonymous transactions, and your money is clean, or hidden, or however you want to put it. And the best way to target this kind of practice in traditional networks was that you targeted the infrastructure, the governments went after the banks. The US government recently put a lot of pressure on Swiss banks to open up and disclose how many Americans are holding funds there. But with Bitcoin you can't do that. If I just pass my funds to a suitable mix, I can anonymise my coins, I can hide whatever funds I have.

This is not a current threat because Bitcoin is very volatile, but the FBI anticipates that to grow, and Europol has already requested greater policing powers for just this.

There's also talk about threats which are non-financial in application, but would use the underlying Bitcoin network. Right now people have discussed using the Bitcoin network and the blockchain as a time-stamping mechanism. You put a hash on there and that's your time-stamp, saying that, here, I have this data. But there was this interesting incident last year where Microsoft Security Essentials suddenly started to send up red flags when scanning Bitcoin wallets. Apparently there's a virus called Stone, which appeared in the 80's, a DOS based virus, it's before my time so I don't really know much about it, but it would show up and your screen would go blank, and then it would say, "You have been stoned, please legalise marijuana". It's very harmless, but apparently traces of that virus, or some segments of code, showed up in the blockchain and Microsoft Security Essentials caught it, and they said this could happen.

And since then Interpol has released a warning, this was last week at Blackhat and they demonstrated the possibility for distributing malware, or harmful content over the blockchain, and they built a prototype. Essentially you'd have a piece of code on your machine, and it would connect to the blockchain, and from certain transactions, it would download some data, and, using that data, construct a virus. And that data could not be removed from the blockchain, because nothing can be removed from the blockchain.

We ourselves did something along these lines, we presented a concept called ZombieCoin at a workshop last month with Financial Cryptography. The idea was that you can use the blockchain to send command and control communications for botnets. If I have bots which are connected to the Bitcoin network, I make a transaction, and in that I tell all the bots to, let's say, send me the credit card information you've collected, and all the bots would receive that instruction. And typically, the only successful way to date to defeat botnets has been to defeat the command and control infrastructure. You make sure the botmaster cannot communicate with his bots. Normally they would communicate over IRC channels and you could take those down, or P2P networks, and you could cripple those. But if they communicate over the Bitcoin network, and if anyone were to do anything about that, that would actually break Bitcoin, so this is something that's very possible as well, and it's dirt cheap, and it's very easy, and very convenient.

So, we're back where we started, which is that we have this paradox, and there doesn't seem to be an easy resolution, and we would hope that people would start to take these things more seriously. Some people have proposed solutions, like online wallets, multisig services, coin tainting techniques, but these solutions, well, except for hardware wallets, they're all deficient in the sense that by targeting some criminal activity over here they necessarily diminish some positive property of Bitcoin. Like, for instance, if I have a multi-signature service, like all my transactions require two or more signatures, I essentially end up compromising on user privacy. Whoever else signs my transactions, they know what I'm doing. So you have that trade-off, and there is no easy solution to this.

Will Technology Make Information Security Impossible? And Must Technology Be Invented Just Because We Can?

Thoughts Occasioned by Brunner's "The Productions of Time" and Asimov's "The Dead Past"

Paul Wernick and Bruce Christianson[⊠]

University of Hertfordshire College Lane, Hatfield, Hertfordshire AL10 9AB, UK
{p.d.wernick,B.Christianson}@herts.ac.uk

Abstract. John Brunner postulates a technology that can record the thoughts and emotions generated by the human brain during sleep, and replay them on demand later for a third party. Isaac Asimov describes a device that can look into the past and display what actually happened. These fictional inventions raise interesting questions about the way we actually handle confidentiality and integrity of information at present, and suggest new threats and countermeasures.

[Major spoiler alert: this paper reveals major plot turns of these stories. If you want to read them for the first time and maintain the element of surprise which Brunner and Asimov achieve, please do not read any further.]

1 Introduction

In his science fiction novel The Productions of Time [2] John Brunner postulates a technology that can record the thoughts and emotions generated by the human brain during sleep, and replay them on demand later for an audience. Isaac Asimov's The Dead Past [1] describes a device that can look into the past and display what actually happened. Brunner's book and Asimov's story raise interesting questions about the confidentiality and integrity of information; how would each be affected by the invention of these devices, and what countermeasures can be envisaged? There is also a deeper question which we do not consider here – what would be the effect on individuals and society of being unable to protect our private thoughts?

A common theme that emerges from these two works of speculative fiction is: can the implications of technical innovations for society be predicted? More generally, can (or should) the invention of devices with extreme implications for privacy and information security be controlled?

© Springer International Publishing Switzerland 2015
B. Christianson et al. (Eds.): Security Protocols 2015, LNCS 9379, pp. 307–313, 2015.
DOI: 10.1007/978-3-319-26096-9_31

2   Plots of the Works

2.1   The Productions of Time

Our hero, Murray Douglas, is given an opportunity to revive his flagging acting career by joining a company for a new production. The brilliant but erratic and controlling director assembles a group of actors in an isolated country house, each of them has had a career-threatening problem. His stated intention is to produce a new play by developing ideas improvised by the cast. At the house, the director provides each actor with the source of their problem – in Douglas' case, caches of alcoholic sprits. It is all very strange …

In his bedroom Douglas finds a strange aerial attached to his mattress, linked to a tape recorder under his bed. Similar systems are in the bedrooms of the other company members. Eventually it turns out that this device is intended to record brain impulses as the sleeper dreams, dreams turned into emotional nightmares by the availability of the source of the sleeper's weakness. The "servants" are actually a group of criminals who have travelled from the future to record these emotions and dreams. The recordings will be taken back to the future where, as most people lead bland lives, they command high prices amongst thrill-seekers who can vicariously experience the raw uncontrolled thoughts. In that future world this mind-reading technology is controlled by the government, and private possession is illegal, but the profit to be made from illicit recordings is sufficient to make the game worthwhile.

Finally, of course, Douglas defeats the criminals and escapes safely – with, inevitably, The Girl.

2.2   The Dead Past

Asimov postulates a device that can look into the past and project the vision on to a screen. The chronoscope' device is operational but its use is under strict government control. A historian cannot understand why the government goes to considerable lengths to prevent him using it. Furious at his research being blocked, he investigates, and works out that a cheap chronoscope can be built by any amateur with sufficient knowledge using easily-available parts. He promptly publishes details of how to make one.

Asimov then has a character point out that anything which happened even a second ago is in the past, and that it can now be seen by anyone with a chronoscope. The inventor, instead of creating a window into the past for historians – indeed, the device can only see 120 years into the past so this is of limited utility – has created the ultimate snooping device, which allows anyone to see what anyone else did a moment ago.

3   Implications of These Inventions – What Are the Threats?

What have these two science fiction works – a 1960s novel and a 1950s story – to do with the theme of SPW 2015? We suggest that together they would pose a great threat to the secrecy and integrity of information. Although secrecy and integrity are conventionally regarded as different security services, current mechanisms for providing one generally rely on the availability of the other at a "lower" level of abstraction, and it is this dovetailing which is threatened.

3.1   Threats to Secrecy

Brunner postulates a device that needs to be close to the victim but, even without a more powerful device that could read minds at a distance, the implications for secrecy as currently implemented are disturbing. If Brunner's thought-reading device were capable of reading a person's thoughts in detail, then it would be impossible for a human to keep any secret, since it could be read directly from the secret-holder's mind. Even if it could only read more general information, this might provide clues to passwords and answers to security questions. Can a system rely on something you know to identify you when an enemy can just read it directly from your brain? Your security question: your dog's name, your mother's maiden name, your school; all can just be read from your brain and repeated as required.

Asimov's invention would bypass the need to read minds, as any security-related actions which took place in the past can be observed. As you type in your password, you can be watched and your keystrokes observed. However well you try to hide your actions it is inevitable that over time your typed passwords will be seen. If you are issued with a security device to plug in to authenticate yourself, the issue process will be visible to enemies, information which can potentially be used in the future to subvert that process. If you try to hide the device, your action will be seen, so no location will be secure by virtue of secrecy. Worse, the design and production of the device will be visible, making duplication much easier. If biometrics are employed, the process of identifying the person with the biometric value will be observable. How valuable is a biometric when an enemy might see the way your details were captured in the first place and subsequently use this information to replace your details with their own (see the discussion on integrity below)? No secure back channel will be free from observation, so any such channel will be vulnerable if it relies on any covert activities.

Any system that relies on the use of specific devices whose presence guarantees that a person is authorised to access secure material is also threatened. Even if an attempt is made to control access to and/or possession of these devices, a sufficiently determined attacker could peek into the minds of their designers, and observe the manufacturing processes. This might enable that attacker to produce illicit copies which would be indistinguishable from newly-made legitimate examples.

In any case, what is the point of trying to maintain information secrecy when the result of somebody reading or hearing the information can be read out of their brain? The only secrets that can be kept are those that nobody ever needs to know. The only reassurance in these circumstances is that the bad guys will be as badly off as the good guys. Forget the master criminal with his[1] secret master plan. The police will have it even as he's thinking of it, and even before he's told his evil henchmen or committed it to paper – assuming that the police are taking advantage of the technology to watch everyone.

3.2   Threats to Integrity

The two inventions make vulnerable any authentication-, confidentiality- or integrity-maintaining system that relies on maintaining a secret.

Current mechanisms for guaranteeing the integrity of information at a distance primarily rely on secrecy. Digital signatures based on public/private key pairs demand that the key part in the hands of the signer be kept secret. But this reliance in practice often relies in turn on another secret – what is the passphrase I use to access my key material, where do I keep the device which contains my secret key? This approach is just as vulnerable as the secrets discussed above.

Biometric-based authentication approaches will also be vulnerable to attack, as the integrity of the information used to confirm identity might be comprised in a similar way. However, there are alternative approaches to integrity preservation which do not rely upon keeping secrets – for example non-repudiable publication of a hash value[2].

4   Potential Solutions – and One Problem Solved?

We have identified two possible means of addressing the threats outlined above. One of these relies on making security mechanisms impossible for an enemy to reproduce by denying them access to useful parts of a previous datastream, whereas the other depends on not revealing a shared secret to a vulnerable party i.e. a human being.

Christianson and Shafarenko's Vintage Bit Cryptography approach [3] is based on the idea of flooding an attacker's information-capturing resource with large amounts of data – far more than can be stored, in which the actual information to be transferred will be hidden at previously-agreed secret locations, with the rest being discarded and not stored by the recipient. The security arises from the attacker not being able to determine in advance which bits of the data stream actually encode information and which do not; the attacker therefore needs to store the entire datastream until this can be determined, whereas the communicators can happily discard irrelevant bits and are thus not faced with the same axiomatically-insuperable data storage problem.

This approach may help resolve the problem arising from Asimov's history reader, as the attacker cannot store all the bits whilst waiting to identify which parts of the datastream are important and which are padding. If we assume

---

[1] Traditionally all (or almost all) master criminals are male, Elementary's Jamie Moriarty being a notable exception.

[2] Jikzi (LNCS 1796, 22–47); DODA (LNCS 2845, 74–95); or a slight re-purposing of the Eternity Service: www.cl.cam.ac.uk/rja14/eternity/eternity.html.

that the covert data channel from the past to the future has large, but not infinite, capacity, it will not be possible for an attacker to extract the useful parts in the same way as the legitimate recipient[3]. It should however be noted that Christianson and Shafarenko still rely on secure bootstrap of an initial weak secret between the communicating parties, which is potentially vulnerable to both types of attack[4].

Despite the concerns raised above it may be possible to resolve the problem of secure communication (although not that of reading information from participants' minds) by the use of tamper-evident boxes. However these boxes must not contain any secrets installed in such a way that this installation may be observed, or depend for security on any action or attribute of a human, or a secret known by a human, as these are all open to reading by one device or the other. (We assume that neither Brunner's nor Asimov's devices can look inside a device and read stored contents not visible to humans without leaving some trace.) We therefore need boxes which leave the factory in a known state and are later brought into agreement to communicate with each other using secrets shared on a one-time basis and impossible to read without affecting the devices, by using some physical mechanism analogous to Kish pairing of devices or quantum entanglement. The secret is thus unreachable and unreadable by the vulnerable element of the security infrastructure, i.e. people.

After one-time mutual initialisation a pair, or larger group, of these boxes could authenticate within the group by some challenge/response mechanism, and then communicate securely, all on the basis of their shared secret. Even if attackers could see the boxes and their operation, or perhaps even obtain them in factory-fresh condition, without the one-time physically shared key they would not be able to communicate with a specific set of boxes, as they are not in possession of the shared secret held in the boxes. The only remaining issue would be that of maintaining the physical security (secrecy and integrity) of boxes, as a member of a group in an attacker's hands would be sufficient to make all authentications and communications insecure.

Paradoxically, we consider that one security-related problem will be solved by Asimov's device. His invention would allow us to literally see with whom we are communicating in almost-real time, which may help resolve the issue of authentication[5].

Regardless of whether the technology described by Brunner and Asimov becomes science or remains fiction (but see below!), we believe that it is a profitable exercise to re-evaluate our security infrastructure, including physical as

---

[3] Whereas even a low-bandwidth covert channel from the attacker's future into their past breaks most security protocols.

[4] Unless this was done before the inventions can be deployed, whence the term "Vintage".

[5] Indeed, it could help solve the data integrity problem, providing we make strong assumptions about the integrity of the data supplied by the chronoscope. Such assumptions are unnecessary for secret sniffing, because in current protocols a correct guess for a secret can usually be verified independently of how the guess was obtained.

well as cryptographic security, from the point of view of the threat model which they would enable.

5   Wider Implications

Brunner's criminals use unlawfully-obtained technology to further their mind-ripping crimes. Asimov's history reader is suppressed for the best of reasons. In both cases, future society apparently suffers from the same issues we currently face; that devices which are safe in the hands of the good guys are very useful for criminals who will therefore expend considerable effort to obtain them and the knowledge needed to use them. A current instance is the spate of thefts of high-value cars using stolen technology which enable thieves to clone the immobiliser-disabling devices needed to operate the car. Once technology is readily available it becomes not just a source for good – Brunner's mind-reading technology could be employed by mental health practitioners to help treat people – but an enabling technology for the bad guys.

If at some future time a technology appears that can read the minds of people without their permission and then replay the recordings to others for surveillance or entertainment purposes, how would society change if this equipment was in the hands of a government which claimed to be working for the good of society as a whole or of private corporations, or of criminals, who do not have this defence? And if this device is invented, can we provide sufficient countermeasures to maintain our privacy against these scanners? And, if privacy protection technologies to defend ourselves against this snooping are invented, who will control access to them? Will mere possession of such a defence without suitable authorisation be seen as an indication of criminal intent?

Asimov's story poses a different problem. His is a technology which may actually be of little value to the bad guys in the long term, since anyone – including the police – can keep an eye on them as they plan and execute their illegal operations, but which will change society as anyone can see anyone else's activities. Blackmail will be impossible as everyone will know that they are being observed all the time – Bentham's Panoptikon made real. The threat of blackmail will be removed, but at the price of a complete loss of privacy as everything will be known anyway – there are no unshared secrets left to reveal.

Both Brunner and Asimov assume that the technology is nominally under government control, as are, for instance, today's information interception technologies, but in both cases the government's attempts to control the technology are failing. What if these get into the hands of the wrong people (or, depending on your opinion of governments, other wrong people), as from past experience seems inevitable? Are some inventions too dangerous to invent? Should the development of some technologies be banned entirely because of their implications for society and/or for individual freedom and privacy? If not, who should control access to this technology? And what actions should they be allowed to undertake in order to maintain this control?

Research has been recently published [4] that allows human thoughts to control external processes beyond game-playing using an EEG headset. Other research described in the same report allows a mouse's brain to be influenced by a surgical implant controlled by a human's brainwaves, control which can change the animal's emotional state. This is turn triggers observed chemical changes in the mouse's physiology. We are already demonstrating an ability to control external events by reading human thought processes using technology. This is equivalent to Brunner's much cruder manipulation of his hero by the provision of alcohol. We are now one step closer to being able to manipulate people and record the resulting patterns. That the results of the experiment have been observed by the researchers is another step towards Brunner's dystopian vision.

As we look back 60 or more years to the stories we started with, we can see that the issues they raised are even more relevant – and even more all-embracing – than they were then. Can we maintain any privacy at all as new technology emerges, or will we have to pull down the net curtains, replace all our walls with glass windows, and let everyone see everything we do? When Steven Rambam said, "privacy is dead, get over it," was he being more prescient than even he realised?

References

1. Asimov, I.: The Dead Past. In: Earth is Room Enough, Panther Books Ltd, London (1956). Reprint 9–52 (1971)
2. Brunner, J.: The Productions of Time. Penguin Books Ltd, Harmondsworth (1967). Reprint 1970
3. Christianson, B., Shafarenko, A.: Vintage bit cryptography. In: Christianson, B., Crispo, B., Malcolm, J.A., Roe, M. (eds.) Security Protocols. LNCS, vol. 5087, pp. 261–265. Springer, Heidelberg (2009)
4. ETH. Controlling genes with your thoughts (2014). https://www.ethz.ch/en/news-and-events/eth-news/news/2014/11/controlling-genes-with-thoughts.html. Accessed 14 November 2014 (formal publication in Nature Communications online at http://www.nature.com/ncomms/2014/141111/ncomms6392/full/ncomms6392.html)

Will Technology Make Information Security Impossible? And Must Technology Be Invented Just Because We Can? (Transcript of Discussion)

Paul Wernick[✉]

University of Hertfordshire, Hatfield, UK
p.d.wernick@herts.ac.uk

I took the title for the theme of this workshop absolutely literally because I've been using fiction as a starting point. I've taken a couple of items of technology created in the minds of science fiction writers and walked them forward and just seen what the implications would be for information security. So, just to give you an idea of what I'm going to be talking about I'll outline the stories. This is going to be a complete spoiler for both of these stories, so apologies to anybody who will actually want to read them later on. I'll talk about the technologies, what threats they pose to information security separately, and possibly when used together, and some possible countermeasures that we've thought up, though hopefully you will come up with others.

Both of these by the way are quite old stories. John Brunner's is from 1967, Asimov's from the 1950s. So firstly, John Brunner's Productions of Time, our hero, who is an actor, joins a company being set up in a house somewhere to improvise a new production. Turns out that all the members of the cast have some weakness or other, our hero drinks a lot, somebody else has a drug problem, someone has an interest in young boys, etc. And our hero finds that each member of the company is actively given access to whatever it is their weakness. Even more puzzling there's some sort of wire grid on the beds where they sleep at night, and what he finds out eventually is that some people have come back from the future, and they're using technology to capture the thoughts of each actor as they relive their experiences, to take them back to the future and market them to people who enjoy these sorts of vicarious pursuits. A bit by accident, a bit by bravery, he foils the plot, gets away, and of course he gets out with the girl.

So we've got a technology that must be capable of capturing mental patterns. There's more to it than this, and Brunner's idea is that it captures emotions. The technology he envisages has to be able to identify which particular mental patterns go with particular activities, or particular relived experiences, and to be able to record them in such a way that you can play them back when our villains go back to the future, so that the people who are buying these sort of black market things can enjoy them.

Frank Stajano: It is also a requirement that the technology must be able to allow the guys to go back in time?

Reply: This is true.

© Springer International Publishing Switzerland 2015
B. Christianson et al. (Eds.): Security Protocols 2015, LNCS 9379, pp. 314–324, 2015.
DOI: 10.1007/978-3-319-26096-9_32

So let's have a look at the other story, Asimov's Dead Past, which is a novella. Here our hero is an historian and Asimov postulates a device, I presume some sort of television screen device, using which you can look back and see what's happened in the past. And our historian thinks, this is absolutely brilliant, I'll be able to go back and look at all the unexplored areas of history, and all the controversial elements, go back and see what *actually* happened. It will open the world of history to reality rather than the conjecture of historians based on poor documentation. Not only that, but this thing's comparatively cheap to make. You can buy the bits easily, and you can put them together, and you can then have your 'view of the past' device, wonderful. So why hasn't anybody done this, why hasn't anybody published the details of it? So our hero decides to do something about this.

All of a sudden the government are stamping all over him and saying, "how dare you do this, you're not allowed to do this," but the government won't say why. Eventually the historian manages to publish the design, and the government then points out two important flaws in his reasoning, one of which is, Asimov's take on the technology, that it only goes back a certain short time, well a hundred years, short for an historian, into the past, and therefore you can't actually see what happened a long time ago. Secondly, that of course everything that happened a moment ago is in the past, so you can see anything anywhere. Somebody could replay the last sentence I've just spoken. So everything in the past is available. Privacy has disappeared, there is a device snooping on everybody, permanently. And that was the reason why the government said they didn't want this thing published. And the denouement of the story, there you are, privacy is gone.

So what sort of technology have we got here? Well, something that can observe the past, can see what's going on, on Earth at least, it doesn't take it beyond that. It could be projected in sufficient detail for viewers to recognise what's going on. Asimov's idea is, as you go a hundred years into the past it fades, but what happened five minutes ago is nice and clear. And for this purpose we're going to assume that this is good enough to be able to see, for instance, what keys somebody hit on a keyboard, so you can literally look over anybody's shoulder and see what they've typed in, and see what they get back on their display.

So what are the implications of these for information security? Let's think about confidentiality. Well firstly, is it possible for a human to keep any secret, if you can just look in their mind and read it out. Let's put to one side the idea that you needn't bother with any other technology than just read it out of the secret-holder's mind.

Let's think about what happens perhaps when secrets are in transit. You use devices to implement security features, you've got black boxes, you've got some software, crypto, things running on machines. Brunner's device allows you to read the mind of the designer and say, how do you design this? What features have you put into it? There's this black box, but you just look in the designer's mind and there it is, now you know how it works. You can also read out passwords from somebody's mind, and indeed their answers to their security questions; what was your dog's name? just read it out of somebody's mind; what's your mother's maiden name? read it out of their mind. It is possible to read all of that information that we commonly use to maintain some level of confidentiality straight out of people's minds.

Asimov's history viewer, you can see any actions that relate to confidentiality. If somebody is typing in their password, you just look over their shoulder and you see what they've typed, nice and easy. And if you didn't get it first time, you just replay it until you've got all of it. What about the security device? Well you can see how it was issued. Somebody gets a particular device, they work for a company perhaps, or work for an intelligence agency, how do they get their device, let's look at the detail, and the issuing process, so we can replicate it. How is it used: are there any special tricks? If you hide it because you don't want to carry it on you, where is it hidden? Nice and easy to see. How did they make it? Well, let's have a look in the factory and see what happened, or look on the designer's board. And any secrets that are entered into it to make it secure by a person, well let's have a look and see what they did. Let's say something is individualised by somebody connecting it to a computer and typing something, we'll see what it says.

The one saving grace here is that the good guys can also see what the bad guys are doing. If you've got the criminal mastermind sitting in his – it is usually *his* – lair, usually dark, somewhere underground, laughing hideously, and sending his minions out to do bad things, well the police can watch what he's doing, and it makes detection a bit easier.

What about the implications for integrity? Well, a lot of integrity protection is based on the confidentiality of something anyway, so really the same issues apply. You've got a wallet, you've got all these wonderful security features, but you roll it back far enough and eventually it's something somebody has, or something somebody knows, or something measurable about them.

Ross Anderson: I'm not sure I buy this. In a world with total pervasive surveillance, like David Brin's proposal where everybody can see everybody else as a design feature, there's no need for particular controls and integrity, because if you want to know what I agreed with Mr. Bloggs at 3 pm last Wednesday at a car dealer in Leicester you just turn on this chronoscope and you look back, sorted, finished. There is no more need for digital signatures, there's no need for message authentication codes, all that just can get tossed.

Reply: As long as you're dealing wih stuff that can be actually put up on a screen and read.

Mark Lomas: Even then you have to look through the entire history because the information that they had five minutes ago may be corrupted ten minutes ago. And therefore you'd have to go through the entire system backwards.

Ross Anderson: Well, a contract is just a crystallization of what people agree to, the agreement was at a particular period of time and they would start doing stuff about it. Where people dispute contracts, you typically resolve that by looking at the correspondence that went before, and the delivery notes that went afterwards. Once you have got that all completely visible in plain sight, and once you've got an ongoing relationship between people, if somebody says, "no I never said that", then at that point you go back and you verify, just as you would if ...

Mark Lomas: What you're saying is you can verify an individual piece of information, but if you want to verify the totality of something you have to go back to its independent ...

Ross Anderson: Well that's the case, even if everything is legitimately signed, you end up with terabytes of stuff that you've got to wade back through, and ...

Bruce Christianson: But one of the things that you can do with digital signature is agree a chain, or a local tree of what's included and what isn't included.

Ross Anderson: And then of course the dispute is not whether the contract is signed, but whether the executive that signed it had the proper authority of the company to do so.

Bruce Christianson: And so forth. So the counter-point of an integrity property is being able to prove that a particular document *wasn't* annexed to the contract, it wasn't around at the time the contract was signed.

Keith Irwin: So, the integrity stamp in this case is going to be the exact time and location where you can go back and see this signed. You can still do a chain, you just say, oh I'll go back and look at this one, and you can see when I'm signing this, it shows the integrity stamp, which says, well when this part came it was here, and you can work your way back, it's a little longer to validate but it's still doable.

Max Spencer: But it's like just going back and looking at the time when the agreement was made. It's slow, you just have to actually go and observe, check that the thing really was actually the same, and surely that's a good argument for using some kind of digital mechanism.

Reply: Which is great until you're actually digitally signing a bag of bits of some sort ...

Bruce Christianson: Yes, precisely.

Reply: ... which represents something else. If it's something you could actually see in front of you, we sit down, and we sign the contract, great, wonderful, you can look over a person's shoulder and see what it is. But if it's a large data store being transferred it's a bit more difficult to work out what was there.

Ross Anderson: I think there's a broader point here. *If* we understand that integrity becomes a different kind of problem, because the cryptographic keys that we currently use for signatures and MACs are no longer relevant, so we just look at the original source materials. *Then* there's a similar criticism of the argument in respect of confidentiality, which is that if you can observe the plaintext being generated by people opening their mouths and talking, then whether you've got access to the keys you used to encrypt the data becomes entirely moot ...

Reply: Yes.

Ross Anderson: ... and this reflects the policy discussions that we're having nowadays with the run up to, the next snoopers' charter. Twenty years ago it was all about whether the government would have access to keys; now who cares? It's all about the government having access to the plaintext that's kept on the servers of Google, Facebook, and so on. And whether that was encrypted on its way to the datacentre in Oregon using SSL is almost an irrelevance.

Reply: Yes. As long as you can demonstrate that the plaintext you're looking at, and the stuff that was sent, and the stuff that was received, are the same thing.

Ross Anderson: But in that case the TLS is the policeman's friend rather than his enemy. It means that when he does seize information from Google through M-Lab he can then wave it in front of the magistrate and the defence lawyers have a harder time quibbling it.

Reply: Well, let me press on. Another issue for integrity is that of biometric-based information, which again, has to be captured and entered in some way, and suffers from exactly the same issues as any other information. But again, it's something that isn't actually directly readable by people and therefore able to be confirmed that it is in fact the right information.

We have thought of a couple of potential solutions for this, one of which actually was prefigured a couple of minutes ago, which is vintage bit cryptography[1], it was Bruce and Alex Shafarenko was it not? The idea is that you just send masses and masses of bits, and only a few of them will actually contain the information, the rest of it is just padding. And the poor attacker is left trying to capture all this stuff, and there's just too much, too many bits being passed down the line for him to capture it all and analyse it, or to keep enough information that's sufficiently far in the past to be useful.

Bruce Christianson: The argument is that the bandwidth from the past to the future, although large, is not actually infinite.

Reply: As the good guy you don't have to worry about all the extra bits, you don't have to worry about keeping them. The bad guy has to keep them all on the off-chance that some of it will in fact be relevant. So that would get round some of the issues there. However much you look into the past all you're seeing is this incredibly long bit stream that you can't capture anyway.

Another possibility is to have devices that don't actually reveal anything to a person, or reveal anything in public. One of these technologies relies on looking inside somebody's head, if the information that's maintaining the security isn't in anybody's head, that's not going to work. The other technology relies on

---

[1] LNCS 5087 pp 261–275.

what can be seen outside physical devices, externally visible phenomena. If the connection doesn't produce any phenomena like this then that can't be seen either.

Ross Anderson: Well at present if you sign an international treaty, or if the President of the USA signs an Act of Congress, then this is video recorded, right, and it's put on the TV. And given that the cost of videoing stuff and saving it are dropping precipitously, the prospect exists that you could record all contracts forever in this way. If you buy insurance from a telephone call centre, they tape record the conversation and keep it for seven years. Maybe this is just how everything will operate in the future.

Reply: A system of connected devices that don't produce any external phenomena, as I'm suggesting, would at least allow secure communication.

Bruce Christianson: What Ross is saying is you don't actually need to keep secrets. Is that right, Ross?

Ross Anderson: Well, if I'm running an insurance company and I have an archive of the recordings of every transaction of any of my call centre operators has ever made with a customer or a prospective customer, I can do some very lightweight things to guarantee the integrity of that. I could put a hash of it in the New York Times every morning, and I can keep my backup tape with my lawyer, whatever, that's a minor engineering detail. The fact that I've got all the plaintext is what I rely on. If there's a dispute I pull the recording and I play it.

Bruce Christianson: There is still a question about how you verify that it really was me at the other end of the phone call.

Reply: Or somebody else who looked over my shoulder when I typed in my password.

Ross Anderson: But there's no password, I have the recording of your voice.

Bruce Christianson: Yes, but the question is whether it really is me.

Frank Stajano: It's increasingly possible, plausible let's say, to have synthetic generation of videos of things that never happened.

Ross Anderson: Do I care.

Frank Stajano: Yes, if you're relying on that as evidence.

Ross Anderson: But my evidence I secure by computing a SHA-512 of all yesterday's communications and publishing to the newspaper.

Frank Stajano: Yes but, if it's in an adversarial context, you could still have done this with synthetic videos and published the thing in the New York Times. There's no guarantee to someone who doesn't believe you that these were things where you *actually* interacted with a client, as opposed to a reconstruction.

Ross Anderson: Now we're getting to somewhere useful, because how a transaction between me and a call centre disadvantages me is that they've got a copy of the contract but I don't. So the policy intervention here might be to say that you make a copy of the contract available to the customer as a condition of its future enforceability, and you can then talk about the technology and the infrastructure necessary to do that. And then I keep a copy of the contract if I want to rely on it, and you keep a copy of the contract if you want to rely on it, and if we argue about who's lying later then a judge looks at us and looks at the evidence, and looks at the available forensics, and makes his mind up in the context.

Bruce Christianson: But that evidence includes the video recording of you giving me the copy of the first video recording.

Frank Stajano: I think it's a good idea. I would prefer the version where I, the customer, make my own recording of the call with the call centre; because I envisage, since we are talking science fiction, that the call centre could *in real time* create a different one, and send me that different one. And then not only would I have to have the stupid call with the call centre, which probably involves 30 min of muzak, but also I'd have to re-watch it *again* to make sure that they sent me the same thing that actually happened! If I record it myself, at least I don't have to do that.

Ross Anderson: So what happens at the moment if you buy insurance is they send you a certificate of insurance with a schedule, and you may then find that they've got some of the details wrong, so you phone them up and you do it again. Now it's only if you've got a dispute later, if you crash your car and there's an argument over who said what when you registered the claim, that the recordings as a practical matter has to be replayed. Do we want to think of some infrastructure to make this easier?

Reply: Yes.

Ross Anderson: Do we want to have a central government repository where people could lodge copies of their recordings, or copies of hashes of their recordings. What's the appropriate technology here?

Alastair Beresford: Both parties could record what they thought the conversation was, and swap, and maybe with enough sensible audio processing you might automatically be able to check they're similar enough to say that you don't have to listen to them again, so that might be an alternative.

Bruce Christianson: But the slight difficulty is the case where my end of the recording was in fact made by a simulacrum of me, and the reason I don't have a copy of the recording is because I wasn't involved in the transaction, and that's why I can't produce my copy, but the court's not going to believe that.

Alastair Beresford: But I guess the insurance company would have two copies, neither of which would involve you at this stage if it was some other criminal that produced it.

Ross Anderson: What actually happens is that two people have a different view of what was said, because each person has a different mental makeup, different things are salient to them, important or unimportant, so if they write up minutes of the conversation afterwards you may get two completely different descriptions of the same process, which is why you have written contracts in the first place.

Alastair Beresford: Or what people say is ambiguous like the phrase "don't stop", which can be interpreted as "carry on" or "*don't! Stop!*"

Ross Anderson: Exactly so.

Reply: Actually now I think maybe Asimov's device sorts this out, because all the caller has to do is to know when I phone up the insurance company ...

Bruce Christianson: He just needs to know the coordinates.

Reply: ... and then just watch the transaction going through, play it back, play back history.

Bruce Christianson: But I like Ross' idea of saying, let's think about what the infrastructure would be to have a distribution mechanism that essentially assigns coordinates to all these things.

Ross Anderson: Well, we're actually building this infrastructure because we're all carrying around lots of devices with cameras and microphones, and they're all backing up in Google's datacentre in Oregon. So just wait twenty years and Google maps will become clickable, and replayable, and then we can show you what happened here 17 h ago. The Chronoscope is being built, and it lives in Oregon, and it's free so long as you pay for ads.

Joan Feigenbaum: So I heard a talk by Bruce Schneier in which he considered not the continuous Chronoscope but just the little pieces of it, which Ross just alluded to, that already exist. He was most intrigued by the potential effect on families and, in particular, the potential effect on marriages. You have all these conversations in marriages that consist mostly of "no you said this, no you said that, no you said this." What if couples could actually resolve all those disputes? Suppose they could answer the question "What did you actually say three days ago when we were discussing this thing that you're supposed to be doing right now?"

Bruce Christianson: I predict the divorce rate would go up.

Joan Feigenbaum: Right. Schneier said "My relationship with my wife would not improve if we could always *prove* that what we think the other person said is *actually* what the other person said."

Reply: I think we'd just move the argument a bit rather than resolving it.

Jeunese Payne: There was an interesting mini series on Channel 4 where they showed these sorts of scenarios. One of the scenarios was what if you could record absolutely everything, through your eyes, and then you could play it back. And there was a marriage scenario in this, where some guy's wife had been cheating on him, and he made her play it back, and they even played back previous sexual encounters while they had sex, instead of actually having sex with each other, and all sorts of creepy stuff. The mini-series is called Black Mirror, and most of the episodes to me are very creepy, but they all play with this idea of what happens if technology goes a little bit step further, and that's one of the possibilities that they do. Also whenever someone goes to the airport they have to play back their last 24 h or whatever, for the security guy to see.

Reply: I think we're getting back almost towards the vintage bit cryptography, because if I've got to play my last 24 h back in real time then we'll stand at the airport for 24 h.

Jeunese Payne: No, not real time, the speed's sped up, and he and you would have to view it.

Frank Stajano: Well if you know in advance it's 24 h, just do the nasty thing 25 h before!

Jeunese Payne: Well I don't know if it was 24 h, but basically you have to play it back. The whole point was that nothing was really private anymore, peoples previous recordings were taking over their life, and their current situation, so this guy had gone on holiday and he was complaining about the hotel, and he was playing it back on the TV through his eyes saying, can you see the mess on the floor, can you see this. Instead of actually just living in the present, everybody's living in the past.

Joan Feigenbaum: So nothing is private, and nothing is ambiguous.

Reply: But society relies on ambiguity.

Joan Feigenbaum: Exactly.

Frank Stajano: Most of your life recording will be of you watching the TV of the previous recording.

Reply: Yes, watching your TV, and you're watching a previous recording, not quite infinitely, but just 61 years of it.

Keith Irwin: I had a question about the second solution. Are we assuming that the Chronoscope can only see people going back in time?

Reply: Well I assumed it could see anything.

Keith Irwin: The question is are we talking about only light, or do we have a wider electromagnetic spectrum? Do we have tempest attacks into the past? I just wanted to ask what the assumption was.

Reply: The poor man was writing in the 1950s, give him a break.

Keith Irwin: I'm asking how *you're* defining it.

Reply: Video and I'm assuming audio as well, and that's about as far as it gets. So no, nothing further into the electromagnetic spectrum.

So therefore you have two devices that talk amongst themselves without actually producing any external phenomena, and don't have any human input into their setting up.

Keith Irwin: Right, so they mustnt have like the transistor buzz depending on their calculations and that sort of thing.

Reply: Well, yes exactly, and no light displays that say what they're going to do, just as a way of transmitting stuff at least outside the Chronoscope.

So there are some other implications here. The first thing is ...

Dylan Clark: I just wanted to revisit the idea that video would remove ambiguity. I don't think it necessarily would, because I think it depends on the viewpoint of the observers. I can, I had some training in the professional use of violence, now my friend showed me videos of what they term police brutality, and to them it is police brutality, to me, from things I know, it's clear that the police are trying to disable the person without hurting them. And yet, from each of our viewpoints, it's the same video, but it's totally ambiguous.

Reply: Well, back to treaties again, as Ross pointed out, their wording is often ambiguous to get both sides to sign them.

Anyway, another issue that I touched on with Asimov's device. Both authors have said these devices have to be illegal, or controlled by the government for the public good. Brunner's criminals have stolen technology, and they know when they go back to the future they're going to get picked up by the police unless they are fairly swift of foot. The government knows that Asimov's device exists but deliberately suppresses it because of the effect on society.

Another thought, which is that both authors postulate a future society that suffers from the same problems that we have. There is some privacy but both are subject to technology-based attacks. That technology being distributed, despite the fact the government wants to control it, does leak out sooner or later. And the technology that can do good, such as the police watching the criminals preparing to commit their crime – this is the map of where their armoured car goes, oh good, the police can see where they're going to hit it – but can also have bad effects.

The question of how it would actually change society, we've already had this discussion. If these devices existed what effect would there be on society, going beyond any of the technological aspects of it? And would we be able to devise countermeasures to protect our privacy? There have been some suggestions that we keep our own copy of the record, or maybe that we have an edited copy of the record – are we actually allowed to cut stuff out of our past, not be 100 %? And who controls access to their devices – will it actually be illegal to have a device that stops somebody else from looking at your past? In a way for me the technological aspects are less interesting than the societal ones, and I think if these devices existed, life would be interesting. Thank you very much indeed.

Ross Anderson: There was an interesting article in The Guardian a couple of days ago called The Future of Loneliness and Internet Isolation[2]. It talks about these issues, and it has to a link to a YouTube video, which brings out the way in which pervasive surveillance changes people's behaviour.

Reply: Yes, if you know you're being watched . . .

Ross Anderson: Absolutely. You change what you do.

---

[2] www.theguardian.com/society/2015/apr/01/future-of-loneliness-internet-isolation

Information Leakage Due to Revealing Randomly Selected Bits

Arash Atashpendar[1]([⊠]), A.W. Roscoe[2], and Peter Y.A. Ryan[1]

[1] SnT, University of Luxembourg, Luxembourg City, Luxembourg
{arash.atashpendar,peter.ryan}@uni.lu
[2] Department of Computer Science, University of Oxford, Oxford, UK
bill.roscoe@cs.ox.ac.uk

Abstract. This note describes an information theory problem that arose from some analysis of quantum key distribution protocols. The problem seems very natural and is very easy to state but has not to our knowledge been addressed before in the information theory literature: suppose that we have a random bit string y of length n and we reveal k bits at random positions, preserving the order but without revealing the positions, how much information about y is revealed?

We show that while the cardinality of the set of compatible y strings depends only on n and k, the amount of leakage does depend on the exact revealed x string. We observe that the maximal leakage, measured as decrease in the Shannon entropy of the space of possible bit strings, corresponds to the x string being all zeros or all ones and that the minimum leakage corresponds to the alternating x strings. We derive a formula for the maximum leakage (minimal entropy) in terms of n and k. We discuss the relevance of other measures of information, in particular min-entropy, in a cryptographic context. Finally, we describe a simulation tool to explore these results.

Keywords: Information leakage · Quantum key distribution · Entropy · Subsequence · Supersequence · Deletion channel · Simulation

1 Introduction

The problem that we investigate here arose from some analysis of quantum key distribution (QKD) protocols. We do not go into the details of the motivating context here, more detail can be found at [1]. For the moment we just remark that in QKD protocols it is typical for the parties, after the quantum phase, to compare bits of the fresh session key at randomly sampled positions in order to obtain an estimate of the Quantum Bit Error Rate (QBER). This indicates the proportion of bits that have been flipped as the result of either noise or eavesdropping on the quantum channel. This serves to bound the amount of information leakage to any eavesdropper, and as long as this falls below an appropriate threshold the parties continue with the key reconciliation and secrecy amplification steps.

B. Christianson et al. (Eds.): Security Protocols 2015, LNCS 9379, pp. 325–341, 2015.
DOI: 10.1007/978-3-319-26096-9_33

Usually, the sample set is agreed and the bits compared using un-encrypted but authenticated exchanges over a classical channel, hence the positions of the compared bits are known to a potential eavesdropper and these bits are discarded. In [1], it is suggested that the sample set be computed secretly by the parties based on prior shared secrets. They still compare the bits over an un-encrypted channel, but now an eavesdropper does not learn where the bits lie in the key stream. This prompts the possibility of retaining these bits, but now we must be careful to bound the information leakage and ensure that later privacy amplification takes account of this leakage.

Further advantages of the above approach are that it provides implicit authentication at a very early stage and it ensures fairness in the selection of the sampling, i.e. neither party controls the selection.

In practice it would probably be judged too risky to retain these bits on forward secrecy grounds: leakage of the prior secret string at a later time would compromise these bits. Nonetheless, the possibility does present the rather intriguing mathematical challenge that we address in this paper.

The structure of the paper is as follows: in the next section we give the problem statement, some notation and the necessary background theory. Section 3 presents our approach for solving the problem as well as the obtained results, followed by a few discussions on privacy amplification and alternative approaches in Sect. 4. Section 5 describes how we use simulations to obtain numerical results and to tackle some of the problems addressed in this paper for which deriving analytic expressions proved to be difficult. Finally, we conclude by summarizing our contributions in Sect. 6.

2   Problem Statement

Given an alphabet $\Sigma = \{0,1\}$, Σ^n denotes the set of all Σ-strings of length n. Consider a bit string y of length n chosen at random from the space of all possible bit strings of length n, i.e. $y \in \Sigma^n$. More precisely, we assume that the probability distribution over the n-bit strings is flat. We assume that the bits are indexed 1 through n and a subset S of $\{1, ..., n\}$ of size k $(k \leq n)$ is chosen at random and we reveal the bits of y at these indices, preserving the order of the bits but without revealing S. Call the resulting, revealed string x. We assume that S is chosen with a flat distribution over the set of subsets of $\{1, ...n\}$ of size k, thus every subset of size k is equally probable. As an example, suppose that for $n = 12$ and $k = 4$ we have:

$$y = \langle 011000011001 \rangle$$

and we choose $S = \{2, 4, 5, 8\}$, then $x = 1001$.

The question now is, what is the resulting information leakage about y? We assume that the "adversary" knows the rules of the game, i.e. she knows n and she knows that the leaked string preserves the order but she does not know the chosen S mask. In particular, can we write the leakage as a function purely of k

and n or does it depend on the exact form of x? If it does depend on x, can we bound this?

To illustrate: if you reveal 0 bits then obviously you reveal nothing about the full string. If you reveal just one bit ($k = 1$) and suppose that it is a 0, then essentially all you have revealed about the full string is that the all 1 string is not possible. At the other extreme, if you reveal all the bits ($k = n$) then obviously you reveal all n bits of the original string. For $k = n/2$, we see that from Theorem 1 the number of possible y strings is $(2^n)/2$, which for a flat distribution would correspond to exactly 1 bit of leakage. However, in our problem the distribution departs from flat so the leakage is in fact a little more than 1 bit. So intuitively the function starts off very shallow but rises very fast as k approaches n.

2.1 Notation

Let us introduce some notation. First we define $x = Mask(y, S)$ to mean that the string y filtered by the mask S gives the string x. Now we define the *uncertainty set*: given an x and n, this is the set of y strings that could project to x for some mask S.

$$\Upsilon_{n,x} := \{y \in \{0,1\}^n, \exists S \bullet Mask(y, S) = x\}$$

- Let $\omega_x(y)$ denote the number of distinct ways that y can project onto x. We will refer to this as the weight of y (w.r.t x).

$$\omega_x(y) := |\{S \in \mathcal{P}(N) : Mask(y, S) = x\}|.$$

- and $\mu_{n,x}$ the number of configurations for n and x, i.e. the number of pairs $\{y, S\}$ such that $Mask(y, S) = x$. It is easy to see that this is given by:

$$\mu_{n,k} = \binom{n}{k} \cdot 2^{n-k} \tag{1}$$

The concepts presented here are closely related to the notions of subsequences, here denoted by x strings, and supersequences (y strings), in formal languages and combinatorics on words. They also crop up in coding theory as a maximum likelihood decoding in the context of deletion and insertion channels.

2.2 Related Work

The closest results to our work are mainly found either in studies dealing with subsequences and supersequences or in the context of *deletion channels*. However, the questions addressed in this paper remain open in related studies. The main problem boils down to determining the probability distribution discussed in the previous section. Here we give a brief survey of the most relevant and closely related results in the literature.

Subsequences and Supersequences: Despite their rather simple descriptions, the spaces of subsequences and supersequences remain largely unexplored and present many unanswered questions. Fundamental results can be found in the works of Levenshtein, Hirschberg and Calabi [2–5] who provide tight upper and lower bounds on the number of distinct subsequences. Furthermore, it was proved by Chase [6] that the number of distinct k-long subsequences is maximized by repeated permutations of an alphabet Σ, i.e. no letter appears twice without all of the other letters of Σ intervening. Flaxman et al. [7] also provide a probabilistic method for determining the string that maximizes the number of distinct subsequences. Results for the mean and the variance of subsequences for the sequence searching problem, also known as the hidden pattern problem, can be found at [8].

For a thorough presentation of efficient algorithms for computing the number of distinct subsequences, e.g. using dynamic programming, and related problems in the realm of DNA sequencing, we refer the reader to [9–12].

Maximum Likelihood Decoding in Deletion Channels: In a deletion channel [13], for a received sequence, the probability that it arose from a given codeword is proportional to the number of different ways it is contained as a subsequence in that codeword. This translates into a maximum likelihood decoding for deletion channels as follows: For a received sequence, we count the number of times it appears as a subsequence of each codeword and we choose the codeword that admits the largest count. The problem of determining and bounding these particular distributions remains unexplored and presents a considerable number of open questions. Case-specific results for double insertion/deletion channels can be found in [14]. Moreover, improved bounds for the number of subsequences obtained via the deletion channel and proofs for how balanced and unbalanced strings lead to the highest and lowest number of distinct subsequences are given in [15].

2.3   Entropy Measures

The obvious follow-on question to the problem posed at the start of this section is: what is the appropriate measure of information to use? Perhaps the simplest measure is the Hartley measure, the log of the cardinality of the uncertainty set. This coincides with the Shannon measure if the probability distribution is uniform. In this case the solution is simple as we will see below: the cardinality of the uncertainty set is a simple function of n and k. However, the probability distribution turns out to be rather far from uniform, so Hartley does not seem appropriate here.

Thought of purely as an information theory puzzle, the standard commonly used measure is Shannon's [16]. For this we have a number of interesting results and observations. In particular, our observations suggest that the maximum leakage for all n and k occurs for the all zero or all one x strings and we have a formula for the leakage in these cases. However, we have not yet been able to prove this conjecture, although we do have intuitions as to why this appears to be the case.

Given the cryptographic motivation for the problem, it is worth considering whether alternative information measures are in fact more appropriate. The Shannon measure has a very specific interpretation: the expected number of binary questions required to identify the exact value of the variable. In various cryptographic contexts, this might not be the most appropriate interpretation. For example, in some situations it might not be necessary to pin down the exact value and a good approximation may be damaging. In our context, the session key derived from the key reconciliation phase will be subjected to privacy amplification to reduce the adversary's knowledge of the key to a negligible amount. What we really need therefore is a measure of the leakage that can be used to control the degree of amplification required. This question has been extensively studied in [17–21], and below we summarize the key results.

Various measures of entropy may be applicable depending on the parameters of the context in question, such as the scheme used for privacy amplification, e.g. universal hashing vs. randomness extractors or whether a distinction is made between passive adversaries and active adversaries [17]. As noted in the works of Bennett et al. [21,22], the Rényi entropy [23,24] provides a lower bound on the size of the secret key s' distillable from the partially secret key s initially shared by Alice and Bob. Moreover, it is shown in [17], that the min-entropy provides an upper bound on the amount of permissible leakage and specific constraints are derived as a function of the min-entropy of s and the length of the partially secret string. More recently, Renner and Wolf show in [18] that the Shannon entropy H can be generalized and extended to two simple quantities, H_0^ε and H_∞^ε, called smooth Rényi entropy values, which provide tight bounds for privacy amplification and information reconciliation in contexts such as QKD, where the assumption of having independent repetitions of a random experiment is generally not satisfied.

For the purpose of our study, we consider the following measures of information, which can be considered as special cases of the Rényi Entropy.

Rényi Entropy of order α. For $\alpha \geq 0$ and $\alpha \neq 1$, the Rényi entropy of order α of a random variable X is

$$H_\alpha(X) = \frac{1}{1-\alpha}\log_2 \sum_{x \in \mathcal{X}} P_X(x)^\alpha. \tag{2}$$

Hartley Entropy. The Hartley measure corresponds to Rényi entropy of order zero and is defined as

$$H_0(X) := -\log_2 |\mathcal{X}|. \tag{3}$$

Second-order Rényi Entropy. For $\alpha = 2$, we get the collision entropy, also simply referred to as the Rényi entropy

$$R(x) = H_2(X) := -\log_2 \sum_{x \in \mathcal{X}} P_X(x)^2. \tag{4}$$

Shannon Entropy. As $\alpha \to 1$, in the limit we get the Shannon entropy of a random variable X

$$H(X) = -\sum_{x \in \mathcal{X}} P_X(x) \cdot \log_2 P_X(x). \tag{5}$$

Min-Entropy. In the limit, as $\alpha \to \infty$, H_α converges to the min-entropy of a random variable X

$$H_\infty(X) := -\log_2 \max_{x \in \mathcal{X}}(P_X(x)). \tag{6}$$

As noted in [17], the entropy measures given above satisfy

$$H(X) \geq H_2(X) \geq H_\infty(X) \tag{7}$$

3   Information Leakage

In this section we show that the size of the uncertainty set only depends on n and k and provide an expression for computing its cardinality, followed by a proof. We then analyze the amount of information leakage and observe that the maximal leakage corresponds to the x string being all zeros or all ones and that the minimum leakage corresponds to the alternating x strings. We also derive closed form expressions for the maximum leakage (minimal entropy) in terms of n and k for the measures of entropy introduced in Sect. 2.

3.1   Cardinality of the Uncertainty Set

Theorem 1. *For given n and k the cardinality of $\Upsilon_{n,x}$ is independent of the exact x string. Furthermore, $|\Upsilon_{n,x}|$ is given by:*

$$|\Upsilon_{n,x}| = \sum_{r=k}^{n} \binom{n}{r} \tag{8}$$

Proof. $\gamma_{n,k}$ satisfies the following recursion:

$$\gamma_{n,k} = \gamma_{n-1,k} + \gamma_{n-1,k-1} \tag{9}$$

with base cases: $\gamma_{n,n} = 1$ and $\gamma_{n,0} = 2^n$.

The base cases are immediate. To see how the recursion arises, consider the following cases:

- Partition the y strings into those that have a mask overlapping the first bit of y and those that do not.
- For the former, we can enumerate them simply as the number of y strings of length $n - 1$ with ≥ 1 projections to the tail of x, i.e. $x*$, i.e. $\gamma_{n-1,k-1}$.
- For the latter, the number is just that of the set of y strings of length $n - 1$ with ≥ 1 projection to x, which has length k, i.e. $\gamma_{n-1,k}$.

The solution to this recursion with the given base cases is:

$$\gamma_{n,k} = \sum_{r=k}^{n} \binom{n}{r} \tag{10}$$

This is most simply seen by observing that the recursion is independent of the exact x, hence we can choose the x string comprising k 0s. Now we see that $|\Upsilon_{n,x}|$ is simply the number of distinct y strings with at least k 0s, and the result follows immediately. □

If the conditional distribution over $\Upsilon_{n,x}$ given the observation of x were flat, we would be done: we could compute the entropy immediately. However, it turns out the distribution is far from flat, and indeed its shape depends on the exact x string. This is due to the fact that given an observed x, the probability that a y gave rise to it is proportional to the weight of y, i.e. the number of ways that y could project to x, i.e. $|\{S|Mask(y,S) = x\}|$. This can vary between 1 and $\binom{n}{k}$.

3.2   Shannon Entropy

Here we will assume that the leakage is measured as the drop in the Shannon entropy of the space of possible y strings. Clearly, before any observation the entropy is n bits. We observe that the maximal leakage occurs when x is either the all 0 or the all 1 string and we derive an expression for the corresponding entropy of $\Upsilon_{n,x}$.

3.3   Minimal Shannon Entropy

Assuming that the maximal leakage occurs for the all zero (or all one) x string we derive the formula for the maximal leakage (minimum entropy of $\Upsilon_{n,x}$) as follows: observe that the number of elements of $\Upsilon_{n,k}$ with j 1's is $\binom{n}{j}$. Note further that for given j the number of ways that a y string with j 1's can yield x is $\binom{n-j}{k}$. Consequently, the probability that y was a given string with j 1's given the observation of x is:

$$P(y_j|x) = \frac{\binom{n-j}{k}}{\mu_{n,k}} \tag{11}$$

where $\mu_{n,k}$ is the normalization, i.e. the total number of configurations that could give rise to a given x:

$$\mu_{n,k} = \binom{n}{k} \times 2^{n-k}$$

Now, inserting these terms into the formula for the Shannon entropy given in Eq. 5, we get:

$$H_{n,k} = -\sum_{j=0}^{n-k} \binom{n}{j} \times \frac{\binom{n-j}{k}}{\mu_{n,k}} \times \log_2\left(\frac{\binom{n-j}{k}}{\mu_{n,k}}\right) \tag{12}$$

For the original cryptographic motivation of this problem, more specifically in the context of privacy amplification, it is arguably an upper bound on the maximum leakage or the amount of information that Eve has gained that we are after [25]. However, it is also interesting to better understand the mean and range of the entropy for given n and k, but coming up with analytic forms for these appears to be much harder. We switch therefore to simulations to give us a better feel for these functions.

3.4 Minimal Rényi Entropy

The expression provided here is also based on the empirical results that conjecture that the minimal Rényi entropy is attained by 0^k or 1^k.

Inserting the derived expression given in Eq. 11 corresponding to the maximal leakage into the formula of the second-order Rényi entropy given in Eq. 4, we obtain the following expression for the minimal Rényi entropy:

$$R(X) = H_2(X) := -\log_2 \sum_{j=0}^{n-k} \binom{n}{j} \cdot \left(\frac{\binom{n-j}{k}}{\mu_{n,k}} \right)^2 \tag{13}$$

The derived expression agrees with the experiments driven by the numerical computation presented in Sect. 5.

3.5 Min-Entropy

The most conservative measure of information in the Rényi family is the min-entropy, and this is of interest when it comes to privacy amplification.

This turns out to be more tractable than the Shannon entropy. In particular it is immediate that the smallest Min-Entropy is attained by the all zero or all one x strings: the largest weight of a y string, and hence probability, is $\binom{n}{k}$ and this is attained by $x = 0^k$ and $y = 0^n$. Thus we can derive an analytic form for the minimum Min-Entropy $H_\infty(X)$ by inserting the derived term for maximal probability given in Eq. 11 into Eq. 6, and thus we get:

$$Min(H_\infty(X)) := -\log_2 \left(\frac{\binom{n}{k}}{\mu_{n,k}} \right) \tag{14}$$

and this immediately simplifies to:

$$Min(H_\infty(X)) := n - k \tag{15}$$

It is clear that this indeed corresponds to the most pessimistic bound of the leakage and can be thought of as assuming that the adversary gets to know the exact positions of the leaked bits.

The Min-Entropy, $H_\infty(X)$, is based on the most likely event of a random variable X. Therefore, this term sets an upper bound on the number of leaked bits, which can be then used in the parameterization of the compression function used in privacy amplification as described in [22].

Using Eq. 7 and the analytic forms given above for the lower bound on the Shannon entropy as well as the min-entropy, we can effectively set loose upper and lower bounds on the Rényi entropy.

3.6 Maximum Entropy

Another observation derived from empirical results obtained by simulation is that it also appears that the minimal leakage (max H) occurs when x comprises alternating 0s and 1s, e.g. $x = 101010...$, as shown in Fig. 3. We have seen that for a given n and k, the total number of masks and the number of compatible y strings are constant for all x strings. Therefore, the change in entropy of the Υ space for different x strings is solely dictated by how the masks are distributed among the compatible y strings, i.e. the contribution of each $y \in \Upsilon_{n,x}$ to the total number of masks.

4 Privacy Amplification and Alternative Approaches

This section gives a brief overview of the context to which this study applies and also analyzes the presented problem from a Kolmogorov complexity point of view. We then propose an approach for estimating the expected leakage, and finally we point out a duality between our findings and similar results in the literature.

4.1 Privacy Amplification

PA involves a setting in which Alice and Bob start out by having a partially secret key denoted by the random variable W, e.g. a random n-bit string, about which Eve gains some partial information, denoted by a correlated random variable V. This leakage can be in the form of some bits or parities of blocks of bits of W or some function of W [22]. Provided that Eve's knowledge is at most $t < n$ bits of information about W, i.e. $R(W|V = v) \geq n - t$, with R denoting the second-order Rényi entropy, Alice and Bob can distill a secret key of length $r = n - t - s$ with s being a security parameter such that $s < n - t$. The security parameter s can be used to reduce Eve's knowledge to an arbitrarily small amount, e.g. in the context of universal hash functions, it can be used to adjust the reduction size of the chosen compression function $g : \{0,1\}^n \mapsto \{0,1\}^r$.

The function g is publicly chosen by Alice and Bob at random from a family of universal hash functions, here denoted by the random variable G, to obtain $K = g(W)$, such that Eve's partial information on W and her complete information on g give her arbitrarily little information about K. The resulting secret key K is uniformly distributed given all her information. It is also shown by Bennett et al. in [22] that $H(K|G, V = v) \geq r - 2^{-s}/\ln 2$, provided only that $R(W|V =$

$v) \geq n - t$. The value of s can be considered a fixed value and comparatively small, typically not larger than 30, as the key length increases.

It is worth noting that the measure of information used in privacy amplification for defining the bound on leakage or the minimum length of the secret key that can be extracted, may vary depending on criteria such as the algorithms used in the amplification scheme and the channel being authenticated or not. For instance, as shown in [17], when randomness extractors are used instead of universal hash functions, the bound for secure PA against an active adversary is defined by the adversary's min-entropy about W. Various schemes for performing PA over authenticated and non-authenticated channels have been extensively studied in [17,21,26].

In QKD, privacy amplification constitutes the last sub-protocol that is run in a session and thus it takes place after the information reconciliation phase. The leakage studied in this paper deals with reduced entropy before the information reconciliation phase. However, this simply means that the leakage quantified here would in fact contribute to the t bits leaked to Eve.

4.2   Kolmogorov-Chaitin Complexity

From a purely information theoretical point of view, quantifying the amount of information leakage in terms of various measures of entropy such as the Shannon entropy is arguably what interests us. However, from a cryptographic standpoint, a complexity analysis of exploring the search space by considering the Kolmogorov complexity, provides another perspective in terms of the amount of resources needed for describing an algorithm that reproduces a given string.

In such a context, what matters for an attacker is how efficiently a program can enumerate the elements of the search space. In other words, whether it can enumerate the space in the optimal way, to minimize the expected time to terminate successfully. To illustrate this point, consider the case of the all 0 x string for which we can start with the all 0 y string, then move to y strings with one 1, then two 1s, and so on and so forth. For other generic x strings, carrying out this procedure in an efficient manner becomes more involved.

4.3   Estimating Expected Leakage

Our primary goal was to compute the leakage for a given x and the maximum leakage for given n and k, however, estimating the average leakage might also be of some interest. Since an exact computation depends on a rigorous understanding of the Υ space and its governing probability distribution, we suggest an approach that moves the problem from the space of supersequences to that of subsequences such that further developments in the latter can enable a more fine-grained estimation of the expected leakage.

Let Y be the random variable denoting the original random sequence of n bits and X the random variable denoting the k bits of leakage from Y. The average leakage can be expressed in terms of the entropy of Y minus the conditional entropy of Y conditioned on the knowledge of X, i.e. $H(Y) - H(Y|X)$. While

$H(Y|X)$ may seem hard to compute without the joint probability mass function of X and Y, we can use Bayes' rule for conditional entropy [27] to reformulate the expression as follows.

$$H(Y) - H(Y|X) = H(X) - H(X|Y)$$

With random Y, X is a uniformly distributed k-bit string and thus we have $H(X) = k$. This leaves us with $H(X|Y)$, and this reformulation allows us to define the entropy space in terms of projection weights, $\omega_x(y)$, assigned to the subsequences of each $Y = y$. Currently, as shown in [3], we only know the expected number of distinct subsequences given an n and t:

$$E_t(n) = \sum_{i=0}^{t} \binom{n-t-1+i}{i} \lambda^i.$$

with t being the number of deleted bits from the n-long y string, i.e. $t = n-k$, and $\lambda = 1 - \frac{1}{|\Sigma|}$, which in the binary case, $\Sigma = \{0,1\}$, would simply be $\lambda = 1 - \frac{1}{2}$. With this measure, we can get a rough estimate on the expected weight, which can then be used to estimate the average entropy, but this only gives us a very coarse-grained estimation of the expected leakage. Therefore, a better understanding of the exact number of distinct subsequences would lead to a more fine-grained estimation of the expected leakage.

4.4 Duality: Subsequences vs. Supersequences

An interesting observation resulting from our findings is that the two x strings of interest in the space of supersequences, i.e. the all zero or all one strings (single run) $0^+|1^+$, denoted here by σ and the alternating x strings: $(\epsilon|1)(01)^+(\epsilon|0)$, denoted here by α also represent the most interesting strings in the space of distinct subsequences.

More precisely, in our study we observe that single run sequences σ lead to the least uniform distribution of masks over the compatible supersequences, whereas the alternating sequences α yield the distribution of masks closest to the uniform distribution. Similarly, in the space of subsequences, σ lead to the minimum number of k-long distinct subsequences and α generate the maximum number of k-long distinct subsequences.

5 Simulations

In this section we first give a brief description of how our simulator [28] carries out the numerical experiments and then we discuss the obtained results with the help of a few plots that are aimed at describing the structure of the Υ spaces. We will refrain from elaborating on all the functionalities of the simulator as this would be beyond the scope of this paper. Instead, we focus on a select few sets of empirical results that were obtained from our experiments. We refer to [28] for more information and details.

The main motivation behind the numerical approach driven by simulations lies in the rather complicated structure of the Υ spaces. As deriving analytic forms for describing the entire space seems to be hard, we rely on simulating the spaces of interest in order to explore their structure.

5.1   Methodology

The simulator relies on parallel computations for generating, sampling and exploring the search spaces. The numerical experiments are carried out in two phases: First the simulator generates the Υ spaces that have various structures satisfying predefined constraints and then it proceeds to performing computations on the generated data sets.

The pseudo-code given in Algorithm 1 provides an example that illustrates one of the main tasks accomplished by the simulator: Given an n and an x string, we generate the corresponding Υ space containing the compatible y strings, compute the projection count $\omega_x(y)$ of its members, and compute its exact entropy.

Algorithm 1 Compute $H_\alpha(\Upsilon_{n,x})$

1: **function** COMPUTEUPSILONENTROPY(n, x)
2:     $SN \leftarrow$ Generate the space of bit strings of length n
3:     $\Upsilon_{n,x} \leftarrow$ Filter SN and reduce it to $\{y \| |y| = n, \exists S \bullet Mask(y, S) = x\}$
4:     $probArray \leftarrow []$
5:     **for** y_i in $\Upsilon_{n,x}$ **do**
6:         $\omega_x(y_i) \leftarrow computeProjectionCount(y_i, x)$
7:         $probArray[i] \leftarrow \omega_x(y_i)/N$
8:     $H_\alpha \leftarrow computeH_\alpha(probArray)$
9:     **return** H_α

5.2   Results Discussion

In this section, we present and discuss a select subset of our results with the help of plots generated by the simulator that provide a better insight into the structure of the Υ spaces.

As mentioned before, one of the main observations resulting from numerical simulations is that the shape of the probability distributions leading to the entropy values of x strings for a given n and k, is mainly determined by how evenly the number of projecting y strings are distributed across the possible projection counts for a given n and k. This observation is illustrated in Fig. 1.

Following from Theorem 1, for a given n and k, the observables computed and plotted in Fig. 1 for any x string satisfy the following

$$\sum_{i=1}^{g(n,x)} c_i = |\Upsilon_{n,k}| \tag{16}$$

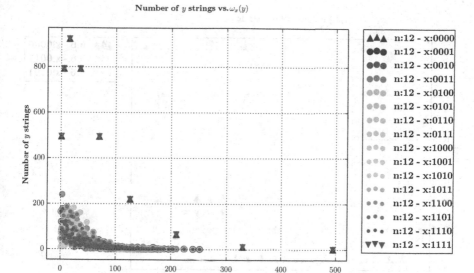

Fig. 1. Distinct count of y strings admitting the same $\omega_x(y)$ for $n = 12$ and $k = 4$.

Furthermore, the sum of the product of c_i and $\omega_x(y_i)$ is equal to a constant for all x strings:

$$\sum_{i=1}^{g(n,x)} c_i \cdot \omega_x(y_i) = \eta_{n,k} \tag{17}$$

With c denoting the values on the y-axis, i.e. the count of y strings projecting $\omega_x(y)$ times, and with $\omega_x(y)$ denoting the number of distinct ways that y can project onto x, and finally with $\eta_{n,k}$ being a constant for any given n and k and $g(n,x)$ being a function of n and x that denotes the number of data points corresponding to the distinct count of y strings that have the same $\omega_x(y)$.

This means that for a given n and k, the total number of projection counts in the corresponding $\varUpsilon$ space is independent of the x strings. We can see that for the x strings yielding the maximum amount of leakage, i.e. $x = 1^k|0^k$, the lower number of data points is compensated by larger values for the distinct number of y strings admitting larger projection count values, hence showing a much more biased structure in the distribution with respect to generic x strings. Conversely, the distributions for the remainder of the x strings are considerably dampened and noticeably closer to a flat distribution and are thus less biased compared to $x = 1^k|0^k$ strings, which in part explains the correspondingly higher entropy values. In particular, the alternating ones and zeros string admits the highest degree of dispersion in terms of the distribution of the masks and thus yields the lowest entropy.

The resulting probability distributions leading to the computed entropy values are illustrated in Fig. 2. An immediate observation is that the distribution of

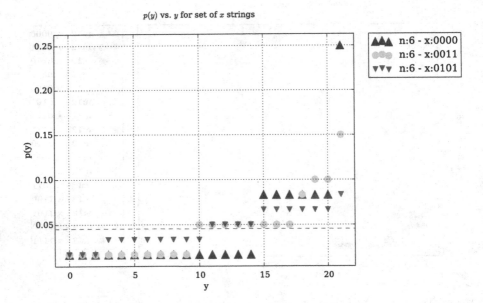

Fig. 2. Probability distributions of Υ spaces for given n and x with y strings enumerated by indices and the red dotted line showing the uniform distribution (Color figure online).

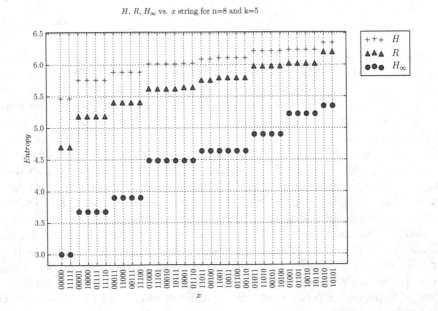

Fig. 3. H (Shannon), R_2 (second-order Rényi entropy) and H_∞ (min-entropy) vs. x strings for $n = 8$ and $k = 5$.

the projecting y strings for the 0^k or 1^k strings has the largest outliers. However, this alone does not capture the role of the shape of the probability distribution. Therefore, one could argue that the probability distribution that admits the largest Kullback-Leibler distance from the uniform distribution, i.e. the most biased distribution, yields the lowest entropy, and the conjecture that we put forth is that this distribution is given by the all 0 or all 1 x strings.

The plot shown in Fig. 3, illustrates three measures of entropy, namely the Shannon entropy (H), the second-order Rényi entropy (R) and the min-entropy (H_∞) as a function of n and k for all the 2^k x strings for $n = 8$ and $k = 5$. The presented empirical results validate our conjecture that the all zero or the all one strings yield the minimum entropy and that the alternating zeros and ones string gives the maximum entropy.

6 Conclusions

We have described an information theory problem that arose from some investigations into quantum key establishment protocols. As far as we are aware, the problem, despite its seeming to be very natural and simple to state, has not been investigated in the mathematical literature. We have shown that the maximum leakage, measured in terms of the drop in the entropy of the space of compatible y strings, corresponds to the all zero or all one observed strings.

We have presented analytic forms for the Shannon entropy, the second-order Rényi entropy, and the min-entropy for these cases. Moreover, we have discussed the relevance of these measures specifically in the context of privacy amplification in QKD protocols. We have also noted that the simulations suggest that the minimal leakage corresponds to the x strings comprising alternating zeros and ones. Moreover, we pointed out an interesting duality between our results and existing results in the literature for the space of subsequences.

We have also described a simulation program to explore these results. This is available at [28].

Acknowledgments. We would like to thank Philip B. Stark, Jean-Sébastien Coron, Marc Pouly and Ulrich Sorger for all the helpful comments and discussions.

References

1. Ryan, P.Y.A., Christianson, B.: Enhancements to prepare-and-measure based QKD protocols. In: Christianson, B., Malcolm, J., Stajano, F., Anderson, J., Bonneau, J. (eds.) Security Protocols 2013. LNCS, vol. 8263, pp. 123–133. Springer, Heidelberg (2013)

2. Hirschberg, D.S.: Bounds on the number of string subsequences. In: Crochemore, M., Paterson, M. (eds.) CPM 1999. LNCS, vol. 1645, pp. 115–122. Springer, Heidelberg (1999)

3. Hirschberg, D.S., Regnier, M.: Tight bounds on the number of string subsequences. J. Discrete Algorithms **1**(1), 123–132 (2000)

4. Calabi, L., Hartnett, W.: Some general results of coding theory with applications to the study of codes for the correction of synchronization errors. Inf. Control **15**(3), 235–249 (1969)
5. Levenshtein, V.I.: Efficient reconstruction of sequences from their subsequences or supersequences. J. Comb. Theory Ser. A **93**(2), 310–332 (2001)
6. Chase, P.J.: Subsequence numbers and logarithmic concavity. Discrete Math. **16**(2), 123–140 (1976)
7. Flaxman, A., Harrow, A.W., Sorkin, G.B.: Strings with maximally many distinct subsequences and substrings. Electron. J. Comb. **11**(1), R8 (2004)
8. Flajolet, P., Guivarc'h, Y., Szpankowski, W., Vallée, B.: Hidden pattern statistics. In: Orejas, F., Spirakis, P.G., van Leeuwen, J. (eds.) ICALP 2001. LNCS, vol. 2076, pp. 152–165. Springer, Heidelberg (2001)
9. Middendorf, M.: Supersequences, runs, and cd grammar systems. Dev. Theor. Comput. Sci. **6**, 101–114 (1994)
10. Lothaire, M.: Applied Combinatorics on Words, vol. 105. Cambridge University Press, Cambridge (2005)
11. Rahmann, S.: Subsequence combinatorics and applications to microarray production, DNA sequencing and chaining algorithms. In: Lewenstein, M., Valiente, G. (eds.) CPM 2006. LNCS, vol. 4009, pp. 153–164. Springer, Heidelberg (2006)
12. Elzinga, C., Rahmann, S., Wang, H.: Algorithms for subsequence combinatorics. Theoret. Comput. Sci. **409**(3), 394–404 (2008)
13. Mitzenmacher, M., et al.: A survey of results for deletion channels and related synchronization channels. Probab. Surv. **6**, 1–33 (2009)
14. Swart, T.G., Ferreira, H.C.: A note on double insertion/deletion correcting codes. IEEE Trans. Inf. Theory **49**(1), 269–273 (2003)
15. Liron, Y., Langberg, M.: A characterization of the number of subsequences obtained via the deletion channel. In: 2012 IEEE International Symposium on Information Theory Proceedings (ISIT), pp. 503–507. IEEE (2012)
16. Shannon, C.E.: A mathematical theory of communication. ACM SIGMOBILE Mob. Comput. Commun. Rev. **5**(1), 3–55 (2001)
17. Maurer, U., Wolf, S.: Privacy amplification secure against active adversaries. In: Kaliski Jr., B.S. (ed.) CRYPTO 1997. LNCS, vol. 1294, pp. 307–321. Springer, Heidelberg (1997)
18. Renner, R.S., Wolf, S.: Simple and tight bounds for information reconciliation and privacy amplification. In: Roy, B. (ed.) ASIACRYPT 2005. LNCS, vol. 3788, pp. 199–216. Springer, Heidelberg (2005)
19. Maurer, U.M.: Secret key agreement by public discussion from common information. IEEE Trans. Inf. Theory **39**(3), 733–742 (1993)
20. Cachin, C.: Entropy measures and unconditional security in cryptography. Ph.D. thesis, Swiss Federal Institute of Technology Zurich (1997)
21. Cachin, C., Maurer, U.M.: Linking information reconciliation and privacy amplification. J. Cryptology **10**(2), 97–110 (1997)
22. Bennett, C.H., Brassard, G., Crépeau, C., Maurer, U.M.: Generalized privacy amplification. IEEE Trans. Inf. Theory **41**(6), 1915–1923 (1995)
23. Renyi, A.: On measures of entropy and information. In: Fourth Berkeley Symposium on Mathematical Statistics and Probability, vol. 1, pp. 547–561 (1961)
24. MacKay, D.J.: Information theory, inference, and learning algorithms, vol. 7. Citeseer (2003)
25. Bennett, C.H., Brassard, G., Robert, J.M.: Privacy amplification by public discussion. SIAM J. Comput. **17**(2), 210–229 (1988)

26. Carter, J.L., Wegman, M.N.: Universal classes of hash functions. In: Proceedings of the Ninth Annual ACM Symposium on Theory of Computing, pp. 106–112. ACM (1977)
27. Cover, T.M., Thomas, J.A.: Elements of Information Theory. Wiley, New York (2012)
28. Atashpendar, A., Ryan, P.Y.A.: Qkd and information leakage simulator, September 2014. http://www.qkdsimulator.com

Information Leakage Due to Revealing
Randomly Selected Bits
(Transcript of Discussion)

Arash Atashpendar[(✉)]

University of Luxembourg, Luxembourg City, Luxembourg
arash.atashpendar@uni.lu

What I am going to talk about is far from fiction, but the theme was fact or fiction, so I guess we are just on the fact side of things. This is joint work with Peter Ryan and Bill Roscoe from Oxford. First, I am going to briefly provide the context in which we faced this issue. It is an information theory puzzle that arose from a study, which resulted in a modification of one of the sub-protocols of quantum key distribution. The modification was suggested in a paper[1] by Peter Ryan and Bruce Christianson, which was presented here two years ago. I am going to explain how things are normally done in this sub-protocol and then explain what the suggested scheme changes.

Essentially, in quantum key exchange protocols, past the quantum phase, when the two parties discard the qubits that were not measured using the same measurement basis, they end up with a partially secret key. Now in the absence of channel noise or an eavesdropper, the error rate in the key should be zero. What the two parties typically do is that they estimate the amount of error in their keys to figure out whether or not there was an eavesdropper. We skip the details here but the way it is usually done is that the two parties communicate over a public channel and compare a small subset of their key strings. The scheme is quite simple: they either randomize their bit strings and pick a fixed chunk or they just take a random subset of their keys and then they compare the subsets to estimate the error rate. If it is below a certain threshold, typically around 12 %, they move on to error correction, otherwise, they assume that the error is entirely due to the adversary's eavesdropping and abort the protocol.

This means that when the two parties communicate over the public channel, since it is all unencrypted, they would have to discard everything, as they are leaking all this information to Eve. One requirement in all QKD protocols is that the two parties start out with a pre-shared secret key, which is mainly used for authentication. In the new scheme, the idea is to use a portion of this key here to secretly and locally compute the bits that the two parties want to compare. This way they won't have to transmit the actual bits over the public channel. They can compute the subset that they want to compare as a function of a small chunk of their pre-shared key.

I won't go into the details, but essentially, it boils down to Alice and Bob sending bits over a public channel without revealing the exact positions of these

---

[1] LNCS 8263 pp. 123–133, 2013.

B. Christianson et al. (Eds.): Security Protocols 2015, LNCS 9379, pp. 342–349, 2015.
DOI: 10.1007/978-3-319-26096-9_34

bits. Alice sends to Bob a string of length n, with a flat distribution so there is no bias. What happens is that a subset of size k of this bit string is leaked and Eve can see this leaked string. Another important aspect of this is that the bits are leaked in order, so you don't know the exact position of the bits, but you know that they're leaked in order.

Here is a specific example to illustrate this point. Consider the space of all bit strings of size $n = 12$, that is to say 2 to the power of 12 bit strings. Here S indicates the indices of the bits that are revealed to Eve. y is the source string or the original string that was transmitted over the channel. Eve gets to see these bits, denoted by x, but she doesn't know where they are, she just knows that they are leaked in order. This scheme offers several advantages: first in terms of consuming less key material because while in existing schemes you have to throw away all the bits that you reveal, here this is not the case as you're not actually telling Eve where the bits are, you're just revealing the fact that they are leaked in order. Plus, it has the advantage that it gives you implicit authentication, but I guess that's not within the scope of this talk.

Now it is important to know how much we're actually leaking because later on in the final step of quantum key distribution protocols, we do privacy amplification, which involves reducing the amount of leakage or the information that's been leaked to Eve to an arbitrarily small amount. In a cryptographic context, it was important for us to figure out, given n the size of the source string, and an x string that is revealed, but not knowing the mask, how much information about the original string we are revealing to Eve. In our work, we decided to use some of the members of the Renyi family of entropy measures, mainly because in the QKD literature various orders of the Renyi entropy are used depending on the context in question. Later on we'll talk about whether or not it's the appropriate measure.

Going back to our notation: you'll get x if you apply the mask S to filter your original y string. Next, we have the uncertainty set, Υ, that contains all the y strings for which there is at least a mask such that when you apply it to y, you get the resulting x string. For given n and x, Eve knows n, and the x string that is revealed. Υ contains all the possible y strings that admit at least one projection to the x string. For a given y string and x string, $\omega_x(y)$ denotes the number of ways the y string can project to the x string. μ denotes our normalization, which is the number of configurations or pairs of y strings and masks that lead to the x string. The normalization is equal to n choose k times 2 to the power of $n - k$. This gives the number of ways you can choose k bits of mask out of the n bits, and for each case, you end up with $n - k$ extra bits, and you compute all the possible values that these configurations could take.

This was the starting point and the first thing we wanted to compute was the number of strings we get for a given n and x. In other words, what's the size of this uncertainty set? And to our surprise, we found out that it's actually completely independent of the chosen x string. In other words, the size of this set is purely a function of n and k, which was a little bit surprising. Now I'll go over the proof of this and then I'll explain the formula itself.

We can describe this set in a recursive manner and once we have that, everything else falls into place. The recursion is $\gamma_{n,k} = \gamma_{n-1,k} + \gamma_{n-1,k-1}$ with base cases $\gamma_{n,n} = 1$ and $\gamma_{n,0} = 2^n$. You can partition all your y strings into two categories or two partitions. In one partition, there is a mask overlapping the first bit of the y strings, and in the other one it is the other way around. In the first case, you end up with y strings of length $n-1$ with more than one projection to the tail of x, that gives you $\gamma_{n-1,k-1}$. In the other partition, we have strings of length $n-1$ again, but here with masks of size k, because they do not overlap with the first bit. These two partitions give you closure, that is to say that they describe the entire space of possible y strings. What you notice here is that this description is entirely independent of the actual x strings, it's only dependent on n and k. So with that, we can just consider an arbitary string. We take the all 0 x string, which has k 0s, and from there it's just a matter of taking all possible combinations starting from k 0s to n 0s. In other words, the number of distinct y strings with at least k 0s.

The distribution of the number of ways each y string projects to a given x is not flat as it is different for varying x strings. This number varies from 1 to n choose k, which is the number of possible projections. Since dealing with this space proved to be quite intractable, we decided to adopt an experiment-based approach. In fact it's very much a physics-based approach as we ended up generating the entire space and simulating all the properties, in the hope of deriving analytic forms afterwards. For a given x, we generate the space of all possible bit strings of length n, then we filter this set and reduce it to the set of compatible y strings. These are the strings that yield at least one projection to the given x string.

Then we go through this list and compute the projection count for each y string but I'm not going to explain the details of the involved algorithms here. Then we normalize the computed projection counts and assign them as probabilities, and now we have our probability distribution. Using this probability distribution, we choose different orders of the Renyi Entropy, mainly focusing on the Shannon Entropy to compute the entropy of the space of y strings to find out how much information we are leaking as a function of different x strings. What you see here is that the minimum entropy or maximum leakage is given by the all 0 and all 1 string, and the alternating strings such as 10101, leak the least.

In the context of quantum key establishment, what matters most is deriving bounds for the maximum amount of leakage. The reason for this is that using this bound we can reduce the amount of leakage by applying privacy amplification. However, understanding the rest of the space is not so obvious. Here is another example that also shows the other formula that I explained. In this matrix[2], the first column shows the y strings of length n and the first row gives the possible x strings of size 3, here n is 4 and k is 3. For a given y string and the corresponding x string, you see how many times the y string projects to the x string. The value in each column varies from 1 to n choose k, which is the maximum value we get for the case of all 0 strings, that is, for $y =< 0000 >$ and $x =< 000 >$. The

---

[2] This matrix can be found at http://qkdsimulator.com/plots.

distribution here helps us understand why we have this trend in the entropy space.

Alastair Beresford: In the top left hand corner, why is it not 5, you know, why is it 4?

Peter Ryan: 4 choose 3.

Alastair Beresford: Maybe it's something I got wrong, because I imagine mapping x and I can find 5 different ways of putting the three 0s. I have the 3 0s on the left, and I could have 2 on the left and one on the far right, I made it across and I end up with 5 different ways rather than 4 or I misunderstood something?

Peter Ryan: It's four ways.

Alastair Beresford: So I thought the idea was that you're saying that x can be any 3 bits out of the 4 that's in y.

Reply: Revealed in order! so let's take an example and I will refer to the indices of the mask applied to y. You can have $S = \{0, 1, 2\}$, $S = \{0, 1, 3\}$, $S = \{0, 2, 3\}$, and $S = \{1, 2, 3\}$.

Peter Ryan: You're just dropping one, and there's only 4 ways you can drop.

Reply: It's OK now, right? OK, good. Here k is small but I couldn't make it bigger for this slide. What matters is how these values are distributed. For the all 1s and 0s you can already see a little bit of bias. In terms of probability distribution, as you go towards the alternating 1s and 0s, you approach a flat distribution.

This is another plot, a box-plot[3], which I could come back to, but for now I'm going to skip it. It tells the same story in terms of distributions and the outliers that you get for the all 0 and the all 1 string. But the most interesting plot that I think explains why you get this trend in the entropy space is this one[4], and I will explain what we're plotting here. On the y-axis you have the number of y strings and the x-axis gives you the projection count. For instance, for the all 0 string, you've got around 100 y strings that project around 200 times to this given x string. If you take the sum of the product of the number of projections and the number of y strings, it's always equal to a constant. It's not a continuous space, you can't think of it as the area below the curve, but it is the same idea.

So for different x strings, you get different numbers of data points and this is compensated by the fact that for strings that leak less, you have more data points, that is to say, more possible y strings, but smaller number of projections. So it's closer to a flat distribution in terms of how the configurations are scattered across the possible y strings. Whereas here, for the all 0 string, as you go from left to right, the Hamming weight goes down to 0 and the number of

---

[3] The box-plot can be found at http://qkdsimulator.com/plots.
[4] This refers to Fig. 1 in the paper.

distinct projection counts goes up until you get a single string that projects 495 times, that's 12 choose 4. This next plot[5] shows examples for the probability distributions that are directly used in the formula for the Renyi entropy and the other measures of information that we use. The blue triangles show the all 0 string and I think the rest speaks for itself, it's self-explanatory, but if there are any questions I can come back to this.

Finally, these are the three curves[6] showing the three different orders of the Renyi entropy. The first order, which is equivalent to the Shannon entropy, is the blue curve. The red one is the second-order Renyi entropy. I'll explain why we have chosen these orders. Finally, the green curve shows the Min-entropy. In the QKD literature, the two most important measures are the Renyi entropy and the Min-entropy. During the last phase of QKD, when you want to perform privacy amplification, there are two different schemes that one can use. One is based on universal hash functions and the other one is based on randomness extractors. In the context of randomness extractors, all you need is the Min-entropy. If you put a bound on the Min-entropy, then that's all you need to be able to do your reduction.

So far, what we have seen is that the size of this Υ set is independent of the x string that you choose. But we see that the probability distribution is not flat, and how it varies depending on the x string that you choose. We also see that the alternating 1s and 0s yield the minimum amount of leakage. Intuitively, one way to look at this is the following and I'm open to any sort of criticism or input: for the all 0 and all 1 string, you can think of the bias in the bits, just the bit probability, and think of it in terms of constraints. The all 0 string and the all 1 string are the most biased strings. If you think of the event as the bit being equal to 1 or 0, the bit probability is 1 or its complement, 0. However, when you go to the other extreme, with the alternating 1s and 0s you have a completely unbiased string, where the bit probability is 50 %. So in a sense, intuitively, if you think of the space of y strings that project to it, for the all 0 string, you're imposing a lot of constraints in terms of bias on a specific set of strings in such a way that the all 0 y string gives you the maximum number of projections, which is n choose k. Whereas here, since there is no bias, you scatter your projections across all possible y strings, in such a way that it's closer to a flat distribution.

Initially, one might just want to compute the average leakage[7] and it's not that hard to compute. We can take the entropy of the y string and then subtract the conditional entropy of the y string given an observation of x. We use Bayes' rule to move these terms around and then since we have a uniformly distributed k-bit string, we can just say the entropy of x is equal to k. We can compute the conditional entropy knowing that it's only dependent on the Hamming weight of the y strings. But the average leakage is not really what interests us, what

---

[5] This refers to Fig. 2 in the paper.

[6] This refers to Fig. 3 in the paper.

[7] This refers to an earlier version and no longer applies to the corrected post-proceedings version of the paper.

we're interested in is: given an n and an x, how much we're actually leaking, and what's the maximum amount of leakage for a given k.

Assuming that the maximum leakage observation is correct, we want to compute the corresponding entropy. This is the bound that we want to put on all orders of the Renyi entropy under the assumption that the conjecture is correct. We can see that for the all 0 string, the number of elements in the Υ set with j 1s, is n choose j, and for a given j, the number of times that this y string can yield x is $n - j$ choose k, that is, once you remove the j 1s. Dividing the weight by the normalization gives you the probability for each y string. μ is the normalization that I introduced at the very beginning. Once you have this, plus the count of the number of elements in the Υ set, you insert these terms in the formulae for the Shannon entropy and the second-order Renyi entropy to get the analytic forms for the bounds on leakage. Finally, for the Min-entropy, there is no j anymore because it's all 0s and it boils down to leaking all the elements. Looking at the plot (See footnote 6), for $n = 8$ and $k = 5$, as you can see the maximum leakage is 3, so you're basically leaking all 5 bits.

One of the things that we have been trying to prove is the observation that the all 0 string yields the maximum amount of leakage. One possible approach would be to use the properties of the Renyi entropy. Knowing that this is something that is derived from Jensen's inequality: you have this inequality between the different orders of the Renyi entropy $H(X) \geq H_2(X) \geq H_\infty(X)$, with the function being a non increasing function in α. But are these properties enough? To show that the minima are actually preserved by all the different orders or not. This is a question that we have been thinking about.

As I said before, depending on the use-case and how you want to do your privacy amplification, the appropriate measure of entropy might be different. For instance, in the case of randomness extractors, we are already happy as we know how to quantify the maximum amount of leakage using the Min-entropy. But for universal hash functions, this is not quite the case. Another perspective would be to look at all this from a cryptographic standpoint. That is, to look at this whole thing from a Kolmogorov-Chaitin complexity point of view. If an attacker were to reconstruct the y string, how much computation time would be needed? or what is the required logical number of enumerations for the string to be reconstructed. Let's take an example, we can think of the all 0 x string: If an attacker were to efficiently enumerate this space, they can just start with the y strings of all 0s and then start adding 1s to this string by flipping the bits one by one, the obtained strings would all be valid. But for a generic x string: it's not so obvious anymore, in terms of how you would go about enumerating this space in an efficient manner.

So what we would like to have is a proof for the alternating 1s and 0s, to show that they actually yield the minimum amount of leakage. To have analytic forms and asymptotic expressions for the amount of leakage and to also better understand the rest of the Υ space and to see what happens in-between the two extremes and how the entropy varies. Finally, what is the appropriate measure of information in such a context and with that I think I'm done.

Bruce Christianson: So what are the implications of this for the issue that you started with, because initially you were looking at the standard quantum key agreement scenario, and there surely you would be able to say: well the chances of the bias being significant get small very quickly. So if I get a large bias I'll just drop this run and start another one.

Peter Ryan: The bias in the x string?

Bruce Christianson: Yes, so can you use the results you've got to give an indication of how much bias I can safely have?

Reply: You mean, given that we know what the bias is, whether or not we can continue or abort the protocol?

Bruce Christianson: Yes, is it safe to continue given some value?

Reply: Well to be honest, I guess in a realistic scenario, the strings are quite long, and unless k is really large with respect to n, which is unrealistic, it wouldn't really matter. Again, another thing that I have to admit is that in the literature, when you look at similar problems, for instance, in the existing schemes, you have different types of leakage, for instance, you leak parities of blocks, of binary blocks, or different functions of your bit string. And essentially what they do is that they don't even try to quantify this distribution space, they look at the worst case scenario, or sometimes in a simplistic manner, they say, OK, I'm revealing 20 parity bits, I'm leaking 20 bits, I'll just throw away the 20 bits. So the way it's usually handled is quite different.

Peter Ryan: I think in practice, if you found you had a heavily biased x string I think that should ring alarm bells anyway, so probably you should stop going into this...

Bruce Christianson: It would be nice to have some sort of practical guidelines on how much bias should ring the alarm.

Peter Ryan: Yes, OK, well that's a good point, we didn't particularly look at that. In a sense, we were partly playing with this as a mathematical game.

Bruce Christianson: Oh sure.

Peter Ryan: In fact, for the all 0 string, it's extremely unlikely and probably you would panic if you got it anyway.

Bruce Christianson: Yes, but the question is, you know, if I've got 10, if I've got 90 % bit strings 0 should I be worried yet.

Peter Ryan: Yes, good point, that's something we should think about.

Bruce Christianson: That would actually make a difference. Any other comments?

Sasa Radomirovic: How small is k compared to n? What does the size of k depend on?

Reply: Well usually this is also subject to heuristics. If you're transmitting a million qubits, and say half of it goes away just because of the way your protocol is set up, then you take a small portion of this for error estimation, it could be 10 %, or 8 %, so you can already see that it is small with respect to the entire string.

Peter Ryan: Well this is another thing which is rather unclear in the literature.

Reply: Yes, it seems to be just arbitrary.

Peter Ryan: Well this is another thing which is rather unclear. It's not clear what percentage you typically sample, and as far as we can tell in the literature it's very vague. It seems to relate to actually what you were saying earlier about the need to get the appropriate confidence level.

Bruce Christianson: Yes, you're in a race with Moriarty about who's got the better estimate for thermal noise.

Reply: I mean, most of the time in the absence of an eavesdropper, you're basically throwing away all these bits. Just because you don't know how much you exactly need to estimate the amount of error.

Peter Ryan: So another line of thought, which we haven't really pursued, is to do something like a risk limiting audit, an idea that Philip Stark has used in voting systems. So you get to potentially adaptively decide how large a sample to take, you start initially with 10 % or whatever, but if you find out that doesn't give you enough confidence level, perhaps you increase it a bit, that's another game you could play. My guess is that typically you would have a sampling set that is probably fairly small, probably in the order of 10 % or something.

Bruce Christianson: If the error rate gets too small, the engineers will just turn up the transmission rate until the error rate goes back up to whatever it is you can live with. So, yes, in practice, you can assume this.

Efficient Data Intensive Secure Computation: Fictional or Real?

Changyu Dong[✉]

Department of Computer and Information Sciences,
University of Strathclyde, Glasgow, UK
changyu.dong@strath.ac.uk

Abstract. Secure computation has the potential to completely reshape the cybersecruity landscape, but this will happen only if we can make it practical. Despite significant improvements recently, secure computation is still orders of magnitude slower than computation in the clear. Even with the latest technology, running the killer apps, which are often data intensive, in secure computation is still a mission impossible. In this paper, I present two approaches that could lead to practical data intensive secure computation. The first approach is by designing data structures. Traditionally, data structures have been widely used in computer science to improve performance of computation. However, in secure computation they have been largely overlooked in the past. I will show that data structures could be effective performance boosters in secure computation. Another approach is by using fully homomorphic encryption (FHE). A common belief is that FHE is too inefficient to have any practical applications for the time being. Contrary to this common belief, I will show that in some cases FHE can actually lead to very efficient secure computation protocols. This is due to the high degree of internal parallelism in recent FHE schemes. The two approaches are explained with Private Set Intersection (PSI) as an example. I will also show the performance figures measured from prototype implementations.

1 Introduction

In the past a few years, we have seen a dramatic increase in the scale and financial damage caused by cyber attacks. Data security is now of paramount importance for most organizations. Compounding the problem, changes in computing – particularly the booming of Cloud computing and collaborative data analysis – has added another layer of complexity to the security landscape. Traditionally, an organization can lock their data in secure storage and process it within an in-house facility operated by trusted staff. But increasingly, data processing is moving out of the trusted zone and security mechanisms that used to be effective do not work any more. A promising solution to solve this problem is *secure computation*. Secure computation allows for computation of arbitrary functions directly on encrypted data and hides all information about the data against untrusted parties, even if the untrusted parties are involved in the computation. It is a transformative technology that will completely change the game.

© Springer International Publishing Switzerland 2015
B. Christianson et al. (Eds.): Security Protocols 2015, LNCS 9379, pp. 350–360, 2015.
DOI: 10.1007/978-3-319-26096-9_35

One prediction says that within 15 years, the secure computation sector will be bigger than the anti-malware sector which currently has the largest share of the IT security industry [1].

Secure computation research started in the 1980s. Yao first defined the concept of secure computation in his seminal paper [2]. The goal of secure computation is to allow multiple parties to jointly compute a function over their inputs, and keeping these inputs private. There are several different approaches for achieving this goal. One prominent secure computation technique is Yao's garbled circuits protocol [3]. In this protocol, a function converted into an encrypted Boolean circuit and the parties evaluate the circuit with encrypted inputs. Another Boolean circuit based technique is the GMW protocol by Goldreich et al. [4]. Also Cramer et al. showed that secure computation can be done with arithmetic circuits and secret shared inputs [5]. Gordon et al. proposed a technique for secure computation in a von Neumann-style Random Access Machine (RAM) model by using an Oblivious RAM [6]. Recently, the development of Fully Homomorphic Encryption (FHE) provided a new direction in secure computation [7]. Apart from those generic secure computation techniques, there are also many special-purpose protocols that are designed for specific secure computation problems, e.g. private set intersection [8] and oblivious polynomial evaluation [9]. Secure computation is an obvious solution for a class of problems in which parties must provide input to a computation, but no party trusts any other party with that data. Examples include e-voting, auctions, information retrieval, data sharing, data mining and many more. Despite the fact that it has so many potential applications, secure computation has remained purely theoretical for many years. Efficiency is one of the main reasons.

Recently there have been a few efforts aiming to turn secure computation from a theorists' toy to a real world tool. Significant progress has been made in the last five years to improve the efficiency of secure computation by algorithmic advancements. For example, various protocols designed to efficiently compute a specific function securely; improvements on garbled circuits including free XOR [10], efficient OT extension [11] and fast cut-and-choose [12]; more efficient share-based multiparty secure computation protocols including Sharemind [13] and SPDZ [14]; more efficient RAM program based secure computation [15]; optimizations for FHE including SIMD operations [16] and polylog FHE [16]. The improvement is significant. Taking garbled circuit based secure computation as an example, after integrating many optimizations to date, the FastGC framework [17] is 10^4 times faster than FairPlay [18] which was implemented in 2004.

That said, secure computation is still far from being practical. Despite all the improvements, secure computation is still tens of thousand to billions times slower than computation in the clear. The overhead might be acceptable if the data to be processed were small, but can be prohibitive when the data is big. Imagine we have a secure computation mechanism which slows down the computation by 10,000 times, then what we can do in the clear in 10 seconds now needs more than 1 day to complete, and what we can do in the clear in 10 hours now needs more than 10 years! Paradoxically, when talking about the killer apps of secure computation, people often use examples such as companies having so much data that they do not have resources to process and have to process it in untrusted clouds, or two mutually untrusted parties have to mine their massive datasets together. Although the examples show the necessity of secure computation, current secure computation technology is incapable of handling such data-intensive applications. This becomes a major impediment to widespread use of secure computation.

How to make data intensive secure computation practical? In the rest of this paper, I will show two new approaches that have great potential: by designing data structures and by using newly developed FHE techniques. I will present the ideas using Private Set Intersection (PSI) protocols as an example.

2   Private Set Intersection: Background

A PSI protocol is a two-party protocol in which a client and a server want to jointly compute the intersection of their private input sets in a manner that at the end the client learns the intersection and the server learns nothing. PSI protocols have many practical applications. For example, PSI has been proposed as a building block in applications such as privacy preserving data mining [19, 20], human genome research [21], homeland security [22], Botnet detection [23], social networks [24], location sharing [25] and cheater detection in online games [26]. Many applications requires massive datasets as inputs. The first PSI protocol was proposed by Freedman et al. [8]. There are several approaches for PSI protocols. Some of them are based on oblivious polynomial evaluation [8, 27, 28], some are based on oblivious pseudorandom function (OPRF) evaluation [22, 29–31], and some are based on generic garbled circuits [32].

3   Data Structural Approach

In computer science, traditionally an effective approach to improve the efficiency of data intensive computation is by using an appropriate data structure, but in secure computation, the power of data structures has been largely overlooked. The reason for that is probably because in the past secure computation research focused on showing feasibility and the use cases were limited to those with small data input. But when we are moving towards real world applications in which data plays the central role and drives the computation, data structural design will become an indispensable part of secure computation. A good example of this data structural approach is the garbled Bloom Filter and the PSI protocol based on this data structure [33].

3.1   From Bloom Filter to Garbled Bloom Filter

A Bloom filter [34] is a compact data structure for probabilistic set membership testing. It is an array of m bits that can represent a set S of at most n elements.

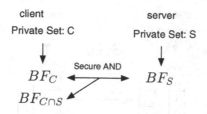

Fig. 1. The naive PSI protocol based on bloom filters.

A Bloom filter comes with a set of k independent uniform hash functions $H = \{h_0, ..., h_{k-1}\}$ that each h_i maps elements to index numbers over the range $[0, m-1]$ uniformly. Let us use BF_S to denote a Bloom filter that encodes the set S, and use $BF_S[i]$ to denote the bit at index i in BF_S. Initially, all bits in the array are set to 0. To insert an element $x \in S$ into the filter, the element is hashed using the k hash functions to get k index numbers. The bits at all these indexes in the bit array are set to 1, i.e. set $BF_S[h_i(x)] = 1$ for $0 \leq i \leq k-1$. To check if an item y is in S, y is hashed by the k hash functions, and all locations y hashes to are checked. If any of the bits at the locations is 0 , y is not in S, otherwise y is *probably* in S.

A standard Bloom filter trick is that if there are two Bloom filters, each encodes a set S_1 and S_2, and both are of the same size and built using the same set of hash functions, we can obtain another Bloom filter $BF_{S_1 \cap S_2}$ by bit-wisely ANDing BF_{S_1} and BF_{S_2}. The resulting Bloom filter $BF_{S_1 \cap S_2}$ encodes the set intersection $S_1 \cap S_2$. It seems that we can obtain an efficient PSI protocol (Fig. 1) immediately from this trick. However, this naive protocol is not secure. The reason is that due to collisions, the resulting Bloom filter $BF_{C \cap S}$ usually contains more 1 bits than the Bloom filter built from scratch using $C \cap S$. This means $BF_{C \cap S}$ leaks information about elements in S.

To avoid information leakage, we designed the garbled Bloom filters (GBF). A garbled Bloom filter is much like a Bloom filter: it is an array of size m with k hash functions. The difference is that at each position in the array, it holds a λ-bit string rather than a bit, where λ is the secure parameter. The bit string is either a share of a set element or a random string. To encode a set S, each element $s \in S$ is inserted as follows: initially all positions in the GBF is set to NULL. We then hash the element using the k hash functions. For $0 \leq j \leq k-2$, If $GBF[h_j(s)] = NULL$ then we put an λ-bit random string at this position, and then we set $GBF[h_{k-1}(s)] = s \oplus (\bigoplus_{j=0}^{k-2} GBF[h_j(s)])$. We can see that each of the k position $GBF[h_j(s)]$ holds a share of s. The shares has the property that if all k shares are present, we can reconstruct the element from the shares $s = \bigoplus_{j=0}^{k-1} GBF[h_j(s)])$; however any subset that has less than k shares reveals no information about the element. After inserting all elements in s to the GBF, we put a λ-bit random string at each position that is still NULL. To query an element y, y is hashed by the k hash functions and we test $\bigoplus_{j=0}^{k-1} GBF[h_j(y)] \stackrel{?}{=} y$. If the test is true, then y is in the set S.

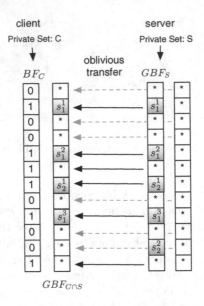

Fig. 2. The oblivious bloom intersection protocol.

A secure PSI protocol can then be built using a Bloom filter and a garbled Bloom filter (Fig. 2). In the protocol, the client encodes its set into a Bloom filter BF_C, the server encodes its set into a garbled Bloom filter GBF_S. The server also generates an array contains m random bit strings of length λ. For each position $0 \leq i \leq m - 1$, the client and server run a (2,1)-Oblivious Transfer protocol [35] such that if the bit $BF[i] = 1$, the client receives $GBF[i]$, if the bit $BF[i] = 0$, the client receives the ith string from the random string array. At the end of the protocol, the result is a garbled Bloom filter $GBF_{C \cap S}$ that encodes the intersection.

By using a garbled Bloom filter, we fix the information leakage problem. In the intersection garbled Bloom filter $GBF_{C \cap S}$, there might still exist residue shares that belong to elements not in the intersection. However, if an element s is not in $C \cap S$, then the probability of all its shares remain in $GBF_{C \cap S}$ is

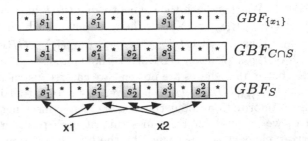

Fig. 3. Indistinguishability of the intersection garbled bloom filter.

negligible. Then by the property of the shares, the residue shares of s in $GBF_{C\cap S}$ leak no information about s. For example, in Fig. 3, s_2^1 in $GBF_{C\cap S}$ is a share of x_2 which is not in the intersection. The element x_2 has 3 shares and one of the share s_2^2 is not transferred to the client in the protocol. Then the other two shares remain in $GBF_{C\cap S}$ look uniformly random and do not leak information about x_2.

3.2 Performance Comparison

The PSI protocol obtained from garbled Bloom filter has many advantages: it has linear complexity, is easy to parallelize, relies mainly on symmetric key operations and it is much efficient than previous best protocols. We compared the performance with the previous best protocols. One protocol is by Huang et al. based the garbled circuits approach [32], and another is by De Cristofaro et al. based on ORPF evaluation [22]. Figure 4 shows the performance improvement at 128-bit security. The numbers displayed in the figure are ratios of running time (previous protocol to our protocol).

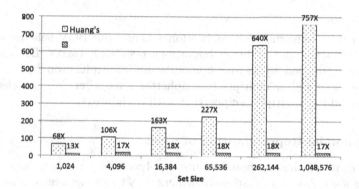

Fig. 4. Performance comparison.

4 Fully Homomorphic Encryption Approach

FHE is a newly established area in cryptography. An FHE scheme allows (any) computation to be carried out on encrypted data directly. FHE is a powerful tool and at the same time is notorious for its inefficiency. It is a common belief that FHE is too inefficient to be practical yet. However, this common belief is not always true. In this section I will show how to build a more efficient PSI protocol using fully homomorphic encryption.

4.1 The BGV FHE Scheme

In 2009, Gentry [7] developed the first FHE scheme. Following the breakthrough, several FHE schemes based on different hardness assumptions have been proposed, e.g. [36, 37].

The RLWE variant of BGV [37] is among the most efficient FHE schemes; it operates in certain polynomial rings. Namely, let $\Phi_m(x)$ be the m-th cyclotomic polynomial with degree $\phi(m)$, then we have a polynomial ring $\mathbb{A} = \mathbb{Z}[x]/\Phi_m(x)$, i.e. the set of integer polynomials of degree up to $\phi(m) - 1$. Here $\phi(\cdot)$ is the Euler's totient function. The ciphertext space of the BGV encryption scheme consists of polynomials over $\mathbb{A}_q = \mathbb{A}/q\mathbb{A}$, i.e. elements in $\mathbb{A}$ reduced modulo q where q is an odd integer[1]. The plaintext space is usually the ring $\mathbb{A}_p = \mathbb{A}/p\mathbb{A}$, i.e. polynomials of degree up to $\phi(m) - 1$ with coefficients in $\mathbb{Z}_p$ for some prime number $p < q$.

There are three basic algorithms in the BGV scheme:

- $G(p, \lambda, L)$: The key generation algorithm. Given p, λ and L such that p is the prime number that defines the plaintext space, λ is the security parameter and L is the depth of the arithmetic circuit to be evaluated, generate a secret key, the corresponding public key and a set of public parameters.
- $E_{pk}(\bar{m})$: The encryption algorithm. Given a public key pk, encrypt an element $\bar{m} \in \mathcal{A}_p$.
- $D_{sk}(c)$: The decryption algorithm. Given the secret key sk, decrypt a ciphertext c.

Being a fully homomorphic encryption scheme, the BGV scheme supports both multiplication and addition operations over ciphertexts. Let us denote homomorphic addition by $\boxplus$ and homomorphic multiplication by $\boxtimes$. We can homomorphically add or multiply two ciphertexts together. We can also homomorphically add or multiply a ciphertext with a plaintext.

4.2   Polynomial Representation of a Set

Freedman et al. [8] first proposed to use a polynomial for representing a set in PSI. Given a set S, we can map each element in S to an element in a sufficiently large field R. Then S can be represented as a polynomial (in a ring $R[x]$). The polynomial is defined as $\rho(x) = \prod_{s_i \in S}(x - s_i)$. The polynomial $\rho(x)$ has the property that every element $s_i \in S$ is a root of $\rho(x)$. For two polynomials ρ_1 and ρ_2 that represent the two sets S_1 and S_2 respectively, the the greatest common divisor of the two polynomials $gcd(\rho_1, \rho_2)$ represents the set intersection $S_1 \cap S_2$. Based on this, we can design protocols to securely obtain the set intersection. Without loss of generality, let both ρ_1 and ρ_2 to be of degree δ and let γ_1 and γ_2 to be two uniformly random degree δ polynomials in $R[x]$, Kissner and Song proved in [27] that $\gamma_1 \cdot \rho_1 + \gamma_2 \cdot \rho_2 = \mu \cdot gcd(\rho_1, \rho_2)$ such that μ is a uniformly random polynomial. This means if ρ_1 and ρ_2 are polynomials representing sets S_1 and S_2, then the polynomial $\gamma_1 \cdot \rho_1 + \gamma_2 \cdot \rho_2$ contains only information about $S_1 \cap S_2$ and no information about other elements in S_1 or S_2. This forms the basis of their PSI protocol in which a party obtains $\gamma_1 \cdot \rho_1 + \gamma_2 \cdot \rho_2$ to find the set intersection but learns nothing more about elements in the other party's set.

---

[1] In the BGV encryption scheme, there are actually a chain of moduli $q_0 < q_1 < \cdots < q_L$ defined for modulus switching. But for simplicity we just use q throughout the paper.

However, Kissner's protocol is not practical due to the facts that it uses expensive Paillier encryption and the computational complexity is quadratic in the size of the sets.

4.3   The Private Set Intersection Protocol Based on FHE

We parallelize computation by utilizing the native plaintext space of BGV to load multiple data items. The native plaintext space of BGV is a polynomial ring, therefore a set can be easily represented in the plaintext space. To simplify the description, I will start from the case where $|C| = |S| = \frac{\phi(m)}{2} - 1$. In the protocol, the client has a BGV key pair (pk, sk) and a set C. The server has a set S. The two parties encode their sets into ρ_C and ρ_S that are polynomials in $\mathbb{A}_p$. The protocol is shown in Fig. 5:

1. The client encrypts its set polynomial ρ_C and sends the ciphertext c to the server.
2. The server chooses random polynomial γ_c and γ_s in $\mathbb{A}_p$, each of degree $\frac{\phi(m)}{2} - 1$, then the server computes homomorphically $c' = (c \boxtimes \gamma_c) \boxplus (\rho_s \cdot \gamma_s)$. The server sends c' to the client, who then decrypts the ciphertext and obtains the polynomial $\rho_C \cdot \gamma_c + \rho_s \cdot \gamma_s$.
3. The client then evaluates the polynomial obtained in the last step with elements in C. For each element, if it is a root then it is in the intersection. The client then outputs the intersection $C \cap S$.

To compute the intersection of sets whose sizes are larger than $\frac{\phi(m)}{2} - 1$, we can use bucketization. Bucketization is a process to partition a large set into disjoint subsets (buckets). The two parties use a public uniform hash function $H : \{1, 0\}^* \to [1, k]$ to map their set elements into k buckets. This is done by hashing each element to get a bucket number and putting the element into the bucket with this number. If the size of the set to be bucketized is n, then each bucket will have around n/k elements. The two parties can choose k so that with a high probability, each bucket has no more than $\frac{\phi(m)}{2} - 1$ elements. To prevent information leakage through bucket size, the two parties pad each bucket with random elements so that all buckets have the same size $\frac{\phi(m)}{2} - 1$. They then run the PSI protocol k times. In the ith run, each party uses its ith bucket as the input to the PSI protocol. The union of outputs is the intersection of the two sets.

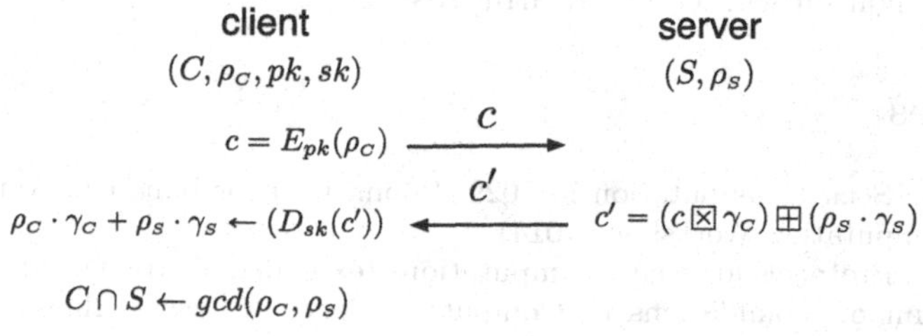

client   server

(C, ρ_C, pk, sk) (S, ρ_S)

$c = E_{pk}(\rho_C) \xrightarrow{\quad c \quad}$

$\rho_C \cdot \gamma_c + \rho_s \cdot \gamma_s \leftarrow (D_{sk}(c')) \xleftarrow{\quad c' \quad} c' = (c \boxtimes \gamma_c) \boxplus (\rho_s \cdot \gamma_s)$

$C \cap S \leftarrow gcd(\rho_C, \rho_s)$

Fig. 5. The PSI protocol.

4.4   Efficiency

The protocol is very efficient. This is due to the high degree of parallelism provided by the BGV scheme. In the protocol, we process a set of $\frac{\phi(m)}{2} - 1$ elements in one go, rather than processing them individually. Therefore the total computational cost is amortized by $\frac{\phi(m)}{2} - 1$. The parameter $\phi(m)$ is large, therefore the amortized cost is small.

Table 1. Performance of PSI protocols.

	2^{10}	2^{12}	2^{14}	2^{16}	2^{18}	2^{20}
GBF-PSI	0.67	1.99	8.21	32.41	130.42	530.36
FHE-PSI	0.11	0.14	0.45	1.55	5.91	23.48
Improvement	6X	14X	18X	21X	22X	23X

* Running Time in seconds

Table 1 shows the performance comparison of the GBF based and the FHE based PSI protocols. In the experiment, security parameter is set to 128-bit. The parameters for the BGV keys were $|p| = 32, L = 1, |q| = 124, \phi(m) = 5002$. The set size varied from 2^{10} (1024) to 2^{20} (1,048,576). As we can see, the FHE based PSI protocol is much faster. For two 1 million elements input sets, the running time is less than half a minute, which is only 1 - 2 orders of magnitude slower than the computation in the clear.

5   Conclusion

In this paper, I presented two approaches that could lead to practical data intensive secure computation. One approach is by designing better data structures. The rationale behind this approach is that when the data to be processed is big, arranging it into certain data structures may make it more amendable for computation. Another approach is by using fully homomorphic encryption. Recent fully homomorphic encryption schemes provide us facilities to parallelize computation, which can greatly reduce the overall cost if the computation task is data parallel. The two approaches can be combined. For example, when using bucketization in the PSI protocol, the list of buckets is essentially a hash table data structure. The research along these two lines is still in an early stage, but further investigation will lead to fruitful results.

References

1. Evans, D.: Secure computation in 2029: Boom, bust, or bonanza. Applied Multi-Party Computation Workshop (2014)
2. Yao, A.C.: Protocols for secure computations (extended abstract). In: 23rd Annual Symposium on Foundations of Computer Science, Chicago, Illinois, USA, 3–5 November 1982, pp. 160–164 (1982)

3. Yao, A.C.: How to generate and exchange secrets (extended abstract). In: 27th Annual Symposium on Foundations of Computer Science, Toronto, Canada, 27–29 October 1986, pp. 162–167 (1986)
4. Goldreich, O., Micali, S., Wigderson, A.: How to play any mental game or a completeness theorem for protocols with honest majority. In: Proceedings of the 19th Annual ACM Symposium on Theory of Computing, 1987, New York, USA, pp. 218–229 (1987)
5. Cramer, R., Damgård, I.B., Maurer, U.M.: General secure multi-party computation from any linear secret-sharing scheme. In: Preneel, B. (ed.) EUROCRYPT 2000. LNCS, vol. 1807, pp. 316–334. Springer, Heidelberg (2000)
6. Gordon, S.D., Katz, J., Kolesnikov, V., Krell, F., Malkin, T., Raykova, M., Vahlis, Y.: Secure two-party computation in sublinear (amortized) time. In: ACM Conference on Computer and Communications Security (2012)
7. Gentry, C.: Fully homomorphic encryption using ideal lattices. In: Proceedings of the 41st Annual ACM Symposium on Theory of Computing, STOC 2009, Bethesda, MD, USA, 31 May–2 June 2009, pp. 169–178 (2009)
8. Freedman, M.J., Nissim, K., Pinkas, B.: Efficient private matching and set intersection. In: Cachin, C., Camenisch, J.L. (eds.) EUROCRYPT 2004. LNCS, vol. 3027, pp. 1–19. Springer, Heidelberg (2004)
9. Naor, M., Pinkas, B.: Oblivious transfer and polynomial evaluation. In: Proceedings of the Thirty-First Annual ACM Symposium on Theory of Computing, 1–4 May 1999, Atlanta, Georgia, USA, pp. 245–254 (1999)
10. Kolesnikov, V., Schneider, T.: Improved garbled circuit: free XOR gates and applications. In: Aceto, L., Damgård, I., Goldberg, L.A., Halldórsson, M.M., Ingólfsdóttir, A., Walukiewicz, I. (eds.) ICALP 2008, Part II. LNCS, vol. 5126, pp. 486–498. Springer, Heidelberg (2008)
11. Asharov, G., Lindell, Y., Schneider, T., Zohner, M.: More efficient oblivious transfer and extensions for faster secure computation. In: ACM Conference on Computer and Communications Security (2013)
12. Lindell, Y.: Fast cut-and-choose based protocols for malicious and covert adversaries. In: Canetti, R., Garay, J.A. (eds.) CRYPTO 2013, Part II. LNCS, vol. 8043, pp. 1–17. Springer, Heidelberg (2013)
13. Bogdanov, D., Niitsoo, M., Toft, T., Willemson, J.: High-performance secure multiparty computation for data mining applications. Int. J. Inf. Sec. 11(6), 403–418 (2012)
14. Damgård, I., Pastro, V., Smart, N., Zakarias, S.: Multiparty computation from somewhat homomorphic encryption. In: Safavi-Naini, R., Canetti, R. (eds.) CRYPTO 2012. LNCS, vol. 7417, pp. 643–662. Springer, Heidelberg (2012)
15. Liu, C., Huang, Y., Shi, E., Katz, J., Hicks, M.W.: Automating efficient ram-model secure computation. In: 2014 IEEE Symposium on Security and Privacy, SP 2014, Berkeley, CA, USA, 18–21 May 2014, pp. 623–638 (2014)
16. Gentry, C., Halevi, S., Smart, N.P.: Fully homomorphic encryption with polylog overhead. In: Pointcheval, D., Johansson, T. (eds.) EUROCRYPT 2012. LNCS, vol. 7237, pp. 465–482. Springer, Heidelberg (2012)
17. Huang, Y., Evans, D., Katz, J., Malka, L.: Faster secure two-party computation using garbled circuits. In: 20th USENIX Security Symposium, San Francisco, CA, USA, 8–12 August 2011, Proceedings (2011)
18. Malkhi, D., Nisan, N., Pinkas, B., Sella, Y.: Fairplay - secure two-party computation system. In: Proceedings of the 13th USENIX Security Symposium, 9–13 August 2004, San Diego, CA, USA, pp. 287–302 (2004)
19. Aggarwal, C.C., Yu, P.S.: Privacy-Preserving Data Mining - Models and Algorithms. Advances in Database Systems, vol. 34. Springer, USA (2008)

20. Dong, C., Chen, L.: A fast secure dot product protocol with application to privacy preserving association rule mining. In: Tseng, V.S., Ho, T.B., Zhou, Z.-H., Chen, A.L.P., Kao, H.-Y. (eds.) PAKDD 2014, Part I. LNCS, vol. 8443, pp. 606–617. Springer, Heidelberg (2014)

21. Baldi, P., Baronio, R., Cristofaro, E.D., Gasti, P., Tsudik, G.: Countering gattaca: efficient and secure testing of fully-sequenced human genomes. In: ACM Conference on Computer and Communications Security, pp. 691–702 (2011)

22. De Cristofaro, E., Tsudik, G.: Practical private set intersection protocols with linear complexity. In: Sion, R. (ed.) FC 2010. LNCS, vol. 6052, pp. 143–159. Springer, Heidelberg (2010)

23. Nagaraja, S., Mittal, P., Hong, C.Y., Caesar, M., Borisov, N.: Botgrep: finding p2p bots with structured graph analysis. In: USENIX Security Symposium, pp. 95–110 (2010)

24. Mezzour, G., Perrig, A., Gligor, V., Papadimitratos, P.: Privacy-preserving relationship path discovery in social networks. In: Garay, J.A., Miyaji, A., Otsuka, A. (eds.) CANS 2009. LNCS, vol. 5888, pp. 189–208. Springer, Heidelberg (2009)

25. Narayanan, A., Thiagarajan, N., Lakhani, M., Hamburg, M., Boneh, D.: Location privacy via private proximity testing. In: NDSS (2011)

26. Bursztein, E., Hamburg, M., Lagarenne, J., Boneh, D.: Openconflict: preventing real time map hacks in online games. In: IEEE Symposium on Security and Privacy, pp. 506–520 (2011)

27. Kissner, L., Song, D.: Privacy-preserving set operations. In: Shoup, V. (ed.) CRYPTO 2005. LNCS, vol. 3621, pp. 241–257. Springer, Heidelberg (2005)

28. Hazay, C., Nissim, K.: Efficient set operations in the presence of malicious adversaries. In: Nguyen, P.Q., Pointcheval, D. (eds.) PKC 2010. LNCS, vol. 6056, pp. 312–331. Springer, Heidelberg (2010)

29. Hazay, C., Lindell, Y.: Efficient protocols for set intersection and pattern matching with security against malicious and covert adversaries. In: Canetti, R. (ed.) TCC 2008. LNCS, vol. 4948, pp. 155–175. Springer, Heidelberg (2008)

30. Jarecki, S., Liu, X.: Efficient oblivious pseudorandom function with applications to adaptive ot and secure computation of set intersection. In: Reingold, O. (ed.) TCC 2009. LNCS, vol. 5444, pp. 577–594. Springer, Heidelberg (2009)

31. De Cristofaro, E., Kim, J., Tsudik, G.: Linear-complexity private set intersection protocols secure in malicious model. In: Abe, M. (ed.) ASIACRYPT 2010. LNCS, vol. 6477, pp. 213–231. Springer, Heidelberg (2010)

32. Huang, Y., Evans, D., Katz, J.: Private set intersection: Are garbled circuits better than custom protocols? In: NDSS (2012)

33. Dong, C., Chen, L., Wen, Z.: When private set intersection meets big data: an efficient and scalable protocol. In: ACM Conference on Computer and Communications Security (2013)

34. Bloom, B.H.: Space/time trade-offs in hash coding with allowable errors. Commun. ACM 13(7), 422–426 (1970)

35. Ishai, Y., Paskin, A.: Evaluating branching programs on encrypted data. In: Vadhan, S.P. (ed.) TCC 2007. LNCS, vol. 4392, pp. 575–594. Springer, Heidelberg (2007)

36. van Dijk, M., Gentry, C., Halevi, S., Vaikuntanathan, V.: Fully homomorphic encryption over the integers. In: Gilbert, H. (ed.) EUROCRYPT 2010. LNCS, vol. 6110, pp. 24–43. Springer, Heidelberg (2010)

37. Brakerski, Z., Gentry, C., Vaikuntanathan, V.: (leveled) fully homomorphic encryption without bootstrapping. In: ITCS, pp. 309–325 (2012)

Efficient Data Intensive Secure Computations: Fictional or Real? (Transcript of Discussion)

Changyu Dong[✉]

University of Strathclyde, Glasgow, UK
changyu.dong@strath.ac.uk

[Omitted explanation of the paper.]

Ross Anderson: Well Craig Gentry's work is very impressive, and there is the problem of fully homomorphic encryption as to what applications you use it for, because even if it all works it becomes equivalent to a good hardware security module which will run faithfully a program on private data and give an output. The question then of course is whether any of the private data are leaked as a result of the design of the program. And this brings in all the problems studied in the field of inference control and statistical database security, so it's only part of a potential solution that would involve direct computation between Amazon and Facebook.

Reply: Yes, I think that's a problem, and I think cryptography can do something but not everything. There are always application scenarios where you can handle something in secure computation, and something you can't handle. For example, if you want to hide the algorithm, secure computation doesn't really support that and we usually assume the algorithm is public. If you want to hide it you might need to use other things rather than secure computation, and it might be possible later we find out that these two things can be combined together and then give you a better solution.

Max Spencer: So apart from the private set intersection example you gave here, are there any new examples like that?

Reply: Yes, actually I do have more examples. Another example is a paper we published last year in ESORICS, about private information retrieval. In that paper we used a tree, binary tree, plus fully homomorphic parallelisation, and that is probably currently the fastest private information retrieval protocol. One more example is ORAM (oblivious RAM). Currently the most efficient ORAM construction is based on a binary tree structure, that's a data structure. And here is another example. Last year there were two papers, one in CCS, one in Asiacrypt. They are about oblivious data structures, i.e. building data structures over ORAM and making use of these structures. We have some other papers, currently in submission, about fully homomorphic encryption, how it can be used in secure computation, and make secure computation protocols more efficient. So it is not just a single case, although still it's in a very early stage and there are a lot of things that need to be done.

Mark Lomas: This question is, partly to make sure that I understand what the underlying problem is. Let's imagine that we each hold a set, and we want

© Springer International Publishing Switzerland 2015
B. Christianson et al. (Eds.): Security Protocols 2015, LNCS 9379, pp. 361–363, 2015.
DOI: 10.1007/978-3-319-26096-9_36

to find the intersection between them, but neither of us wants to reveal any of the elements that the other doesn't know. But I want to cheat. So I take my set and I add a set of elements that I think are in your set, and then I participate in the protocol, and we find the intersection. I know which elements I've lied about so I can subtract those from the intersection to know more elements that were in your set.

Ross Anderson: Well this exactly is an inference attack on your database security, and if you look at your anonymous medical database before and after, you add a false record that the prime minster being prescribed an aspirin. Now that cannot be solved with cryptography.

Reply: That cannot be solved by cryptology. In the definition of secure computation, the parties can always change their inputs before engaging in the computation, because that is not preventable. You can always change your set, unless the set is somehow certified by some trusted party.

Ross Anderson: Or you have a commitment.

Reply: Yes, otherwise if without a trusted party or commitment or something like that, the best we can do is to trust that the users use their own sets. That's really an attack we cannot prevent in secure computation.

Keith Irwin: You sort of have this game theory problem, right, where if both of them are trying to do the same thing, and screw the other one over, and both end up submitting all of the items, and you compute the intersection and you say, yes, you both have all possible things and that's what happens every time. So you have to kind of break that socially, anyway.

Joan Feigenbaum: There is actually work on combining secure multiparty computation with incentive compatibility, and there is some subtlety in how to combine the two.

Reply: Yes, crypto cannot solve every problem, we need other parts.

Daniel Thomas: So if two companies have two big sets of IP addresses and they want to see what the intersection of those two sets is, would this work simply for that?

Reply: Yes.

Peter Ryan: Well partly a follow-on to previous comments, it depends a little bit of what's done with the resulting computation presumably. If that's handed on to some third party for something or other, then presumably there might be an incentive not to do so.

Reply: Secure computation is defined in a general way so you can evaluate any function. So the output might not be set intersection directly, you might apply another function that securely post processes the set intersection without revealing the intersection. Then the secure function is composed of the intersection function and the other function. In this way you can hide the intersection. That might be able to solve some of the problems, but it still depends on applications.

Peter Ryan: So you listed three ways of speeding things up, and there's a fourth way, right, you use a quantum computer.

Reply: Yes.

Peter Ryan: As I think about it I'm not quite sure what secure quantum computation means.

Reply: If you have a quantum computer then a lot of things you can't really do because the crypto may be broken, although fully homomorphic encryption probably will remain secure. But I guess quantum computers, maybe as a fourth way to improve secure computation, because it's really something different, and in the protocol design we need to consider some special features of quantum computers.

Bruce Christianson: Taking Mark's point a little bit further, it seems these techniques are really only useful against a data that's easy to guess, because if you have data that's hard to guess, you can just connect to hash values and then reveal the hash values of clients. So it's only worth doing this where it's easy to guess candidates for missing data.

Reply: Yes, but if we assume all the data inputs are hard to guess then it's really a very strong assumption. In a real case we can't assume anything about the distribution of the data.

Epilogue

... there is an osmosis from fiction to reality, a constant contamination which distorts the truth behind both and fuzzes the telling distinctions in life itself, categorizing real situations and feelings by a set of rules largely culled from the most hoary fictional cliches ...

– Iain M. Banks, The State of the Art, 1989

© Springer International Publishing Switzerland 2015
B. Christianson et al. (Eds.): Security Protocols 2015, LNCS 9379, pp. 365, 2015.
DOI: 10.1007/978-3-319-26096-9

Author Index

Printed in the United St...
F...Bookbinders...

Printed in the United States
By Bookmasters